CRUSADING LIBERAL

CRUSADING LIBERAL

Paul H. Douglas
of Illinois

Roger Biles

NORTHERN
ILLINOIS
UNIVERSITY
PRESS
DeKalb

© 2002 by Northern Illinois University Press

Published by the Northern Illinois University Press, DeKalb, Illinois   60115

Manufactured in the United States using acid-free paper

Library of Congress Cataloging-in-Publication Data

Biles, Roger, 1950–

Crusading liberal: Paul H. Douglas of Illinois / Roger Biles.

   p.   cm.

Includes bibliographical references and index.

ISBN 0-87580-304-0 (alk. paper)

1. Douglas, Paul Howard, 1892– 2. Legislators—United States—Biography. 3. United States—Congress—Senate—Biography. 4. African Americans—Civil rights—History—20th century. 5. African Americans—Legal status, laws, etc.—History—20th century. 6. Civil rights movements—United States—History—20th century. 7. Liberalism—United States—History—20th century. 8. United States—Race relations—Political aspects. I. Title.

E748.D68 B45 2003

328.73´092—dc21

[B]   2002067767

Contents

Acknowledgments

• Over the course of the several years that this book gestated, I bene-fited from the generous assistance provided by a number of organiza-tions and individuals. The Division of Research and Graduate Studies at East Carolina University awarded me a Research/Creative Activity Grant that helped defray the cost of travel to libraries and archives. Another travel grant came from the Everett M. Dirksen Congressional Center. The Department of History at East Carolina University provided a Re-search Assignment Leave so that I could devote an entire summer and the following fall semester to writing. I also profited from the criticisms offered by several historians who read all or portions of the manuscript. Brian Deeson and Richard Fry read the chapter on the 1954 election and gave me the benefit of their knowledge of Illinois politics. Alonzo Hamby, David Kyvig, and Iwan Morgan read the entire manuscript with care, pointing out careless errors and asking insightful questions that forced me to sharpen the prose. Librarians and archivists at several repositories were helpful; I am especially indebted to Archie Motley at the Chicago Historical Society who demystified the confusing organiza-tion of the Paul H. Douglas Papers.

The historian's craft is necessarily a solitary enterprise. Poring over manuscript materials and peering at computer screens, the scholar neces-sarily spends countless hours working alone. Still, I always feel that the products of my labor substantially reflect the other times spent with my wife and children. They have contributed to the making of this book in ways that they surely do not recognize. My most heartfelt thanks then go to my wife, Mary Claire, and to my children, Brian, Jeanne, and Grant.

CRUSADING LIBERAL

Professor and Social Activist

1

A professor has a basic and scholarly responsibility to serve as a critic of the society in which he lives toward the end of improving it for the welfare of his fellow man.

—Paul H. Douglas[1]

• Paul Douglas, university professor, renowned economist, three-term U.S. senator, and one of the foremost spokesmen for liberalism in the post–World War II era, launched his journey toward prominence from exceedingly humble origins. Although his modest beginnings offered little hope of future greatness, Douglas's early life hinted at a number of character traits that would be fully evident in later years—an intense intellectual curiosity, a remarkable capacity for hard work, a fierce competitiveness and drive to succeed, and a devotion to the underdog and a commitment to aid the downtrodden. A fragmented family life and hardscrabble existence in a primitive environment bred in Douglas a drive to succeed and compassion for others in dire circumstances. The rudiments of his character could be glimpsed and the future course of his public career foreseen during his formative years.

The second son of James Douglas and Annie (Smith) Douglas, Paul Howard Douglas was born on March 26, 1892, in Salem, Massachusetts. His father's Scottish forebears had come to America at the end of the seventeenth century and engaged in fishing, shipbuilding, and other maritime pursuits along the coast of Maine. His mother's ancestors had been New England Tories who fled to Canada during the American Revolution. Annie Smith left New Brunswick to attend Vassar College and, running out of money, found a teaching position in Buckport, Maine, where she met and married James Douglas. In 1896, when Paul Douglas was four years old, she died of tuberculosis, and Paul and his older brother, John, went to live with a distant cousin. The following year, James Douglas married a young woman from Maine, Florence Young, and the family settled in Saratoga Springs, New York.[2]

Having twice failed in the dry goods business, James Douglas became a drummer for a Providence, Rhode Island, firm and for twenty years roamed a vast sales district in upstate New York. During his brief stays at home, he exhibited a violent temper and drank excessively. The loneliness and strain of a traveling salesman's life, Paul Douglas later thought, caused his father's drunkenness and shortcomings as a husband and parent. Unable to tolerate her situation any longer, Florence Douglas left her husband and, taking her two stepsons, moved to a remote area of central Maine near Moosehead Lake to live with her brother, who had recently opened a resort hotel. In subsequent years, James Douglas rarely wrote to his sons and saw them infrequently. Dismissive of his father's lifestyle, Paul Douglas was "repelled by his taste for low life" and claimed that he "always feared the emergence of some of [his] traits in me."[3]

For eight years, young Douglas lived with his family in the Maine backwoods a dozen miles from the nearest town. The isolation was such, he later remembered, that a person could travel 150 miles north to the Canadian border without seeing another person or other sign of human life. Only the daily whistles of the Canadian Pacific Railroad trains on the main line from Montreal to Halifax, Nova Scotia, interrupted the bucolic stillness. Supplementing the modest cash income earned from summer guests, the Douglas family achieved self-sufficiency by clearing forested land and growing much of their own food. For Paul, life on the farm meant a daily regimen of chores, such as gathering maple sap and milking cows. The latter task, he later commented, "should be requisite for all aspiring politicians, for it strengthens one's hand for handshaking, and the hand movement is nearly the same." During the summers, when guests at the hotel arrived from Boston and New York City, he toted bags, cut firewood, carried water, and attended to all of the tasks assigned to him as the only bellboy.[4]

In such harsh and primitive conditions, Paul Douglas experienced a rural poverty that no doubt accounted for the empathy for society's unfortunates that he evinced throughout his political career. Similarly, his interest in industrial relations and his lifelong dedication to improving the lives of the laboring classes owed much to his observation of workers in early-twentieth-century Maine. He watched the exploitation of the French Canadian lumberjacks who worked long hours, often performing dangerous jobs that resulted in loss of life, for a dollar a day. The absence of workmen's compensation or burial provisions for those who suffered industrial accidents left the workers and their families vulnerable. In his autobiography, Douglas recounted his sympathy for the railroad section hands working in the vicinity who fought unsuccessfully for higher wages and better conditions; he wondered why the train crews failed to join in a strike that would have compelled the railroad's ownership in Montreal and England to negotiate with the workers.[5]

Douglas's spirited defense of minorities likewise could be attributed in part to the opprobrium his family suffered as staunch Democrats in overwhelmingly Republican Maine. At a time when the remaining members of the Grand Army of the Republic still exercised great influence in state and community affairs and local leaders continued to label the Democrats the party of disunion, annual pageants like the Memorial Day celebration kept issues of patriotism and loyalty alive. Douglas remembered:

> This annual parade became a Republican affair in Maine. There were a few kids in our town, I think only one other when I got to high school, who were known to be members of Democratic families. We were always allowed to march too, but they put us at the end of the line, so as not to contaminate the rest of them. Gradually we realized that we were always put at the end of the line and we got sore about it.

In a 1950 profile, a *Time* writer suggested that the Memorial Day parade experience left Douglas "a rebel, a reformer, a crusader for the boys at the end of the line. . . . He never got over being sore at injustice, wherever he found it."[6]

During the winters, Florence Douglas operated a small school for her youngest son and the children of the French Canadian railroad workers who lived nearby. She taught vocabulary with the use of McGuffey's *Readers* and the novels of Charles Dickens, and Douglas became a voracious reader. Borrowing copies of popular magazines left behind by the hotel's guests, he pored over issues of *McClure's, Collier's,* and the *Progressive.* Reading exposés by Lincoln Steffens, Ray Stannard Baker, Ida Tarbell, and other muckrakers, he developed a keen interest in politics and a lasting antipathy for corruption and malfeasance—attitudes reinforced by reading the daily issues of Joseph Pulitzer's crusading *New York World.* In all, Douglas estimated, his early schooling amounted to no more than a year and a half of classroom instruction, yet the breadth and scope of his reading prepared him well for secondary education.[7]

With the finalization of her divorce on the grounds of desertion, Florence Douglas left the hotel, remarried, and settled on a farm outside of Newport, Maine. For the next four years, Paul attended the high school in Newport where he studied traditional subjects like history, chemistry, physics, algebra, and geometry as well as French and Latin. He read insatiably, his interests ranging from poetry to English literature to world history to the New England transcendentalists. A middling athlete, young Douglas competed on the school's baseball and football teams. In his spare time, he worked in the baggage office of the Maine Central Railroad in Newport and continued to perform his chores on the family farm.[8]

In 1909 Douglas matriculated at Bowdoin College, a liberal arts school in Brunswick, Maine; originally founded by the Congregational Church, it had by the early twentieth century become nondenominational. He could afford to begin his studies because his older brother, John, had parlayed an engineering degree from the Massachusetts Institute of Technology into a lucrative job with the General Electric Company and could provide financial support. During the first year, however, the financial aid ceased as his brother began to pay for the care of their ailing father. To discharge the cost of his tuition, room, and board, Douglas waited on tables, mixed concrete, sold gelatin desserts, and performed a series of odd jobs; in the summers, he sold extracts door-to-door. With the collective sums his many odd jobs generated and a modest inheritance from his father, who died in 1912, he pieced together enough money to attend four years of college.[9]

"Intellectually," Douglas later recalled, "I found the college placidly stimulating." He read widely in history, economics, and politics, citing as especially influential Henry George's *Progress and Poverty,* James Bryce's *American Commonwealth,* and Abbott L. Lowell's *Governments and Parties in Continental Europe.* He also pored over the biographies of great American statesmen such as Thomas Jefferson, Abraham Lincoln, George W. Norris, and Robert M. La Follette, Sr. His interest in politics and forensics led to participation on the college's debate team where he argued the leading issues of that time—federal income tax, popular election of U.S. senators, tariff revision, workmen's compensation, minimum wage legislation, the direct primary, and trust regulation. In debating all of these issues, Douglas eagerly defended the more progressive and frequently less popular points of view.[10]

Outside the classroom, Douglas engaged in a number of activities that made him a leading figure on campus. He played on the Bowdoin football team for four years, the last two as the starting center. At six feet two inches tall and well over two hundred pounds, he was a strong and determined if not particularly skillful player. He brought the same qualities to the college boxing team. In later years, he testified that the lessons learned in athletic competition—perseverance, dedication, discipline, and resilience—aided him in his political career. He also became well known as a political activist who frequently championed unpopular causes. A Bowdoin classmate characterized Douglas as a "radical campus leader" who was "rather to the left of Eugene V. Debs." His activism frequently involved the pursuit of better treatment for minority groups and other underdogs. In his senior year, for example, Douglas launched a crusade on behalf of the forty or fifty "untouchables" who had been excluded from the eight social fraternities that dominated the social life on campus. A member himself of one of the college's less prestigious fraternities, he persuaded the college to buy a house for a nonfraternity club and helped charter new fraternities. "We at least enlarged the circle of the privileged," he remembered, "making even the lower social depths more endurable."[11]

In 1913 Douglas graduated with a Phi Beta Kappa key from Bowdoin College as an economics major. With what remained of his inheritance and a $500 fellowship award, he enrolled later that year in the Graduate School of Economics and Political Science at Columbia University. Douglas took courses from a number of Columbia's distinguished economics professors, studying public finance with E. R. A. Seligman, statistics with Robert E. Chaddock, and economic theory with John Bates Clark. He also attended the lectures of historian Charles A. Beard and philosopher John Dewey (with whom he would later serve in the League for Independent Political Action). Most influential, however, was economics professor Henry R. Seager, whose courses on labor problems helped determine Douglas's future specialization in the discipline. Seager's examination of labor relations advanced beyond economic theory to emphasize the impact of legislation on workers' lives.[12]

During his two years at Columbia, Douglas found in New York City much fertile ground for his growing interest in labor relations and his long-standing commitment to progressive politics. As at Bowdoin College, he became a social activist who devoted much of his time to activities outside of the classroom and the library. He frequented Greenwich Village coffee shops and studios where the public-spirited discussed the issues of the day and read the provocative editorials of Herbert Croly, Walter Lippmann, and other leading progressives. In the November 1914 elections, he served as a poll watcher to curtail vote theft by the notorious Tammany Hall machine. In the wake of the Triangle Shirtwaist Company fire, in which more than two hundred young women workers had been burned to death because of inadequate safety provisions in the workplace, Douglas enlisted as a labor organizer for the International Ladies' Garment Workers' Union (ILGWU). On one occasion, police arrested him for blocking traffic while giving an organizing speech to an audience of six persons. At the subsequent trial, one of the arresting officers testified falsely that Douglas had attracted a crowd of more than one thousand and had cursed and struck the policemen when they had attempted to unclog the traffic. Despite Douglas's denials and the testimony of other witnesses, the judge found him guilty and levied a fine. The episode proved instructive. "I realized the practical pressures being used against the organization of workmen into unions," Douglas said. "I could also understand the feeling of the workers that the law and, indeed, government itself were hostile to them."[13]

While at Columbia, Douglas fell in love with Dorothy Wolff, a brilliant student from a prominent New York family whom he later described as "the most generous and altruistic person I had ever met." She shared with him not only many scholarly interests but also a passion for progressive politics. Looking forward to, as Douglas put it, "a life of high academic endeavor and social crusading," they married in 1915. Over the next eleven years, they had four children—Helen, John, Dorothea, and Paul—and Dorothy Douglas managed to complete a doctorate in sociology. The inability to find two teaching positions at the same institution, a difficulty common to academic couples, caused strain in the marriage, and other personal problems arose over the years as well. The marriage eventually lapsed into a protracted separation and ended in divorce in 1930.[14]

In 1915 Douglas completed his master's degree in economics at Columbia and accepted a graduate scholarship to continue his studies at Harvard University. He chose Harvard in order to strengthen his knowledge of economic theory and profited from the teaching there of Professors F. W. Taussig, T. N. Carver, and C. J. Bullock but overall found his year in Cambridge very disillusioning. Douglas abhorred the "deep-rooted provincialism and social snobbery" that he encountered among the students and faculty in Cambridge. In particular, he rejected the very conservative approach to labor-management relations that predominated in the classrooms there. He said: "The economics department at Harvard, with only one or two notable exceptions, on the whole disliked poor people and sided with the wealthy and powerful, and those of social importance. This repelled me, and I have never felt too warmly toward Harvard since."[15]

With a growing family to support and disenchanted with his studies at Harvard, Douglas decided to postpone the completion of his doctoral work and begin a teaching career. In 1916 he accepted an instructorship at the University of Illinois and, a year later, an assistant professorship at Reed College in Portland, Oregon. America's entry into the First World War in 1917 intervened, however, and provided for Douglas a difficult decision. Originally unclear about the culpability of the Allies and the Central Powers, he followed Woodrow Wilson's strictures urging strict neutrality in thought and action. After the Treaty of Brest-Litovsk, which concluded the alliance between Germany and Russia, he feared the likely triumph of Prussian militarism and began speaking of the need for victory by England and France. Yet his religious beliefs left him opposed to the taking of human life, and he initially registered his pacifism with government authorities. By the second year of U.S. participation in the conflict, his heightened commitment to the Allied cause and sense of duty overrode his earlier misgivings, and he sought to enlist in the army. Rejected by the military because of poor eyesight, he considered serving in the Canadian Army (which had lower standards) but opted instead to work for the federal government settling labor disputes. Douglas and his family spent the duration of the war in Philadelphia where he served as a labor disputes adjustor for the Emergency Fleet Corporation.[16]

During his brief residence in Pennsylvania, Douglas and his wife visited the Quaker school at Westtown where he read the *Journal of John Woolman*. Learning about Woolman, an eighteenth-century Quaker who devoted his life to freeing the slaves in America, led Douglas into a deeper examination of the Quaker faith. His bent toward pacifism dovetailed with the Quaker belief in redemptive love as the superior alternative to violence. His inclination to champion the rights of the unfortunate in unpopular causes found eloquent statement in the Quaker call for speaking truth to power. His desire to reform society made perfect sense in the context of the Quaker doctrine of good works. Finally, the Quaker belief in the innate power of good will reinforced the essential optimism in Douglas's personality that allowed him to suffer many defeats yet not lose faith in the righteousness of his cause. He later explained how the Quaker concept of good will profoundly affected his life:

> In the Quaker tenets, for the first time I realized the contagious power of good will. If like a biologist, one views life as a struggle between bacteria, still one must admit that ill will is divisive and destructive, and good will is uniting and constructive. The problem of life, then, is to increase the "bacteria," the infective centers of friendliness. . . . In brief, I do have great faith in the power of friendliness and good will to touch other people and change many of their attitudes.[17]

In 1920 he joined the Society of Friends and, although in the next decades the rise of bellicose totalitarian states led Douglas to renounce the doctrine of nonresistance and to attend meetings for worship less frequently, he remained nominally a member of the sect. Most important, even though his connections to the Society of Friends became more attenuated with time, Quaker tenets continued to inform his concept of service to society. "With all their imperfections," Douglas noted of the Quakers, "they are, I believe, the best corporate body of men and women with whom it has ever been my privilege to be associated."[18]

After concluding his work with the Emergency Fleet Corporation, Douglas taught for a year at the University of Washington in Seattle. Burdened with a heavy teaching assignment, he nevertheless managed to write a number of scholarly articles that year on labor topics, most notably concerning the federal government's role in arbitrating labor disputes and the relationship of newly developing shop committees to established trade unions. Adjunct teaching at the Seattle Labor College allowed him to learn more about the Pacific Northwest's dynamic labor movement. The following year, Douglas joined the economics faculty at the University of Chicago and established a home there for the remainder of his academic career. Founded by John D. Rockefeller in 1892, the University of Chicago had quickly become a first-rate institution of higher learning, and its economics department had earned the reputation of being among the nation's best. Douglas loved the university, savoring its commitment to academic freedom and appreciating the opportunity to work alongside distinguished colleagues. Settling into the academic community in the Chicago neighborhood of Hyde Park, he became a member of one of the city's staunch reform enclaves in the historically progressive Fifth Ward. He also established a spiritual home, attending Society of Friends meetings along with Jane Addams and the rest of the small but vibrant Quaker meeting at Hull House.[19]

Through his association with Jane Addams, Douglas became a member of Chicago's vital reform community. He developed lasting friendships with Julia Lathrop and Grace and Edith Abbott and, at their invitation, offered lecture courses at Hull House and to union study groups. He became acquainted with the leadership of such labor unions as the Amalgamated Clothing Workers and the International Ladies' Garment Workers, and his contacts with the immigrant patrons of Hull House heightened his interest in the perils confronting the teeming masses in America's heterogeneous metropolises. Similarly, increased contact with members of the Brotherhood of Sleeping Car Porters and the National Association for the Advancement of Colored People led to a growing concern with the circumstances of Chicago's rapidly expanding African American community. Douglas's involvement with reform causes and his burgeoning network of associations outside of Hyde Park played a large role in his decision to remain at the University of Chicago when other academic job offers materialized.[20]

In 1921 Douglas took a leave of absence to complete the requirements for the Ph.D. degree from Columbia University. His doctoral dissertation, "American Apprenticeship and Industrial Education," examined the eighteenth-century rise and twentieth-century fall of apprenticeship in American industry. The nearly seven-hundred-page tome went beyond a historical study of a changing labor practice, advocating greater vocational education for children as a necessary replacement for the outmoded apprenticeship system. Denouncing the impersonality of work in the modern factory and excoriating the pervasive role of the profit motive in labor-management relations, he sought a way of humanizing the work experience for the masses. His seventeen-point program called for such items as raising the age of compulsory education to sixteen years, free tuition and financial aid to children of poor families, revision of public school curricula to include prevocational guidance counseling, and other programs to be administered by a federal department of education. Such initiatives would be funded by federal taxes on personal income, excess profits, and inheritances. The obscure doctoral dissertation in economics attracted scant attention at the time of its completion, and its ideas seemingly left little imprint on Washington policymakers, but it serves as a convenient summary of many of the economic nostrums Douglas propounded in later years. The dissertation bore the unmistakable imprint of the idealistic Quaker reformer.[21]

At the University of Chicago, Douglas moved quickly up the academic ranks, achieving promotion from assistant to associate professor in 1923 and to full professor in 1925. He devoted considerable time to his classes and became known as an excellent instructor. In his early years of teaching, Douglas ruefully acknowledged, he had driven his students hard and been known as something of a martinet in the classroom. Reflecting his growing attention to Quaker principles, he softened his approach while at the University of Chicago by encouraging his students to work with him and not for him. Determined to cultivate personal relationships with his students so that the large and imposing university would not seem too impersonal, he set aside times each week for individual conferences and invited every student in his classes to his home at least once per term. He took great pride in the achievements of his students, three of whom—Paul Samuelson, Gregg Lewis, and Jacob Mosak—later achieved great distinction as economists.[22]

While attending to his teaching and other faculty duties, Douglas established himself as a prominent economist and specialist in labor relations. Although he did not see his published work belonging to any formal "school" of economic thought, it seems clear that his research reflected the influence of Henry Seager, Wesley Mitchell, and others who closely studied the impact of economic forces on the lives of laboring men and women. Like other economists interested in examining national income aggregates, he became an avid practitioner of econometrics (the application of mathematical and statistical techniques in testing economic theories). Toiling sixty and seventy hours a week to sustain an ambitious research program along with his teaching, he published several articles per year and a book every two or three years during the 1920s. (Altogether, he published more than 300 articles and twenty books in an academic career that spanned nearly two decades.) Frequently Douglas found it possible to publish scholarly treatises that echoed his concern with social welfare issues and reinforced his progressive political views. In 1921, for example, the *American Economic Review* awarded an article he coauthored with his wife first prize in a contest. The 118-page article, "What Can a Man Afford?" called for increased charity to aid society's unfortunates and for more efficient administration of philanthropic institutions. A book he coauthored in 1923 with two other economists, *The Worker in Modern Economic Society,* sharply criticized conditions in the workplace and called for laborers to receive more compensation for their efforts.[23]

In 1925, working in conjunction with the International Labor Organization, Douglas published *Wages and the Family,* a detailed analysis of family income that attracted much attention from social scientists and commanded laudatory reviews in professional journals and popular periodicals. Having carefully described the difficulties encountered by families attempting to live on workers' meager wages, he offered as a solution the payment of a "family-based wage." According to Douglas's blueprint, the family and not the individual worker would be the unit of calculation for wage rates. Employees would receive a minimum wage along with an additional sum for other dependents that would be paid to their wives; single men would receive no additional stipends. In order to forestall any potential abuses by employers who might shortchange workers, he prescribed federal legislation and supervision. Although, as Douglas argued in the book, precedent for such payment plans existed in France by mutual agreement between workers and employers and in Australia by law, his design for ameliorating the harshness of capitalism's wage system never attracted much support in the United States.[24]

Throughout the 1920s, Douglas focused much of his scholarly attention on a detailed examination of wages and their adequacy for workers. To compute the actual amounts of goods and services workers could purchase based upon their hourly, weekly, and annual earnings for each year since 1890, he employed a number of research assistants whose salaries he paid by adopting a rigorous public speaking schedule in Chicago and the Midwest. He published the result of this laborious research, *Real Wages in the United States, 1890–1926,* in 1930 to much acclaim. Among Douglas's conclusions, several assumed importance in the context of the Coolidge-era boom and the collapse of prosperity at decade's end. From 1923 to 1927, workers' real earnings remained stagnant even while stock market values increased dramatically. Despite the great disparity between profits and wages, he argued, net incomes of all classes increased most when labor unions exerted influence—or when the threat of unionization kept the corporate world honest. In all, Douglas concluded that a more equitable distribution of income and government restrictions on market speculation would have significantly mitigated the economy's breakdown at the end of the 1920s. A companion volume published the following year, *The Movement of Money and Real Wages in the United States, 1926–1928,* affirmed these findings with particular attention to the years immediately preceding the stock market crash.[25]

Douglas's growing reputation in the field of labor relations resulted in business and the unions agreeing to his selection as chairman of the newspaper industry's national board of arbitration in 1925. Because the arbitration decisions frequently involved much acrimony and the chairman often held the deciding vote on a board evenly split between business and labor partisans, arbitrators seldom served for a great length of time. The fact that the newspaper publishers and the printing unions requested Douglas's retention as chairman for sixteen years before America entered the Second World War was a testament to his reputation for fairness and impartiality. The generous compensation for his arbitration services proved a welcome supplement to the professor's modest salary, and he found the work stimulating. Moreover, the success he enjoyed reinforced his faith in collective bargaining as an effective means of resolving labor-management disputes.[26]

While Douglas's career flourished, his marriage faltered. "We were two people with some common interests but with strong wills and dissimilar temperaments," he concluded. His wife became restive in Chicago, a city that she quickly came to dislike. The University of Chicago prohibited the employment of faculty wives, and she failed to secure a teaching appointment at any other institution in the area. A promising writer and social critic, she chafed at forced inactivity at the same time that her husband's teaching and public activities increasingly kept him away from home. He admitted subsequently to shirking family responsibilities, the decision to devote more time to his work having estranged him from his wife and growing children—just as his own father had done decades before. "In later years," he lamented, "I paid a heavy price for the tenuousness of my relations with the children." The marriage also suffered from widening political differences between a wife whose radicalism was becoming more doctrinaire and a husband whose progressivism remained tempered by his Quaker beliefs. (By the 1930s, according to the Federal Bureau of Investigation, Dorothy Wolff Douglas was secretly a member of the Communist party.) In 1927, at his wife's urging, he accepted a visiting lectureship at Amherst College. When she received a job offer from another institution, they agreed on a separation.[27]

With the four children, Dorothy Wolff Douglas established a new life at Smith College in Newburyport, Massachusetts. She purchased a seventeenth-century mansion where Puritan divine Jonathan Edwards had been married, turning it into a salon for left-wing intellectuals and campus radicals that (the FBI reported) became known in Newburyport as the "Little Kremlin." In 1930 Dorothy Wolff and Paul Douglas obtained a divorce, and she subsequently entered into a long-term intimate relationship with one of the boarders at her sprawling home, avowed communist Katharine Du Pre Lumpkin. (In later years, during her testimony before the House Committee on Un-American Activities, Dorothy Wolff invoked the Fifth Amendment to the Constitution and refused to say whether she was or had ever been a member of the Communist party.) In 1931 Douglas married Emily Taft, the daughter of renowned sculptor Lorado Taft and an actress whose credits on stage included performances in stock companies and in Broadway productions. A University of Chicago graduate and seasoned political activist, Emily Taft held a prominent position in the Illinois League of Women Voters. Their marriage lasted until his death more than forty years later.[28]

Douglas took time off from the visiting lectureship at Amherst College to serve as an economic adviser to a trade union delegation touring the Soviet Union. Organized by Albert F. Coyle, the editor of the *Locomotive*

Engineer's Journal, the delegation included among its members John Brophy, president of the United Mine Workers Union; James Maurer, president of the Pennsylvania Federation of Labor; Columbia University professor Rexford G. Tugwell; and Stuart Chase, best-selling author and economist. Douglas agreed to go only with the assurance that no communists would be included in the trip. To ensure that no questionable organizations contributed to the cost of the excursion, he paid his own travel expenses. During the visit, the Americans toured collective farms in the Ukraine and met with Joseph Stalin and Leon Trotsky in Moscow. At an airplane factory where Douglas gave a brief speech, Russian workers harangued him over the sensational Sacco and Vanzetti trial in which the two immigrants had been found guilty and sentenced to death. Citing the outcome of the proceedings as an example of corrupt American jurisprudence and unfair treatment of the proletariat, the workers went on to criticize capitalism for its inherent exploitation of workers. Forcing an interpreter to translate, Douglas responded with a spirited defense of American institutions in which he admitted his belief in the innocence of Sacco and Vanzetti but argued for the inherent soundness of American democracy. The debate became more intense, and with the agitated crowd shouting revolutionary slogans the tour guide hurriedly adjourned the meeting.[29]

Douglas came away from his visit to the Soviet Union with decidedly mixed impressions. On the positive side of the ledger, the admittedly low standard of living in the country had nevertheless shown evidence of some improvement in recent years, and despite the existence of a totalitarian government he did not find stark economic inequality there. Railroad and factory workers, in particular, enjoyed much better purchasing power than they had before the revolution. A measure of private enterprise clearly survived in farming and some service trades and to good effect. Moreover, he observed, there seemed to exist a "spiritual unity among the people" that impressed the American visitors. On the other hand, Douglas deplored the Communist party's authoritarian control of every aspect of the people's lives. In the delegation's report of the visit, "Russia after Ten Years," Douglas wrote a scathing condemnation of the Soviet government's violations of civil liberties only to find that section of the document considerably softened in the final version edited by Coyle. Based upon his observations there, Douglas expressed hope that the USSR and the United States could find common ground for economic cooperation despite their very different systems of government and assented to the recommendation that the United States recognize the Soviet Union as a sovereign state.[30]

After his return from the Soviet Union, Douglas resumed his reform activities. In 1928 he became a contributing editor for the *World Tomorrow,* a journal founded during World War I by the Fellowship of Reconciliation to protest the incarceration of conscientious objectors. A target of the Justice Department during the Red Scare of 1919–1920, the publication continued in the next decade to be a forum for pacifists who sought social reform in America as well as peace abroad. Douglas's essays and editorials in the *World Tomorrow* criticized the backward policies of both political parties and urged thoroughgoing economic reform. He severed his ties with the journal in the early 1930s when the rising fascist menace in Europe led him away from his earlier isolationist position in foreign affairs.[31]

Through his association with the Fellowship of Reconciliation, Douglas became acquainted with Socialist Norman Thomas. In the 1928 presidential election, he repudiated the candidates of the two major parties and publicly supported Thomas. Speaking for thirty-six leading educators who urged votes for the Socialist candidate as a protest against the sorry state of the nation's politics, he acknowledged that Republican candidate Herbert Hoover and his Democratic counterpart, Al Smith, were "men of honor" but nevertheless argued that the two presidential aspirants were backed by "sterile and corrupt groups." In an article in the *New Republic,* Douglas argued against the prevailing liberal wisdom that a vote for a third-party candidate like Thomas was a waste. Admitting that Thomas had no realistic chance of being elected, he nonetheless noted that support of a real reformer outside of the entrenched political system constituted the best means of wrenching concessions from the two parties. Fearful of losing their progressive wings, he argued, the Democratic and Republican leaderships would have to consider policies they otherwise would dismiss and "a liberal can, therefore, exercise more influence upon the old parties from without." Most important, the support of the Socialist party would help lay the groundwork for the creation of a labor party in America. Douglas declined to join the Socialist party—he rejected the key party tenet that class struggle was inevitable—but concluded that it temporarily offered the best venue for replicating the kind of labor party that thrived in England.[32]

In 1929 Douglas contributed an essay to a book edited by Norman Thomas and Harry W. Laidler, executive director of the League for Industrial Democracy, which provided a clear statement of his reform views at that time. First, he dismissed Karl Marx's dialectical theory that forecast the inevitable destruction of capitalism. Economic evolution, he believed, was not a "blind force" that inexorably determines the fate of nations. War rather than economic determinism posed the gravest threat to American democracy. Second, while stating that socialism presented a more humane and equitable economic system than capitalism, he rejected the totality of state control practiced in the Soviet Union. Voluntary associations would be essential to protect workers, farmers, and consumers from a potentially oppressive state. From a totally pragmatic standpoint, moderate differences in wages would have to be tolerated in order to recognize skill levels and to foster initiative. Most important, regardless of capitalism's many flaws, the people must willingly choose socialism; democracy and not dictatorship should be the avenue for change. Douglas rejected the substitution of socialism for capitalism through violent revolution as impractical as well as immoral. These principles suggest that his inchoate view of socialism placed him at the radical fringe of the American polity on the eve of the Great Depression. His commitment to socialism largely theoretical, he declined to join the Socialist party and fiercely opposed communism. At the same time, he felt that socialism had much to offer a capitalist society that bred inequality and failed to care adequately for its unfortunates. His Quaker beliefs and innate optimism led him down a path of social activism that emphasized service to the community.[33]

According to Douglas's political views, nothing damaged the public interest more than monopoly capitalism, and beginning in 1929 he became involved in a populist crusade against one of the nation's most powerful tycoons, utilities magnate Samuel Insull. The struggle against Insull lasted for years, ended in a surprising victory for the antimonopoly forces, and made Douglas a prominent national figure for the first time. Known as the uncrowned king of Chicago, Insull wielded influence that extended throughout the state and much of the nation as well. He owned the Windy City's two purveyors of electricity (Commonwealth Edison and Public Service of Northern Illinois), the gas company, and the elevated traction lines. His national corporations, Insull Utility Investments and Corporation Securities, managed a byzantine network of holding companies that in turn controlled dozens of utility companies throughout the country. Insull safeguarded his economic interests through a series of alliances with Illinois's most powerful politicians, beginning with Chicago's Republican mayor, William H. "Big Bill" Thompson, and Democratic leaders Anton Cermak and George Brennan. He also provided huge sums of money for the election of Frank L. Smith to the U.S. Senate. Smith's chairmanship of the Illinois Commerce Commission allowed the Insull concerns to maintain high utility rates despite reduced costs and soaring profits.[34]

Douglas and other reformers targeted Insull because of the expiration of Chicago's traction franchises in 1927. The utilities magnate owned the city's elevated lines while, pursuant to the franchise ordinance of 1907, different companies owned the various streetcar lines. By the mid-1920s, all lines needed improvements and extensions, and a growing sentiment existed for more efficient service through the reorganization and unification of all the companies. In 1929 a five-man committee appointed by a federal judge concluded its investigation and proposed the following solution: All lines would be consolidated as a private corporation with total assets valued at $264 million under an "indeterminate franchise" with Insull as manager. To safeguard the public interest, the arrangement required enabling legislation from the state legislature in Springfield, similar ordinances from the Chicago City Council, and approval by a popular referendum. Chary of vesting such power in one person, members of the Cook County Real Estate Board approached Douglas and asked him to determine whether the proposal truly served the public interest.[35]

Douglas spent the winter and spring months of 1929 carefully scrutinizing the proposed legislation, especially the valuation claims. He uncovered a report, which had been prepared earlier by the chairman of the New York Public Utility Commission for Chicago mayor William E. Dever and suppressed by a city council subcommittee, which proved especially helpful in exposing falsehoods and exaggerations in the Insull proposal. The report showed that the estimates of the value of the transit equipment ignored years of wear and tear and offered no deductions for the deterioration of the property. Insull listed among the inventories tracks and cars no longer in use along with horses long deceased. Affixing more realistic values to the transit lines' assets, Douglas estimated the total worth of the companies to be about $130 million. Insull's suggested valuation of $264 million therefore contained $134 million of water. Douglas warned that the bill under consideration also failed to grant the city power to terminate franchises for misuse, thereby limiting accountability on the operation of public transit. Finally, the bill obligated the city to construct a subway that would be given to Insull's traction holdings at no cost. In short, Douglas reasoned, "The ordinance gives away the city's rights in the street in perpetuity and returns to the city virtually nothing in exchange."[36]

Douglas's findings galvanized the opposition to Insull's plan. In 1929 several of the city's most prominent reformers, including Harold L. Ickes, Charles E. Merriam, and Donald Richberg, formed the People's Traction League (PTL) to educate the public and to lobby state and local legislators against the traction proposal. Former mayors Carter Harrison and Edward F. Dunne, though well advanced in years and no longer active in public affairs, lent their names to the reform cause, and William Randolph Hearst provided the editorial backing of his two Chicago daily newspapers, the *American* and the *Herald and Examiner.* Harold Ickes assumed the chairmanship of the fledgling organization. As the PTL's chief economic authority, Douglas gave public speeches and testified before the state legislature and the city council throughout the summer of 1929. In August, when Ickes suffered recurring hemorrhaging that required him to curtail his public activities, Douglas devoted himself fulltime to PTL business. The efforts of the reformers notwithstanding, the state legislature passed the enabling legislation by a four-to-one margin, and the Chicago City Council concurred with but one dissenting vote.[37]

In the spring of 1930, as the Insull forces and the PTL waged a public relations war prior to the public referendum, Douglas was absent from Chicago while he served as acting director of the Swarthmore College Unemployment Study. (Douglas's marriage had just ended in divorce, and he accepted the temporary appointment at Swarthmore, he said, because it "permitted me to lick my wounds in private while I worked on a new set of [economic] problems.") Ickes and Douglas corresponded regularly during those months, the former reporting on the PTL's activities and the latter drafting speeches, letters to the editor for publication in Chicago newspapers, and position papers he had written for the reformers' use. In these essays, Douglas systematically attacked the particulars of the ordinance approved by the city council, predicting that popular approval of the measure would not only arrogate unrestrained authority to the Insull concerns but also inevitably result in increased fares on surface and elevated lines. As an alternative, Douglas proposed municipal ownership with the regulating body composed of public-minded citizens rather than elected municipal officials. Again, however, the efforts of the reformers ended in abject failure. The Insull propaganda campaign and a rumored wholesale purchase of votes, activities generously underwritten by local bankers, resulted in a lopsided referendum vote— 325,468 in favor and 58,212 opposed.[38]

Although they seemed to be more casualties of the Insull steamroller, the Chicago reformers refused to surrender and continued in the next few years to scrutinize the operations of the local utilities industry. As conditions worsened in the Great Depression, Insull's far-flung empire began to crack as many of his corporate holdings elsewhere went bankrupt. Believing that Insull was using the profits from his comparatively healthy Chicago businesses to subsidize failures nationwide, Douglas and his cohorts charged that the Illinois Commerce Commission had guaranteed exorbitant profits for the Insull corporations by failing to provide rate reductions for consumers. In 1931 Douglas, Ickes, Richberg, Merriam, Clarence Darrow, and several utilities experts organized the Utility Consumer and Investors League of Illinois as a watchdog agency devoted to the protection of consumer interests. The following year, the organization lodged a vigorous protest when the Illinois Commerce Commission approved without warning a $72 million bond issue for intercorporate transfers among holding companies. Here, charged Douglas, was a classic example of how funds were being drained from Illinois enterprises to undergird the shaky substructure of the Insull empire.[39]

In the summer of 1932, the Illinois Commerce Commission belatedly held hearings on the proposed bond issue. From the outset of the proceedings, members of the commission sought to divert attention from substantive issues and instead discredit the motives of the reformers. Douglas became the principal target, the object of a red-baiting attack based upon his 1927 visit to the Soviet Union and alleged communist sympathies. Commission members even impugned Douglas's Quaker beliefs. Upon the advice of Harold Ickes, who served as his legal counsel, Douglas refused to respond to hostile questions and demanded that the matter of the bond issue alone be addressed. The session degenerated into a shouting match, Ickes pronounced the proceedings unfair and biased, and he and Douglas stormed out of the room. Outside the hearing, Douglas suffered as well. The *Chicago Tribune* accused him of undermining both the public's faith in the regulatory process and investors' confidence in the utilities industry. La Salle Street bankers and other prominent businessmen called for Douglas to lose his teaching position, but University of Chicago president Robert Maynard Hutchins resisted the pressure to initiate dismissal proceedings.[40]

Once again, the quixotic campaign against Insull seemed to be running aground, and Douglas's spirits sank. One day, as he was preparing to leave Chicago for Springfield to testify before the Illinois Commerce Commission, the harried Douglas discovered that he had sent his only good pair of pants to the cleaners. Finding the shop closed, he frantically searched for the owner and persuaded him to open the shop and retrieve the pants. As the train pulled out of the station bound for the state capital and he reflected on the absurdity of the day's events, he recalled thinking to himself: "Oh, what a fool you are Douglas. Only one good pair of pants to your name and here you are trying to fight the whole Insull empire!"[41]

Two days after the conclusion of the hearings, however, Insull fled to Paris. The financial news for the utility tycoon's distended empire had been steadily worsening, and the muckraking efforts of the Utility Consumer and Investors League had begun to pay huge dividends. As Insull fled from Paris to Greece and finally returned to the United States under arrest, Douglas and his cohorts produced proof that members of the City Council Committee on Transportation and the Illinois House of Representatives had purchased stock in Insull corporations at bargain rates before voting for the traction legislation. In addition, they showed that a number of leading bankers who supposedly safeguarded the interests of stockholders in Insull companies had themselves received sweetheart deals on the very same stock. The collapse of the Insull conglomerate occurred rapidly amid a rush of disclosures concerning corruption and influence peddling. Indicted but not convicted of mail fraud and embezzlement, Insull lost his fortune and became one of the fallen idols of the 1920s business culture. "I do not claim to be the cause of his downfall and flight," Douglas said, but clearly the reformers' efforts played a significant role in Insull's dramatic plunge.[42]

Best of all, in Douglas's view, the Insull struggle led to genuine reform in Chicago. In the spring of 1933, newly elected Illinois governor Henry Horner telephoned Douglas at home and asked him to draft a model utilities bill for the state. Based upon the existing New York legislation, Douglas's version broke new ground in two ways. First, the proposed law allowed the Illinois Commerce Commission to initiate rate actions against utility companies and not just act as an impartial tribunal when consumer groups sought relief. Second, the bill gave the commission greater authority in assessing the valuation claims of the corporations. Douglas testified before the Utilities Committee of the state senate and again suffered harsh treatment at the hands of several legislators who enjoyed close relations with utilities interests. But with Governor Horner's ardent backing and the Hearst papers marshaling public support, the Illinois Utilities Act of 1933 passed without amendment. In the next few years, the Illinois Commerce Commission moved slowly and made infrequent use of its new authority to supervise the utilities industry, but the situation gradually improved. Governor Horner prodded the recalcitrant members of the commission into action by periodically threatening to appoint Douglas chairman.[43]

The Insull imbroglio proved to be a milestone in the city's reform history. Sustained by his Quaker belief in speaking truth to power, Douglas took on not only Insull but also many of the city's most influential citizens. "We . . . made many highly placed Chicagoans squirm," he remembered some years later. Eventual success after years of disheartening setbacks reinforced his belief in the efficacy of their cause specifically and the need for vigilant oversight of society's rich and powerful generally. As well, collaboration with Ickes, Richberg, Merriam, and other luminaries expanded Douglas's network of associations with the leading reformers of the age. He had provided the invaluable economic expertise necessary to dissect the Insull interests and established himself in the forefront of the reform movement. The protracted struggle, which had been covered extensively by the press, transformed the obscure college professor into a public figure.[44]

As the crusade against Insull concluded, Douglas's interest turned increasingly to the presidential election of 1932. The massive unemployment and widespread suffering of millions of Americans during the Great Depression left him convinced of the necessity of new leadership in Washington. "Hoover was oblivious to both the causes and the means of alleviating the depression," concluded Douglas. He had been consistently critical of Hoover's ineffectual economic policies and helped to draft an appeal signed by 1,028 economists that unsuccessfully urged the president to veto the disastrous Smoot-Hawley Tariff. A staunch advocate of public power, Douglas excoriated Hoover for his veto of the Muscle Shoals bill. The liberal economist especially rued Hoover's steadfast refusal to expand significantly the activities of the federal government during the crisis. Like Republican presidents Harding and Coolidge before him, Douglas charged, Hoover simply allowed the nation's industrial tycoons to make decisions about the government's economic policies.[45]

As in 1928, however, Douglas also expressed disappointment with the Democratic alternative. He knew Franklin D. Roosevelt moderately well, having accepted the New York governor's invitation to serve as a consultant to the New York Committee to Stabilize Employment in 1930 and having helped him prepare an economic conference for governors in 1931. Douglas genuinely liked Roosevelt and admired the way he had battled against polio to remain an active political figure. He believed that Roosevelt had taken progressive stands on some issues such as compulsory unemployment insurance and public power but had shied away from confrontations with the powerful Tammany Hall machine in New York City. Generally he saw the well-intentioned Roosevelt as the captive of a Democratic party whose policies differed little from those of the Republicans. "While one can understand Governor Roosevelt's position," concluded Douglas, "farmers, workers, and liberals should beware of placing excessive reliance upon a well-meaning though ambitious man to effect a deep-sea change in the Democratic party."[46]

In 1932 Douglas continued to advocate the formation of a third political party, one that would truly serve the interests of the nation's progressives. That year, he published *The Coming of a New Party,* in which he called for old-age pensions, unemployment compensation, national health insurance, improved child labor legislation, and minimum wage and maximum hour laws. He again proposed his family wage plan as the centerpiece for economic reform. Douglas recommended close cooperation with the Socialist party in the short term but felt that ultimately a new progressive party (which he declined to name) would be needed. Fearing that communists would attempt to infiltrate the new party and assume control of it, he urged that they be excluded explicitly from membership. In a passage that his political enemies later unearthed to embarrass him, Douglas wrote:

> There is indeed no logical place in American life for the Democratic party. The Republican party has a definite place and a real function to perform. It represents the conservative elements and the propertied classes. There is room for one such party. But there is not room for two.

In 1932, as he had done four years earlier, Douglas voted for Norman Thomas for president. As vice-chairman of the League for Independent Political Action, an organization whose members included John Dewey, Fiorello LaGuardia, Thomas R. Amlie, and Oswald Garrison Villard, he helped in 1933 to organize a national conference of progressives who remained interested in forming a farmer-labor party to challenge the Democrats and Republicans.[47]

Douglas's highly publicized battles with the Insull conglomerate had attracted much attention nationally, ratifying his progressive credentials as a fearless reformer and cementing his reputation as one of the nation's foremost economists specializing in consumer issues. As a result, the Roosevelt administration appointed him a member of the fledgling Consumer's Advisory Board of the National Recovery Administration (NRA). Douglas accepted the appointment despite his suspicion that the NRA's governmentally supervised cartels would prove to be an ineffective panacea and despite his low regard for the agency's chief administrator, General Hugh S. Johnson. A series of disappointing experiences confirmed his doubts about the NRA's worth and his specific fears that consumer issues would be lost in the rush to serve business interests. The codes of fair competition negotiated by NRA committees allowed price-fixing and restricted output, he believed, while organized labor sought higher wages for its members but ignored the welfare of consumers. Douglas told newspaper editor William Allen White that he hoped to create a consumers' movement equal to the trade union movement, but he encountered insuperable obstacles. The Consumer's Advisory Board repeatedly challenged the more onerous provisions of the codes but without success, leading Douglas to conclude that a U.S. Department of the Consumer should be created within the president's cabinet. In attempting to muster support for consumers, he encountered the long-standing problem of defending the interests of an amorphous group with no political influence. As he put it, "We were disregarded because we had no organized constituency behind us and represented only the diffused interests of uninformed and otherwise occupied consumers."[48]

At the direction of the Consumers' Advisory Board chairman, Mary Harriman Rumsey, Douglas established a national chain of nearly one hundred consumer councils. These local councils received and forwarded consumers' complaints, demanded accurate advertising and labeling of goods, and, perhaps most important, sought to arouse public concern with consumer issues. The vast majority of the councils disappeared when the Supreme Court found the NRA unconstitutional in 1935, so improvements tended to be short-lived. Douglas also served on the NRA's code authority for the consumer-finance industry, where his suggestions for the drafting of the codes were poorly received. Convinced that common practice in the credit industry allowed for exorbitant interest rates, Douglas proposed at the code authority's first meeting a series of reforms on behalf of consumers. The meeting promptly adjourned, and a few days later he received a letter urging his resignation from the group. A disenchanted Douglas left the NRA altogether and returned to his teaching duties in Chicago. A quarter of a century later, he revived his interest in the consumer credit industry and fought for the very same reforms that the NRA code authority rejected in the 1930s.[49]

Despite his increasing political activism and a demanding teaching load, Douglas continued to be an extraordinarily productive scholar. In order to continue publishing at such a rapid rate while engaging in so many other activities, he maintained an exhausting work schedule. A custodian at the University of Chicago reported that Douglas placed a washstand in the hallway, and two or three times late at night he would emerge from his office, soak his head in cold water to keep himself awake, and go back inside to continue writing. Such dedication resulted in the publication of a series of books in the 1930s, his scholarly work reflecting an ongoing commitment to improve workers' lives. In 1931 he coauthored *The Problem of Unemployment,* a careful look at the role played by new technology in the displacement of workers during the Great Depression's early years. Thanks to a Guggenheim Fellowship, he spent part of 1931 in Europe studying joblessness patterns and unemployment insurance. In his 1933 book *Standards of Unemployment Insurance,* which he dedicated to University of Wisconsin economist John R. Commons, the leading advocate of unemployment insurance, Douglas argued the case for its implementation in the United States. He lauded Commons's pioneering efforts on behalf of unemployment insurance but took exception with the Wisconsin economist's specific prescriptions for implementation. Whereas Commons argued that employers should bear the financial burden for unemployment insurance, Douglas called for a state-pooled fund.[50]

In 1934 Douglas published *The Theory of Wages,* the final version of a manuscript he had revised continuously for the previous eight years. In 1926 a committee of distinguished economists had awarded the original version of that manuscript the $5,000 first prize in an international competition sponsored by the Hart, Schaffner, and Marx Company. Concerned that his earlier studies of wage rates suffered from the lack of a comprehensive theory of production, he had continued to refine the analysis and withheld the manuscript from publication as he conducted additional research in a number of different nations. Collaborating with mathematician Charles W. Cobb, Douglas devised a formula for determining the relative contributions made by labor and capital on production. After presenting a paper on the "Cobb-Douglas function" at the annual meeting of the American Economic Association in 1927, he continued to experiment with different data sets to refine the conclusions. Finally published in 1934, *The Theory of Wages* received widespread acclaim and became, Douglas felt, his chief claim to scholarly distinction. Building upon his earlier work on wages, most notably *Real Wages in the United States, 1890-1926,* he attributed much of the distress in the Great Depression to the inefficiency of a capitalist system that produced massive surpluses and disappointingly small returns on investments. *The Theory of Wages* called for a redistribution of income in favor of wage earners and the indigent, an eventuality that would benefit all classes.[51]

Douglas's *Controlling Depressions,* published in 1935, attributed capitalism's periodic economic crises to the rigidity of wages and prices and the corrosive influence of monopolies; his solution centered on increased government regulation and "pump priming" measures (deficit spending on relief and public works) by the federal government to stimulate spending. He argued that, although federal deficits could not be sustained over the course of major economic cycles, no need existed for a perfectly balanced budget each fiscal year. Douglas's economic prescriptions for the United States far outdistanced the relatively cautious measures undertaken by President Roosevelt. Along with other economists such as Marriner Eccles, Lauchlin Currie, and, most famously, John Maynard Keynes, Douglas earnestly called for more extensive deficit spending by government as the best response to the Great Depression's lingering effects.[52]

Increasingly in the early 1930s, Douglas's research centered on the issue of social security. As early as 1921, during the severe economic contraction following the First World War, he had advocated unemployment insurance—and had been labeled a Bolshevik by his conservative foes. He had also been a forceful proponent of old-age pensions, workmen's compensation, and unemployment compensation, measures that were all included in the omnibus legislation passed by Congress in 1935 as the Social Security Act. Initially, as he explained in *Standards of Unemployment Insurance,* Douglas believed that the unlikely passage of such laws in Washington, D.C., meant that reformers should confine their activities to the state level. In subsequent years, therefore, he drafted the Illinois Old Age Pension Act of 1935, the Illinois Unemployment Insurance Act of 1937, and the 1939 revision of the original Illinois Social Security Act. By middecade, however, he came to believe that such nettlesome problems as old-age and unemployment insurance, as well as hour and wage legislation, could not be dealt with solely by state legislation and would have to be handled by the federal government as well. Accordingly, through his scholarly publications and his consulting work in Illinois, New York, and Pennsylvania, he became one of the foremost spokesmen for national social security legislation.[53]

Not all the experts agreed upon the particulars of how best to implement unemployment insurance, however, and Douglas figured prominently in the disjunction that opened between two groups of economists. On the one hand, the adherents of University of Wisconsin economist John R. Commons believed in assigning the cost of unemployment insurance to the employers. On the other hand, Douglas and other supporters of the "Ohio plan" such as I. M. Rubinow and Abraham Epstein noted the helplessness of many businessmen in the face of cyclical unemployment and questioned whether the "Wisconsin plan" placed unrealistic expectations on employers in an unpredictable economic system; they preferred instead a pooled reserve fund based upon employer and employee contributions. For Douglas and his cohorts, total reliance on employer contributions would inevitably result in a modest fund, limited benefits, and the economic burden falling most heavily on those who often lacked the means to bear it. Their more liberal approach called for financial contributions by government as well as a measure of economic redistribution made possible by a more generous reserve fund—a goal that the economists favoring the Wisconsin plan rejected. In July 1930, Douglas attended a meeting of twenty-three leading economists at the Yale Club in New York City to attempt a reconciliation of the two factions. After a spirited argument that lasted for hours, the group voted 21–2 in favor of the Wisconsin plan.[54]

In 1934 President Roosevelt named the Committee on Economic Security to develop social security legislation. Significantly, Secretary of Labor Frances Perkins selected to serve on the committee a group of economists who favored the Wisconsin plan. Although some New Dealers like Rexford Tugwell and Henry Wallace argued for a federally administered system of unemployment insurance with national standards, the committee opted for a joint national-state system with no minimum standards of benefits prescribed. Excluded from the key policy-making group that fine-tuned the social security bill, Douglas continued to urge a more aggressive approach in a series of articles and speeches and in his testimony before congressional committees considering the legislation. Extremely bitter at their exclusion from the Committee on Economic Security, Epstein and Rubinow denounced the compromise legislation that it produced. Stung by the committee's rejection of his views, Douglas nevertheless stopped short of the public criticism of the Social Security Act engaged in by some of the other dissidents. His 1936 history of the struggle for social security legislation, *Social Security in the United States,* noted the law's shortcomings but also hailed its pathbreaking achievements. From 1935 to 1937, he served on a committee that advised the U.S. Senate and on the Federal Social Security Board for the purpose of revising the original law. In later years, he felt vindication in the widespread recognition of the law's inadequacies regarding unemployment insurance and, as a U.S. senator, helped to pass legislation that would shore up some of those deficiencies.[55]

Rebuffed in his efforts to shape social security legislation along what he considered truly progressive lines, Douglas rekindled his interest in local affairs. The defeat of the Insull interests had been a great victory, but Windy City reformers continued to chafe at the corruption and venality rampant in local government. Republican Mayor Big Bill Thompson, an Insull crony and longtime bête noire of good-government crusaders, lost his bid for reelection in 1931 to Democrat Anton Cermak, but this changing of the guard hardly seemed like progress to the reform community. Indeed, Cermak forged an alliance of Chicago's varied ethnic groups into a powerful Democratic machine that lasted until after Richard J. Daley's death in the 1970s. Cermak died after only two years in office, the victim of an unsuccessful attempted assassination of president-elect Franklin D. Roosevelt. Patrick J. Nash, chairman of the local Democratic party, chose Edward J. Kelly to replace him. The chief engineer of the Sanitary District and the president of the South Park Board, Kelly had never held elective office in Chicago, but his business ties with Nash and strong connections with the Democratic party's dominant Irish leadership made him the choice for mayor. The Kelly-Nash machine ruled Chicago every bit as autocratically as had Cermak and his lieutenants.[56]

For the 1935 municipal elections, a citywide network of reformers fashioned a bipartisan fusion movement patterned after the alliance of Republicans and Democrats constructed in New York City to unseat Tammany Hall officeholders. The fusionists announced a platform that promised reduction of utility rates and fares, cessation of the use of city police as strikebreakers, application of the merit system to appointments and promotions in municipal employment, and elimination of tribute paid from liquor, gambling, and vice syndicates. On February 15, boasting of having collected more than forty thousand nominating petition signatures in seven days, they announced that Paul H. Douglas would be the fusion candidate for mayor against Kelly. Less than two weeks later, however, fusion spokesmen announced that their ticket would include no candidate for the mayor's office. Douglas had reconsidered and withdrawn from candidacy for reasons that he never addressed publicly. In all likelihood, his initial reforming fervor waned as he soberly considered the futility of a race against the powerful Democratic machine.[57]

Kelly won the election handily, defeating his Republican opponent Emil Wetten by a vote of 799,060 to 167,106, and Douglas ended up playing a leading role in a bizarre episode that enlivened an otherwise uneventful campaign. Douglas continued to pillory the Democratic machine yet came to Kelly's defense when independent mayoral candidate Newton Jenkins charged that a cabal of Jewish financiers and lawyers had conspired to reelect the incumbent. Douglas likened Jenkins's campaign to the kind of Hitlerism and Nazism flourishing at that time in Europe. Noting that, like the Nazis, Jenkins's hate-filled campaign relied heavily on anti-Semitism, Douglas called for an end to divisive racial and ethnic politics. Jenkins responded with assertions that a sinister Russian was controlling Douglas and with other thinly veiled references to the University of Chicago professor's alleged communist connections.[58]

Although Douglas's brief foray into independent politics in 1935 proved fruitless, he remained interested in the possibility of effecting reform outside the traditional two-party system. Disappointed with the modest achievements of the New Deal generally and personally frustrated with the limited influence his progressive views had enjoyed in the NRA and the drafting of the Social Security Act, he lacked enthusiasm for the reelection of Franklin D. Roosevelt in 1936. Accordingly, he participated in a summer 1935 gathering in Chicago of approximately 250 self-styled "native American radicals" who founded the American Commonwealth Political Federation. The delegates included New York Representative Vito Marcantonio, Wisconsin Representative Thomas Amlie, and Minnesota Farmer-Laborite Ernest Lundeen. Elected chairman of the conference, Douglas eagerly took part in the acrimonious debate over whether communists should be allowed membership in the new organization. He expressed disappointment that the conference failed to adopt a resolution barring communists outright but took solace in the passage of a motion that excluded from membership all those who did not advocate change through peaceful and democratic measures. After the Chicago gathering, Douglas continued to proselytize for the third-party movement. For the remainder of 1935, as he reported to Thomas Amlie, he corresponded with a host of potential recruits for the American Commonwealth Political Federation.[59]

As one of Chicago's leading liberals, Douglas became embroiled in one of the decade's most sensational labor conflicts. On Memorial Day in 1937, when striking steel workers staged a demonstration in front of the Republic Steel plant in the neighborhood known as South Chicago, police fired into the crowd and then beat retreating strikers. Ten people died in the "Memorial Day Massacre," and although Mayor Kelly defended the police action the outraged public clamored for an impartial investigation. After viewing a newsreel film of the episode that clearly showed policemen shooting into the crowd and later clubbing the wounded on the ground, Douglas agreed to preside at a protest meeting in the Chicago Opera House and to serve as chairman of a citizens' investigating committee. (He consented to undertake these tasks only after receiving assurances that no communists would be admitted to the meeting or be allowed to join the committee.) In its report, the committee condemned the police and recommended the dismissal of two captains who had issued the attack orders. Mayor Kelly took no action against the policemen but promptly met with local union leaders to discuss ways of improving relations between organized labor and local officials. Best of all to Douglas and other liberals, Chicago police stopped employing violence against striking workers.[60]

Though immersed in the local reform scene, Douglas's interest in foreign affairs increased significantly in the mid-1930s. In the fall of 1935, he and his wife, Emily, went to Europe for an extensive vacation and saw firsthand the specter of fascism in Italy. In Rome, the Douglases joined the huge crowd that gathered outside the Palazzo Venezia to hear Benito Mussolini announce the Italian invasion of Ethiopia. The mass hysteria that accompanied Mussolini's theatrical speech and the perfervid displays of nationalism that followed convinced the visiting Americans that the Mussolini dictatorship barely resembled the benign regime portrayed in U.S. newspapers and magazines. "From that afternoon on," Douglas explained, "I realized the threat which Hitler and his ally [Mussolini] had become to the free people of the world." Observing the passive response of the western democracies to Italian aggression and the ineffectualness of the League of Nations, Douglas became convinced that totalitarianism must be thwarted at all costs. Returning to the United States, he became an outspoken critic of the Hitler and Mussolini regimes while urging the British and French to assume more stalwart positions in opposition to the fascist advances. When the Spanish Civil War erupted in 1936, he joined the North American Committee to Aid Spanish Democracy and chaired the Committee on Medical Aid to Spain. In both of those organizations, he fought hard to curtail communist influence for, as firmly as he believed in the antifascist struggle, he believed equally strongly in the need to oppose communism.[61]

The rise of European dictatorships and Douglas's attendant conversion from pacifism to interventionism resulted in his abandonment of socialism in favor of the Democratic party. His association in the early 1930s with such radical organizations as the League for Independent Political Action, the Farmer-Labor Political Federation, and the American Commonwealth Political Federation lapsed as he drifted toward the political mainstream. Douglas's reluctant vote for Franklin D. Roosevelt in 1936 can be explained in part by the administration's spate of liberal legislation in 1935 (the so-called Second New Deal) and, more important, by his belief that the president showed greater awareness than his opponent of the threat to American sovereignty posed by Hitler and his potential allies. Douglas's break with socialist groups owed more than anything else to what he regarded as their misguided naïveté in dismissing the increasing danger of totalitarianism.[62]

By the late 1930s, Douglas was recognized as an influential figure in a number of different arenas. An esteemed professor at the University of Chicago, he was a prolific writer and nationally renowned authority on such economic matters as unemployment, wages, and social security. His expertise in those areas brought him to the attention of policymakers in Washington, D.C., and a number of state capitals where he delivered expert testimony on pending legislation. Because of his many years of service as chairman of the board of arbitration for the newspaper publishing industry, he had become widely known and respected in labor relations circles. The prominent role he played in the campaign against Samuel Insull burnished already impressive reform credentials and elevated his public profile. His understanding of economic principles and commitment to humane causes defined a political outlook forged in the Progressive era, informed by socialism, and shaped by the Quaker notion of good works. An early flirtation with socialism gave way to dissent in closer proximity to the political mainstream. Throughout the 1920s and early 1930s, Douglas could best be characterized as a social democrat. At the same time, even as he became a prominent intellectual of the left, Douglas firmly rejected communism. Convinced that the brand of Marxism practiced in the Soviet Union amounted to a form of totalitarianism, he repudiated its political regimentation while affirming his devotion to freedom and democracy. Douglas had largely remained on the sidelines, confining his activities to writing, theorizing, and championing liberal programs, but his background and devotion to public service made a plunge into electoral politics seem almost inevitable.

Into the Political Arena

2

When I went to the Chicago Board of Aldermen many years ago, I had to decide whether I would try to represent the best interests of the people or be a good fellow with the ruling club. I made my decision, and have never regretted it, nor have I in the Senate. It does not hurt to be a bit lonely.

—**Paul H. Douglas**[1]

• During the Roaring Twenties, rampant corruption in city hall and gangland slayings in the streets earned Chicago the reputation as the nation's wickedest city. In the 1930s, the end of Prohibition led to a decrease in the more sensational episodes of lawlessness, but the city remained a haven for gambling, prostitution, and other varieties of vice. Corruption permeated the police department, the courts, and the ruling Democratic organization. Not only policemen and firemen but even public school teachers had to pay bribes to get their jobs and continue paying tribute to retain them. Reformers blanched when Mayor Edward J. Kelly pugnaciously promised that Chicago would not become a "bluenose" town where the government kept the citizens from enjoying their leisure time. From Washington, D.C., where he served as the secretary of the interior in the Roosevelt administration, Harold L. Ickes observed that the Kelly-Nash machine had "brought Chicago to the lowest ebb in its history. There probably isn't any community in the whole United States that is so abjectly rotten, so dominated by a corrupt and stinking political machine." Ickes complained bitterly to Roosevelt about the unsavory dealings of the Chicago Democratic machine, but the president refused to intervene in local affairs on behalf of good-government legions. After all, the Kelly-Nash machine turned out huge Democratic majorities at election time and publicly supported New Deal policies without reservation. As offensive as the venal machine was to Chicago reformers, its leaders had reached a rapprochement with the Roosevelt administration.[2]

In 1939 Chicago's reformers determined to challenge Mayor Kelly's reelection. Democratic state's attorney Thomas Courtney broke with the machine and declared his mayoral candidacy, but reformers regarded "Fighting Tom" as an opportunist whose record as Cook County's top law enforcement official seemed no better than Kelly's and declined to support him. Instead, they hoped that Courtney's candidacy might split the regular Democratic vote and allow a real reformer such as Harold L. Ickes to win the party primary. Without Ickes's consent, they established a fund-raising committee and opened temporary headquarters from which to conduct his mayoral campaign. Paul Douglas badgered Ickes relentlessly, trying to convince him to resign his post in Washington and return to Chicago to fight the good fight against the hated machine. Although Ickes admitted to being sorely tempted and believed that he could win, an Illinois statute requiring candidates for political office to have resided in their communities for at least a year prior to the elections disqualified the secretary of the interior. Douglas and Ickes then urged Roosevelt to persuade Kelly and Courtney both to withdraw from the race in favor of a liberal Democrat such as Judge John Gutknecht. The president refused to get involved. Both Kelly and Courtney remained in the race, and—unable to arrange for Ickes to oppose them—the reformers finally fielded no candidate for mayor that year.[3]

Meanwhile, as part of their plan to contest the election of Kelly-Nash candidates citywide, reform Democrats sought a candidate to run against the incumbent alderman in Douglas's own Fifth Ward. Along with other members of the Fifth Ward nominating committee, Douglas identified a number of potential candidates, only to have each refuse to make the race. Citing a host of reasons—some claimed lack of time, some declared financial exigency, and others sheepishly referred to skeletons in their closets that they did not want exposed in a hard-fought political campaign—more than a dozen men and women rebuffed the committee's entreaties. With the filing date imminent, the other members of the committee turned to Douglas and urged him to run. Having been critical of the others who had refused to do their civic duty, his reform colleagues reminded Douglas, how could he decline to serve? Douglas initially said no, referring to his already overwhelming schedule of teaching, writing, and other political activities, and his wife, Emily, agreed. But after a sleepless night in which Douglas and his wife concluded that it would be hypocritical of him not to answer the call to service he had just put to others, he announced his willingness to run. Later he explained his decision to enter the contest by saying: "In a city which is not conspicuous for civic probity, I wanted to dramatize the fact that I considered the aldermanic appointment a public trust and not a plum tree."[4]

The Republicans nominated a young lawyer, Noble Lee, to run against the incumbent alderman, Democrat James Cusack, who had allied with the Courtney faction of the party. The regular Democratic organization would also field a candidate, so it seemed like an uphill battle for the politically inexperienced professor. The political calculus changed dramatically, however, when the Kelly-Nash machine offered to support Douglas. In a city hall meeting attended by ten independents, ten Kelly-Nash regulars, and the mayor himself, Douglas noted the incongruity of his representing such disparate groups and offered to withdraw. At the climax of the meeting, Douglas agreed to remain in the race under one condition—that, if elected, he would always be free to follow the dictates of his own conscience and be accountable to no one else. At that, Douglas remembered, Kelly pounded his fist on the table and exclaimed, "That's what I want!" Explaining that the city council had become complacent and one-sided, the mayor said that it needed someone who was unafraid to roil the waters. (Cynics suggested that, facing a potentially tough race against Courtney and worried about the machine's sullied reputation, Kelly hoped his association with a candidate of spotless reputation like Douglas would help with liberal voters.) Subsequently, Douglas filed as an independent with city hall's endorsement. Justifying his alliance with the political machine he had so vigorously tried to topple, he noted the enlightened actions recently taken by Mayor Kelly on a number of issues—striving to provide more adequate relief to the jobless, safeguarding the civil liberties of protesting unemployed groups, and restraining the police from strikebreaking activities during a stockyards strike. "In justice to Ed Kelly," Douglas remarked, "it must be said that he kept his word. Although later we often clashed, he never hit me below the belt, and he kept his followers within the limits of moderation."[5]

Adjacent to Lake Michigan several miles south of Chicago's central business district, the Fifth Ward had long been known as the city's foremost haven for independent politics. From 1909 to 1917, the voters had elected Charles E. Merriam, a University of Chicago political scientist, to the city council and, in the 1920s, had elected two women, Flora Cheney and Katherine Goode, to the state legislature. Yet by the late 1930s demographic changes and shifting political allegiances made the Hyde Park neighborhood something of an electoral enigma. The area west of Washington Park, once predominantly Irish, had become inhabited primarily by African Americans. Whereas black voters had earlier been loyal Republicans, the benign policies of the Roosevelt and Kelly administrations had begun to make the Democratic party a more alluring alternative. Although many affluent Jews had begun to emigrate from the area, Hyde Park remained one of the city's predominant Jewish enclaves. A large Irish Catholic population remained near the lake, and, in the deteriorating Woodlawn neighborhood to the south, rooming houses began to crowd out single-family homes. Of the ward's 126 precincts, only 10 fell within the university community. In such a polyglot and changing community, Douglas's status as an esteemed professor was a limited asset and, given the normal town-and-gown tensions, occasionally a liability. Douglas would have to convince the Fifth Ward's heterogeneous voting blocs that a university professor could effectively represent their disparate interests in the city council.[6]

To reach the thousands of voters scattered throughout the ward who had never heard of him and to scotch notions that he was an ivory tower intellectual out of touch with the real world, Douglas campaigned tirelessly. After completing his classes at the university, he rang doorbells and dropped in to introduce himself at area businesses. In the evenings, he attended a series of teas and other small gatherings of women voters usually scheduled by his wife, a veteran of League of Women Voters activities. In order to dispel rumors that he was a former prohibitionist and devout nondrinker, he made the rounds of Sixty-third Street taverns to share a beer with late-night revelers. (In fact, Douglas was a moderate drinker who limited himself to a half-glass of beer at each bar he visited.) A halting and excessively formal public speaker at first who tended to lecture audiences, he improved his delivery as the campaign proceeded and became much more relaxed at the dias. His energy and sincere interest in the people became evident, and he found that he genuinely liked campaigning.[7]

Even though most of the labor for the campaign came from volunteers, the cost for posters, pamphlets, and telephone charges mounted quickly. Douglas contributed $2,000 of his own money and borrowed $3,000 from his wife's savings. He calculated that friends provided another $2,000 in small contributions and a rich former student gave $3,000. To that sum of $10,000 scraped together by the independents, the Kelly-Nash organization added about twice as much. (With the backing of Courtney Democrats, Cusack probably spent $40,000.) Even though the local press pilloried Douglas for having "sold out" to city hall, the financial resources provided by the Democratic machine proved essential. Moreover, he said, the money from city hall came with no strings attached, and he retained full independence to spend it as he pleased.[8]

On the day of the primary election, the indefatigable Douglas paid a final visit to each of the ward's 126 precincts. He received 15,896 votes to 10,343 for Cusack but, because five other candidates obtained a total of 7,063 votes, narrowly failed to secure the necessary majority for outright victory. He suspected that city hall had held back votes in some precincts to prevent him from winning immediately and thereby force his participation in a runoff election. Kelly-Nash insiders conceded privately that the alliance with the independents had allowed the mayor to win the Fifth Ward and had probably helped with liberal voters in other parts of the city—an advantage Kelly would need in the April election against a formidable Republican candidate, Dwight Green. In the ensuing campaign, the desperate Cusack forces resorted to red-baiting to discredit Douglas. According to his opponent, the professor's 1927 trip to the Soviet Union and his subsequent support for diplomatic recognition of the USSR served as evidence of his communist sympathies. So did his and Emily's "adoption" through a foster parents' organization of a child orphaned during the Spanish Civil War. According to the Republicans, the provision of financial support to an orphan somehow revealed unsavory connections to the communist-aided Loyalists in Spain. Easily discrediting such baseless allegations, Douglas defeated Cusack by a comfortable margin of 22,862 votes to 16,431.[9]

Douglas immediately became something of a curiosity in the city council, an idealistic newcomer to politics surrounded by, as he phrased it, "the cunningest body of legislative bastards to be found in all of the western world." The aldermen, many of whom possessed no more than a grade school education, beheld the "perfessor" with some bemusement. At least initially, he felt very much out of place among the experienced, hardened politicos. Some of the aldermen, salty old pols like Michael "Hinky Dink" Kenna of the First Ward and Mathias "Paddy" Bauler of the Forty-third Ward, were openly hostile to him at first. Bauler often stopped by Douglas's seat in the council chambers to offer him a "Mickey Finn" or threaten to have him beaten. In time, though, most of the aldermen came to appreciate Douglas's hard work, integrity, and good humor in the face of repeated setbacks. While he vigorously disagreed with their policies, he adhered strictly to the practice of never leveling personal attacks against his opponents. Douglas said that, although he disagreed with their views on the issues, he liked nearly all of his colleagues and respected their legislative acumen.[10]

Even though Douglas won the grudging respect of the other aldermen, he remained very much an idealistic crusader who exercised decidedly little influence in city government. Years later, a *Time* article referred to Alderman Douglas as a "gadfly," a "wind-mill-tilter," a "nagging conscience," and a "sponsor of lost causes." During his first year, he repeatedly lost votes in the city council by margins of 49–1. In his second year, John Boyle of the Sixteenth Ward fashioned a reformist alliance with Douglas on matters concerning the municipal budget and public transit; thereafter, they commonly lost 48–2. Douglas and Boyle rejoiced when reaching the high-water mark of their apostasy, once marshaling 9 votes in a losing cause. They could take some satisfaction in sparking lively debate on issues that otherwise would have been rubber-stamped in silence and thereby making the city council something of a deliberative body. If nothing else, Douglas used the city council floor as a convenient forum to advocate ideas and policies of importance to him—and occasionally to good effect. When the city cut the relief budget by 40 percent, Douglas carried to the city council rostrum a market basket with a week's ration of food for five people. After he removed 40 percent of the eggs, milk, bread, and meat to demonstrate how little remained, a number of aldermen expressed their outrage at what the new budget would mean to relief recipients. Within minutes, Mayor Kelly rushed in from his office to announce that he had found an additional million dollars in the treasury that would be added to the relief budget.[11]

The lingering Great Depression dominated Douglas's years in the city council, forcing him to devote considerable time to the relief crisis. With thousands of Chicagoans unemployed and inadequately housed, city, state, and federal relief allotments remained hopelessly inadequate. Douglas and his aides worked closely with the city relief bureau and the Work Projects Administration (WPA) in an attempt to help as many of the ward's unfortunates as possible. In cooperation with the Friends Service Committee, they converted vacant lots in black residential neighborhoods into recreation areas. They planted vegetable gardens in other deserted spaces and helped organize community groups to take care of them. To replace many of the trees that had been cut down for kindling, the city provided saplings that able-bodied relief clients planted. Douglas provided grass seed to be planted in vacant lots and bought 250 garbage cans for families that could not afford them. He soon found that the sum of his many charitable contributions exceeded his aldermanic salary and that he was paying as much as $250 a month from his university salary. Unable to satisfy the philanthropic demands of Hyde Park churches and other charitable institutions, he demonstrated the extent to which he was subsidizing his aldermanic salary by having his income audited and published each year; his first year in the city council, his net income after expenses totaled $16.72.[12]

Leaving Hyde Park and touring nearby neighborhoods in Chicago's South Side, Douglas inspected the wretched conditions in the sprawling African American ghetto. After viewing the black slums that he described as "sodden, dismal, depressing, and filthy beyond words," Douglas returned home "feeling both physically and mentally befouled." Relying on the same "environmental" arguments employed by the Progressive-era housing reformers, he called for an attack on slums that would benefit all citizens indirectly—that is, better living conditions for the poor would improve public health, reduce crime and juvenile delinquency, and cut police, fire, and hospital costs. Publicizing his slum tours, Douglas prescribed joint activity by local, state, and federal governments to initiate large-scale slum clearance efforts followed by the construction of public housing. His dedication to slum clearance produced few immediate gains as local realtors decried public housing as socialistic and relied on racially restrictive covenants to maintain segregation. His commitment to progressive reform in the areas of race and housing remained firm, however, as later evidenced by his activities in the U.S. Senate.[13]

During his years in the city council, Douglas devoted much of his time to Chicago's lingering traction problem. In 1941 Mayor Kelly asked the city council to approve a new franchise for public transportation. The surface and elevated companies declared the value of their holdings to be $220 million, less than the $264 million Samuel Insull had claimed a decade earlier but (in Douglas's estimation) still grossly inflated. Calculating the value of the transit companies at an estimated $100 million, he predicted that the award of a franchise under the mayor's plan would quickly result in a fare hike from 7 cents to 8 or 9 cents for the ridership and exorbitant profits for the private companies—as well as a fiscal crisis for the city, which was experiencing financial difficulties over the completion of the State Street subway. He contended that the proposed ordinance, with its grant of a perpetual franchise and no requirement for improvements, would even have pleased earlier traction magnates like Samuel Insull and Charles Tyson Yerkes. Douglas called for the city to purchase the companies and turn them over to a public authority specifically created for the provision of public transportation in the city. Defeating each of the fifteen amendments that Douglas offered, the city council voted 40–6 to award the franchise renewal according to Mayor Kelly's proposal.[14]

Douglas enjoyed no more success in his efforts to ease the city's budget deficit by reducing wasteful expenditures. Espousing the virtues of economy, he contended that as much as $3 million could be saved annually through more efficient delivery of services and the dissolution of anachronistic agencies. He recommended, for example, eliminating the Board of Local Improvements, a municipal bureau that once served a useful function but had become a dumping ground for political appointees. At a time when six workers raised and lowered each of the many bridges spanning the Chicago River, his proposal to discharge a number of bridge tenders similarly promised to save money but threatened to trim loyal members of the Democratic machine from city payrolls. In a series of lopsided votes, the city council rejected Douglas's budgetary amendments and preserved the inefficient operation of a local government based heavily upon patronage.[15]

During 1941, Douglas took time out from his aldermanic duties for a series of activities on behalf of President Roosevelt's foreign policy. Adolf Hitler's defeat of France, the Nazi-Soviet Pact of 1939, the German invasion of the Soviet Union, and other setbacks for Europe's democracies convinced him of the need for action to thwart the Nazis. Living in Chicago, the midwestern capital of isolationism, he read with disquietude the attacks on Roosevelt's foreign policy initiatives published by the anti-interventionist *Chicago Tribune* and the Hearst papers. Challenging the positions of America First, the isolationist organization headquartered in Chicago, he joined William Allen White's Committee to Defend America by Aiding the Allies and drilled once a week with the volunteer Home Defense Unit at the University of Chicago. His total rejection of the Quaker commitment to nonviolence became evident in a debate with Norman Thomas at which he accused isolationists of trying to "avoid an unpleasant happening by burying their heads in the sand." Affirming the necessity of American involvement in the European crisis, he said: "Personal pacifism is impossible for any nation to follow." The Nazi-Soviet alliance confirmed Douglas's distrust of communists and led him to resign from organizations like the International Labor Defense, the National Emergency Conference for Democratic Rights, the Council for Pan American Democracy, and the American Committee for Democracy and Intellectual Freedom that he suspected had fallen under communist influence. Similarly, he resigned from the Institute for Propaganda Analysis, which he felt had become too critical of President Roosevelt's internationalism. After Germany invaded the Soviet Union, he accepted the strategic necessity of supplying aid to Stalin, but did so reluctantly.[16]

Even though Douglas distanced himself from organizations whose patriotism could be questioned, his long-standing involvement in leftist politics made him an inviting target for red-baiting conservatives whose anticommunism remained rabid despite the rise of fascism in Europe. In 1941, citing national security concerns and Douglas's reputed involvement with Communist party "front groups," the Federal Bureau of Investigation (FBI) conducted a formal investigation of his political activities. On July 17 he spoke at length with Bureau agents and denied ever having been a Communist party member or sympathizer. The FBI's investigation concluded that, from 1921 to 1941, Douglas had belonged to such Communist party "front groups" as the American Youth Congress, National Negro Congress, American League Against War and Fascism, American Student Union, and the National Association for the Advancement of Colored People, among others, but that he had not been a member of the Communist party. Bureau reports also noted that Douglas had bitterly denounced the Communist party and its influence on American life. Although political opponents continued to raise questions during the early cold war years about Douglas's putative softness on communism, no evidence exists to indicate that the federal government investigated him again after 1941.[17]

After the Japanese attack on Pearl Harbor that brought the United States into the conflict, Douglas felt very strongly that he should contribute in some way to the war effort—either by serving in the national government or by enlisting in the armed forces. He had for some time considered seeking the Democratic nomination for the U.S. Senate in 1942, a determination influenced in part by the extreme isolationism of the incumbent, Republican C. Wayland "Curly" Brooks.

In January 1942, he wrote to Adlai Stevenson, with whom he had become acquainted on the William Allen White Committee and the Chicago Council on Foreign Relations, about the political situation in Illinois. Acknowledging the unlikelihood that the Kelly-Nash machine would support him for U.S. senator, Douglas suggested that he would seek the nomination regardless. Anticipating that he would lose to the Kelly-Nash candidate in the Democratic primary, he enlisted the aid of Stevenson (who was then serving as special assistant to Secretary of the Navy Frank Knox) in having the age requirement waived for military service. Douglas would be fifty years old in March of that year but claimed to be in splendid physical condition. "I want desperately to get in as an ordinary sailor or soldier," he wrote Stevenson, "and find that the age limits are more generous in the navy and Naval Reserve than in the Army. When the time comes, I hope you will be willing to help me with the Department." Stevenson suggested to Douglas that he might have to settle for a teaching position in one of the navy's training schools, to which Douglas responded that he still aspired to active service.[18]

Douglas announced his candidacy for the U.S. Senate on January 14, 1942, and prepared to wage an uphill campaign against whomever the Chicago Democratic organization endorsed. Rumors abounded that Kelly himself intended to make the race for the Senate, a chilling prospect to influential Illinoisans in Washington like Harold Ickes and Frank Knox who registered their opposition in the White House. Facing hostility from downstate Democrats and lacking President Roosevelt's blessing, the sixty-five-year-old Kelly finally demurred. Instead, the Chicago Democrats endorsed Raymond S. McKeough, U.S. congressman from the Second Illinois District located on Chicago's South Side. A reliable party stalwart, McKeough had compiled an undistinguished record in Washington but enjoyed the lavish support of the Kelly-Nash legions and received the endorsement of the Illinois Democratic Central Committee.[19]

Largely unknown outside of Chicago, opposing the nation's most powerful political machine, without the rudiments of a campaign staff, and desperately lacking money, Douglas had good reason to consider the defeatism he had expressed to Adlai Stevenson well founded. The independent's campaign spent only $20,000 while the regular Democratic organization reputedly spent several times that amount. Franklin D. Roosevelt insisted on neutrality in the Illinois primary, a crushing blow to Douglas and other liberals who hoped for the president's imprimatur in their reformist crusade. Harold L. Ickes reported to Douglas that Kelly had convinced the president that McKeough would make the best candidate. "[Roosevelt] needed Kelly far more than he needed me," glumly concluded Douglas.[20]

Despite the overwhelming odds against him, Douglas waged a rousing and increasingly effective campaign. Beginning at 6:00 A.M., he passed out literature, shook hands, and greeted workers at factory gates and mine entrances throughout the state. Regaling audiences from a loudspeaker affixed to a Jeep, he gave speeches to crowds of all sizes. Usually he spoke extemporaneously, and newspapermen covering the campaign noted that the quality of his talks improved as the campaign progressed. To the surprise of many onlookers, the academician mingled easily with the crowds of curious voters and genuinely seemed to enjoy the opportunity to share his views. Throughout the state, he articulated his campaign themes—opposition to machine politics, integrity and honesty in government, and, most important, unqualified support for President Roosevelt's conduct of the war. Even though he regularly disparaged the Kelly-Nash machine, he spoke highly of McKeough and strove to conduct a campaign based on issues rather than personalities.[21]

Douglas favorably impressed many voters and received high marks from reporters who covered his whirlwind campaign but, as an independent bucking the Democratic party machinery of Illinois, received short shrift from the professional politicians. One local Democratic leader repeatedly refused even to talk with Douglas until mutual friends intervened to arrange a meeting. "Okay," the boss relented, "tell him to come to my house at midnight, but tell him we're going to murder him in the primary." The two men met, and after several drinks and a cordial conversation the local boss patted Douglas on the shoulder and said: "You're not such a bad so-and-so after all. I can't support you this election, but I'll tell you what I'm going to do. I'm going to let you have twenty-four hundred votes here." Douglas received 2,413 votes in that community's primary election.[22]

Douglas's 1942 campaign earned him the grudging respect of the state's Democratic leaders and a wellspring of goodwill throughout Illinois. Still, as he knew all along, no independent could beat the Kelly-Nash machine. Douglas carried 90 of the state's 102 counties and won the election outside of Cook County by a three-to-two margin, but saw his chances expire in Chicago. He lost all of the city's 50 wards except his own, many of them by overwhelming margins, and netted 285,000 votes statewide to McKeough's 570,000. The night of the primary election, after the results showed that he had lost, Douglas delivered a brief radio speech thanking his supporters and congratulating his opponent. Noting that the election of Brooks would be a "calamity," he pledged to work hard for McKeough's election. In a taxi ride home later that evening, he spoke to his wife about enlisting for military service.[23]

The next day, Douglas submitted his application for combat duty in the U.S. Marine Corps and quickly renewed his correspondence with Adlai Stevenson. He also wrote to Harold L. Ickes, who promptly interceded with Secretary of the Navy Knox on Douglas's behalf. Within a week, Knox assented to Douglas's request to have the age limit waived, subject to his passing a routine physical examination. (Knox also dismissed the normal admission standards for teeth and eyesight.) The Marine Corps accepted the fifty-year-old Douglas and ordered him to report in one month for basic training at Parris Island, South Carolina. During that time, he attended a daily physical fitness class at the University of Chicago's Stagg Field and swam in Lake Michigan to prepare for the rigorous training ahead. He took a leave of absence from teaching, resigned from the city council, put his financial affairs in order, and on May 15 boarded a train at Union Station for the journey to South Carolina.[24]

In later years, Douglas was often asked why a man of his age and religious beliefs would enlist in the Marines and specifically request to be assigned to a regular infantry platoon. The answer was complicated. He believed strongly that police states bent on conquest had to be stopped and that the task inevitably fell to democracies like the United States. The doctrine of nonresistance no longer seemed to be a plausible alternative. In the hierarchy of Quaker beliefs, nonviolence ranks high, but the paramount authority is the individual conscience. "My conscience told me I had to fight," Douglas remembered. "I had advocated resistance to all aggression. I could find no peace of mind without backing up my views physically." Disappointed that he had failed to act accordingly during World War I, he saw an opportunity in 1942 to make amends. Red-baited because of his leftist political views, he hoped that he could put to rest any questions about his patriotism by fighting for his country. Finally, he disputed charges that his enlistment was a grandstand play to cultivate support for postwar political ambitions, pointing out that he refused a safe desk job in Washington in favor of genuinely hazardous duty overseas. In a letter to Adlai Stevenson, however, Douglas cryptically noted that "enlistment as an ordinary seaman might have some symbolic value which would not be useless," a likely reference to the political benefit accruing to the path he had chosen. In all, however, any political considerations seem to have been secondary to a genuine desire to serve his country and oppose totalitarianism.[25]

At Parris Island, Douglas initially found himself in a platoon of sixty recruits with an average age of nineteen. Not surprisingly, the strenuous physical training in the merciless South Carolina summer heat proved to be his greatest challenge. He survived basic training and reveled in his acceptance by the other members of his platoon. Douglas earned a series of promotions to the rank of captain, all the while refusing permanent assignments to administrative positions and continuing to plead for frontline duties. After months of inactivity at the base's training center, he appealed successfully (with his commanding officer's permission) to Secretary Knox for a combat assignment in the Pacific theater of operations. For several months he served in various posts as an adjutant helping to process paperwork for the Marine divisions scattered throughout the Pacific. He appreciated being overseas but continued to chafe at being relegated to clerical duties. In August 1943, he wrote to Harold Ickes and, in September 1943, to Adlai Stevenson, asking for their help in being sent to a combat area. Specifically, he hoped that he could be named a regimental adjutant, which would necessitate movement closer to the front. "To be overseas and yet not see battle is a frustrating experience," he explained, "and I shall not feel content until I have shared the hardships and some of the dangers of the men up in the front." Ickes and Stevenson recommended the change, and Secretary Knox complied.[26]

Douglas's first action came almost a year later in September 1944 on the island of Peleliu in the Carolines near Mindanao. Ordered to secure the small island, the Marines fought a dwindling but determined force of Japanese soldiers for six weeks before securing their objective. Douglas received a Bronze Star for carrying ammunition to the front lines under fire and suffered a minor wound, for which he was later awarded a Purple Heart citation, when struck by shrapnel from an exploding mortar shell. When the medics arrived with orders to evacuate officers first, Douglas insisted that the enlisted men be carried away before he allowed himself to be touched. In April 1945, Douglas's regiment participated in the invasion of Okinawa. A U.S. flotilla of 1,200 ships transported 250,000 troops, a joint Army and Marine force that had been training for three months for the invasion, to the island. After a successful landing on the beaches, Douglas's First Marine Division edged slowly inland for the next two weeks in the face of murderous enemy fire. His assignment as a staff officer required that he remain at the back of the line, but Douglas removed his major's insignia and moved to the front to serve as a rifleman. Apparently, his superiors had resigned themselves to tolerating the reckless eccentricities of the white-haired soldier. He killed at least one enemy soldier in battle, the circumstances of which he pondered sadly: "Here is man right back on his belly in the primeval ooze—and the sniper I just killed after he shot at me in the entrance of a cave may well have been a professor of economics at the University of Tokyo."[27]

On May 9 the First Marine Division launched an attack on a hill near the Naha-Shuri line, the site of an intense and prolonged engagement. Advancing into heavy fire, Douglas suffered a horrible wound when a burst of machine gun bullets shredded his left arm from elbow to wrist and severed a main artery. A group of Marines dragged him down the hill to a crude medical aid station set up in a cave nearby. Chaplain Berman of the Sixth Marine Division described the situation there:

> Chaplain Thompson greeted me with: "I've got a friend of yours over here," and he pointed to a grimy, blood covered man lying on a stretcher. "I don't recognize him," I said. "That's Paul Douglas, who has been badly hit, as you can see. When they brought him in and asked him his name,

he said, 'Private Douglas,' and it was only when I recognized him that I saw to it that the record was corrected to 'Major.'" "When I asked Douglas," Chaplain Thompson continued, "why he had indicated he was a Private, he told me that he didn't want to get any special consideration or treatment."[28]

After Douglas underwent an emergency operation in an Army field infirmary, he sailed for the United States on a hospital ship that arrived in San Francisco in mid-June. Following a brief stop in Norfolk, Virginia, he settled in at the Naval Hospital in Bethesda, Maryland, where he remained for more than thirteen months. Four additional operations failed to regenerate the nerves that had been frayed in his left arm. Even after completing extensive physical therapy treatment, he never regained use of his left forearm and hand. Thereafter, he remarked, his left hand served only as a good paperweight. In November 1946, Douglas received an honorable discharge as a lieutenant colonel. A gaunt, ashen figure who weighed forty-five pounds less than he had at the time of enlistment, he left the Marine Corps with two Purple Hearts, a Bronze Star, and a disability pension based upon his classification as 75 percent disabled. Unwilling to accept a disability check when he could make a living as a professor and legislator, Douglas later attempted to renounce the pension. When the Marine Corps refused to terminate the monthly payments, he placed the money in an account under the following conditions—interest on the deposits would be paid to his wife and daughter after his death and then, after they died, to the U.S. government for the purchase of recreational land in Chicago.[29]

After serving briefly on a committee to determine the agenda for President Truman's Labor-Management Peace Conference that sought to rationalize postwar industrial relations, Douglas resumed his teaching duties at the University of Chicago. He continued to publish the findings of his research on wages and won election to the presidency of the American Economic Association, but he struggled to ease back into academic life. The university seemed very different to him, and he felt uneasy in the intellectual climate that predominated on campus after the war. He rued the fact that conservatives who extolled the virtues of the free market and rejected the efficacy of governmental activism had taken over the economics department. To him, it seemed that a new obeisance to big business and an indifference to the injustices of modern industrial society dominated his immediate environment—just as he sensed that a rising wave of reaction embracing the same values threatened postwar America. "I found myself increasingly out of tune with many of my faculty colleagues and was keenly aware of their impatience and disgust with me," he recalled. Most of his like-minded colleagues had retired or departed, and he found himself isolated in his economic and political beliefs. His growing despondency with academic life made politics all the more appealing.[30]

During his absence from Chicago, his wife had been elected U.S. congresswoman-at-large from Illinois—Emily Taft Douglas had defeated isolationist Republican Stephen A. Day by 200,000 votes in 1944—and Douglas announced that he would not attempt to revive his own political career as long as she served in Washington. Initially, she felt confident about her prospects for reelection in 1946, but postwar disillusionment against the party in power and President Truman's plummeting popularity threatened a Republican resurgence that year. Refusing to bow to the groundswell of support for rushing U.S. servicemen home, Emily took the unpopular position of urging measured troop withdrawals from Europe and Asia because of the continued need for collective security abroad—a position in stark contrast to her isolationist Republican opponent, William G. Stratton. In decrying her liberal voting record in the House, Stratton accused Emily of following the Communist party line. Citing a report that Radio Moscow had endorsed candidates for office in the United States who had received the backing of the Congress of Industrial Organizations' (CIO) Political Action Committee (PAC), Stratton argued that Emily's association with the PAC made her one of "Russia's candidates for the American congress." Engulfed by the antiadministration torrent that swept the nation that year, the Democrats surrendered control of Congress for the first time since 1930. Emily lost by nearly 350,000 votes and announced her intention to leave politics behind.[31]

For Douglas, his wife's defeat and the uncongenial climate at the university made the resuscitation of his political career an attractive option. In late 1946, he became involved in the latest incarnation of the crusade for good government in Cook County. By that time, Mayor Kelly and Twenty-fourth Ward Alderman Jacob M. Arvey were heading the Democratic machine. (Following Pat Nash's death in 1943, Kelly served as both mayor and county Democratic party chairman; he fared so poorly in his attempt to handle both jobs that Arvey replaced him as party chairman in 1946.) A septuagenarian of failing health who seemed to have lost much of his political acumen, Kelly made an inviting target for reformers on the eve of the 1947 mayoral election. Douglas threatened to run for mayor as an independent unless the Democrats dumped Kelly and nominated either John Boyle or civic-minded businessman Martin Kennelly. It remains unclear whether Douglas would have followed through on his threat—he clearly had his sights set on higher elective office—but he believed that his putative candidacy may well have played a role in Kelly's demise. Convinced that Kelly's flagging popularity could cost the Democratic machine control of city hall, Arvey persuaded the mayor to step aside and selected Kennelly as the party's candidate. Kelly became expendable to the Democratic machine leadership in large measure because of his support for open housing and public school desegregation, liberal measures that the party's dominant Irish contingent would not countenance. Ironically, then, the insurgents succeeded because the mayor defended positions central to the reform crusade—positions that Douglas would champion throughout his senatorial career. To the delight of Douglas and the reformers, Kennelly won handily.[32]

In short order, a number of leading Illinois Democrats approached Douglas about running for either governor or U.S. senator in 1948. Although it remained uncertain whether he would receive the nomination for either office, he gave speeches throughout the state on weekends throughout 1947 to lay the groundwork for a potential candidacy. From their wartime correspondence, Douglas knew that Adlai Stevenson had somewhat passively pursued the Democratic nomination for governor in 1944. He also heard Stevenson's name mentioned for both offices in 1948. Stevenson announced a preference for the U.S. Senate because of his interest in international affairs but refrained from discouraging speculation about whether he would assent to running for governor. The Americans for Democratic Action (ADA), the organization of liberal Democrats and independents formed in 1947 to preserve the gains of the New Deal and Fair Deal, favored Douglas for senator; the Independent Voters of Illinois (IVI), the ADA affiliate in that state, informed Arvey that it would support Douglas and Stevenson for the two offices in any combination. Douglas told Leo Lerner of the IVI that he preferred to run for the Senate. Good-government Democrats had identified two candidates for the two major offices to be contested in 1948, but both men preferred to run for senator rather than governor.[33]

Jacob Arvey, boss of the Cook County machine and chairman of the Democratic slate-making committee, perceived the need for change in Illinois politics. The 1946 elections had been a bonanza for the Republicans, and the pundits were predicting more success for the GOP in 1948. The Democratic party in the state suffered from the stigma of the Chicago machine, and Arvey realized the importance of nominating candidates untainted by charges of corruption and scandal. He had taken the first step in salvaging the Democratic party's sullied reputation by replacing Ed Kelly with the squeaky-clean Martin Kennelly in 1947 and intended to do much the same the following year. Having Douglas and Stevenson at the top of the ticket excited Arvey, and although he remained silent publicly he decided early on that Douglas would be the better choice to run against the Republican incumbent senator, Curly Brooks. Arvey explained his reasoning:

> I thought I had Brooks—I had made up my mind in 1946 that it should be Paul Douglas against Brooks. In 1946, Douglas came to a mass meeting in uniform. He did not make a speech but he waved a greeting to the crowd. I

saw his withered hand [wounded in the war]. Brooks never made a speech without saying, "I got shrapnel in my back at Chateau-Thierry and I learned what it means to serve our country." I knew the shattered hand would dispose of that.[34]

Arvey's explanation sounded unconvincing to many political observers who thought that the Chicago boss assembled the Democratic ticket the way he did for other reasons. According to *Time* magazine, Arvey remembered Douglas's fierce independence in the Chicago City Council and hoped to send him far away to Washington, D.C., where he could do the machine little harm. As governor, Douglas would have a direct say in the dispensation of statewide patronage, and his well-known independence would be a problem. The politicians considered Stevenson, who had not held elective office and was more of a political unknown, less savvy than Douglas about how politics worked and potentially more malleable. The two candidates suspected as much. Stevenson thought that he was being denied the chance to run for the Senate "because they want Douglas out of their hair." Douglas agreed, saying, "the Chicago organization, not wishing to tangle with me on the state level, would be more likely to select me for the Senate. Also, a junior senator had neither patronage nor political power." In all likelihood, such considerations figured in Arvey's calculations.[35]

On December 29, 1947, just moments before Douglas delivered the presidential address to the annual meeting of the American Economic Association in Chicago, Arvey informed him that the Democratic state committee had selected him to run for the U.S. Senate. Douglas turned to his wife and quoted from Shakespeare's *Othello:* "Oh, now forever / Farewell the tranquil mind!" Arvey made the official announcement the next day, prompting Democratic Senator Scott Lucas of Illinois to refer to the Douglas-Stevenson pairing as a "dream ticket." Liberals greeted the announcement with enthusiasm, but the prospects for progressive Democrats in 1948 seemed dim. With the full support of the influential *Chicago Tribune* in what was shaping up as a Republican year, Senator Brooks quickly emerged as the heavy favorite in the election; Douglas's chances, opined *Time* magazine, "looked as hopeless as Harry Truman's."[36]

Douglas harbored no illusions about the uphill battle facing him. He recognized the low regard in which the electorate appeared to hold President Truman and feared that the president's unpopularity would harm all Democratic candidates. (In fact, along with many other leading Democrats, Douglas had urged Truman to step aside for the good of the party and yield the presidential nomination to World War II hero Dwight D. Eisenhower.) He expressed concern that his advocacy on behalf of society's unfortunates, a position that resonated with much of the general populace during the Great Depression, would fall flat in an age of emerging prosperity and ambition; conversely, Brooks's conservative Republican nostrums seemed better suited to the times. Brooks could rely on the financial backing of Chicago's banks and large corporations and, as a popular incumbent, would have no trouble raising funds for the campaign. In addition to the *Tribune,* the *Chicago Daily News* provided the incumbent its editorial endorsement. Douglas also thought that his relative inexperience would contrast sharply with Brooks's comparatively gaudy political resume.[37]

Brooks owed his elevation to the U.S. Senate directly to the benevolence of *Chicago Tribune* publisher Robert R. McCormick. In 1931 Brooks had successfully prosecuted the case against Leo Brothers, the murderer of *Tribune* reporter Jake Lingle, and a grateful McCormick had become his political patron. Elected in 1940 to fill the unexpired Senate seat of J. Hamilton Lewis, who had died the year before, Brooks became McCormick's mouthpiece in Washington, opposing lend-lease and the military draft while praising the isolationist pronouncements of America First. Focusing his 1942 reelection campaign on the tyranny of wartime controls and the "Gestapo tactics" imposed by the Roosevelt administration, Brooks defeated Raymond McKeough by a comfortable margin. McCormick's biographer caustically noted that Brooks "rarely expressed a thought that hadn't first occurred to [the *Tribune* publisher]." One of the most reactionary members of Congress and the bête noire of the Democratic party's liberal wing, Brooks anticipated reelection in 1948 as a potential springboard to the vice presidency.[38]

To compound the Democratic nominee's problems, not all members of Illinois's liberal community favored his candidacy. In effect, many of the members of the Progressive Party of Illinois (PPI) considered Douglas not liberal enough. They accused him of being too chummy with Arvey and the hated Cook County machine. (Others hinted that the Chicago boss had offered up the naive university professor as a sacrificial lamb to the unbeatable Brooks.) The PPI questioned Douglas's commitment to civil liberties and his support for trade unionism, but primarily attacked him on foreign policy issues. A strong supporter of the Marshall Plan and critic of Soviet expansionism, Douglas was simply too much of a cold warrior for the organization pledged to the presidential candidacy of Henry Wallace. Earlier Douglas had denounced Wallace for proposing a policy of appeasement that would "permit Russia to take over all of Europe and much of Asia as well." His refusal to condemn President Truman's developing containment policy made him acceptable to the ADA but not to the PPI, which endorsed the candidacy of Curtis D. MacDougall instead. Responding to the doubts regarding his liberal credentials, which had been fully aired early in the campaign by the *New Republic,* Douglas published in a later issue of that journal a detailed outline of his positions on domestic and foreign policy issues. In short, he affirmed his support for liberal reform at home as well as his vigilant opposition to communist aggression abroad.[39]

Douglas believed that his brand of liberalism simply made more sense in the postwar world, and he took his case to the voters of Illinois in 1948. As he had when seeking the senatorial nomination in 1942, he crisscrossed the state speaking to as many voters as possible. From early in the morning until well past midnight, he introduced himself at factory gates, street corners, shopping centers, gas stations, and anywhere else people congregated. Driving a Jeep station wagon equipped with a loudspeaker and a phonograph, he traveled rapidly from one community to the next and during the summer became a fixture at the state's many county fairs. Meanwhile, his wife met with women's groups in community centers and private homes. Everywhere he repeated essentially the same messages—a vigorous defense and extension of the New Deal along with an unvarnished opposition to communism everywhere. To create a more humane society in America, he favored additional price supports for farmers, repeal of the antilabor Taft-Hartley Act and protection of the right to collective bargaining, increased federal aid to education, expanded social security benefits, the construction of fifteen million new homes over the next decade along with federal aid for slum clearance in large cities, federal checks on monopoly and inflation, and protection against discrimination for racial and religious minorities. As domestic anticommunism intensified, he demanded that individuals who found themselves the subjects of congressional investigating committees conducting loyalty probes be guaranteed the right to exonerate themselves by issuing public statements.[40]

To advance the nation's interests abroad, Douglas advocated the Marshall Plan, full support of the United Nations, the international control of atomic energy, and opposition to communist aggression in Iran, Hungary, Czechoslovakia, and wherever else American military forces might be needed. In speech after speech, he reiterated his profound aversion to communism. Characterizing the cold war as a moral struggle between the forces of democracy and despotism—indeed, between light and darkness—he predicted that "a glacial age would descend upon the earth were the police state of communism to be triumphant." Arguing that the isolationism of his Republican opponent would be disastrous in the international struggle against America's enemies, Douglas affirmed the efficacy of the containment policy recently implemented by the Truman administration. "For this election at least," he intoned, "the extreme reactionaries and the Communists are allies. We are opposed to them both."[41]

Douglas described politics in the vast expanses of Illinois as having been determined by geologic and historical forces. In prehistoric times, he told campaign audiences, glaciers extended roughly as far south as Springfield in the middle of the state. When the glaciers receded, they left deposits of rich black soil in the northern half of Illinois. The southern portion of the state, burdened with less fertile land and settled primarily by migrants from Virginia and Kentucky, had long been a Democratic stronghold. In central and northern Illinois, the home of New Englanders and New Yorkers who had migrated directly westward and become prosperous farmers in an agricultural showplace, the Republican party had predominated. Speaking in Bloomington, Peoria, Champaign-Urbana, and other central Illinois communities, he urged embattled Democrats to take heart; they were really fighting against the mighty glaciers. This analysis, a staple of Douglas's campaign oratory in 1948 and subsequent elections, elicited knowing looks and nods from listeners in all corners of the state.[42]

In July Douglas attended the Democratic National Convention in Philadelphia, a tumultuous affair that left the party in disarray over the issue of civil rights. The controversy began with the attempt by the convention's liberal wing to unseat the Mississippi delegation, a group that had been chosen by dubious methods and that refused to support all Democratic candidates. The insurgency failed amid charges of dishonest vote counting and served as a prelude to the main event, a struggle over the civil rights plank in the party platform. Challenging the innocuous plank approved by a majority of the Resolutions Committee, the young mayor of Minneapolis, Hubert Humphrey, delivered a passionate plea on the convention floor for the party's adoption of a bold, straightforward pledge of civil rights for all Americans. In the Illinois delegation, Douglas asked Ed Kelly to lead a demonstration in favor of Humphrey's exhortation. The ailing Kelly declined, and he then placed the state standard in Douglas's hands, motioning the Illinois delegates to follow him in an impromptu parade. Following the Illinois contingent down the center aisle came delegations from California, New York, and a host of other states, and soon the convention was in an uproar. In the voice vote that followed, the Humphrey amendment carried overwhelmingly. Delegations from Georgia, South Carolina, Louisiana, Alabama, and Mississippi marched out of the convention and later broke away from the Democratic party to nominate Strom Thurmond for president. As the southerners left the convention hall, Ed Kelly remarked to Douglas: "Paul, those fellows look just like the APA'ers who used to stone us Catholic kids when I was a boy. We can do without them."[43]

The defection of the Dixiecrats, along with the dissidents who broke away from the party to support Henry Wallace, seemingly left Truman's candidacy in a precarious state. Hoping to avoid a break with the southerners, Truman's representatives in the Resolutions Committee had stifled a strong civil rights plank, but the president's men could not control events on the convention floor. To his credit, Douglas commented later, Truman loyally defended the party's daring civil rights position during the campaign—and ultimately to good effect. Although many Democrats feared that the convention's impetuous embrace of the civil rights cause would undermine their chances of winning the election, Douglas supported the decision without reservation. He thought that it would help the Democratic party politically by cementing its hold on black and liberal voters, and, perhaps more important, he believed that it was the right thing to do. As in many other instances, he believed, taking the high road meant good politics.[44]

Douglas returned to Illinois with a renewed sense of purpose, eager to resume the uphill struggle against his seemingly invincible opponent. Bookmakers quoted ten-to-one odds against a Douglas victory, and the Democrat's campaign suffered from severe financial shortcomings. By the end of the summer, his campaign treasury was empty, and he had no money for radio time or billboards. With Douglas's supply of campaign literature depleted, the printer would accept no more orders on credit. Campaign workers had not been paid for a month, and those who remained on the job did so only out of a sense of loyalty. To keep the campaign afloat, the Douglases scraped together about $25,000 by mortgaging a cottage they owned in the Indiana Dunes and borrowing on their modest cache of stocks and bonds. This last infusion of money allowed Douglas to reimburse his staff, print new circulars, and purchase $10,000 worth of radio advertising.[45]

The campaign suffered a blow when the *Bloomington Pantagraph,* the most influential newspaper in central Illinois, came out for Brooks. This endorsement shocked Douglas, because Adlai Stevenson and his sister owned 49 percent of the newspaper's stock. Stevenson maintained that he had been powerless to forestall the negative endorsement, but Douglas partisans found his denials unconvincing. The incident underscored the divergence in the campaigns of the state's two leading Democratic office seekers that year. On the surface, at least, it would have seemed that Stevenson and Douglas had much in common and could comfortably have worked together against their Republican opponents. Relative newcomers to politics who had never held major elective offices before, they came from good-government backgrounds, enjoyed the backing of Jacob Arvey and the Chicago Democratic machine while remaining distant from them, and shared the reputation of being thoughtful and articulate intellectuals. Yet the two went their separate ways in the 1948 campaign, primarily at Stevenson's insistence. Douglas suggested that they pool their campaign resources but, no doubt feeling that his wealth and social standing gave him greater access to financial contributions, Stevenson declined. Whereas Douglas always said good things about all the candidates on the Democratic ticket, Stevenson did not mention Douglas at all in his speeches except on the rare occasions when he spoke to partisan labor groups or Democratic rallies. Douglas concluded that Stevenson was not a real Democrat and that he seemed more interested in pleasing his affluent Lake Forest peers than in genuine reform. Their relationship, strained during the 1948 campaign, remained uneasy thereafter.[46]

In September, speaking in Champaign at a meeting of war veterans, Republican congressman Fred E. Busbey introduced into the campaign the issue of Douglas's earlier expressions of radical politics. He charged that the Democrat's trip to the Soviet Union and his publication of *The Coming of a New Party* bespoke his latent communist sympathies. Decrying Douglas's membership in such "communist-front" organizations as the American Civil Liberties Union, Busbey called him "a friend of communism and a colleague of the enemies of our republic." The *Chicago Tribune* quickly picked up the story, trumpeting the allegations in a series of front-page headlines. At a DuPage County Republican rally at which Busbey spoke, Emily Taft Douglas asked to reply to the charges but was denied the opportunity to speak. Shortly thereafter, Paul Douglas formally responded before a huge audience in Urbana. He carefully reviewed his anticommunist credentials and recited in detail the communists' published attacks on him during the campaign. He defended *The Coming of a New Party* as a harmless anachronism that had been published before the New Deal and averred that its political philosophy bore very little resemblance to his current ideas. The book's only relevance to the 1948 campaign, Douglas added puckishly, rested in the fact that his enemies' dramatic references to its publication had rejuvenated sales and that the sudden increase in royalties helped him defray mounting campaign expenses. Accusing Brooks and the *Tribune* of red-baiting, Douglas suggested that he might file charges of slander in the future but vowed not to address the issue of his alleged communist inclinations again during the campaign. Busbey stopped talking, and the issue disappeared from most of the state's newspapers. For the balance of the campaign, however, the *Chicago Tribune* continued referring inaccurately to Douglas as a former Socialist party leader.[47]

Impervious to the distractions and his disheartening underdog status, Douglas continued the frenetic pace of his campaign. In all, he delivered more than 1,300 speeches in 300 towns and cities and spoke to an estimated 600,000 people. By late summer, he sensed a change in the size and temper of the crowds that came to his public appearances. Reporters covering the campaign noted that the crowds seemed to respond to Douglas's impassioned, colorful, decidedly unprofessorial orations. One national publication described Douglas as "a big, 6 ft. 2 1/2 in., 235-pounder with simplicity and integrity sticking out all over him, a scholar who looked equally at home in the coal fields of Little Egypt and the tenements of South Chicago." A steelworker commented: "That guy's no politician. He doesn't try to con you." Becoming more of an extrovert as the campaign progressed, Douglas began responding to cheers from the audience by clasping both hands over his head in the classic prizefighter's pose. When Brooks refused to debate the issues in person, Douglas borrowed an old ploy used by Al Smith—he addressed his remarks to an empty chair on stage, referring to a nonexistent Senator Brooks. Sometimes he conducted an imaginary conversation with Brooks, alternately delivering the lines for both men. He often ended by singing, "We shall meet, but we shall miss him. There will be a vacant chair." Invariably, he got the better of these "debates," and the crowds roared their approval.[48]

Douglas's determined effort notwithstanding, Illinois Democrats remained pessimistic about the outcome of the Senate race. In the closing weeks, oddsmakers still made Douglas a four-to-one underdog. Republicans acknowledged that Brooks would probably not carry Illinois as handily as their presidential candidate, Thomas E. Dewey, but still predicted a comfortable victory margin of between 250,000 and 300,000 votes over Douglas. *Newsweek* reported that the Democrats had conceded defeat in the Senate race but thought that Stevenson still had an "outside chance" in the gubernatorial contest. President Truman made a final appearance in Chicago a week before the election. Although Douglas thought the crowd large and enthusiastic, the newspapers reported a much different story. (Perhaps not wanting to be associated with Truman and Douglas, Stevenson failed to attend.) When a pollster told him the Sunday before the election that he would win the election by 400,000 votes, an astounded Douglas replied that he expected to lose by 50,000 or so. He would not lose by the landslide the newspapers were predicting, he felt, but a victory seemed unrealistic. The persistent pollster stuck to his forecast and urged Douglas to bet heavily on himself. The candidate declined, chuckling that he did not have a dollar left to wager.[49]

The Douglases voted early on election day, then visited several precincts on Chicago's South Side. Exhausted from the weeks of nonstop campaigning, Douglas went home when the polls closed and took a long nap. Awakening later that evening, he listened disbelievingly to the radio report of his and Truman's substantial leads in Illinois. On the way to his campaign headquarters, he saw the early edition of the next day's *Chicago Tribune* with its famous front-page headline proclaiming Dewey's defeat of Truman—the paper similarly reported a substantial Brooks win over Douglas—and tempered his optimism with the knowledge that a number of Republican strongholds in the state had not yet submitted their vote counts. As Douglas and his supporters closely monitored the election returns throughout the night, his lead not only held firm but steadily lengthened. At four A.M., Brooks conceded defeat. The final totals had Douglas winning Cook County by 435,000 votes and losing downstate by only 28,000 for a net victory margin of 407,000—the second-largest majority by any senator in the state to that time. Stevenson won by more than 570,000, and Truman by 31,000.[50]

How to explain Douglas's improbable victory? Undoubtedly, the Democrat's exhaustive campaign made a positive impression on the electorate. Douglas's whirlwind coverage of the state overcame the handicap of his relative anonymity, and his surprisingly engaging performance as a speaker left the professional politicians surprised and the voters enchanted. The contrast with Brooks, who conducted the same type of subdued campaign that led Thomas Dewey aground in the presidential race, could not have been sharper. Brooks's torpor surely played a role in the remarkably light Republican turnout that year—67 percent of registered Republicans in Illinois failed to cast ballots in November—as the expectation of a certain victory led many Republicans to forgo voting. Brooks enjoyed the backing of the *Chicago Tribune* and the state's other leading Republican organs, but Douglas picked up the support of a number of important newspapers such as the *Chicago Sun, Chicago Times,* and *Chicago Daily News.* His reputation as a friend of workers, bolstered by his many years of distinguished service as a labor arbitrator, resulted in solid support from the trade unions; he garnered the endorsements of the CIO, American Federation of Labor (AFL), and a number of independent locals. The Republican Eightieth Congress's drastic reduction of Commodity Credit Corporation aid to farmers no doubted harmed Brooks's position in agrarian downstate Illinois as well. Contrary to the suspicion that Arvey and Chicago's party leaders would do less than their best for Douglas, the Cook County machine turned out the vote with its customary efficiency. Douglas was convinced that even Ed Kelly, still active in politics as Democratic National Committeeman for Illinois, worked on behalf of his former–city council antagonist. Finally, Douglas's message of domestic liberalism and containment abroad resonated with many voters that year—much as Harry Truman's similar campaign did on a national scale. Douglas found a comfortable niche between the dubious foreign policy of Henry Wallace's communist-tainted Progressives and the reactionary anti–New Dealism of Curly Brooks and the *Tribune*'s Colonel McCormick. It was, as Douglas liked to say, a liberalism that made sense to the voters.[51]

Douglas's victory triggered a celebration among liberals not only in Illinois but also throughout the nation. On December 2, 1948, James Loeb, Jr., executive secretary of the ADA, wrote Douglas about a conversation he and two other ADA leaders (Joseph Rauh and James Wechsler) had recently had about Douglas's future in the Senate. The ADA leadership urged Douglas to seek appointment to the Banking and Currency Committee or, secondarily, the Committee on Labor and Public Welfare. "Never in our generation," wrote Loeb, "has there been a liberal member of the United States Senate with the knowledge, the background, and the convictions that are yours, particularly in the whole field of domestic economic policy." Loeb and his cohorts downplayed the need for Douglas's services in the area of foreign affairs where a bipartisan cold war consensus seemed to be functioning smoothly. He added: "We believe that, in any key Committee spot, you would naturally become the greatest legislator of our time, the most competent spokesman for the people of America on economic policy." Douglas's victory had given hope to liberals everywhere that the New Deal and Fair Deal legacies would be protected and advanced. "All of this boils down," concluded Loeb, "to the single point that we look to you for the most effective liberal leadership in our generation in the United States Senate."[52]

3

Precocious Freshman Senator

Support one's party in all procedural matters everywhere. Argue substantive programs within party councils in the hope of gaining a majority within the party. But when the chips are down in the Senate, a Senator should vote his profound individual convictions on substantive matters regardless of who is with or against him.

—**Paul H. Douglas**[1]

• As an extension of Franklin D. Roosevelt's New Deal, Harry Truman's Fair Deal had been a thorough disappointment. In the years 1945 to 1948, the president submitted to Congress an ambitious legislative agenda that included a full-employment bill, a permanent Fair Employment Practices Committee (FEPC) to combat discriminatory hiring practices, a continuation of farm price supports, an increase in the minimum wage, public housing, a national health insurance program, and federal aid to education. Faced with the nettlesome problems of demobilization at the end of the Second World War, striking labor unions, and a hostile Congress dominated by Republicans and conservative southern Democrats, Truman achieved few successes in his attempt to, in the historian Alonzo Hamby's apt phrase, "adapt the New Deal tradition to postwar prosperity." Congress either rejected Truman's initiatives outright or, as in the case of the Employment Act of 1946, passed watered-down legislation that bore scant resemblance to the robust measures conceived at the other end of Pennsylvania Avenue.[2]

The outcome of the 1948 election gave liberals hope, however, for along with Harry Truman's improbable victory the Democrats won control of both houses of Congress. The freshman class of '49 included Hubert Humphrey of Minnesota, Estes Kefauver of Tennessee, Clinton Anderson of New Mexico, and Paul Douglas of Illinois in the Senate as well as Richard Bolling of Missouri, Eugene McCarthy of Minnesota, Sidney Yates of Illinois, and Abraham Ribicoff of Connecticut in the House of

Representatives. The Democrats held a 54–42 majority in the Senate, a source of much optimism among Fair Dealers, but regional, economic, and racial cleavages in the party still allowed the Republicans to mount effective coalitions that blocked legislative initiatives. Bourbon Democrats often allied with their Republican counterparts to defeat Fair Deal measures that threatened to redistribute wealth. Similarly, conservative Republicans found common cause with southern Democrats in opposition to civil rights legislation. At the same time, the structure, institutions, and practices of the Senate combined to protect its conservative leadership and safeguard the status quo. The system of seniority allowed Democrats elected from one-party states in the South, who won reelection after reelection through the decades, to secure appointment to key committees and eventually to the chairmanships of those committees. The filibuster also allowed the minority to engage in unlimited discussion as a means of thwarting the will of the majority. So, despite the apparent advantages enjoyed by liberal Democrats as the Eighty-first Congress convened in the spring of 1949, the path to reform remained strewn with imposing roadblocks.[3]

Paul Douglas arrived in Washington, D.C., dedicated to fighting the good fight for liberal reform, but he also insisted on maintaining the rugged independence of thought and action for which he had been known in Chicago. He intended to be a trustworthy team player for the Democrats, but he also determined to exercise his own judgment rather than blindly following the dictates of his party's leadership in all matters. He confirmed his fealty to the broad domestic and foreign policy platforms announced at the Philadelphia convention in 1948, but allowed that he might deviate a bit from legislative particulars. To forestall any charges of conflict of interest, he placed his own meager stock holdings into a broad-based mutual fund. Chagrined at the enormity of the task facing him and not altogether knowledgeable about the mores and folkways of the Senate, he vowed to conquer ignorance with hard work and undivided attention to the new tasks facing him. "All I want," he said plaintively, "is to be a damn good Senator." Later he amended his statement to: "All I want is to be half as good a Senator as old George Norris." For inspiration, he placed on his office wall the portraits of two Renaissance scholars, an oil painting of Erasmus and a pencil drawing of Sir Thomas More. "These two old fellows are important to me," he explained. "They are a good brake, or a sort of warning signal at least. You see, both of them were professors of sorts. One went into politics and lost his head. The other stayed out and kept his. I find it very useful at times to ponder which was the smarter of the two."[4]

At first, Douglas felt overwhelmed by the frenetic pace and crushing burden of work that befell a U.S. senator. Because his wife had served a term in the U.S. House of Representatives and he had testified several times at congressional hearings, Douglas thought he possessed a good sense of what the job of congressman entailed. Very quickly he learned that his earlier impressions had not been at all accurate—or, as he put it, "only the toad beneath the harrow can really feel the sharpness of the prongs." Contemplating the daily rounds of committee hearings, staff meetings, visits with constituents, and mountains of letters and telegrams that needed to be read and answered, he despaired of ever having the study time necessary to master the many pieces of legislation he must evaluate. "I am frank to say," he lamented early on, "that I do not know for how long a man can keep up such a pace."[5] Amazed at the number of social engagements he found himself having to attend when more serious work beckoned, Douglas complained to a group of newspaper reporters: "The trouble with Washington is that there is too little time for work and too much time devoted to cocktail parties. Something ought to be done to get these cocktail hour hostesses off our necks."

As the reporters eagerly took down his impolitic remarks, Douglas realized his mistake and turned in exasperation to his wife. "Emily," he bleated. "Please come help me. I've put my foot in it again."

"Don't worry about the invitations, dear," his amused wife responded. "People are curious because you're new, but your glamour will soon wear off."[6]

Making the necessary concessions to Washington nightlife, Douglas worked hard each day to familiarize himself with the issues and plunged headlong into the legislative maelstrom. At the outset of the session, Senate liberals brought the issue of civil rights to the floor. In 1947 President Truman's Commission on Civil Rights had recommended national legislation to secure equality for blacks in public life, a goal seconded at the 1948 Democratic National Convention. Truman took the first step by issuing an executive order desegregating the armed forces, and liberal Democrats in the Eighty-first Congress prepared to continue the drive for civil rights by removing the filibuster as an effective roadblock in the Senate. Liberals realized that any antidiscrimination legislation they introduced would founder as long as southerners could hold the floor and endlessly delay a vote. Filibustering southerners enjoyed such latitude because of Rule XXII, the celebrated measure that allowed cloture to debate on the Senate floor only after a two-thirds vote of the membership. Because of Rule XXII, a mere third of the Senate could prevent a vote on any bill even if a majority clearly favored its passage. Between the adoption of Rule XXII in 1917 and 1949, only one of the many attempts to invoke cloture had been successful. Protective of the principle of unlimited debate and fearful that a more generous cloture provision could be used against them, many senators outside the South had for years put aside their apprehensions about the filibuster and resisted any tampering with Rule XXII. In the spring of 1949, for example, conservative Republicans allied with southern Democrats to preserve the two-thirds cloture rule in return for their promise to oppose revision of the Taft-Hartley Act.[7]

At the direction of President Truman, Senate Majority Leader Scott W. Lucas (Democrat, Illinois) introduced a motion that a simple majority, rather than two-thirds, be the necessary number to end debate and call a vote. After a full discussion of the merits of Lucas's motion but before a vote could be taken, southerners launched a filibuster. To combat this tactic, Lucas could have demanded that the Senate remain in session around the clock until discussion ended. But recognizing that such a regimen might prove harmful to some of the aging and infirm southerners— elderly Georgia Senator Walter George suffered from a heart condition, for instance—he allowed recesses late at night with the resumption of the filibuster the following mornings. (A moderate who had been appointed party whip in 1946 and majority leader in 1948 with the full support of the Democratic party's southern wing, Lucas had promised to offer just token resistance to filibusters.) After several days, southerners and their allies introduced a countermeasure that would make cloture even more difficult to achieve. A resolution offered by Kenneth Wherry (Republican, Nebraska) required a two-thirds vote of all members of the Senate, not just two-thirds of the members present at the time, to invoke cloture. Under Wherry's proposal, all absentees would be counted as no votes, making cloture harder to invoke than ever before.[8]

Flouting the tradition that consigned newly elected members to an initial period of silence on the chamber floor, Douglas delivered his maiden speech as a U.S. senator on March 17 in opposition to the Wherry resolution. Condemning the "marriage of conservatism" and "sectionalism which has always cursed American political life," he explained in detail why the practice of filibustering subverted the institutions of representative democracy. He said:

> The Wherry Resolution gives to 33 Senators, now and almost forever more, the power to kill any measure. This means that 17 states can act to preserve a filibuster. This means that a combination of the 17 smallest states, with less than 8 per cent or 1/13 of the population and less than 7 per cent or 1/15 of the income can tie up the Senate and the country and defeat the will of over 90 per cent of the people. If we continue along this line, the great qualifications of a Senator will be his ability to speak for 24 hours without stopping. . . . Everyone in his heart knows that it is a disgrace.[9]

Disgraceful or not, the Senate voted to reduce the possibility of invoking cloture. After three weeks of proposals and counterproposals, along with a healthy dose of filibustering, the Senate rejected Lucas's call for a simple majority and voted instead for a new rule requiring a two-thirds vote of the total membership. "It is hard to recall a more discouraging, a more complicated, or a more fantastic legislative picture," lamented James Loeb of the Americans for Democratic Action (ADA). The setback on Rule XXII demoralized civil rights advocates inside and outside of Congress, for they felt that the long, hazardous journey they were commencing had faltered with the very first step. Douglas offered a more optimistic interpretation. Before this highly publicized defeat at the hands of the conservatives, he argued, few people outside of Washington understood the essentiality of abrogating Rule XXII. "A necessary education of the American people was begun," he said.[10]

The Democrats' liberal initiatives continued with an attempt to repeal the Taft-Hartley Act, the antiunion measure passed by the Republican-dominated Congress over Truman's veto in 1947. Although repeal of the Taft-Hartley law had become a shibboleth for liberals and Douglas had endorsed that plank in the Democratic platform during his senatorial campaign, he expressed a slightly different view in early 1949. Decrying many aspects of the law for its decided unfairness to organized labor, most notably the prohibition of the union shop, he still approved of the power afforded government by Taft-Hartley in dealing with national emergency strikes and secondary boycotts. Instead of supporting outright repeal, therefore, he favored an extensive list of amendments that targeted the law's onerous features. At odds with the leadership of his party, the AFL, and the CIO, Douglas refused to support a new administration bill that lacked his amendments. The bill failed to pass in the Senate and the House, and the Taft-Hartley Act remained on the books unchanged. In the aftermath of the vote, several labor leaders acknowledged that Douglas's measured approach might well have been better strategy than the all-or-nothing tack taken by the administration. The episode demonstrated that Douglas intended to be as independent in the halls of Congress as he had been in the Chicago City Council.[11]

On the issue of public housing, Douglas not only supported the liberal position but also took an active leadership role. Based upon his experiences in Chicago, he believed firmly in the need for the federal government to subsidize slum clearance and low-income housing construction. The Taft-Ellender-Wagner Housing Act, which proclaimed its goal to be "a decent home and suitable living environment" for every American family, provided for the building of 810,000 low-income units in the next six years, an impressive rate of 135,000 units per year that dwarfed the earlier public housing appropriations of the 1930s and 1940s. At the same time, Title I of the law offered generous subsidies for urban redevelopment whereby slum clearance would elevate depressed property values, boost property tax revenues, and encourage private investment in beleaguered central business districts. The bill contained something for everyone—unprecedented amounts of public housing for liberals and vast moneymaking opportunities for downtown developers under the rubric of redevelopment—and it passed the Senate Banking and Currency Committee with only modest changes. As a member of that committee, Douglas insisted on the retention of the act's provisions for housing the poor. Assigned the job of floor manager for Title I of the bill, he spoke to the entire Senate about slums as a "moral cancer, a health hazard and an economic loss" and hung enlarged photographs of some of the nation's worst slums throughout the Senate chamber. To dramatize further the intolerable conditions prevalent in the slums, Douglas guided six senators on a highly publicized tour of some of the District of Columbia's most blighted neighborhoods, including the infamous "Schott's Alley" area within one hundred yards of the Senate Office Building. Title I carried without significant amendment.[12]

The bill's commitment to public housing generated considerable opposition, however, as conservatives railed that "socialized housing" meant yet another step in the erosion of local control and the insidious expansion of federal power in Washington. The attack on public housing came somewhat subtly in the form of an amendment offered by two Republicans, John Bricker of Ohio and Harry Cain of Washington. The Bricker-Cain Amendment, introduced by two steadfast opponents of civil rights, prohibited any racial or ethnic discrimination in any of the housing units constructed under the bill's auspices. The Republicans knew that such a proviso would be unacceptable to southern senators, many of whom had originally allied with northern liberals in support of the measure. To the charge that the housing bill could not pass saddled with his amendment, Bricker smugly responded:

> If it does not pass, there is something wrong with the bill, something wrong with the Constitution of the United States, or something wrong with the platforms of the Democratic and Republican Parties, both of which parties came out frankly and without any equivocation in favor of civil rights. Here is one chance for the Members to vote their belief and stand up for or against it.[13]

Throughout a long weekend, Douglas agonized over whether to vote for the amendment, thereby affirming his commitment to racial equality and almost surely defeating the housing bill, or to increase the possibility of attaining meaningful housing legislation by rejecting a measure that articulated heartfelt principles. Many of his Senate colleagues advised him not to address the issue on the floor, because members of the public who were unaware of the entire situation could misconstrue any comment. Just before the vote, however, he spoke against the Bricker-Cain Amendment. Douglas managed to utter but a few sentences when he yielded the floor to a hostile questioner. Ten minutes later, he regained the floor only to speak briefly before being interrupted again.

This pattern of harassment persisted for two hours as Douglas bantered with his principal antagonists, Republicans Kenneth Wherry of Nebraska and Homer Capehart of Indiana. (Senators Claude Pepper of Florida, Hubert Humphrey of Minnesota, and Charles Tobey of New Hampshire offered comments supportive of Douglas's position.) Calm and composed throughout the exchange, Douglas carefully explained the reasons for his vote. He excoriated the cynicism underlying the amendment, noting indignantly Senator Bricker's avowed intention of voting against the Taft-Ellender-Wagner Act even if his amendment carried. Douglas pointed out that Mary McLeod Bethune, president of the National Council of Negro Women, and the *Chicago Defender* had condemned the Bricker Amendment because of the deleterious effect it would inevitably have on housing for the poor. "Probably having cut my political throat from ear to ear," Douglas said, he must vote against what seemed on the surface to be civil rights legislation. "As for me, the choice is clear. I want slum clearance and housing for four million people. I want it for all groups, regardless of race, creed, or color. I should like to point out to my Negro friends what a large amount of housing they will get from this act."[14]

Southern Democrats and northern liberals following Douglas's lead defeated the Bricker-Cain Amendment 49–31; the next day the Taft-Ellender-Wagner Housing Act passed in the Senate by a 57–13 margin. Thereafter, Douglas spent months defending his vote to some liberals and African Americans who somehow failed to understand the quandary he and others had faced. Mary McLeod Bethune avidly defended Douglas, and as the full complexity of the situation came to be understood his standing with those groups improved. The protracted controversy owed to the fact that Douglas had been in the Senate for such a short time and had not yet had the opportunity to establish his liberal credentials. In later years, the same groups that questioned him in 1949 would no doubt have readily accepted his explanation.[15]

If Douglas's performance perturbed some civil rights advocates, the story of his leadership in the defeat of the Bricker-Cain Amendment made him an instant celebrity on Capitol Hill. Seldom did freshman senators play a leading role in such dramas, a fact made clear to him during his rough questioning by Republicans who suggested that he should be listening to the discussion from his seat at the back of the chamber. His poised reaction to the hectoring of Senators Capehart and Wherry won plaudits from Democrats and Republicans alike. "There was no doubt at all at the end that something new had been added to the Senate," enthused the *New Republic*'s Richard L. Strout. "Liberals at last had a spokesman of intellectual stature equal to [Ohio Senator Robert A.] Taft on the conservative side." Thomas Sancton, writing in the *Nation,* observed that Douglas was "emerging as one of the great figures in the Democratic Party" who "would make a powerful Presidential candidate for liberal forces."[16]

During the Eighty-first Congress's first session, the junior senator from Illinois took the floor often to espouse causes he favored and did so with flair. He again became the center of controversy by daring to question aspects of the traditionally sacrosanct rivers and harbors bill. Each year like clockwork, Senator Kenneth D. McKellar (Democrat, Tennessee) introduced an appropriations bill that doled out funds to all states containing seaports or navigable rivers, ostensibly to be used for public works improvements. Some projects were clearly legitimate, but others constituted nothing more than pork-barrel awards to the Tennessee patriarch's acolytes. To the disbelief of the Senate body, Douglas introduced an amendment that pared by roughly 40 percent the sums to be spent on navigation improvements and arrogated to the executive branch the authority to determine where the cuts would be made. Reminded by his colleagues that Illinois usually received a considerable portion of the allotments and would have much to lose if his amendment carried, Douglas rejoined that legislators must sometimes rise above parochial concerns and act in the national interest. His home state would sacrifice along with all the others for the sake of economy and fairness.[17]

Asked to cite specific examples of undeserving projects that would be funded by the bill, Douglas quickly mentioned the proposed deepening of the Josias River in Maine at a cost of $33,000. He had grown up in Maine, Douglas reminded the audience, and he had never heard of the Josias River. Pulling a magnifying glass out of his pocket, he painstakingly examined an atlas for any sign of the river and then invited others to do the same. (Douglas had originally planned to bring a meat axe and scalpel to the rostrum to illustrate the proper technique of budget cutting, but his staff convinced him to rely instead upon the atlas and magnifying glass as props.) After a lengthy discussion with Maine senators Margaret Chase Smith and Owen Brewster about the possible significance of a body of water too small to be included in an atlas, Douglas surrendered the floor. The Senate overwhelmingly voted down his proposed reductions, but he vowed to continue scrutinizing the annual rivers and harbors bills.[18]

The junior Illinois senator promptly resumed his campaign against government inefficiency, advocating cuts to the budget proposed by President Truman. Calling on his expertise as an economics professor, Douglas presented on the Senate floor a detailed explication of the federal budget, including income, expenditures, and the national debt. Identifying waste and inefficiency in the administrative cost of government, he recommended a cut of at least $3 billion from a proposed budget of $42.2 billion that Truman had earlier characterized as "skin and bones." It was possible to balance the budget, Douglas averred, and that could most painlessly be achieved through spending reductions rather than tax increases. Virtually every federal bureau could absorb a 5 to 10 percent reduction without a loss in the delivery of services, he maintained, simply by not replacing some of the workers who left their positions. At least $1 billion could be pared from the military budget without jeopardizing national security, chiefly through more careful oversight of purchasing. To the consternation of the Democratic administration, Douglas voted with the Republicans for a 5 percent budget cut. Questioned about whether his vote had been contrary to liberal principles, he responded: "Liberalism and conservatism, like 'the flowers that bloom in the spring,' have nothing to do with this case. . . . To be a liberal, one does not have to be a wastrel. We must, in fact, be thrifty if we are to be really humane."[19]

Douglas demonstrated his commitment to economy in government again in 1949 when the Senate considered annual appropriations for the U.S. Department of Labor. Republicans called for a 5 percent cut in the Labor Department's proposed budget, and Douglas concluded that the agency could indeed operate more efficiently. He agreed with the Republicans that cuts in overhead could be made without endangering any of the agency's worthwhile programs. When he supported the reduction in the roll call vote, a number of Democrats on the Senate floor expressed their dismay. As Douglas left the floor that day, a group of reporters asked him to explain why he had deviated from the Democratic party line. He brusquely suggested that they investigate his voting record in the Chicago City Council regarding budgetary allotments.[20]

Douglas found himself at odds with the administration again when he failed to support the Murray-Dingell Act, the omnibus health care legislation endorsed by the president. Introduced into the Senate in April 1949, the Murray-Dingell bill provided for federal aid to medical education, the establishment of medical research institutes, federal grants to the states for the improvement of public health systems, additional funds for hospital construction, and, most controversially, comprehensive national health insurance. The health care package called for free medical care—payment for doctor bills, hospital charges, prescription medicine, and all the rest—at no additional charge to all workers, the cost to be funded by a 3 percent payroll tax (half paid by the employer and half by the employee). Immediately, the American Medical Association (AMA) mounted a massive lobbying campaign against the bill based largely on the charge that national health insurance constituted socialized medicine. The measure stalled for months in the Senate Labor and Public Welfare Committee.[21]

Douglas balked at the "tremendously broad coverage" of the administration bill and, although he favored some form of national health insurance, feared that the Murray-Dingell version tried "to do too much too soon." He urged Truman to compromise, warning that an all-or-nothing approach would likely result in no progress toward national health insurance being made for a long time. "The two sides are now at a point where they are more interested in hitting each other than in finding some solution," Douglas lamented. As a countermeasure, he suggested a more limited form of national health insurance that would cover only catastrophic illnesses and be available only to families that had already spent a specific portion of their incomes on medical expenses; his less costly program would be funded by a half-and-half, 1 percent payroll tax and be administered privately rather than by the government. By scaling back in that fashion, he hoped to convince the medical lobby to accept some sort of compulsory program as an alternative to a fully nationalized health care system. The AMA remained steadfast in its opposition to any and all proposals, however, and Douglas's efforts did nothing to clear away the legislative logjam. His proposal of a compromise without consulting with supporters of the administration's bill merely antagonized James E. Murray, John Dingell, and, in all likelihood, the president himself.[22]

Late in the first session, Douglas had the opportunity to reaffirm his liberalism by taking a stand against monopolies and protecting the interests of small businessmen. He did so by opposing a "basing-point" bill that threatened to restore monopolistic conditions and harm consumer interests. The basing-point system originated with the steel industry in the nineteenth century. Prices throughout the nation would be fixed at the local market price plus the freight rate to a basing point—Pittsburgh, in the case of steel. Such a system eliminated competition and allowed for monopolistic control of prices that may have varied from place to place but became uniform in any given city. Companies that attempted to charge less found themselves subject to reprisals, and consumers in protected markets naturally paid higher prices. When the Federal Trade Commission (FTC) outlawed the Pittsburgh-plus system in 1924, the steel industry concocted a multiple basing-point system that allowed prices to be determined according to freight rates from a number of bases, and the result continued to be the elimination of competition. The U.S. Supreme Court declared the single and multiple basing-point systems a violation of antitrust laws in a number of industries, but the battle shifted to the U.S. Senate where Douglas, Russell Long of Louisiana, Estes Kefauver of Tennessee, and William Langer of North Dakota manned the antitrust ramparts.[23]

On June 1, 1949, Senator Joseph C. O'Mahoney (Democrat, Wyoming), long one of the legendary leaders of the antitrust forces, introduced a basing-point bill that would have amended antitrust statutes to legalize single and multiple systems. O'Mahoney characterized his bill as antitrust, and Douglas and his cohorts, reluctant to challenge one of the lions of the antimonopoly movement in the twentieth century, raised no objections as the bill passed by voice vote. On August 10, having read the entire bill thoroughly and finding it surprisingly inimical to the antitrust cause, Long called for reconsideration. Careful not to impugn O'Mahoney's intentions, Douglas delivered a passionate forty-five-minute address in which he laid bare the full implications of the law's intent. "If we enacted the basing point system as provided for in this bill," he charged, "we would legitimize monopoly or cartel fixing of prices and we would help strangle competition." Nevertheless, the motion to reconsider failed 49–28, and the bill proceeded to a conference committee where its supporters further reduced the government's power to declare price-fixing illegal. Back in the Senate, Douglas and Long maneuvered to delay action on the bill and managed to postpone a vote until January 1950, but they could not alter the outcome; the measure passed 42–27. President Truman vetoed the bill on June 16, and its sponsors lacked the necessary two-thirds vote to override. Douglas and the other antimonopolists won a Pyrrhic victory, however, for a similar basing-point bill became law over Truman's veto in 1951.[24]

Nor did Douglas and his fellow liberals triumph in their quest to pass legislation authorizing federal aid to education. The bill introduced in the Senate by Elbert Thomas of Utah, Lister Hill of Alabama, and Robert Taft of Ohio provided federal grants to the states that would have dramatically increased the amount of money spent on education in the poor southern states. Long a firm believer in addressing regional inequities through federal disbursements, Douglas worked assiduously for the bill's passage. The legislation quickly became embroiled in a religious controversy as the nation's Roman Catholic leadership insisted that direct aid be provided to parochial as well as public schools, a position that the National Education Association (NEA) and a number of Protestant churches adamantly opposed. Douglas helped craft a compromise whereby money for pedagogical purposes would be spent only on public schools, but separate legislation would allow federal aid to both public and private schools for transportation and health expenditures. These measures passed in the Senate but found more treacherous going in the House where religious divisions ran deeper. There, Protestants refused to allow spending of federal dollars for ancillary activities like transportation to and from schools, and Roman Catholics rejected legislation that offered parochial schools no funding at all. The breakthrough on federal aid to education came years later as part of Lyndon Johnson's Great Society reform program.[25]

Truman's Fair Deal may not have fared well in the first session of the Eighty-first Congress, but Douglas enjoyed a remarkable freshman year in the Senate. Disregarding the custom that relegated first-year solons to the margins of legislative life, he delivered nine speeches to the assembled body and participated fully in the debates on the major issues considered that year. In short, he acted like a veteran from the beginning. In the heated debate over the Bricker-Cain Amendment, he stood his ground against seasoned adversaries and became an instant hero to the nation's liberals. Yet, at the same time, he established his independence on several occasions by going his own way and breaching party unity. Hailed by some journalists as the Fair Deal's answer to Robert Taft, he quarreled with the Truman administration often enough to convince discerning observers that he prized freethinking more than partisanship. In September 1949, a poll of 211 political correspondents from Washington's newspaper and radio community ranked him the third-best senator (behind Robert A. Taft of Ohio and Arthur H. Vandenberg of Michigan, respectively).[26]

During the second session of the Eighty-first Congress, Douglas continued to maintain an unusually high profile for a newcomer to the Senate. He repeatedly found himself in the limelight, defending liberal causes and opposing bills proposed by conservative legislators. The first battle came in March 1950 when he led the fight against a bill that exempted natural gas producers from federal regulation. First introduced the previous year by Senators Robert Kerr and Elmer Thomas of Oklahoma and Representative Orren Harris of Arkansas, the bill prohibited the Federal Power Commission (FPC) from regulating the prices charged by independent gas producers to interstate pipeline operators who supplied the product to consumers. Such a change appealed to conservatives of both parties who regularly condemned governmental presence in the marketplace and especially to the congressmen of the great natural gas–producing states, Texas, Oklahoma, Louisiana, Arkansas, and Kansas; legislators from the populous midwestern and eastern states where the natural gas would be used in greatest quantity expressed concern about the impact on consumers. The big winners in deregulation figured to be the mammoth oil companies—Standard, Gulf, Shell, Texaco, Sinclair, Phillips, Cities Service, and the like—that monopolized the production of natural gas as well as petroleum. Without government limits on the prices charged on the gas as it entered the pipelines, economists predicted, profits would rise $600 million the first year and continue to increase as more and more homeowners used natural gas nationwide.[27]

Robert Kerr became the bill's champion in the Senate. Principal owner of the Kerr-McGee Company, which manufactured drilling equipment and marketed oil and natural gas, he knew the industry better than anyone in Washington. A multimillionaire who boldly claimed to oppose "any deal I am not in on," Kerr took pride in his reputation as a spoilsman who jealously protected the economic interests of Oklahoma and the Southwest. Intelligent, hard working, and widely respected, he became known as the principal congressional spokesman for the oil, gas, lead, uranium, and zinc interests. By the 1950s, the highly influential Oklahoman had become known as the uncrowned king of the Senate.

Fully committed to the deregulation of natural gas, he confidently predicted the bill's passage with no more than twenty dissenting votes.[28]

Even before the fate of the bill had been decided, Kerr took the first step toward deregulation by opposing the reappointment of FPC chairman Leland Olds. An advocate of public regulation, Olds had spoken out against the Kerr bill even though his confirmation hearing was forthcoming. At the reappointment hearings before a subcommittee of the Senate Committee on Interstate and Foreign Commerce, Lyndon Johnson of Texas grilled Olds about anticapitalist beliefs he had espoused in the 1920s. Despite the committee's recommendation against confirmation by a 10–2 vote, President Truman called upon Senate Democrats to approve the reappointment. Speaking in the nominee's behalf, William Langer said that "the case against Leland Olds smells strongly of oil" and, labeling the charges of 1920s radicalism a smear, noted that "not one iota of information was brought out which reflected on the record of this man as a public-power commissioner." Having been the target of similar attacks himself, Douglas dismissed the relevance of any remarks made a quarter of a century earlier and praised Olds as an able and honorable public servant who had compiled an excellent record as chairman of the FPC. Unlike some of his colleagues, Kerr refrained from red-baiting and confined his remarks to criticisms of Olds's opposition to deregulation. The Senate rejected Olds's reappointment 53–13, and the FPC chairmanship subsequently went to someone more acceptable to Kerr and the southwestern oil interests.[29]

Douglas spoke for the opposition when the Kerr bill came before the Senate in March 1950. He admitted to feeling overmatched in a debate with Kerr over the technical aspects of oil and natural gas production and recognized that the Oklahoman had the reputation of being a fierce advocate with a "unique capacity for brutal and caustical argument." Douglas prepared feverishly for the encounter and benefited from the tutelage of an FPC employee who painstakingly explained the minutiae of British thermal units, pipe widths, and gas rates computations. On March 20, the fourth day of the Senate debate on the bill, Douglas obtained the floor and for the next three days sparred verbally with Kerr and his principal allies, Lyndon Johnson and Democratic Whip Ernest W. McFarland of Arizona. Noting that 18,000 miles of pipeline had been laid or authorized in the preceding two years, Douglas sketched out a future of explosive growth for the natural gas industry and concomitant price increases for consumers if government ceased to supervise. The way natural gas was distributed made it a public utility subject to monopolistic control, he concluded, and competition would not modulate the price. Quoting data gleaned from U.S. Bureau of Mines reports, he said that 3 percent of the 2,300 natural gas producers would sell 80 percent of the product in 1952 and warned

Alderman Douglas addresses the Chicago City Council, 1940. Although always heavily outnumbered and frequently taunted by his city council colleagues, he continued to speak out for the causes in which he believed. (Chicago Historical Society)

At the age of fifty, Douglas enlisted in the U.S. Marine Corps and subsequently saw combat duty in the Pacific theater during World War II. (Chicago Historical Society)

Severely wounded in combat, Douglas returned to the United States and underwent extensive rehabilitation lasting thirteen months at Bethesda Naval Hospital. He never recovered full use of his left forearm, which had been sprayed by machine gun fire. (Chicago Historical Society)

Before the 1960 election, Douglas accompanied Democratic presidential nominee John F. Kennedy during his campaign swings through Illinois. Here, Douglas listens intently to Kennedy on the courthouse steps in Geneva. (Chicago Historical Society)

Douglas receiving a pen from President Lyndon B. Johnson at the ceremonial signing of civil rights legislation. Johnson singled out Douglas for special recognition after the passage of the Civil Rights Act of 1964 and the Voting Rights Act of 1965. (Chicago Historical Society)

Douglas speaks to a gathering of voters in 1966. He campaigned as ardently as he had in previous years but lost to Republican Charles Percy. (Chicago Historical Society)

Re-Elect PAUL H. DOUGLAS THE PEOPLE'S SENATOR
VOTE DEMOCRATIC · TUES. NOV. 8th 1966

Douglas and his wife, Emily Taft Douglas, talk with Vice President Hubert Humphrey. Like Douglas a devoted liberal, Humphrey had long been a friend and trusted ally in the civil rights struggle in Congress. (Chicago Historical Society)

that the profits would go not to "men in overalls" but to "giants operating under near monopoly conditions."[30]

The natural gas bill passed the Senate but by a much narrower margin than Kerr had predicted, 44–38. The measure at first failed in the House 178–172, but four representatives changed their votes so that the bill finally passed 176–174. Hopeful that the narrowness of the votes and the rising tide of public indignation against the oil companies might convince Truman not to sign the bill, Douglas and Democratic National Committee chairman William Boyle, Jr., conducted a campaign to request a presidential veto. The ADA, which was holding its annual convention when the bill passed in Congress, adopted a unanimous resolution calling for Truman to veto the measure. The mayors of the nation's eighteen largest cities, most of them situated in the Northeast and Midwest, sent a petition to the White House urging the same course of action. The AFL sponsored a series of nightly radio addresses in which Douglas urged the public to inundate the White House with letters calling for a veto of the "ripper" gas bill. Confident that he had bested the liberal forces arrayed against him, Kerr told other senators of the president's assurances that he would sign the bill. Ten days after receiving the bill from Congress, however, Truman vetoed it with a forceful statement that affirmed the government's intention of regulating natural gas in the public interest.[31]

Liberals rejoiced over what they perceived to be a great victory over the oil interests. Truman, they believed, had been predisposed to sign the bill but had not been able to withstand the withering political pressure applied from the left. In their view, the true Fair Dealers had been forced to nudge Truman back into the fold. Liberals and conservatives agreed that Paul Douglas's three-day clash with Kerr on the Senate floor had focused national attention on the issue and made natural gas regulation a cause célèbre. After the bill had passed in both houses of Congress, Douglas's dogged determination to force a presidential veto galvanized the opposition forces into an effective lobby. Douglas hailed Truman as "the true defender of the common people," but in liberal circles the Illinois senator received the lion's share of the credit for the stunning outcome of the natural gas battle.[32]

In the spring of 1950, Douglas devoted his attention to the creation of a sound national budget. He searched carefully for instances of inefficiency and waste that could be curtailed to the taxpayer's benefit, and again he found countless examples in the annual rivers and harbors bill. With much fanfare on the Senate floor, he cited case after case of pork-barrel politics contained in the $1.5 billion measure and listed $840 million—spanning dozens of proposed projects from Prouts Neck, Maine, to Westport Slough, Oregon—that could be eliminated without harm to the commonweal. He poked fun at the tens of thousands of dollars authorized for the improvement of bathing facilities at Palm Beach,

Florida, yachting at Stonington Harbor, Connecticut, and crabbing at Twitch Cove, Maryland, while other senators merely sat and listened in stony silence. When a senator petitioned that several inlets in his state be dredged to keep motorboats from disturbing the crabs, Douglas wearily asked, "Must we extend welfare-state benefits to crustacean life?" The Senate systematically voted down Douglas's many amendments and then passed the bill in its original form, 53–19. To the great annoyance of his colleagues, the persistent Douglas suggested as a cost-cutting measure the elimination of free shaves and haircuts for senators.[33]

Douglas was fashioning amendments to the administration tax bill when the United States became involved in the war in Korea and it became evident that additional revenue would have to be raised. On July 5, nine days after Truman announced that U.S. troops would participate in the "police action" against North Korea, Douglas vigorously defended the president's decision. Citing legal and constitutional grounds for executive action apart from a declaration of war, he emphasized the need for a quick and decisive response to communist aggression. Fully supportive of the massive commitment of soldiers and materiel to the United Nations fighting force, Douglas nevertheless insisted that U.S. military action be funded through progressive taxation. It was essential, he argued, that the fighting in Korea not result in windfall profits for big business or a crushing tax burden borne disproportionately by the lower economic classes. He even blamed the Treasury Department for not having foreseen the likelihood of hostilities in Korea and formulating excess-profits taxation to handle the sudden need for revenue—a charge that endeared him to no one in the administration.[34]

Preparing to challenge the tax bill that emerged from the Senate Finance Committee, Hubert Humphrey arranged for an informal tax seminar to be conducted by Department of the Treasury staff members who had worked on the original bill and could identify all of its inequities. Meeting surreptitiously at night at locations far removed from Capitol Hill, the Treasury Department experts dissected the tax code with Senators Humphrey, Douglas, Langer, and Herbert Lehman of New York. For several days thereafter, Douglas and the others conducted a floor fight on a series of provisions in the tax bill. Douglas spoke in favor of an excess-profits tax, arguing that such a measure would equalize the tax burden significantly and also curb inflation, but the measure failed. He offered an amendment that would disallow a family partnership provision whereby adults avoided the payment of taxes by creating "partnerships" with wives and infant children who actually contributed no services or capital to the business. Douglas claimed that the closing of this loophole would save at least $100 million annually, but again the Senate voted no. The longest and most animated discussion occurred with regard to the new depletion allowances proposed for oil and gas. Douglas argued strenuously that those industries already enjoyed excessive tax favors and that the new legislation would allow "a change of oil into gold" to the extent that "the dream of the alchemist had been realized." The Senate not only approved the new measures for the oil and gas industries but also extended the depletion principle to include such commodities as sand, gravel, and oyster- and clamshells. In the rush to provide revenue for the fighting in Korea in 1950, the Senate passed legislation that gave scant attention to Douglas's call for more equitable rates.[35]

During the rest of the nation's involvement in Korea, Douglas, Humphrey, Lehman, and a handful of others sought to amend the taxation legislation passed each year by Congress. In each instance, the dissidents called for equity and efficiency, and in each instance the administration's tax bills passed without amendment. Douglas proposed an increase in the capital gains rate that he said would add $87 million in revenue annually, a critical sum when the fighting in Korea engendered a huge federal budget deficit. In 1951 Douglas's amendment to reduce the percentage depletion on oil and gas from 27 1/2 to 15 failed by a vote of 71–9. Even his proposal to limit deductions for business entertainment expenses, most notably the total elimination of any deduction for the purchase of alcohol, ran aground. Douglas believed that the nation's regressive tax structure should be altered to achieve what he called "horizontal equity," but Truman and healthy congressional majorities did not see the war in Korea as the appropriate backdrop for pursuing the Fair Deal's goal of tax reform.[36]

The war in Korea sparked concerns about internal security. In 1940 Congress had passed the Smith Act, which made it illegal to advocate the overthrow of the U.S. government or to join any organization that did so. In the 1944 presidential campaign, Republican candidate Thomas Dewey had charged that communists had infiltrated the upper echelons of the Democratic party. After the conclusion of the Second World War, as the tenuous alliance with the Soviet Union crumbled, concerns about a communist presence within the United States intensified. In 1947 President Truman ordered loyalty investigations of the more than three million U.S. government employees, and subsequently the government discharged security risks judged to be especially susceptible to blackmail because of their alcoholism, homosexuality, or indebtedness. In 1950 a jury convicted Alger Hiss, an aristocratic former State Department official accused of passing classified documents to a communist spy, of perjury because the statute of limitations on treason had expired. Later that year, Senator Joseph McCarthy of Wisconsin leveled a series of charges against the U.S. State Department, which he claimed was honeycombed with subversives, and rapidly emerged as the foremost spokesman for the Republican right's crusade to purge the nation of the communist menace. McCarthy's rise to prominence elevated the fear of traitors in government to new heights.[37]

In 1950 Congressman Richard Nixon of California and Senator Karl Mundt of South Dakota revived a bill, which the two Republicans had first proffered in 1948, to require the registration of Communist party members, bar them from government employment, and incarcerate anyone attempting to foment the overthrow of the government by violent means. President Truman publicly condemned the Mundt-Nixon bill, calling its provisions cumbersome and ineffectual, and warned that such a blunt antisedition instrument would only drive communists underground. Pat McCarran, the Democratic senator from Nevada who chaired the Judiciary Committee, so altered the bill that his name superseded those of Mundt and Nixon. The McCarran Internal Security Act, which liberals saw as a threat to civil liberties and predicted would be an administrative nightmare, required the Justice Department to register all communists, denied them employment in the federal government, and barred all aliens who advocated a one-party form of government. "It is so clumsy in operation," said Douglas, "and will create such protracted delays that it will be ineffective in detaining or exposing Communists or in protecting the country against sabotage and espionage." Along with many other liberals, Douglas believed that the poorly drafted bill would allow real security threats to escape detection while branding innocent persons as subversives.[38]

Seeking to offset the more onerous provisions of McCarran's bill but recognizing the need for some legislation that balanced the need for security with the protection of civil liberties, Senate liberals huddled to create alternative legislation. Douglas, Hubert Humphrey, Estes Kefauver, Herbert Lehman, Frank Porter Graham of North Carolina, William Benton of Connecticut, and Harley Kilgore of West Virginia united behind a variation of a bill that had originally been proposed by Warren Magnuson of Washington. The resultant Kilgore bill authorized the U.S. attorney general to seize and detain anyone believed to be engaged in subversive activities during an internal security emergency as declared by the president. Douglas defended what Senator Homer Ferguson of Michigan called a "concentration camp bill" by saying that the Kilgore bill would deal with the real threat of sabotage rather than impose unenforceable limits on propaganda. "Defamation of character is worse than detention," Douglas said in all sincerity but with questionable logic. "That is something which seems very difficult for certain persons to understand. Defamation is really more injurious than detention." Speaking for the Kilgore bill on the Senate floor, Humphrey boasted of its toughness and derisively dismissed the McCarran Act as a "creampuff special." Douglas, Humphrey, and other liberals vigorously opposed the McCarran bill but wanted substantive legislation of some sort—if for no other reason than to safeguard their own reputations at a time of heightened fear of radicalism. A majority of the Senate disapproved of the Kilgore bill, however, and the measure failed by a vote of 50–23.[39]

Senate Majority Leader Scott Lucas, who was engaged in a tough reelection campaign against conservative Republican Everett M. Dirksen and thought it helpful to burnish his anticommunist credentials then, moved to attach the Kilgore measure to the McCarran Act as an amendment. Perhaps buoyed by the addition of the forcible detention provision and doubtless intimidated by the prevailing political climate—he admitted that "to oppose the bill would mean being labeled pro-Communist"—Douglas voted for the McCarran Act "as a practical matter." Only seven senators (Frank Porter Graham, Theodore Green, Estes Kefauver, Edward Leahy, Herbert Lehman, James Murray, and Glen Taylor) voted no. Humphrey later told Kefauver he was "very proud" of him for voting no and added, "I wish I could say the same for myself." Douglas immediately expressed regret at having voted for a bill that he knew to be deeply flawed and, admitting to a failure of courage, said that he had "failed morally." The casting of this vote, he averred, was one of his worst moments in the Senate.[40]

Truman's veto of the measure provided Douglas with an opportunity to atone at least partially for his mistake, and he began immediately to work for a vote that would sustain the president. He joined with Humphrey, Lehman, Kefauver, Kilgore, and Langer in a thirty-hour filibuster on the floor to delay the vote so that public pressure could be applied to wavering legislators. Langer held the floor for more than five hours before collapsing from exhaustion. Douglas stepped over Langer's body, began speaking so that their opponents could not obtain the floor, and then talked for an additional four hours. In decrying the McCarran Act's inadequacy, he noted both the threat to individual liberty inherent in the registration of suspected communists and the weakening of the emergency detention provisions by the bicameral conference committee. Thus, even as he eagerly took advantage of a second chance to condemn the bill's assault on civil liberties, he still defended the substance of the Kilgore amendment. He worried about internal security and sought appropriate legislation—just not the McCarran bill. When the liberals ended the filibuster, the McCarran bill became law with the Senate voting 57–10 to override the president's veto and the House following suit, 286–48.[41]

When Congress adjourned and he left Washington to campaign for Scott Lucas and other Illinois Democrats in the fall 1950 elections, Douglas could reflect back upon another year of accolades from a variety of sources. Earlier that year, *Time* selected Douglas one of the ten "most valuable" U.S. senators, calling him "the ablest, best-balanced liberal Democrat in the Senate and its most impressive freshman in years." The magazine referred to him as a "maverick liberal who also insists on prudent spending" and praised his "notable capacity for collecting, sifting and appraising facts." Douglas also received the Congressional Distinguished Service Award from the American Political Science Association in recognition of his penchant for advocating unpopular causes, his unceasing vigilance of government inefficiency, and his advocacy of social reform.[42]

When the Eighty-second Congress convened in January 1951, the Democrats still maintained majorities in both houses, but the Republicans had made significant inroads. The Democratic party held a slim 49–47 majority in the Senate after having lost five seats the previous November, one of the chief casualties having been Senate Majority Leader Scott Lucas, who had lost to Republican Everett M. Dirksen. Lucas's defeat owed to the growing unpopularity of the Truman administration, disappointing military developments in Korea, and the untimely disclosure of scandals in the Chicago Democratic party. Repaying the support he had received from Lucas in 1948, Douglas campaigned extensively for him throughout the state but was unable to offset the Republican resurgence. (Citing his unwillingness to risk losing Republican votes in the future, Governor Adlai E. Stevenson campaigned very little for Lucas, a decision that angered Douglas and contributed to the growing rift between them.) A staunchly conservative critic of the Truman administration, Dirksen called the Fair Deal "socialistic" and the Korean War the result of "diplomatic bungling." He and Douglas settled into an uneasy relationship that lasted during the fifteen years that they served together in the U.S. Senate.[43]

As U.S. involvement dragged on in Korea, congressmen and others in Washington began to ask hard questions about war aims, the role of the nation in the United Nations force, and the length of time necessary to secure a favorable outcome. In January 1951, a number of senators coupled their concerns about Korea with broader queries about America's strategy in the cold war in a lengthy foreign policy colloquy. As the debate raged on the Senate floor, Douglas remained uncommonly disengaged. Closeted in his cramped Senate office for a week, he read voraciously and, aided by four stenographers, wrote and rewrote a series of drafts. On January 15, he emerged from his seclusion and joined the argument with a four-hour speech on the Senate floor that vigorously defended the administration's containment policy against the attacks leveled by Senator Robert A. Taft and former president Herbert Hoover. In a lengthy Senate speech a few days earlier, Taft had questioned not only the wisdom but also the authority of the president to send troops into battle without a congressional declaration of war. For the Taft-Hoover forces, the best cold war strategy entailed withdrawal from Korea, a limited U.S. military presence abroad, and the development of the Western Hemisphere into "the Gibraltar of Western Civilization." If warfare became necessary, the Republicans averred, the United States should fight by sea and air and not on land.[44]

Douglas rejected this neoisolationism, referring derisively to Taft's "speak very loudly and carry a small stick" foreign policy. He argued for a broad interpretation of the Constitution that permitted the president to respond militarily without legislative approval when the nation's interests seemed at risk. He also contended that a reliance on "Gibraltarism" would result in the fall of both Europe and Asia to communist forces. In Douglas's view, the experiences of World War II and Korea clearly showed the inadequacy of sea and air power in modern warfare; infantry and artillery were still indispensable. Nor did he abide the argument advanced by some isolationists that the United States must be prepared to defend Europe or Asia but not both. Instead, he advanced what he termed the "Protect Freedom Everywhere We Can" position, for the protection of freedom and the opposition to despotism demanded no less. Specifically, he proposed a substantial commitment of U.S. ground forces to the North Atlantic Treaty Organization (NATO), a naval blockade of the China coast, a promise of air and naval support against communist advances in Indochina, mobilization of an additional six million men into the armed forces, and an increase in the defense budget to $100 billion (a sum double the amount projected in the famous secret memorandum, NSC-68). It was a bold call to arms worthy of any cold warrior, a tribute to Truman's containment initiatives that urged further action. He concluded:

> Let us determine that our civilization is not to fall, and that the ice cap of the police state shall not descend upon either us or Western culture. Even if open struggle comes, if we are determined to preserve the faith by which we live, we can rebuild much of the damage done and free ourselves and others from the fear of tyranny. . . . Let us resolve to win. Let us have faith and in that faith let us act.[45]

Throughout the spring and summer of 1951, as the hostilities dragged on in Korea and frustrations mounted at home, Douglas defended President Truman's conduct of the war. When the stalemate resulted in a steady stream of American casualties and a disgruntled populace questioned the desirability of sustained action, Douglas preached the need for determination and sacrifice. When Senator Taft acidly referred to the ongoing struggle as "Truman's war," Douglas countered that it was America's war—and a war endorsed by the United Nations. When Truman replaced General Douglas MacArthur for insubordination, Douglas stoutly defended the president's need to do so as commander in chief. In the face of thousands of letters and telegrams condemning MacArthur's removal from command, Douglas steadfastly affirmed Truman's decision. "The issue is one of military discipline and the principle upon which we are waging war," he wrote a constituent, "and not the respective personal merits of General MacArthur and the Commander-in-Chief." He also publicly called for the replacement of Secretary of State Dean Acheson who had become, in Douglas's view, a "political liability." As cease-fire negotiations continued, he questioned the restoration of the thirty-eighth parallel as the dividing line between North and South Korea and suggested instead to Secretary of Defense George C. Marshall that the United Nations should press for a new boundary approximately one hundred miles north of the thirty-eighth parallel as a check against future communist aggression.[46]

Even as he supported the administration's increasingly unpopular position in Korea, Douglas found himself equally unpopular with the president himself. The relationship between the two politicians, which had been uneasy from the start, unraveled entirely in 1951. At the 1948 Democratic National Convention in Philadelphia, Douglas had questioned the likelihood of Truman's reelection and publicly advanced the idea of drafting Dwight D. Eisenhower for president. During the 1948 campaign, Truman wrote Douglas a personal letter congratulating him on an article he had published in the *New York Times Magazine* on the arduousness of campaigning. Desperate for money in the last days of the campaign, Douglas inexplicably sold the letter for fifty dollars to one of his contributors, only to have the contributor advertise it for sale as a collector's item. Truman vehemently objected to the transaction. Though Douglas retrieved the letter, returned it to the White House, and apologized profusely for the unintended slight, the president apparently never forgot the incident. The events left Douglas in an uneasy position with the White House before he first took his seat in the Senate in 1949.[47]

The awkwardness persisted during Douglas's early days in Washington as his repeated demonstrations of independence irritated Truman, a dedicated partisan who believed that Democrats should follow the administration's lead unquestioningly in all matters. Although Douglas almost always supported the president's policies, he deviated in a few well-publicized instances and insisted upon maintaining the right to do so. In 1950 a subcommittee of the Senate Banking Committee chaired by J. William Fulbright of Arkansas launched a high profile investigation of the Reconstruction Finance Corporation (RFC), an independent government agency that dispensed low-interest loans to corporations. Fulbright and Douglas became the members of the committee who pursued the investigation most aggressively. Suggesting that the RFC needed a "thorough housecleaning," Douglas charged that the agency had shown favoritism in its lending decisions by bailing out certain struggling corporations but ignoring others. In some instances, RFC officers had granted generous loans to corporations, resigned from government employment, and then become executives in those firms. Particularly embarrassing to the president, the leading figures in the scandal—White House aide Donald S.

Dawson and a shadowy figure named E. Merl Young, who falsely claimed to be related to Truman—were friends of his from Missouri. In August 1950, Truman responded to the flood of negative publicity by firing several top RFC officials, including the agency chairman. In short order, however, the president nominated several men as RFC directors whom Douglas and Fulbright considered to be of questionable character. Dismissing the objections of the subcommittee members, Truman resubmitted the names of his controversial nominees in December.[48]

In February 1951 the subcommittee issued a report, *A Study of the Reconstruction Finance Corporation: Favoritism and Influence,* that Truman called "asinine." When Fulbright announced that the contentiousness surrounding the report had convinced the subcommittee to conduct hearings, Truman objected and called Fulbright "an overeducated S.O.B." (Douglas believed that "Truman disliked all Ph.D.s, and he thought Bill Fulbright and I were educated beyond our ability.") Truman had his staff examine RFC correspondence and found many examples of congressmen, including Fulbright and Douglas, having recommended that the agency grant loans to their constituents. The irate president called Senator Charles Tobey (Republican, New Hampshire) out of a subcommittee executive session and spoke with him on the telephone about his discovery. A shaken Tobey returned to the subcommittee meeting and reported the substance of the president's conversation: "He told me that the real crooks and influence peddlers were members of this committee, as we might soon find out." Interpreting the president's comments as a threat, Douglas defiantly responded: "Then there is only one thing for us to do. We must go ahead full tilt and summon the crucial administration witnesses to the stand."[49]

That evening, Douglas and his staff examined his correspondence with the RFC and found three letters he had written recommending that the agency grant loans to specific companies. At the next day's hearings, he read all three letters aloud and admitted that he "had probably gone too far" in endorsing the loan requests and should only have recommended that the agency give "proper attention" to the applications. Because Douglas preempted the presidential charges of influence peddling by the senators, the issue quickly faded away. Douglas and Fulbright met privately with Truman in the White House to apprise him of their findings. Douglas told the president that he had been loyal to friends who had not repaid his loyalty with honest service. "I guess you are right," Douglas said the president responded, but no such public admission ever came from the White House. The hearings uncovered a few peccadilloes committed by RFC staffers, but the embarrassment of the disclosures eventually forced Truman to respond. In May 1951, he installed Stuart Symington as the new chief administrator of the RFC with explicit instructions to clean up the agency.[50]

A short time later, an Internal Revenue Service (IRS) agent informed Douglas that his 1949 tax returns would be audited. The IRS called the audit routine and, despite its timing, denied any relationship with the RFC investigation. Douglas thought otherwise. He turned over all his financial records, and a month later the agent returned to report that all was in order. In fact, the embarrassed agent announced, the senator had overpaid by $41.12. Douglas requested not only the refund but also a letter officially stating the outcome of the audit. The agent initially refused but, after consulting with his superiors, produced a statement and a check. Douglas sent the statement to the *New York Times,* which reported the incident in detail. Douglas did not publicly charge Truman with initiating the audit but privately believed he had. "Even Roosevelt had used the Internal Revenue Service as a club over recalcitrant members of Congress," he reflected, "and Truman was following the same tradition."[51]

The feud between Douglas and Truman resurfaced in the summer of 1951 when the two Democrats conducted a very public struggle over a pair of federal judgeship appointments in Illinois. To fill two vacancies on the Northern Illinois District Court, Douglas reached an agreement with the Cook County Democratic leadership in January 1951; he chose William H. King, and the machine selected Benjamin Epstein. As the senior senator from Illinois, Douglas expected to be allowed to recommend judges for the federal bench, but in July, without warning, Truman nominated instead two other jurists, Joseph J. Drucker and Cornelius J. Harrington. Surprised by Truman's breech of custom, convinced of the superiority of his candidates, and unwilling to accede to the president's power play, Douglas determined to fight for his choices. He requested that the Chicago Bar Association poll its six thousand members to determine their preference for the judgeships, and the membership overwhelmingly identified King and Epstein as more qualified. At the same time, the Illinois State Bar Association polled its members in the sixteen northern counties of the state, and the *Chicago Sun-Times* queried a sample of twelve thousand attorneys in the city. In all of these cases, the polls' respondents identified Truman's nominees as decidedly inferior. Claiming vindication, Douglas took his case to the Senate Judiciary Committee and carefully noted his objection to the "methods and manner by which [Truman's] appointments were made." He said that he contested the president's nominations with great reluctance, but "in this matter, God helping me, I can do no other."[52]

Douglas refused to yield on the matter of the judicial appointments, arguing that his choices were simply better than the president's. He and Jacob Arvey conferred with Truman but found him equally adamant. Committed to protecting the Senate's exercise of its powers of "advice and consent" regarding all presidential appointments, the Judiciary Committee upheld Douglas's prerogative and rejected the president's nominees. The judgeships remained vacant until President Eisenhower filled them years later. The clash between the two strong-willed Democrats allowed the appointments to be made by a Republican executive, an outcome that left disturbed Cook County Democrats with no judicial aspirants to reward. To Truman, it was another example of how Douglas's nettlesome independence could be counterproductive.[53]

Truman also resented Douglas's periodic crusades to purify the federal government, an impulse the president felt the senator should suppress when such investigations would only embarrass the administration of his own party. (Douglas saw the root of these antireform feelings in Truman's early association with the corrupt Pendergast machine in Kansas City.) Such negative feelings inevitably worsened when Douglas assumed the chairmanship of a subcommittee of the Labor and Public Welfare Committee charged with reporting on ethical standards in government. Upon learning that Douglas had sent questionnaires on ethics and public morals to members of the president's cabinet, Truman sent him a blistering letter condemning the subcommittee's activities. The president pointedly suggested that the principal problem in the federal government rested with headline-hungry senators who had forgotten that they had been elected to legislate, not to discredit the executive branch. Douglas responded in an equally forceful letter, defending the appropriateness of his committee's inquiries and explaining that he had sent the questionnaires to cabinet members only after having received clearance from Bureau of the Budget officials. "I regret that it has not met with your approval," he closed coolly.[54]

After the subcommittee concluded its investigation, Douglas continued to discuss the topic by delivering a series of lectures at Harvard University and, expanding on those addresses, publishing a book, *Ethics in Government*. In the book, he discussed such topics as the recent RFC investigation, campaign financing, and the growing power of lobbyists in Washington. He also ruminated at length about the troublesome problem of politicians' accepting gifts or entertainment from constituents. The acceptance of valuable gifts was clearly problematic, for, if nothing else, it raised the appearance of impropriety. On the other hand, everyone agreed, the receipt of inexpensive tokens or favors surely raised no great moral dilemmas. So where should the line be drawn? Douglas suggested that public officials should adopt the standard he had employed since arriving in the Senate—$2.50. If a gift worth more than that amount arrived at his office, staff members immediately sent it back. If the gift cost less than $2.50, Douglas sent it to local hospitals or gave it to his staff. Douglas acknowledged the arbitrariness of the figure, just as others ridiculed the paltry amount that he had chosen. To many politicians, including the president, the "Douglas rule of $2.50" smacked of more self-righteousness by the senior senator from Illinois.[55]

Truman's antipathy for Douglas's independent brand of reform politics must have increased as a series of scandals in Washington besmirched the president's reputation in 1950–1951. With the exception of the RFC investigation, Douglas played no role in uncovering the myriad scandals bedeviling the Truman White House, but no one could ignore the stark contrast between the Illinois senator's unblemished reputation for probity and Truman's apparent indifference to the cronyism and corruption surrounding him. Douglas believed Truman to be personally honest, a victim of his association with politicians who used their White House connections for private gain. Overall, Douglas believed the president served the country well under difficult circumstances. On a number of intractable foreign policy problems—the use of the atomic bomb, aid to Greece and Turkey, the Marshall Plan, the development of the hydrogen bomb, Korea, the removal of General MacArthur—he felt that Truman had made courageous and judicious decisions. The Illinois senator approved of the Fair Deal's liberal contours as well. Compared with the monumental decisions he made so effectively, the president's vendettas and excessive partisanship seemed inconsequential. In later years, Douglas regretted that his and Truman's relationship faltered over comparatively minor matters. Indeed, the tension between the two Democrats emanated more from contrasting temperaments than from differences in principle.[56]

At a time of plummeting popular opinion polls for the Truman administration, the Illinois senator's popularity soared and his name frequently arose as a potential presidential candidate in 1952. In a laudatory *New York Times Magazine* profile, Cabell Phillips noted that, with the possible exception of Wendell Willkie, Douglas had achieved more acclaim in a shorter period of time than any other public figure in recent memory and reported that Democratic state leaders listed him as their top choice for president in 1952 if Truman declined to seek reelection. (In fact, his popularity was such in 1951 that Walter Winchell reported in *Life* that he was being promoted for U.S. secretary of state, and the *New York Times* detailed the movement to hire him as commissioner of baseball. In both instances, Douglas declined interest.) The Douglas-for-president movement eventually fizzled because the "candidate" declined to take the bait. In a series of public statements and private letters, Douglas categorically denied any interest in pursuing the presidency and commanded his supporters to cease all activities in his behalf; in a number of instances, he ordered his backers not to enter his name in presidential preference primaries. He simply squashed the movement.[57]

Why did Douglas decline to pursue the highest political prize, especially when his own popularity and Truman's problems seemed to make him a bona fide candidate? Howard Shuman, Douglas's administrative aide for many years, believed that several factors kept the senator from pursuing the presidency. His earlier association with radical politics would undoubtedly resurface in a national campaign, and despite the solidly anticommunist credentials he had amassed since World War II any fallibility on the issue at the height of the McCarthy Red Scare could be lethal. Douglas's divorce constituted another potential public relations problem, particularly because of the rumors concerning his ex-wife's ties to the Communist party. Her politics aside, divorce remained a real liability for politicians as late as the mid-twentieth century, as Adlai Stevenson discovered in 1952 and 1956. Most important, Shuman thought, Douglas—an insomniac who constantly worried about votes he had to cast in the Senate—questioned whether he possessed the decisiveness and toughness for the job of president. Shuman disagreed with that assessment but believed that Douglas seriously doubted that he had the temperament the presidency would require.[58]

In his letters to supporters admonishing them not to advance his candidacy, Douglas cited several reasons but principally emphasized two concerns. First, he said that he very much enjoyed the work of a U.S. senator, had no aspirations to do anything else, and feared that his work in the Senate would be hampered if the public believed him to be angling for higher office. As he had said before, he just wanted to be a damn good senator. Second, he said that he doubted his ability to handle the presidency. In several letters, he emphasized his concerns about the physical and emotional demands on the president. "My nerves and physical strength are already taxed to the very breaking point, " he confided in a confidential letter to the president of the Oregon Young Democrats, "so that the crushing load of the Presidency would, in my judgment, kill me within a few months." He wrote the editor of the *Peoria Journal:*

> I could not stand the strain of the terrible and crushing lonely decisions which have to be made by a President. Some men can make them and then throw them off and sleep. But I worry about decisions for days, even though they are shared by others. In short, I don't think I have the ability to "roll with the punches" which a President or Governor needs, and that one month on the job would quite literally kill me.[59]

Douglas's admitted concerns about his ability to handle stress seemed more valid to observers following an episode near the end of the 1951 legislative session. He took the floor to question the need for specific items in a $61 billion military appropriations bill and offered an outline for reductions totaling approximately $1 billion. Senator Joseph O'Mahoney, chairman of the appropriations subcommittee that had recommended the bill, interrupted repeatedly and suggested that Douglas was impugning the integrity of the military. O'Mahoney said: "I can imagine the words of the senator from Illinois being read tomorrow morning, and, by some representative of Tass, being broadcast behind the Iron Curtain, to indicate a lack of faith among American members of Congress in the men who work, who fight, and who die for them." Douglas suddenly jumped to his feet, grabbed his head, and let out a high-pierced scream of exasperation. He ran crying from the Senate chamber and fled to his office. After reclining on a couch with a cold towel on his forehead for a half hour, he returned sheepishly to the Senate floor. One of Douglas's aides later explained that the senator's overreaction owed to fatigue and disbelief that a colleague would question his patriotism. *Newsweek* suggested that the bizarre outburst irretrievably damaged Douglas's presidential chances by raising questions about his emotional stability, but in fact he had already intentionally halted any momentum his candidacy had achieved.[60]

Douglas's critics had a field day with the "shouting out" incident, calling him high-strung, emotional, overly sensitive to criticism, and the like. On the other hand, he reported receiving a thousand letters of support from citizens who not only sympathized with his emotional outburst but also appreciated his continued efforts to squeeze waste out of flabby federal budgets. In three years as a U.S. senator, Douglas had built a huge national following that viewed him as one of the most capable, honest, and sincere men in Washington. His willingness to put principle before party, his devotion to liberalism, and his fierce opposition to communism accounted for his popularity. He had taken himself out of the upcoming presidential race, a decision that many of his admirers accepted with equanimity because he would be continuing his good work in the Senate. Although Truman and other Democratic loyalists seethed at Douglas's brand of independent liberalism, the public and the press responded with rave reviews.[61]

4 Politics in the Age of McCarthy

The record will show that I have supported [President Eisenhower] on every feature of his foreign policy, such as the Bricker Amendment, broader trade and foreign aid. My opponent, *in his actions, writings and statements,* has taken an exactly opposite course. I have also supported the President on those features of his domestic program which were *in the best interests of the American people,* such as housing, social security, health, etc. . . . I shall support the President when he is right and oppose his policies when I believe them to be wrong. In good conscience I can do no other.

—**Paul H. Douglas**[1]

• The presidential election of 1952 presented Paul Douglas with a series of problems. Throughout 1951, he had publicly and privately renounced any interest in running for president, yet talk of his candidacy persisted. In December 1951, the *New York Times* reported Douglas the overwhelming choice of 150 labor union presidents in a poll to select the Democratic nominee for president should Harry Truman decide not to run for reelection; Douglas finished first with 47 percent of the vote and Estes Kefauver a distant second with 19 percent. Douglas remained steadfast in his determination not to seek the presidency and continued to deflect interest in his candidacy wherever it originated. As late as May 1952, he publicly chastised Edward G. (Pat) Brown for urging California delegates to the upcoming national party convention to vote for him and privately dismissed Adolf Berle's assertion that he was the only Democrat who could defeat Dwight D. Eisenhower in the fall election. At the same time, he contemplated supporting Kefauver even if Truman opted to run again. Complicating the situation was the potential candidacy of Adlai Stevenson, whose eloquence, moderate politics, and fine record as governor of Illinois had earned him a large and loyal following among the nation's Democrats. Douglas preferred the more liberal Kefauver but felt that he could not fail to support Stevenson if he chose to pursue the nomination. In the early months of 1952, with so much uncertainty prevailing, Douglas hoped above all else that the Democrats would nominate their most liberal candidate for president.[2]

To Douglas and many other liberal Democrats, the party's best presidential candidate seemed to be Estes Kefauver. Elected to the Senate from Tennessee in 1948, Kefauver had achieved considerable national prominence in a short time. Like Douglas, he had become known as an independent who did not hesitate to deviate from party orthodoxy when matters of conscience dictated. One of only seven senators to vote against the original McCarran Act, he took a courageous stand for civil liberties when many other liberals (including Douglas) were not as discerning about the internal security legislation they supported. He took a more progressive position on civil rights than any other southern senator, even daring to support the curtailment of the filibuster in the Senate. An internationalist in foreign policy, he became the foremost spokesman in Congress for an Atlantic Union that would link the nations of western Europe, Canada, and the United States in a federated organization designed to foster cooperation in opposition to communism. Most important, Kefauver became a household name in America because of the extensive television coverage afforded the investigation of organized crime conducted by a special Senate committee he chaired.[3]

Truman and other Democrats saw Kefauver as a publicity-hungry demagogue who put his own advancement before the interests of his party, as evidenced by his insistence on conducting the crime investigation in the midst of the 1950 campaign. Convinced that the negative publicity generated by the sensational hearings helped account for the Democrats' dismal performance that year—most damagingly in Illinois, where disclosures of scandals in Chicago supposedly played a major role in the defeat of Senate Majority Leader Scott Lucas—many party regulars saw Kefauver as an irresponsible maverick. On the other hand, Douglas praised Kefauver for his intrepidity and willingness to advance unpopular causes. "He is a loyal Democrat, all right," argued Douglas, "but his loyalty is to the best in our party, not at all to the worst."[4]

Hoping that Kefauver might get the Democratic nomination in an open selection process and deploring the undemocratic convention system of presidential nomination in which the party bosses exerted inordinate influence behind the scenes, Douglas argued strenuously in the early months of 1952 for the adoption of presidential preference primaries in all states. In February, joined in the House by Representative Charles Bennett (Democrat, Florida), Douglas introduced a bill in the Senate whereby the federal government would provide an additional incentive to establish primaries by awarding each state up to 25 cents per voter to offset the cost of an election; the legislation failed. While the bill languished in Congress, Douglas publicly suggested that Truman should run in the primaries if he planned to seek another term. The president initially declined to have his name placed in nomination in New Hampshire, calling the primaries "eyewash" and boldly affirming that he could have the nomination if he wanted it, but relented when his remarks unleashed a flood of negative publicity. On March 11, 1952, Kefauver scored a stunning upset over Truman in the New Hampshire primary, and suddenly the renomination of the president seemed decidedly less than automatic. His candidacy invigorated by the surprising victory in the campaign season's first primary, Kefauver asked Douglas for a formal endorsement. Douglas regretfully declined because of the continued ambiguity surrounding the presidential ambitions of Adlai Stevenson.[5]

Douglas's great affinity for Kefauver notwithstanding, he felt that he could not fail to support the governor of his own state in the presidential contest—even though his already uneasy relationship with Stevenson had deteriorated further in 1951–1952. On October 13–14, 1951, Douglas and Stevenson met secretly at a mutual friend's cottage in the Indiana Dunes to discuss the selection of Illinois delegates to the 1952 Democratic National Convention. Determined not to allow the seamier elements of the party to dominate the selection process, they agreed that each would choose half of the downstate delegates subject to the other's approval. Seeing that the selection would take a considerable amount of time, they broke off the discussion and agreed to submit lists later that their aides would collate, and on October 26 Douglas sent Stevenson his list of delegates. He was shocked when the governor later submitted a slate to the state Democratic committee that contained none of Douglas's nominees. Stevenson's biographer believed that the mix-up resulted from a breakdown in communication within Stevenson's staff and that the governor had not intended to shortchange Douglas. In other words, it was another example of the administrative sloppiness that plagued the Stevenson political operation in 1952 and after. Douglas thought otherwise. In a later discussion, Douglas noted, Stevenson seemed disingenuous in first claiming to have fulfilled his obligation and then denying that any such agreement had been reached at the Indiana meeting. Douglas suspected that Stevenson's repeated declinations of interest in the presidency failed to persuade his aides, and they subsequently acted to ensure that the Illinois delegation only contained their boss's supporters. In all, this episode underscored Douglas's suspicions about Stevenson's abiding if undeclared interest in the presidential race.[6]

At the Democrats' Jefferson-Jackson Day dinner in late March, Truman announced that he would not seek reelection and that he preferred Stevenson to succeed him as president. Stevenson immediately issued a statement denying any interest in the presidency, affirming his singular intention of running for reelection as governor. His announcement seemed entirely unambiguous, but Douglas remained wary and wanted even more assurances. He telephoned a number of the governor's closest confidants in Springfield and Chicago, and they all confirmed that Stevenson genuinely harbored no presidential ambitions at that time. Finally convinced that Stevenson would not be a candidate, Douglas threw himself wholeheartedly into the Kefauver campaign. During the spring of that year, Douglas spoke extensively on behalf of Kefauver who carried primary elections in state after state.[7]

In the weeks leading up to the Democratic National Convention, Stevenson never publicly reneged on his disavowal of interest in the presidency, but many of his friends privately began intimating that he had not intended to shut the door entirely to a possible candidacy. An extensive public speaking tour that took the Illinois governor around the country during the heart of the primary season enhanced speculation that he would bow to a convention draft, as did increasingly ambivalent remarks he made that always seemed to stop just short of a complete refusal to run. Admirers of the Illinois governor contacted Douglas, urging him to discontinue his support for Kefauver and announce his backing for Stevenson. Douglas refused to desert Kefauver, emphasizing that he had given Stevenson every consideration weeks before. Kefauver asked Douglas to nominate him at the convention but Douglas, fully convinced at last that Stevenson would run, had to decline to avoid an open affront to the governor. (The convention, after all, would be held in Chicago.) Because of Stevenson's vacillations, Douglas found himself in an awkward position but intended to honor his commitment to Kefauver.[8]

The Democratic National Convention began on Monday, July 21, at Chicago's International Amphitheater with Douglas addressing the delegates on the first day. He delivered a highly partisan defense of the Truman administration's conduct of the war in Korea, criticizing a number of Republicans, including John Foster Dulles, General Douglas MacArthur, and the party's presidential nominee, Dwight D. Eisenhower, for initially supporting the war only to second-guess the president later for purely political reasons. To the charge that Truman had been inattentive to the security needs of South Korea before the North Korean invasion, Douglas rejoined that the Republican-dominated Eightieth Congress had repeatedly rejected the administration's military and economic aid package for the defense of South Korea. As late as January 1950, just five months before the outbreak of hostilities, Republicans had voted as a bloc to defeat a Korean aid bill—the effort to derail the measure having been eagerly supported by the Republican vice presidential candidate, Richard M. Nixon. "If mistakes were made prior to the invasion of Korea," Douglas told the delegates, "Republicans shared in them even more than Democrats."[9]

During the first three days of the convention, a series of struggles ensued over the seating of disputed delegations and the adoption of rule changes and resolutions; in each instance, northern liberals (including Douglas) vied with southerners and moderates over issues related to civil rights. In the most spirited contest, a resolution introduced by liberals allowed the seating of only those delegates who agreed to the automatic placement on their states' ballots of the party's candidates chosen at the convention—in other words, requiring a binding loyalty oath obviously designed to forestall the kind of walkout conducted by the Dixiecrats four years earlier. The resolution failed narrowly as northern moderates seeking to avoid another rupture allied with southerners. Despite Kefauver's impressive performance in the primaries, the pundits agreed, the defeats suffered by the liberal forces in the convention's opening days damaged his chances and boosted Stevenson's.[10]

On Thursday, July 24, the convention commenced the nomination of presidential candidates, an interminable procedure that began at noon and continued well past midnight. In the midst of the nomination roll call, the civil rights struggle resurfaced as a floor fight broke out over the seating of the Virginia, South Carolina, and Louisiana delegations. Stevenson supporters believed that the northern liberals had raised the issue in order to unseat the delegates from those three states and thereby precipitate a walkout by other southern delegations. Without the backing of the southern states, Stevenson's candidacy would be fatally wounded. The vote on Virginia proved decisive as party regulars and southerners combined to defeat the resolution. Fearing that the Stevenson forces might be on the verge of a first-ballot nomination, liberals hurriedly caucused and decided to seek an adjournment in order to regroup overnight.[11]

At about 1:00 A.M., Douglas privately informed Sam Rayburn, who was presiding in his role as permanent convention chairman, that he intended to move for a recess until noon the following day. According to Douglas, Rayburn stiffly allowed that motions to recess were always in order but only if the chair recognized the delegate who wished to make the motion. From his vantage point in the Illinois delegation directly in front of the speaker's podium, Douglas then attempted to introduce the motion to recess. Denied access to the microphone by Illinois delegates friendly to Stevenson, Douglas climbed onto a chair and shouted, "Mr. Chairman, Mr. Chairman, Mr. Chairman," in a vain attempt to be recognized. Literally a few feet away from the Illinois contingent, Rayburn blithely ignored the calls for recognition as the business of the convention continued. After nearly two hours, during which time Douglas yelled continuously even as he fended off antagonists who tried to knock him off his chair, Rayburn suddenly recognized the Illinois delegate. Disheveled and perspiring from his ordeal, his hands pressed against his chest, Douglas grabbed the microphone, hoarsely moved to adjourn, and then dramatically sank to the floor. The motion carried. Opponents criticized the theatricality of Douglas's performance, calling it another example of his penchant for histrionics. Friends told him that he had "cut a most undignified figure," and he admitted that his performance had been "quixotic." The entire tableau brought no credit to either side.[12]

Defeat for the liberals came the next day. Kefauver led the field during the first two ballots, but a massive swing of votes to Stevenson began during the third. Closely monitoring these developments from the nearby Stockyards Inn, Kefauver and Douglas realized that the tide had turned irrevocably in favor of Stevenson. Kefauver decided to withdraw in favor of Douglas who would, in turn, throw his support to Stevenson; Douglas agreed to accompany him to the convention floor so that he would not face the lonely walk to the podium alone. The two men strode up the center aisle as the roll call continued, only to be denied access to the dais when Douglas informed Rayburn of Kefauver's desire to withdraw in the interest of party harmony. Instead, Rayburn humiliated Kefauver by making him—and Douglas—sit in full view of the convention until the completion of the balloting. Only then did Rayburn allow Kefauver to endorse Stevenson and pledge his support of the ticket. A few days later, Douglas sent Stevenson a congratulatory telegram in which he dryly noted that he had tried to offer an endorsement on the convention floor but had been denied recognition.[13]

After a lengthy trip to Europe, Douglas returned to campaign for the Democrats in the fall election. Admiring of Stevenson's oratorical excellence yet wary that the candidate had made too many bargains with conservative forces in the party in order to receive the presidential nomination, the Illinois senator hoped that he and other liberals would not be too disappointed in the Democratic campaign. To Douglas's great surprise, Stevenson took genuinely progressive positions on most issues. The Illinois governor sounded a clear call for civil rights and took issue with the Republicans' positions on offshore oil and Taft-Hartley Act revisions. As expected, Stevenson's internationalist views on foreign policy dovetailed closely with Douglas's. Pleased with the tenor and substance of Stevenson's campaign, Douglas campaigned extensively for him in Illinois and elsewhere. In a landslide victory for Eisenhower and the Republicans, however, Stevenson lost Illinois by more than 400,000 votes. A dispirited Douglas attributed the defeat to the public's infatuation with Eisenhower, the self-effacing military hero whose common sense and likableness had catapulted him into the presidential race, and a desire for change after two world wars and twenty years of Democratic presidents. "You made a splendid race," Douglas wrote consolingly to Stevenson, "and the nation is the better for you having taught sense to the American people."[14]

During the presidential election year of 1952, the Eighty-second Congress allocated generous sums of money for the national defense budget but ended up, according to Douglas, "an utter flop on domestic legislation." Early in the session, he became concerned about a new immigration bill offered by Senator Pat McCarran of Nevada that perpetuated—and in some cases exacerbated—the inequities of the national-origins quota system for regulating the number of newcomers. (The existing formula permitted annually a number of immigrants from each foreign country based upon the number of immigrants from that country already living in the United States; these quotas discriminated strongly in favor of some nations at the expense of "less desirable" countries-of-origin.) The bill, which maintained inordinately low immigrant quotas for people leaving southern and eastern Europe, seemed particularly wrongheaded to Douglas in its bias against the people most desperate to escape the communist tyranny practiced behind the Iron Curtain. Moreover, he objected to the ethnocentrism inherent in the prevailing origins formulation. "We should not mistake differences for inferiority," he contended. "We should not believe that because people are different from us they are therefore inferior to us." To counter the prejudice against the so-called "New Immigrants" from southern and eastern European nations, he quoted crime and juvenile delinquency statistics that showed no greater lawlessness committed by those immigrants than by other groups in America. Even more worrisome, Douglas believed, the McCarran bill offered scant protection of individual rights for those immigrants facing possible deportation, exclusion, or denaturalization proceedings. Altogether, he saw this cold war measure as flawed in many of the same ways that McCarran's Internal Security Act had been and personally favored an amendment offered by Hubert Humphrey and Herbert Lehman that would have provided less draconian immigration quota reductions and included adequate legal safeguards in deportation cases. Congress passed the McCarran bill and later overrode Truman's veto of it.[15]

Douglas also vigorously opposed the Maguire bill, a measure designed ostensibly to curtail the influence of drugstore chains that was championed by independent pharmacists—and by liquor and tobacco interests who stood to gain from the elimination of retail price wars. The bill allowed manufacturers to fix the price at which their products would be sold at retail and made illegal the sale of that product for less by any retailer. These prices would be binding on all retailers within a state, and the federal government would enforce what Douglas saw as a blatant example of price-fixing. Independent drug stores complained about the use of "loss leaders," the cost-cutting practices of chain stores that lowered the prices on pharmaceuticals to lure customers to their stores and made great profits on the sale of other items. If the smaller independent pharmacies had to maintain comparatively low retail prices on brand products, they would be unable to compete with the chain stores. Passionately committed to competition on behalf of consumers, Douglas opposed price-fixing of any sort and saw the bill as a collusive effort to circumvent antimonopoly statutes by retail druggists, drug wholesalers, and drug manufacturers. He found himself on the opposite side from many of his usual liberal allies, most notably Hubert Humphrey. The son of a drugstore owner and himself a registered pharmacist, Humphrey remembered how his family's small business had almost been driven into bankruptcy by the arrival of a chain store in his parents' neighborhood. Humphrey and other liberals contended that they backed the Maguire bill as protection for small businesses against monopolies.[16]

On July 1, some time after the Maguire bill had passed in the House, Vice President Alben Barkley suddenly introduced the measure to the floor of the Senate. Without submitting a report from the Committee on Interstate and Foreign Commerce or offering any explanation regarding the contents of the bill, Barkley hurriedly announced, "Without objection, the bill is passed." Before he could finish his sentence, Douglas leaped to his feet, registered an objection, and asked for an explanation. Where was the published record of the committee hearings? What did the chairman of the committee have to report? What were the particulars of the bill? When no one responded to any of his questions, Douglas proceeded to outline the bill's provisions and explained why he stood in opposition to its passage. He proposed a compromise bill that allowed price markups not to exceed 6 percent—a concession he attributed to desperation and later regretted offering—that failed by the vote of 69–12. The original legislation then passed by a vote of 64–16. Douglas could take solace in the fact that the U.S. Supreme Court promptly found the Maguire bill unconstitutional.[17]

Another setback for Douglas came when the Senate rejected statehood for Alaska and Hawaii, a result of rising sectional tensions between the North and South over the nascent civil rights movement. Douglas avidly supported the admission of both territories as states in order to bolster U.S. defenses against communist aggression in the Pacific and to make a bold statement against colonialism. Citing the overwhelming support for statehood in Alaska and Hawaii, he noted that the substantive opposition came from southerners who foresaw the presence of four more U.S. senators who would vote for civil rights legislation. An increase in the number of liberal votes in the upper house would threaten the southern control of the seats necessary (one-third of the total) to prevent cloture in the inevitable debates on civil rights measures. Douglas made an impassioned speech on the Senate floor in which he appealed to the southern states to "place the national interest above its prevailing regional concerns." Douglas's argument that the more populous states in the Northeast and Midwest would have to make economic concessions to support the two new states—that is, states like New York, Pennsylvania, and Illinois would pay for the large grants of federal money that would flow to Alaska and Hawaii—proved unpersuasive to the southern states. Alaska and Hawaii had to wait for statehood until 1959.[18]

The civil rights issue arose immediately in the opening moments of the Eighty-third Congress as the Senate once again considered the fate of Rule XXII. Repeatedly thwarted by the threat of the filibuster, civil rights advocates decided to move for a reconsideration of the Senate's operating rules (including Rule XXII) before the first session of the Eighty-third Congress officially began. The Wherry resolution, which had been adopted in 1949, required a two-thirds vote of all senators to halt a filibuster on any motion to alter the rules, but liberals argued that the incoming Senate had the right to adopt its own rules by majority vote before the official business of the Senate commenced—just as the House of Representatives had always done. Southerners characterized the Senate as a continuous and immortal body with operating rules forever fixed in stone, whereas liberals contended that each Congress existed as separate and distinct from its predecessors and, therefore, possessed the authority to determine its own rules and procedures. Congressional insiders recognized that what might have appeared at first glance to be a dispute over arcane parliamentary matters was actually the key to determining the fate of civil rights legislation in any session. The issue, Douglas noted, was "whether the Senate can ever free itself for decision by breaking filibusters conducted by a small minority."[19]

Douglas planned to introduce the motion allowing consideration of the rules at the start of the session but stepped aside when informed that several senators would be more inclined to vote yes if Clinton Anderson (Democrat, New Mexico) made the motion. (Reflecting the relative insignificance of the issue in his state, Anderson had not been in the forefront of agitation on civil rights as some other liberals—most notably, Douglas—had.) If the motion carried, the Illinois senator planned to propose the amendment of Rule XXII to require only a simple majority for the invocation of cloture; the more moderate Anderson then intended to move for the limitation of debate by just a three-fifths vote. Speaking on behalf of Republicans and southern Democrats, the new Senate majority leader, Robert Taft, defended the principle of unlimited debate and moved to table Anderson's original motion. Douglas spoke at length about the illogic of his opponents' arguments and argued strongly for the modification of the rules to end the tyranny of the filibuster—but without success. Taft's motion to table the Anderson initiative carried 70–21.[20]

The lopsided defeat on the question of Rule XXII not only augured ill for civil rights measures but also served as an indication that little hope for liberal reform existed in the Eighty-third Congress generally. Riding the coattails of the Eisenhower victory in 1952, the Republicans had recaptured the Senate by a 49–47 margin and the House by 221–214. In his study of the Eighty-third Congress, the historian Gary W. Reichard found that the 59 Republican freshmen (9 senators and 50 representatives) shared a number of common beliefs. The newcomers campaigned in

1952 against big government and much of the New Deal while pledging to support their presidential candidate's views on how best to combat communism throughout the world. A number of incumbent Republicans in Congress—the so-called Old Guard—held even more conservative views, favoring more of an isolationist foreign policy than the internationalism espoused by the incoming president. Eisenhower promised "enlightened conservatism," but a survey of the new Republican-controlled Congress suggested more conservatism than enlightenment.[21]

On February 9, 1953, Speaker of the House Joseph W. Martin and Senate Majority Leader Robert Taft included among the eleven pieces of "must" legislation identified by the White House a bill to confer upon the states ownership of all submerged lands within "historic" state boundaries. Such legislation would transfer ownership of offshore lands rich in oil deposits from the federal government to such states as California, Texas, and Louisiana, a bonanza for those states because of the estimated mineral wealth of $300 billion contained in the continental shelf. Although the newspapers referred to the "tidelands" controversy, the ownership rights in question referred not to the lands included within normal tidal action but to offshore land under the ocean extending out to the nation's three-mile legal boundary. To Eisenhower and his supporters, the issue presented an opportunity to advance the conservative cause of states' rights and curtail the involvement of the federal government.[22]

The offshore oil question had gone unresolved for nearly a decade by the time the Republicans regained control of the White House. In 1945 President Truman had claimed federal ownership of all natural resources in the offshore lands, but a series of Supreme Court decisions left the legal title issue unsettled. While oil continued to be extracted from the submerged lands, private concerns with leases from the government had deposited their royalties in escrow until the issue of state and federal jurisdiction could be clarified. In 1952 Congress considered a law granting title of the submerged lands to the coastal states, a bill that Douglas disparaged as an "outright gift" that would shortchange the vast majority of Americans. Why, he asked, should forty-five states be deprived of a veritable treasure for the sole benefit of three states? Instead, Douglas and seventeen other senators proposed that the federal government retain ownership and use the revenue from offshore oil leases exclusively for aid to education. The law favoring state ownership passed, but Truman vetoed what he called the "give-away" measure. Shortly before leaving office, Truman declared all offshore oil a reserve of the U.S. Navy.[23]

The Eisenhower administration moved quickly to revise that policy. Its bill to give jurisdiction of the disputed territory to the states generated a lengthy and heated discussion in the Senate where liberal Democrats and maverick Republican Wayne Morse of Oregon staged a filibuster. Douglas held the floor for ten hours and forty minutes spread out over two consecutive days arguing the bill's illegality and unfairness. In a sweeping indictment of the measure, he warned that such a precedent would not only deprive all of the states of much-needed funds for education ("oil for the lamps of learning") but lead to additional depletion of natural resources. A victory for states' rights in this instance, he warned, would be inimical to the common good as well as an ecological disaster for the submerged coastal lands; he felt that the federal government would be the best steward of the nation's undeveloped natural resources. A disheartened Douglas reported that his constituent mail ran fifty-to-one in opposition to state ownership of the submerged offshore land, but the measure carried in the Senate by a vote of 56–35. The liberals salvaged something two months later with the passage of a related bill, which was patterned after legislation proposed by Douglas and Clinton Anderson, providing for the development of the rest of the continental shelf beyond the three-mile limit exclusively by the federal government. In later years, Douglas happily noted that the overwhelming proportion of offshore oil deposits rested outside the states' domain.[24]

The question of offshore oil having been resolved, Douglas turned his attention to the related issue of depletion allowances for oil and gas. His attempts in 1950 and 1951 to reduce the allowances had been foiled, and so in 1954 he offered with Senators John J. Williams (Republican, Delaware), George D. Aiken (Republican, Vermont), and Herbert H. Lehman (Democrat, New York) a tax bill amendment to cut oil and gas allowances from 27 1/2 percent to 15 percent. When the Senate rejected the amendment by voice vote, Douglas submitted a substitute measure that allowed the full 27 1/2 percent depletion allowance on annual oil and gas incomes that did not exceed $1 million, 21 percent on incomes in excess of $1 million but less than $5 million, and 15 percent on incomes greater than $5 million. Again, the Senate voted no. He introduced taxation amendments calling for the reduction of oil and gas depletion allowances on a graduated scale ranging from 27 1/2 percent to 15 percent in 1957, 1958, 1959, and 1960 with the same negative results.[25]

Although he dedicated most of his time to the consideration of pending legislation, Douglas also became concerned with the abuses of McCarthyism in the U.S. Senate. On July 16, 1953, he delivered a speech on the Senate floor, "Fair Play in Congressional Investigations," which by implication criticized Joseph McCarthy and others who had used congressional forums to conduct improper investigations of American citizens. Emphasizing the damage irresponsibly conducted investigations could do to the reputations of innocent men and women, Douglas observed that the fairness or lack of fairness depended in large measure upon the conduct of the committee members themselves—and particularly upon the committee chairmen who all too often made their own rules, did anything they desired, and behaved as though they had been given unrestricted hunting licenses. The temptation of publicity, he charged, seemed to have led committee members to cut ethical corners as well. At the end of the speech, Douglas offered "ten commandments for fair play" in congressional inquiries that prescribed, among other changes, less public disclosure of derogatory remarks in congressional hearings in order to protect the reputations of witnesses, guarantee of the right of counsel for witnesses, the right of witnesses to cross-examine other witnesses, and more expeditious procedures to shorten the duration of the proceedings.[26]

Unlike some other liberals, Douglas spoke infrequently against the abuses of McCarthyism and never delivered a speech inside or outside of Congress that specifically reproved the Wisconsin senator. Indeed, historians of the domestic anticommunism practiced in the early 1950s have commented on Douglas's surprising quiescence on the issue. In *Senator Joe McCarthy,* for example, the journalist Richard H. Rovere wrote: "Paul Douglas of Illinois, the possessor of the most cultivated mind in the Senate and a man whose courage and integrity would compare favorably with any other American's, went through the last Truman years and the first Eisenhower years without ever addressing himself to the problem of McCarthy." In her discussion of Eleanor Roosevelt's stand against McCarthyism, the historian Allida Black observed: "Senator Paul Douglas . . . whose credentials for liberalism and integrity were heretofore impeccable, refrained from discussing McCarthy until it was politically safe to do so." The historian Richard M. Fried similarly noted the apparent anomaly and provides this explanation: "Paul Douglas (not noted for a lack of courage), while disapproving of McCarthy's methods, had to concede that 'we have had some Alger Hisses in government.'" Fried quoted Douglas as saying: "We were handicapped by the fact that many of the men who McCarthy singled out were implicated to some extent."[27]

The fact that Douglas did not emerge as one of McCarthy's principal antagonists in the Senate and played only a marginal role in the Wisconsin demagogue's demise may be explained by several factors. An avid defender of civil liberties who had been the frequent target of red-baiters during his own political career, Douglas genuinely deplored McCarthy's methods, and yet—as the quotations cited by Fried suggest—he grudgingly admitted that the proven existence of communist spies necessitated the unpleasant kind of investigative work conducted by the red-hunters. Furthermore, Douglas confined himself to taking issue with policies and proposals advanced in the give-and-take of the legislative process but refrained from attacking the veracity or conduct of his senatorial colleagues. Even though McCarthy presented an inviting target and never himself hesitated to attack a colleague, Douglas would not engage in ad hominem verbal exchanges. Thus, he might give a speech calling for the improvement of congressional investigations without directly indicting the primary culprit whose excesses prompted the reproofs. Privately, Douglas expressed his contempt for McCarthy and later reiterated those feelings in his autobiography, but he stopped short of expressing his feelings at the time. He did, however, vote with just eleven other senators for immediate action on Senator Ralph Flanders's Resolution 301 to censure McCarthy, a demand deflected by the referral of the resolution to a six-man select committee chosen by the vice president. Following the select committee's recommendation, Douglas voted for censure.[28]

The controversy swirling around McCarthy provided the backdrop for Douglas's 1954 reelection campaign. Political pundits suggested that McCarthy would respond to the threat of censure in the Senate by lashing out at Democratic senators seeking reelection that year. As embattled as the Wisconsin senator seemed that summer, his name still evoked fear in many quarters. Although scholars later disputed the belief that McCarthy's interventions in a number of state contests in 1950 had been decisive in defeating his Democratic opponents, in 1954 the stories of his influence four years earlier still held currency; in particular, his incursions into the 1950 Maryland and Illinois senatorial races supposedly contributed significantly to the defeat of incumbent Democrats Millard Tydings and Scott Lucas. Douglas seemed a likely target in 1954, and the press reported that McCarthy would campaign in Illinois against him. *Life* suggested that so many (ten) Republicans entered the Illinois senatorial primary that year because, as a "superliberal" and a "superinternationalist," Douglas was an especially inviting target and because the Republican receiving the nomination could expect generous assistance in the campaign from McCarthy.[29]

All of the accolades Douglas had received during his six years in the Senate notwithstanding, many political observers sensed that he might be vulnerable in 1954. Despite the Cook County Democratic machine's continued control of the Chicago electorate, the Republican party controlled 90 of the state's 102 county courthouses. Moreover, demographic trends seemed to be running against the Democrats. The number of registered voters in Chicago fell from 2,077,775 in 1952 to 1,928,102 in 1954, and voters who moved to the suburbs were beginning to vote Republican. In addition to the considerable opposition of Illinois Republicanism, which was underwritten by Colonel Robert McCormick and editorially boosted by his *Chicago Tribune*, Douglas would have to allay the concerns of the state's Democrats. Many party loyalists questioned the independence of a man who maintained an uneasy relationship with Governor Stevenson and openly feuded at times with President Truman. Some liberals felt Douglas too much of a cold warrior, too quick to enlist the military on behalf of containment, and too tolerant of the witch-hunting produced by the fear of communist subversion at home—and too hesitant to speak out against Joe McCarthy and his minions. To be sure, the voters appreciated Douglas's flinty integrity and knew where he stood on the issues, but did they endorse his ideas? Would Douglas's full-throated internationalism seem reasonable to the voters in a state known for its isolationism, or would they prefer to fight communism only at home? What would they think of his brand of liberalism in the conservative Ike Age?[30]

Surviving the crowded Republican primary, Joseph T. Meek emerged as Douglas's opponent that year. (Meek received 300,000 votes while Douglas, running unopposed, won twice that many in the Democratic primary.) A lifelong businessman and lobbyist with no previous political experience, Meek served as president of the Illinois Federation of Retail Associations, a prosperous lobby that served the interests of an estimated forty thousand to sixty thousand members in the state. A jovial glad-hander who referred to himself as "Mr. Retail," Meek explained his initial foray into politics as a patriot's defense of Americanism against the country's insidious drift toward socialism. Although Meek genially assured reporters that he and Douglas were friends who would conduct a civilized campaign—"It's always been 'Paul' and 'Joe' between us," he said—he soon referred to Douglas as "the Senior Socialist Senator from Illinois" and the "Medicine Man from the Midway." Douglas likewise ridiculed his opponent's conservatism, calling Meek "the Republican Rip Van Winkle who has slept twenty years in Lobbyland" and "a man who was dragged screaming into the twentieth century." The two candidates could not have differed more completely in their political views, and the campaign promised to be contentious.[31]

In December 1953, Meek wrote to Senator Everett M. Dirksen, chairman of the Republican Committee on Senatorial Contests, to discuss Douglas's vulnerabilities and propose a strategy for defeating him. Predicting that he would be the Republican candidate the following year, Meek urged Dirksen to keep a careful record of Douglas's statements and senatorial votes so that they could be used against him with the Illinois electorate. Meek called Douglas a "veritable giant of the art of double-talk" who routinely uttered "half-truths" in order to fool the unsuspecting voters. In Meek's view, Douglas received a favorable press because of the widespread perception of him as a "delightful fellow personally, full of good will" despite his many shortcomings. Furthermore, Meek averred, Douglas's record showed an unsettling penchant for government action as the cure for all economic ills and an indifference to rugged individualism. In short, the Democratic senator "is dedicated to installation of the Federal Government as master of our lives." Meek's sulfurous letter closed with his assurance that he could defeat Douglas but only if the national Republican organization provided the necessary support.[32]

Throughout the campaign, Meek projected an image of down-home congeniality. A short, round, rumpled man with horn-rimmed glasses and a ubiquitous smile, he veritably oozed unpretentiousness. Sprinkling his speeches with country aphorisms, especially when campaigning in Illinois's many isolated towns and hamlets, he mocked Douglas's erudition even as he proudly admitted his own intellectual limitations. An energetic campaigner who seemed to enjoy the endless hand-shaking and baby-kissing necessary in a statewide political contest, he impressed onlookers with his apparent modesty and self-effacing wit. "Hell, everybody likes Joe Meek" in downstate Illinois, concluded a *New York Times* reporter assigned to the campaign.[33]

Meek's affability notwithstanding, however, his combative speeches attacked every aspect of Douglas's political career and crackled with right-wing ideology. Referring to his opponent as "Paul the Planner," a "Fabian socialist," and a "high-pressure lobbyist for the overthrow of capitalism," Meek portrayed Douglas as an unwitting dupe of nefarious agents who sought to divert Americans onto the road to communist enslavement. Douglas and the Democrats had aided in this process, the Republican alleged, by supporting the program of Earl Browder, leader of the American Communist party. Meek's list of subversive programs championed by the Democrats revealed the extremism of his thinking. The list included the following:

> Government deficit financing, manipulation of bank reserve requirements, insurance of bank deposits, guarantees of mortgages, control of bank credits, tinkering with the currency system, regulation of installment buying, price controls, price support for farm products, agricultural credits, RFC loans for business corporations, social security systems for workers, various benefits for veterans, government housing, public works projects to provide employment, many projects for conservation of national resources, juggling of the tax structure, new tariff regulations, government organized foreign loans, the employment act, the President's Economic Committee, stimulated war armaments production on a large scale.[34]

In addition to Meek's direct attacks on the Democratic party, Douglas again became the target of rumors and innuendos that questioned his patriotism and cast him as a former socialist. A pamphlet widely distributed by the Abraham Lincoln Republican Club, an independent organization with no direct ties to the Republican party, resurrected charges made against Douglas during his 1939 campaign for alderman and his 1948 senatorial race. The pamphlet listed a number of "communist-front" organizations to which Douglas once belonged, retold the story of his 1927 visit to the Soviet Union, and erroneously reported that he had previously been a member of the Socialist party. The *Chicago Sun-Times* discovered that Meek's campaign manager, Mark G. Van Buskirk, had secretly commissioned the printing and distribution of the material. As before,

Douglas vigorously defended himself, pointing out that he had long ago resigned from leftist organizations that he judged too radical and carefully explained the circumstances under which he had gone to the USSR. He denied ever having been a member of the Socialist party and offered as corroboration a letter from Norman Thomas. Confirming that Douglas had never joined the Socialist party, Thomas concluded: "I should frankly add that I wish [your reform program] came closer than it does to my own socialist point of view." Reiterating his rejection of socialism and communism, Douglas reminded voters that he had demonstrated his patriotism by fighting for his country in the Second World War—a claim that Meek, who had no record of military service, could not make.[35]

The Republicans tried to link Douglas to a scandal in the Federal Housing Administration (FHA) uncovered by a Senate Banking Committee investigation. The Copley Press newspaper syndicate published stories in several northern Illinois dailies alleging that Douglas's campaign had illegally profited from overpayment of an FHA award for the construction of an apartment complex to a Chicago developer. An FHA bureaucrat, a former Republican ward committeeman in Chicago, transmitted a letter supposedly implicating Douglas to the office of Senator Everett Dirksen; a Dirksen aide then leaked the information to the Copley Press's Washington correspondent. Any notion of Douglas's involvement quickly evaporated when the chairman of the Senate Banking Committee, Homer Capehart (Republican, Indiana), clarified the purloined letter's contents. Explaining that the government had not overpaid the developer and that Douglas had not shared in any windfall, Capehart pointed out that the FHA loan actually fell nearly a million dollars short of the cost of construction. Capehart's detailed summary of the project's costs totally exonerated Douglas and exposed the attempt to smear him as an amateurish effort.[36]

Because Congress did not adjourn until late in August, Douglas could not begin campaigning in earnest until after Labor Day. In the weeks that followed, despite a lingering illness that left him listless and occasionally made walking difficult, he campaigned at a torrid pace throughout the state. With unrelenting zeal, he explored the issue of Meek's right-wing extremism. Noting his opponent's opposition to social security, dislike of minimum wages for women, call for the withdrawal of all U.S. troops from Europe, endorsement of Joe McCarthy, support for the Bricker Amendment, and boasts that he had helped defeat three Fair Employment Practices Commission (FEPC) bills in Illinois, Douglas concluded that Meek belonged firmly in the Old Guard wing of the Republican party. Indeed, Douglas claimed, he stood closer than Meek to President Eisenhower and the responsible element in the GOP. Douglas supported the president's foreign policy initiatives to combat communism and selectively backed the domestic policy programs he judged to be worthwhile. A primary example involved public housing. Whereas Eisenhower had agreed with Douglas that the government had a moral obligation to provide some low-income housing and had signed the Housing Act of 1954, Meek contended that "you can't get away from the persistent threat of socialism and communism unless you begin doing for yourself that which you are now willing for the government to do for you . . . including slum clearance." Douglas also cited the case of national health insurance. Recalling that he had opposed the Murray-Dingell bill for going too far, he lauded the more circumscribed Eisenhower medical plan that Congress had recently defeated.[37]

While portraying Meek as drastically out of step with his own party's leadership in Washington, Douglas still took the Eisenhower administration to task over its economic policies. Despite the apparent health of the national economy, Douglas boldly forecast the onset of a recession due to Republican mismanagement during the previous two years. In his travels around Illinois, Douglas informed the voters, he had spotted telltale signs of economic problems—unusually empty parking lots adjacent to the farm-implement factories in Rock Island and Moline, long lines at employment insurance offices, growing inventories of unsold vehicles at downstate automobile dealerships—before economists recognized a national problem. Republican leaders dismissed Douglas's warnings as the gloom and doom of a desperate incumbent fearing defeat at the polls, and the *Chicago Tribune* accused him of using scare tactics for his own personal gain. In *Economy in the National Government*, a book he had published just two years earlier during a Democratic administration, Douglas had termed 6 percent unemployment an acceptable rate. With a Republican in the White House, complained the *Tribune*, Douglas was finding 5 percent unemployment excessive and predicting dire economic consequences. Douglas rejoined that a sophisticated assessment of the national economy had to go beyond a cursory comparison of unemployment data; he continued to cast the putative Republican prosperity as a kind of Potemkin village.[38]

In the campaign's closing days, Meek attempted to position himself nearer to the Republican middle ground. Acknowledging the value of a closer association with President Eisenhower, whose personal popularity remained high with voters, Meek de-emphasized his disagreements with the administration's policies. He persuaded Everett Dirksen to take him to the White House for a fence-mending session with the president, after which Dirksen assured Eisenhower that Meek "is a team player." Likewise, he tempered his enthusiasm for the ruthlessness of Joe McCarthy's red-hunting escapades. Earlier a spirited defender of McCarthy's methods, Meek became increasingly vague about the acceptability of the investigative tactics employed by congressional committees. His strained attempts to drift into the political mainstream seemed calculated and unconvincing, however, as when he said: "The objectives of the McCarthy Committee are very essential. Sometimes the methods of the man are not acceptable. Sometimes they are." Even though his political positions remained contrary to views held by the Republican administration in Washington, Meek handled the awkward McCarthy situation effectively enough to receive Eisenhower's tepid endorsement.[39]

Contrary to the speculation that McCarthy would campaign extensively in Illinois against Douglas in 1954, he never appeared in the state that year. He canceled a September 26 speech in Naperville, citing sinus problems that forced him to check into a hospital for treatment, and similarly backed out of two other scheduled speeches in Illinois that autumn. On October 31 Senator John Bricker and other party stalwarts, who had been dispatched by the Republican National Committee, addressed a rally in Galesburg alongside Meek, but McCarthy was noticeably absent. Everett Dirksen felt that appearances by McCarthy could have aided Meek and other Republican candidates in Illinois and, although he stopped short of publicly criticizing Eisenhower and White House staff, lamented the party leadership's decision not to bring the Wisconsin senator into the state. Wary of the controversy swirling around the embattled McCarthy, Republican leaders seemed to have concluded that his presence in Illinois would potentially have done more harm than good.[40]

The issue of McCarthyism arose one last time when Douglas and Meek appeared on the television news program "Meet the Press" the Sunday before the election. Asked how they would vote on the upcoming resolution to censure the Wisconsin senator, the two candidates gave strikingly different answers. Meek endorsed the beleaguered McCarthy, but Douglas offered a long, rambling response that at first seemed noncommittal but eventually suggested that he would vote for the censure resolution. He began by saying that he would reserve judgment until reading the report of the special committee studying the charges—to do otherwise would be to prejudge the case—but later reminded the audience that he had been one of the few senators who voted for immediate action on the resolution. Douglas indeed seemed to be trying to have it both ways, claiming to have an open mind pending full disclosure of the evidence and yet also hinting that he found McCarthy's conduct censurable. McCarthy fired off an angry telegram to Douglas, charging him with hypocrisy and attempting to deceive the voters when he obviously had already thrown his lot in with the senators favoring censure. Praising the forthright position taken by Meek, McCarthy denounced Douglas in the press and called for his defeat at the polls.[41]

In the campaign's closing weeks, the *Chicago Tribune* likewise weighed in heavily against Douglas. Grudgingly acknowledging the senator's cold war credentials, the newspaper nevertheless criticized his eagerness to commit U.S. military forces in the fight against communism globally.

Even more problematic, the *Tribune* maintained, was Douglas's devotion to government meddling in the economy. His warnings about rising unemployment and the threat of an impending recession made him a demagogue. Though stopping short of overtly red-baiting him, the newspaper continued to refer to his earlier associations with leftist organizations. The virulence of the *Tribune*'s campaign against Douglas peaked with its publication of a critical series of articles just before election day. In one of those acerbic pieces, Republican state auditor Orville Hodge called Douglas "morally unfit" to hold elective office. (Two years later, Hodge was in prison, having been found guilty of embezzling $2.5 million from the state.) The *Tribune*'s endorsement of Joe Meek seemed to be an afterthought, its principal goal the removal of Douglas from office.[42]

Douglas won the election by approximately 237,000 votes. He received 53.6 percent of the votes, about one percentage point less than in 1948, but still won by the largest margin of any Democratic congressional candidate that year. Douglas attributed his success to the rising reaction against McCarthyism and the public's concern about an impending recession brought on by misguided Republican economic policies. In his view, the righteousness of his positions on the issues triumphed over a vacuous but generously funded Republican campaign. "For a second time," he exulted, "I had beaten the moneyed Establishment." Meek naturally saw it quite differently. He pointed to disunity in the Republican party as the salient factor in explaining the election's outcome. He felt unaccepted by both the Eisenhower and Taft wings of the party and rued his inability to heal the rift between the two factions. Most important, he had been unable to alter the perception that he was "pro-McCarthy" and "anti-Eisenhower." These internal fissures, he surmised, explained the low voter turnout in traditionally Republican areas of the state. Disgusted at the party's fractiousness and unsure of Meek's loyalty to the popular Eisenhower, many Republicans simply stayed at home on election day.[43]

Both candidates' analyses contained some perceptive insights, but their brief assessments touched on just a few of the many factors that contributed to the incumbent's reelection. Douglas's decision to emphasize dollars-and-cents issues undoubtedly yielded considerable dividends. His jeremiads about the worsening economic situation seemed to have paid off in the industrial regions of East Saint Louis, Rock Island, Moline, and the southern Illinois coal mines, all of which were already experiencing severe unemployment, but less so in cities like Peoria and Rockford where conditions remained healthy. Organized labor rallied to Douglas's cause, partly because of his many years of support for unions and solid voting record in Congress and also because Joe Meek's twenty-year history of complete opposition to any prolabor legislation in Illinois made him anathema to AFL and CIO officials. Meek's paeans to free enterprise and fulminations against government intrusions into the operations of the free market may have played well with chambers of commerce and other businessmen's organizations, but his strenuous objections to government aid to agriculture struck a discordant note among Illinois farmers. While Douglas's liberalism did not always appeal to all of his constituents, the state's farmers recognized that, at least in this instance, his support of an activist government served their interests.[44]

Although the Cook County Democratic machine had lost some of its power and faced population decline and the concomitant growth of the suburbs, the Chicago organization, which supported Douglas strongly, remained a potent force in state politics. Uncharacteristically unsuccessful in the 1950 and 1952 elections and beset by a series of scandals, the machine valued its association with Douglas more than ever and responded accordingly in 1954. The payoff came in the huge majorities he enjoyed from Chicago precincts on election day. Meek carried suburban Cook County by 80,000 votes and the rest of the state by 68,000 votes, but the Chicago leviathan made the difference for Douglas. (The area immediately surrounding Cook County, the so-called "collar counties" of McHenry, DuPage, Kane, and Lake, gave Meek a plurality of 59,000 votes.) Chicago's continuing loss of population and the growing affinity between the Republican party and suburban voters provided some consolation to Colonel McCormick's partisan *Tribune*, but not enough electoral muscle to save Joe Meek in 1954.[45]

In reelecting Douglas, Illinois voters knew that they were returning to Washington an independent Democrat who would support the Republican administration on some issues, namely in championing a staunch anticommunism in foreign affairs, while demanding more government activism in behalf of social welfare measures. The state's electorate recognized the expediency of Meek's eleventh-hour rapprochement with Eisenhower and understood that he truly occupied a niche much farther to the right on the political spectrum. If Douglas was more liberal than many Illinois voters, he stood less removed than Meek from the state's political epicenter. In the waning days of Joe McCarthy's influence in the Senate, politicians like Meek who were closely associated with the discredited Wisconsin senator could only fare worse than those like Douglas who could claim to have opposed—even in a small way—the excesses of domestic anticommunism. Reelected by a substantial if not overwhelming margin, Douglas returned to the Senate secure in the fundamental soundness of his political beliefs and prepared to resume the struggle for liberal reform.[46]

5

The Civil Rights Movement in the Senate

Surely resistance, defiance and nullification in respect to the country's basic laws are not entitled to special privilege under the guise of "States' Rights." And when threats, intimidation and obstruction to Constitutional rights seek the hallowed sanctuary of a "way of life," out of reach of the Constitution, then it is time for Congress to re-assert by reasonable federal remedies the supremacy of law and order under the Constitution.
—**Paul H. Douglas**[1]

•   The history of the struggle for racial equality in twentieth-century America has been written almost exclusively in terms of court decisions and protest activities staged by civil rights organizations with comparatively little attention paid to events in Congress. Historians have first noted the painstaking legal work performed principally by the Legal Defense Fund of the National Association for the Advancement of Colored People (NAACP) as brilliantly conceived and implemented by Charles Hamilton Houston, Thurgood Marshall, and others. In a series of path-breaking victories culminating in the landmark case of *Brown v. Board of Education of Topeka, Kansas,* NAACP attorneys undermined the legal underpinnings of the separate-but-equal doctrine of segregation. Next came the courageous and inspiring efforts of the organizations and individuals devoted to grassroots protest. For a decade extending from the mid-1950s to the mid-1960s, sit-ins, freedom rides, and protest marches captured the headlines and made civil rights an issue that Americans could no longer ignore. During those years, the moving cadences of Martin Luther King, Jr.'s oratory stirred the nation's conscience. The story of the civil rights movement, according to the standard history, shifts to Capitol Hill only in the mid-1960s with the passage of the key legislation that represented the culmination of a long fight waged elsewhere. Even then, most attention has been devoted to the key role played by the executive branch of the federal government. The assassination of John F. Kennedy and the surprisingly enthusiastic and able leadership provided by his successor, Lyndon B. Johnson, forced a conservative legislature at last to pass such measures as the Civil Rights Act of 1964, the Voting Rights Act of 1965, and the Twenty-fourth Amendment.

In this common description of the civil rights movement, events in Congress during the period are largely ignored. The conventional wisdom suggests that southern Democrats in the Senate used the filibuster and other procedural tactics to stifle any sentiment for reform, the result being the relegation of Congress to the sidelines until events in the eleventh hour at last dictated legislative action, but a careful examination of the Senate yields a more complicated picture. Conditions in the upper house in the 1950s and 1960s set the stage for the legislative breakthroughs of 1964–1965. More specifically, presidential leadership could not have been so effective had it not been for the preliminary groundwork laid in the Senate by a dedicated cohort of liberals who were committed to the cause of civil rights. Paul Douglas believed that the long, seemingly hopeless crusade waged by him and the other devotees of civil rights finally paid off in the legislative cornucopia of the Great Society. Although success hardly seemed likely at the time, he was right in noting the indispensability of the Senate liberals to the civil rights cause.

When the small bipartisan group of civil rights supporters returned to the Senate in January 1955, they did so with a renewed sense of purpose. The *Brown* decision of the previous year had invigorated the liberals, encouraging them to seek follow-up advances in Congress while the spirit of change remained alive. But if the possibility of civil rights breakthroughs seemed greater in the wake of *Brown,* the intractable obstacles were no less daunting. Arthur Krock of the *New York Times* noted that "the Senate was the graveyard of civil rights and Rule XXII was the gravedigger." In the hands of a crafty and dedicated band of southern obstructionists, the filibuster remained a formidable roadblock to civil rights legislation.[2]

The 1954 election had produced slim Democratic majorities in both houses of Congress, giving hope to the small group of Senate liberals that the passage of civil rights legislation might be a more obtainable goal. On January 4, 1955, the evening before the Eighty-fourth Congress convened, the liberal caucus met to consider another assault on Rule XXII. Although such attempts had failed in 1949 and 1953, Herbert Lehman strongly urged an immediate call for revision of Rule XXII as a necessary precursor to any legislative advances. Hubert Humphrey counseled against Lehman's proposal, however, arguing instead for forbearance so that the new majority leader, Lyndon Johnson, could have time to temper the opposition of the Senate's southerners. Arguing that Johnson was sympathetic to the cause of civil rights and would reveal himself as an ally in time, Humphrey posited that the new majority leader must be allowed to consolidate his power before tackling such an explosive issue.

Remembering Johnson's vigorous opposition to the revision of Rule XXII just two years before, Lehman and others expressed skepticism that the majority leader or any other southern senator would desert his compatriots on civil rights matters. Douglas hoped to preserve unity within the liberal caucus, and so, despite his misgivings about Humphrey's assessment of Johnson, he agreed to postpone action on Rule XXII. In the months that followed, Douglas detected no changes in Johnson's stand on civil rights and concluded that Lehman had been right after all.[3]

Early in the Eighty-fourth Congress, Douglas and his allies in the Senate introduced a series of civil rights measures dealing with housing, voting rights, antilynching, and employment. Because President Eisenhower had assented during the 1952 campaign to the need for civil rights legislation, the liberal Democrats publicly and privately sought to enlist the aide of the Republican administration in the drafting and refinement of these bills. Douglas complained that the efforts to force the Republicans to honor their campaign promises, particularly the attempt to obtain cooperation from the attorney general's office, met consistently with indifference. In 1955, as southern opponents to the *Brown* ruling sharpened their dissent to the Supreme Court's supplementary decision calling for public school desegregation "with all deliberate speed," Congress produced no laws to complement the judicial initiative by undercutting the developing "massive resistance" movement in the South.[4]

In addition to the setbacks in the area of civil rights, Douglas's seventh year in the Senate proved frustrating because of a lingering health problem. The extreme fatigue he had experienced during the 1954 campaign persisted and worsened during the early months of 1955. He often had difficulty sleeping and invariably grew weaker as each day progressed. By afternoons, he had to retire to his office and lie down for long naps. Even while lying at rest, his limbs twitched violently, and he sweated profusely. After months of failed attempts to diagnose the mysterious ailment, a physician finally identified the condition as undulant fever and prescribed a battery of drugs that gradually brought relief. For most of the year, however, Douglas struggled to discharge his responsibilities as a senator. Often his aides literally dragged him off the couch in his office and pushed him in a wheelchair to the Senate floor so that he could participate in debates and cast important votes. Reporters and other senators recalled having gone to Douglas's office where he remained lying on his couch, too listless to sit at his desk during their conversations. Not until after Congress adjourned in August did he regain full strength and resume normal activity.[5]

Throughout his senatorial career, but especially during the months he suffered from undulant fever, Douglas relied heavily on his wife Emily for advice and counsel. A sagacious politician in her own right, she had given up a career in public life to support her husband but still retained a keen interest in government affairs. During Douglas's years in the Senate, his wife generally kept a low profile and almost never made headlines on her own. She played an important role in his success, however. Douglas said admiringly: "Emily combines idealism with a woman's sense of caution, and integrity with a politician's sense of timing, qualities that have saved me from many mistakes." She appeared infrequently in Douglas's Senate office, but they conferred often by telephone during the day, and he regularly solicited her views on pending issues. She routinely drove him to work from their home in the northwest section of Washington, D.C.—he did not drive automobiles because of the wound he suffered to his arm during World War II—and they spent those thirty to forty minutes discussing the day's upcoming events. When they were apart, especially when campaigning separately in Illinois during election years, he telephoned her each morning and discussed the upcoming events of the day. A poised and polished public speaker, she gave speeches in his behalf and became especially active during his reelection campaigns. She was, according to members of Douglas's office staff, a considerable political asset and the person whose judgment he valued most.[6]

At the outset of the 1956 congressional session, the Senate liberals drafted a comprehensive civil rights measure that invested the federal government with unprecedented authority to safeguard individual rights against the states in a variety of areas ranging from employment to voting rights. The bill, Douglas later proclaimed proudly, was the quarry from which much subsequent civil rights legislation was mined. Senator Thomas C. Hennings, a liberal Democrat who chaired the judiciary subcommittee to which the bill was referred, produced a favorable subcommittee report but achieved no such success in the committee. Judiciary Committee chairman James O. Eastland of Mississippi presided over a prolonged series of hearings and imposed a number of delays that prevented any action on the bill during the session. He failed to call committee meetings, refused to acknowledge Hennings, recognized motions to adjourn at critical moments, and scheduled committee meetings to coincide with regular Senate sessions so that sparse attendance resulted in the absence of a quorum. The fate of the measure confirmed again why Eastland's Senate Judiciary Committee became known as the graveyard of civil rights legislation.[7]

In January 1956, Douglas turned his attention from civil rights to a natural gas bill that the House of Representatives had passed at the end of the 1955 session. The latest legislation designed to aid the southwestern gas and oil interests, which had been introduced by Senator J. William Fulbright and Congressman Oren Harris, differed only slightly from the bill Robert Kerr had unsuccessfully championed in 1950. Again, Douglas argued for government regulation of the natural gas industry as the only means of keeping prices down and protecting consumer interests, and again he found himself upholding an unpopular position. He scoffed at the characterization of the bill as benign, saying, "A 'protect-the-consumer-by-raising-his-prices-bill' is unique in my legislative experience." The Senate passed the Fulbright-Harris bill, and Douglas fully expected President Eisenhower to sign the measure into law. A scandal arose, however, when Senator Francis H. Case of South Dakota reported having been offered a bribe by a natural gas lobbyist to vote for the bill, and a subsequent investigation disclosed that a number of bribes had been offered to other legislators. With the public duly aroused against the lobbyists' illegal activities, President Eisenhower vetoed the bill. Once more, an unexpected, last-minute presidential veto rewarded Douglas's dark horse struggles against the oil and gas interests.[8]

In April of that year, the Eisenhower administration finally introduced a civil rights bill into the Senate and the House of Representatives but, according to Senator Hennings, several months too late to expect favorable action. Cynics suspected that, in fact, Eisenhower did not want serious consideration of civil rights legislation in an election year and therefore intentionally submitted the measure tardily. In any event, the administration's bill stopped far short of the version introduced into the Senate by the liberal Democrats and met less opposition among congressional moderates. As it became apparent that the House would adopt the measure, the Senate liberals decided to move the bill's consideration by the entire Senate in lieu of its immediate referral to the Judiciary Committee (an unusual but permissible action that would keep Eastland from burying yet another civil rights initiative before Congress adjourned for the summer). When word arrived in the Senate on July 23 that the roll call vote on the civil rights bill in the House was nearing completion, Douglas rushed to the other chamber intent upon accompanying House Resolution 627 back to the Senate so he could immediately file a motion not to assign the bill to the Judiciary Committee. He arrived a few minutes too late, however, only to discover that the bill had already been dispatched to the Senate. Frantically retracing his steps, uttering hasty apologies as he bumped into startled tourists, Douglas breathlessly returned to the Senate floor just minutes after the bill had been assigned to the committee. The unusually expeditious conduct of congressional affairs, an astounded Douglas concluded, could only mean that opponents of the civil rights measure had heard of the liberals' plan and sped up the process accordingly.[9]

Douglas informed the senators present of what had happened and moved to discharge the bill from the committee for consideration by the entire Senate. Richard Russell of Georgia, tactical leader of the southern anti–civil rights forces, quickly acted to defeat Douglas's motion and enlisted the aid of Majority Leader Lyndon Johnson. Russell threatened the immediate use of a filibuster to disrupt the Senate at the end of the session and reminded his colleagues that such a spectacle only days before the opening of that year's Democratic National Convention could seriously damage the party's fortunes. According to Senate Rule XXVI, Section 2, a discharge petition could not be filed on the same day of the bill's referral to committee without unanimous consent. Douglas intended to file his petition the following day, but Johnson moved to recess that night rather than adjourn so that July 24 would still be considered the same "legislative day" as July 23. Johnson's ploy, which he repeated day after day, would forestall the consideration of the discharge petition for the remainder of the legislative session. On July 24 Douglas interrupted one of Johnson's motions to recess and introduced a motion to adjourn for five minutes in order to create a new legislative day. The chairman ruled Douglas's motion out of order, but Johnson agreed to put the matter to a vote—what Senator William Knowland called a vote of confidence on the Senate majority's leadership. "I should like to see how many Members wish to have the Senator from Illinois continue the course he has followed today," Johnson said and requested a roll call vote. Douglas knew that he would lose in defying the majority leader on a technical matter, but the outcome of the vote dismayed him. His motion failed 76–6, as only Lehman, Hennings, and three Republicans (William Langer, Irving Ives, and George Bender) joined Douglas in voting against the majority leader.[10]

Douglas realized that no civil rights legislation would be passed in 1956 and that his insistence upon introducing the discharge petition a few days before the end of the legislative session might have seemed counterproductive to other senators who otherwise supported civil rights. (Calling Douglas's tactical maneuver "doomed to futility," Hubert Humphrey wrote a constituent: "Had I believed that there was any chance for action on civil rights, I would have whole-heartedly supported Senator Douglas.") The Illinois senator believed that champions of a noble cause must fight ceaselessly to achieve their goals, and he could not understand how his purported allies—especially Hubert Humphrey—could contribute to such a humiliating vote on a civil rights matter. In this episode as in other instances when civil rights advocates faced decisions about whether to vote solely on principle, Douglas felt it necessary to declare his intentions unequivocally while Humphrey would countenance tactical retreats if he thought immediate victory unlikely. On his way out of the Senate chamber, he stopped to kiss Humphrey's wife, Muriel, and assure her that all would work out well. As he and members of his staff waited for the elevator, he commented: "Let us punch the bell three times and pretend that I am a senator." (Senators pushed the button three times to inform elevator operators that a senator, not a member of the general public, was waiting.) Alone back in his office, Douglas later recalled, he broke down and cried in utter discouragement. The southern opponents of civil rights had triumphed again thanks to a parliamentary trick, and he blamed himself for not being better prepared. Worse, he despaired at the apparent hopelessness of the cause when so few senators cared enough to stand with him for civil rights.[11]

Word of Douglas's defeat on the Senate floor reverberated throughout the civil rights community. Clarence Mitchell, director of the NAACP's Washington Bureau, wrote Douglas and thanked him for his "gallant efforts" on behalf of their cause. Mitchell noted that many politicians, Democrats as well as Republicans, nominally supported civil rights in their public addresses but stopped short of taking the necessary steps to get legislation passed in Congress. He further surmised that Democratic leaders hesitated to take controversial positions so that they could avoid a party split shortly before the pending nominating convention. But why, Mitchell asked, would black Americans suppose that Democrats would do any more to seek racial equality if they controlled the White House when they achieved so little when they enjoyed majorities in both houses of Congress? Would a Democratic president be any more receptive to civil rights concerns than Eisenhower had been?[12]

From Washington, Douglas and his wife traveled directly to the Democratic National Convention in Chicago. Though still an enthusiastic supporter of Estes Kefauver, Douglas was reconciled to the fact that Adlai Stevenson would receive the Democratic nomination for president. He hoped that the convention would adopt a strong civil rights plank, an eventuality that the Stevenson forces clearly sought to avoid for the same reasons that had prevailed four years earlier—an unwillingness to alienate the southern wing of the party, an essential element of Stevenson's centrist coalition. Aided by Herbert Lehman, Douglas moved from one state delegation to the next on the convention floor, politicking for a stronger civil rights plank than the one proposed by the party's platform committee. Knowing that the convention chairman, Sam Rayburn of Texas, would rule in favor of the weaker civil rights plank if a voice vote were taken, Douglas called for a roll call vote instead. An open declaration, he believed, would at least force the delegations to declare their positions in full view of a national television audience. Douglas's motion failed to receive the support of the necessary eight state delegations to require a roll call vote, and Rayburn administered a voice vote with predictable results. On the losing end of yet another dispiriting referendum on civil rights, Douglas watched as the Democratic delegates chose party unity over principle. Douglas felt that Hubert Humphrey and Adlai Stevenson were willing to cut ethical corners in order to avoid estranging southern Democrats. Joseph L. Rauh, counsel for the Democratic party, wrote that even Eleanor Roosevelt and United Auto Workers president Walter Reuther had conspired to avoid a roll call vote. Douglas wondered if men and women of good intention were squandering the promise of the *Brown* decision in their timidity.[13]

Despite his unhappiness with some of the events at the Democratic National Convention, Douglas believed that the party's ticket of Adlai Stevenson for president and Estes Kefauver for vice president provided the electorate with a superior choice to the Eisenhower incumbency. He and his wife campaigned vigorously throughout Illinois and the Midwest for Democratic candidates, especially for the Stevenson-Kefauver ticket. The vote produced mixed results as Congress remained safely Democratic while Eisenhower again beat Stevenson decisively. For the second time in four years, Douglas sent Stevenson a note of appreciation for the honorable fight he had waged and lost. "You made a splendid campaign and deserved to win," Douglas wrote the defeated candidate. Still, Douglas lamented the kind of campaign the Democrats had conducted nationally to accommodate white southern voters. Stevenson's moderation on the civil rights issue, which had allowed him to carry six of the seven states of the Old Confederacy, continued to nettle Douglas. He believed that the Democratic party should lead the assault on white supremacy in the South and looked forward eagerly to continuing the fight in the Senate.[14]

On January 2, 1957, the day before the opening session of the Eighty-fifth Congress convened, a bipartisan group of senators committed to civil rights met in Douglas's office to plan yet another assault on Rule XXII. (At exactly the same time, southern Democrats huddled in the office of Georgia's Richard B. Russell to discuss how they would blunt this attack.) As in years past, the liberals believed that the key to passing civil rights legislation lay in defusing the filibuster and that that could best be accomplished by reducing the number of votes needed for cloture of debate from the two-thirds established by Rule XXII to a more reasonable number. The following day, Clinton Anderson moved on behalf of himself and twenty-five other senators that, pursuant to Article I, Section 5, of the Constitution, which declares that "each House may determine the rules of its proceedings," the Senate adopt new rules for that session. Anderson's motion elicited a predictable response from the southern Democrats, who recognized that Rule XXII lay at the heart of the liberals' interest in adopting new rules, and triggered a tortuous procedural struggle that consumed the next two days. Lyndon Johnson immediately took the floor and moved to table Anderson's motion, a result that would end the insurgency and allow the Senate session to commence under the existing rules. The liberals duly noted the irony in the proponents of unlimited debate moving quickly to end consideration of a motion that would lead to limitations on debate.[15]

In the ensuing discussion of Johnson's motion, Douglas compellingly argued the case against limitless debate in the Senate. According to the 1949 Wherry amendment of Rule XXII, he noted, sixty-four votes were required to halt a filibuster, instead of two-thirds of those present and voting, as the rule had stipulated between 1917 and 1949. Thus, only thirty-three senators could defeat any motion to limit debate by voting no or, most insidiously, by staying away at the time of the cloture vote. Because senators not in attendance are counted as no votes, Rule XXII as amended in 1949 provided perfect cover for those who wished to uphold the filibuster—or vote against civil rights—without being recorded publicly as doing so. That was why, Douglas argued, it became so difficult to pass civil rights legislation even though the vast majority of the American people desired it. As long as senators were allowed to espouse their belief in civil rights yet not be held accountable because of Rule XXII, the southern minority could continue to hold the nation hostage. Douglas held out little hope that his blandishments would alter the outcome of the pending vote, but he spoke on and off the Senate floor to educate the electorate about the significance of the abstruse parliamentary wrangling that launched the Eighty-fifth Congress.[16]

Johnson used his power as majority leader to oppose any change to Rule XXII, especially utilizing his influence to sway the one-third of the senators who had just been elected in November 1956. He delayed the appointment of new senators to committees until after the vote on Rule XXII was taken, referring all inquiring freshmen to Richard Russell's office. Russell asked them how they intended to vote on the filibuster issue, indicating that the Senate Steering Committee would consider that vote very carefully in making committee assignments. Indeed, those newcomers who voted with the southerners later received choice committee assignments. Those who sided with the liberals disappeared into the anonymity of the District of Columbia and the Rules Committees.[17]

The vote on Johnson's motion carried, 55–38, with three senators who had announced their opposition to tabling unable to attend. With the addition of the 3 absent votes, the supporters of Anderson's motion received a total of 41 votes, only 7 shy of a majority. The liberals had lost a similar vote on Rule XXII at the outset of the 1953 session 70–21, so they had clearly gained ground in the ensuing four years. The southerners witnessed the outcome of the vote with considerable alarm, for they recognized the dwindling support for their last line of defense, the filibuster. Hubert Humphrey wrote Walter Reuther: "We actually gained more votes than we had a right to expect, and surely many more than the opposition had anticipated." In an optimistic report to his constituents, Douglas wrote: "Our near success in this fight gave a new urgency and hope to civil rights prospects which would not otherwise have been the case, and created an atmosphere in which at least some form of bill could be passed."[18]

Senate liberals promptly introduced several civil rights bills, but as in the previous year attention quickly focused on a more moderate measure introduced by the Eisenhower administration. On June 18, 1957, the House of Representatives passed the "Brownell bill" (named for

Eisenhower's attorney general, Herbert Brownell) without significant amendment by the vote of 286–126, at which time the several Senate bills were still mired in the quicksand of the Judiciary Committee. Despite the best efforts of Senator Hennings, hostile rulings by Judiciary Committee chairman James O. Eastland and a series of "committee filibusters" by other southerners kept civil rights bills from being considered by the committee. Legislators and concerned onlookers understood that the hopes of passing civil rights legislation rested with the Brownell bill.[19]

The administration's civil rights bill contained four primary sections: (1) creation of a bipartisan civil rights commission to investigate civil rights violations and to make recommendations for legislation; (2) creation of a Civil Rights Division in the Justice Department to be administered by an assistant attorney general; (3) authorization of the attorney general, under the authority of the Fourteenth Amendment, to seek injunctions from federal courts to prevent local officials or groups from denying equal rights to American citizens; and (4) amendment of laws to permit the federal government to seek injunctive relief from the courts in voting rights cases. The president could arguably have created a civil rights commission and a new division within the Justice Department without legislation, so attention understandably turned to the last two sections of the bill. Douglas and other liberals regretted that, before the federal government could intervene in civil rights cases, individuals must initiate legal proceedings. Moreover, unlike the liberals' bills, favorable court rulings would only benefit individual plaintiffs in specific cases and not classes of aggrieved people—what Douglas referred to as "using a retail remedy to cure a wholesale evil." Nevertheless, despite these flaws, Douglas and his cohorts agreed to support the Brownell bill as the best available alternative.[20]

A few days before the House's passage of the bill, Douglas and fourteen other Democratic senators met to devise a strategy for supporting the legislation when it arrived in the Senate. Some Democrats expressed reservations about working actively to support an administration measure, the success of which would allow the Republicans to take credit for finally passing civil rights legislation. In particular, Democrats from the western states such as Clinton Anderson of New Mexico and Warren Magnuson of Washington balked at cooperating with the Republicans. Douglas strongly urged the acceptance of allies from every quarter, arguing that only a bipartisan coalition of liberals and moderates could hope to defeat the formidable conservative alliance. The caucus sided with Douglas and designated him to work with Republican Minority Leader William F. Knowland. The group also selected Thomas Hennings, a member of the Judiciary Committee and a longtime civil rights partisan, to lead the floor fight for the administration's bill. In the contentious weeks that followed, however, Hennings succumbed to his chronic alcoholism, failing to appear some days on the Senate floor and eventually disappearing altogether from Capitol Hill. Owing to Hennings's absence, Douglas assumed the role of floor leader as well. On June 14 the fifteen Democratic senators issued a formal statement expressing their goal of placing the Brownell bill directly on the Senate calendar rather than having it referred to the Judiciary Committee and declaring their willingness to work with others regardless of party who sought the same result.[21]

To avoid what had happened the year before, the "Douglas-Knowland Axis" organized teams of senators to guard the floor at all times, and sympathetic members of the House sent regular bulletins to the Senate charting the progress of the Brownell bill toward passage. When the Brownell bill reached the Senate floor on June 19, its supporters were fully prepared. On June 20 Knowland objected to the bill's referral to committee, and Senator Russell raised a point of order against the objection. Vice President Richard M. Nixon declined to make a formal ruling on Russell's point of order, instead calling for a vote of the membership. Republicans and liberal Democrats combined to defeat Russell's point of order by a vote of 45–39, and the Brownell bill went directly onto the Senate calendar. Civil rights supporters rejoiced in the victory, for the outcome of the vote meant escape from the clutches of James Eastland's dreaded Judiciary Committee. Knowland later said, "We would not have had a civil rights bill passed that year had this gone to the committee."[22]

Although the civil rights coalition had won the battle to keep the bill out of committee, Douglas worried that four liberal western Democrats— Wayne Morse of Oregon, Warren Magnuson of Washington, and Mike Mansfield and Jim Murray of Montana—had surprisingly voted with the southerners. Douglas recognized the politics at work when Johnson soon thereafter moved to release from committee a bill to construct a dam at Hell's Canyon on the Snake River between Oregon and Idaho. The bill had failed the year before with southern senators voting solidly against it, but in 1957 these westerners were trading their votes on civil rights for southern support of public power. On June 21 five southerners—Richard Russell, James Eastland, Sam Ervin of North Carolina, Russell Long of Louisiana, and George Smathers of Florida—switched their votes from the year before and provided the margin for the bill's passage. The Hell's Canyon bill failed in the House, but the southerners had done their part in the Senate. In return for their support of the Hell's Canyon measure, Douglas believed, the western defectors had agreed to help water down the civil rights bill.[23]

On July 8 the Brownell bill came formally before the Senate, and after eight days of debate the senators voted 71–18 in favor of its consideration. Having narrowly won on the Rule XXII battle and having lost on the votes to place the bill on the calendar and then to consider it, the southerners saw little chance of avoiding the passage of some sort of civil rights legislation. They could always fall back upon the filibuster, but Russell believed that tactic to be increasingly unpopular with the public and hoped to use it only as a last resort. Instead, the southerners sought to dilute the bill so that its passage would inflict minimal damage to the southern schema of race relations. While still brandishing the threat of a protracted debate, Russell began caucusing behind the scenes with members of the opposition to effect a series of compromises that would make a full-blown filibuster unnecessary.[24]

The southerners advanced two principal objections to the bill, charging that the federal government ought not to have the power to initiate suits in cases involving constitutional rights as provided in Section III and that the power of a judge to impose sentence for contempt in voting rights cases violated the right of a man to be tried before a jury of his peers. The deletion of Section III and the addition of a jury trial amendment would make the bill as palatable to the southerners as it would be unpalatable to Douglas and the other longtime civil rights advocates. Yet Russell knew that not everyone in the bipartisan civil rights coalition felt strongly about all sections of the bill; many senators simply wanted to pass civil rights legislation of some kind or other. Acknowledging the sagacity of Russell's strategy, Douglas also understood that only a relatively small number of Democrats would hold out for the programs most likely to foster significant reform in the South. He wrote his wife:

> We are trying to reinforce our lines and keep our group determined, but one difficulty we have is that while most of our people care about civil rights, they don't care deeply; whereas those who are opposed are very intense in their feeling. . . . What I am chiefly afraid of is that we will get some kind of a more or less meaningless compromise in return for which the Southerners will give up their filibuster. I fully expect Lyndon Johnson to spring this toward the middle or end of July and he will try to take our people away from us one by one.[25]

Russell moved first to strike Section III from the bill. Like the other southerners, he feared that that portion of the measure would facilitate the implementation of the recent school desegregation decision. "This was precisely why Russell had apoplexy over Part III," said civil rights attorney Joseph Rauh, "and was willing not to filibuster after his victory on Part III." On July 2, in a melodramatic address on the Senate floor, Russell condemned the "cunningly designed" bill as a devious instrument for "the destruction of any of the local customs, laws, or practices separating the races in order to enforce a commingling of the races throughout the social order of the South." Next, in Douglas's words, Russell "refought the Reconstruction period." The Georgia senator likened this modern force bill to the efforts of Radical Republicans Thaddeus Stevens and Charles Sumner "to put black heels on white necks." His references to "bayonet government" not only conjured up images of the federal occupation of the southern states after the Civil War but also related to the contemporary crisis involving southern resistance to public school desegregation. He skillfully exploited the widespread fear that Section III would inevitably lead to the forced implementation of the *Brown* decision, violence, and possibly even a constitutional crisis. Senators from outside the South should vote to eliminate Section III, Russell argued, in order to preserve sectional harmony and avoid bloodshed. Douglas complained that the press reported the Georgian's presentation as statesmanlike and reasonable.[26]

Russell's arguments resonated even more with wavering senators when, at a press conference the following day, President Eisenhower announced that "there were certain phrases [of the bill] I didn't completely understand." Supporters of the bill in the Senate were dumbfounded to hear the president say that he could not unconditionally support his own administration's bill until he had had more talks with the attorney general. "It was a stunning confession of ignorance," said Eisenhower's biographer, Stephen E. Ambrose. The president "had been pushing the bill for two years . . . and yet now said he did not know what was in it. Eisenhower's admission was an open invitation to the southern senators to modify, amend, emasculate his bill, and they proceeded to do just that."[27]

Russell met with Eisenhower in the White House at length on July 10, and at a press conference shortly thereafter the president admitted to having second thoughts about the efficacy of the bill. The president reiterated that he had intended the measure to be about voting rights only, the implication being that he cared little about Section III. On July 17 Eisenhower further commented that the attorney general should bring desegregation suits only when local school authorities requested federal action. "If you go too far too fast," the president warned, "you are making a mistake." Eisenhower's retreat on Section III undercut the morale of the fragile bipartisan coalition that supported the bill. "Whenever we rise to defend the Administration," lamented Douglas, "the rug is pulled out from under our feet by the Administration which presumably we are defending."[28]

Several senators echoed President Eisenhower's admission that he had not fully understood the bill. These senators, who said they believed that the measure dealt primarily with voting rights, cited Brownell's earlier assurances that Section III instituted no sweeping changes in federal-state relations to justify their confusion. They charged that Brownell had consistently understated the injunctive authority arrogated to the federal government and wondered whether an attorney general guilty of such misrepresentation could be trusted to enforce the provision. Senators Clinton Anderson and George Aiken introduced an amendment that virtually eliminated Section III, and Majority Leader Johnson lent his support to their measure. Retreating somewhat from the original wording that allowed the attorney general to intervene on his own accord, Douglas prepared an amendment that allowed the attorney general to become involved when invited to by local officials or when an aggrieved party sought his intervention. Knowland prepared an amendment, which he believed to be more acceptable to Eisenhower, providing only for intervention by the attorney general at the request of local officials. Because the liberal Democrats and the Republicans could not agree on which of the two amendments to support, they decided not to offer either version but rather simply to oppose the Anderson-Aiken amendment.[29]

On July 24 Douglas urged the Senate to spurn the Anderson-Aiken amendment and vote for the Brownell bill in its original form. His remarks concentrated on the urgent need for arming the federal government with the kind of injunctive power created in Section III. Since the pathbreaking *Brown* decision three years earlier, he informed the senators, no public school desegregation had occurred in eight southern states (Alabama, Florida, Georgia, Louisiana, Mississippi, North Carolina, South Carolina, and Virginia) and in only four states (Arkansas, Kentucky, Tennessee, and Texas) had even token progress been made. In many of these southern states, legislatures had passed laws to resist desegregation. Douglas argued that the events of recent years vividly underscored the need for legislation to ensure the extension of the Fourteenth Amendment's influence into the southern states and to uphold the rulings of the Supreme Court. He reminded those who contended that Section III granted the attorney general "dictatorial powers" that the federal official had only the power to file suits in federal courts and that the merits of the calls for injunctive relief would be decided by the justice system. Douglas's long and impassioned address apparently swayed few senators, for the Anderson-Aiken amendment carried, 52–38.[30]

The second major issue—the right of a jury trial in voting rights cases—generated an equally impassioned dispute. Southern opponents of the bill again raised the specter of tyranny, charging that the prescribed use of injunctions in Section IV, rather than jury trials, threatened liberty. North Carolina's Sam Ervin and Alabama's Lister Hill noted that northern liberals had in the past argued for jury trials and against injunctions in cases involving labor unions but now were willing to deprive southerners of the same right. Richard Russell saw the denial of jury trials as a "gratuitous insult" to every white citizen in the South because of the implication that white juries would not fairly consider cases involving African Americans. In high dudgeon, these southern legislators questioned the honor as well as the wisdom of the Brownell bill's supporters.[31]

Stung by the charge of hypocrisy, Douglas thought at length about the apparent inconsistency between his aversion to the use of injunctions against trade unions and his willingness to countenance their use in civil rights cases. Ultimately, he decided, the blatantly prejudicial legal system and the systematic disfranchisement of African Americans in the South justified the use of injunctions in voting rights cases. In his defense of Section IV before the Senate, Douglas dwelled at length on the repressive system by which whites maintained suzerainty in the South. Through the use of poll taxes, white primaries, understanding clauses, and other subterfuges, the southern states kept voting by African Americans to a minimum. In Illinois, for example, 72 1/2 percent of citizens of voting age actually cast ballots while, in Mississippi, only 22 percent did. Similarly, only 4 percent of African Americans of voting age were even registered to vote in Mississippi, and the figures for other southern states were not much better—10 percent in Alabama, 20 percent in Virginia, and 25 percent in Georgia and South Carolina. In such a repressive environment, political oppression could be countered only with extraordinary help from outside. Douglas added that no constitutional "right" to jury trials existed in contempt-of-court cases when injunctions had been violated, noting that the overwhelming majority of southern state courts allowed judges rather than juries to rule in contempt cases. Clearly, he contended, proposals to broaden jury trial guarantees would deter—not enhance—the pending legislation.[32]

Douglas's comments notwithstanding, Lyndon Johnson confidently assured the press that a jury trial amendment would be added to Section IV. Joseph C. O'Mahoney (Democrat, Wyoming) introduced an amendment providing for jury trials in all contempt cases, a proposal that ignored the distinction between civil and criminal contempt cases. A series of amendments to O'Mahoney's amendment followed as senators seeking compromise added and subtracted to satisfy their peers on both sides of the issue. Douglas complained that the frequent alterations of the amendment left opponents of jury trials "shooting at a moving target." The fourth and final version, offered by Frank Church of Idaho, responded to Douglas's complaint that southern states prohibited African Americans from service on juries and would guarantee "the right of all Americans to serve on [Federal] juries, regardless of race, creed or color."[33]

Douglas suspected that the emendation of the U.S. code would do little to ensure that blacks served on juries in the South, but he opposed Church's amendment for a more fundamental reason: the fourth version of O'Mahoney's amendment mandated jury trials for criminal contempt cases but not for civil contempt cases. In civil cases, the court holds a person in contempt to secure compliance with a specific order, and the person can remove the contempt citation by carrying out the directive. In criminal cases, the subject of a court order has already failed to comply, and the court seeks to punish the offender. In voting cases, as Douglas pointed out, a registrar who failed to obey a court order to allow blacks to vote could be tried for civil contempt with the opportunity to remove the contempt charge by compliance. But if the registrar ignored the court order and blacks did not vote on election day, criminal contempt charges would result and a jury trial would be involved. As Douglas summarized, "With the knowledge that they would be tried by a local jury, can anyone say that this was not an invitation to Southern registrars and other election officials to defy the law until the day of election passed and thereby gain a jury trial and acquittal, as well as preventing Negroes from voting?"[34]

On August 1 the Senate voted to add the jury trial amendment to Part IV by a vote of 51–42. As the spokesman for a bipartisan group, Douglas unsuccessfully sought the floor to offer an amendment reviving parts of Section III that had been eliminated. Instead, at a time of commotion on the floor, the Senate approved Johnson's unanimous consent request that limited further discussion to amendments that had already been offered. Thus, the bill under consideration at that time created a civil rights commission and a new assistant attorney general for civil rights, contained no Section III, and added to Section IV the provision for jury trials in criminal contempt cases. Indeed, the bill had undergone significant change in the preceding weeks, and everyone agreed that it had lost much of its potency. Did the product justify the effort?[35]

As the last speeches concluded on the Senate floor, Douglas grappled with the question of whether to vote for the bill. On August 7, in a speech before the Senate before the final vote, he explained his reasons for deciding in the affirmative. He conceded that "it has been the advocates of segregation and of white domination who have won the major triumph." On the other hand, he expressed hope that the civil rights commission may prove useful in initiating change in the South. Also, despite the limitations imposed on Section IV, he suggested that resourceful judges might find ways to protect voting rights through the aggressive use of injunctions and civil contempt actions. Finally, he noted that the Senate could still strengthen the bill in conference with the House after passage. In short, something was better than nothing. And, as he wrote to Walter Reuther, Douglas believed that "it has been worth the fight, if only to dramatize again for the public the importance of the basic issues at stake."[36]

On August 7, 1957, by a vote of 72–18, the Senate passed the first civil rights bill in eighty-two years. When members of the House rejected the jury trial amendment attached to the bill by the Senate, leaders of the two chambers held informal negotiations for two weeks in an effort to draft a compromise amendment. Joseph Rauh believed that the Republicans, especially Vice President Nixon, wanted the bill buried in conference for the remainder of the session so that they could blame the Democrats in the 1958 elections for the failure to enact civil rights legislation. To keep that from happening, Rauh, Douglas, and Representative

Richard Bolling devised a strategy for amending the bill in the House for return to the Senate. On August 27 the House voted to accept a proposal that limited the use of injunctions to civil rights cases, eliminated jury trials for civil cases, and allowed jury trials in criminal cases only when a federal judge imposed fines in excess of $300 or a jail sentence longer than forty-five days.[37]

Satisfied with the considerable changes effected in the bill since its introduction, Russell and his followers in the Senate agreed not to filibuster but simply to vote against the final version. Such an accommodation proved unacceptable to South Carolina fire-eater Strom Thurmond, however, who conducted a one-man filibuster on August 28–29 that lasted a record twenty-four hours and thirty-two minutes. Normally a filibusterer could expect questions from the floor and other diversions staged by like-minded colleagues to allow him brief periods of rest, but, in this instance, the other southern senators ignored their maverick colleague. Feeling sorry for Thurmond, Douglas brought him a pitcher of orange juice at midnight as a show of good sportsmanship. After Thurmond succumbed to fatigue and surrendered the floor, Wayne Morse of Oregon followed with his own one-man filibuster. Morse characterized the bill as a sham, the product of a sellout by putative civil rights partisans who lacked the courage of their convictions. After having enumerated all of the procedural and substantive flaws in the bill many times over, he finally yielded the floor. On August 29, 1957, the Senate agreed by a vote of 60–15 to the compromise version drafted in the House; President Eisenhower signed the measure on September 9.[38]

Earlier, during the debate over the fate of Section III, Eisenhower had attempted to mollify southerners who feared the intrusion of the federal government to enforce the guarantees of the Fourteenth Amendment, saying: "I can't imagine any set of circumstances that would ever induce me to send Federal troops . . . into any area to enforce the order of a federal court." On September 24, barely two weeks after signing into law the Civil Rights Act of 1957, the president issued an executive order dispatching National Guard troops and U.S. Army forces to Little Rock, Arkansas, to enforce a court integration order. The dramatic events that ensued at Little Rock's Central High School underscored for many liberals the inadequacy of the recently passed civil rights law, providing an immediate demonstration of how southern intransigence had created a need for more substantive legislation. Civil rights advocates lamented how the bill that survived its way into law had failed to justify the promise of its origins, the greatest failure being the elimination of Section III. Douglas said the bill in its final form "was like soup made from the shadow of a crow which had starved to death," and Eleanor Roosevelt called it "mere fakery." How had the bill ended up such a disappointment?[39]

Although the vote on Rule XXII at the outset of the Eighty-fifth Congress indicated that sentiment for civil rights was building in the Senate and that the force of public opinion was gradually turning against the southern Democrats, the filibuster remained a powerful tool for derailing legislative initiatives. Even if the southern leadership avoided prolonged disruptions of senatorial discourse, Richard Russell and other southerners consistently used the threat of the filibuster to discourage their opponents. Russell was, in the words of another senator, "a shrewd politician, a skillful parliamentarian, and a resourceful constitutional lawyer. But he is above all a first-rate dramatist." The emasculation of the Civil Rights Act of 1957 arguably constituted Russell's finest hour as a defender of white supremacy. On the floor of the Senate, he boasted, "The fact that we were able to confine the Federal activities to the field of voting and keep the withering hand of the Federal Government out of our schools and social order is to me, as I look back over the years, the sweetest victory of my 25 years as a Senator from the State of Georgia."[40]

The final version of the Civil Rights Act of 1957 also owed much to the indefatigable efforts of Senate Majority Leader Lyndon Johnson. Most observers have given Johnson high marks, contending that his ceaseless efforts at compromise resulted in the passage of the first civil rights bill in nearly a century. His willingness to sacrifice key elements of the bill has been forgiven as a necessary expedient in the drive to pass some sort of legislation. Douglas found much irony in a fawning press's appreciation of Johnson's statesmanship and his own portrayal as an extremist whose unreasonableness had to be overcome in order to ensure progress. (He bristled, for example, when the journalist William S. White praised Johnson's moderation and called Douglas the "Faubus of the North.") He viewed Johnson in a much different light, as a key member of a dedicated cohort of senators who yielded ground grudgingly to the powerful drive for civil rights while limiting the amount of change foisted upon the South. He saw Johnson working hand-in-glove with Russell to protect his good standing with the southern senators while keeping his own national political ambitions alive by creating the impression that he did as much as any southerner could do to pave the way for change in the area of civil rights. In Douglas's mind, the bill retained its modest value despite Johnson's efforts, not because of them.[41]

The passage of civil rights legislation depended upon the unprecedented achievement of a foreboding task, maintaining a tenuous coalition of Republicans and liberal Democrats. The political compromises that weakened the bill resulted from a series of defections that attenuated the coalition. Richard Russell and Lyndon Johnson played a critical role in skillfully seducing moderates away from the coalition, but—as disgruntled liberals of both parties groused—the failure of presidential leadership also contributed significantly to the outcome. To many observers inside and outside of the Senate, it remained unclear whether President Eisenhower, Vice President Nixon, and Minority Leader Knowland sought a truly meaningful civil rights bill or merely any measure that would fulfill a long-overdue campaign promise.

Civil rights supporters harbored ambivalent feelings about the Civil Rights Act of 1957. After accommodating themselves to the initial disappointment at what might have been, however, many liberals found reasons to celebrate the bill's passage. The NAACP's Roy Wilkins said: "If you are digging a ditch with a teaspoon, and a man comes along and offers you a spade, there is something wrong with your head if you don't take it because he didn't offer you a bulldozer." Despite his initial misgivings, Douglas quickly reconciled himself to the results of the months-long legislative tempest. "I can only say that I did my best," he wrote Norman Thomas, "and have no regrets on what I tried to do." Accepting the Sidney Hillman Award that year from the Amalgamated Clothing Workers Union for his indispensable work on behalf of the bill, Douglas told the assembled labor officials:

> We had some defections from our ranks—whose motives I shall not criticize, but who in the name of procedure strained at a gnat and swallowed a camel. But we were successful, and we broke through the outer defenses of the opponents of civil rights and for the first time in 82 years brought a civil rights bill to a vote on the floor of the Senate.[42]

This historic achievement, Douglas fervently asserted, became possible only because of the concerted efforts of the liberals. Whereas many pundits attributed the bill's passage to the compromises crafted by Johnson and the moderates, Douglas credited the steadfast pressure applied by the civil rights stalwarts. His willingness to accept a flawed bill disproved the charge by some conservatives that doctrinaire liberals like Douglas refused to compromise. Still, the Illinois senator saw the 1957 law as only a temporary expedient on the path to more meaningful legislation. This first chink in the armor of southern resistance to civil rights, he believed, must be followed by continued legislative pressure. Rather than resting on their laurels, congressional liberals should press forward on two fronts, seeking to resurrect Part III in a new bill and continuing to assail Senate Rule XXII so that the filibuster could finally be removed as an instrument for blunting the will of the majority. Although he suspected that many of his Senate colleagues were satisfied with finally having passed a civil rights bill, Douglas saw the Civil Rights Act of 1957 as a beachhead from which to launch more extensive forays onto the contested ground of race relations. The breakthrough in 1957, he concluded, constituted a "modest step forward."[43]

Undaunted Crusader for Civil Rights

6

Against the background of the continuing and urgent needs of millions of our Negro citizens for equal justice, the advocates of human rights cannot afford to retire and lick their wounds, despite this legislative defeat. I believe there are things for all of us to do.
—Paul H. Douglas[1]

• After a decade in the Senate, Paul Douglas had achieved the reputation of an unswerving defender of liberal causes whose flinty integrity and honesty could not be gainsaid. Journalists, colleagues, and Capitol Hill observers remarked about the breadth of his knowledge, and many considered him the most erudite senator of his time. (Intellectually curious about a wide variety of subjects, Douglas devoted portions of his summers and other times between congressional sessions to the study of random topics ranging from U.S. Supreme Court decisions to Italian art to physics to foreign languages.) Careful to avoid any hint of scandal, he released a complete account of his personal finances every year, a practice he had initiated years earlier when serving in the Chicago City Council. Though a relentless debater and hardy partisan, he enjoyed the reputation of a gentleman who scrupulously observed the rituals and folkways of the Senate. "He's so damn polite while he's sticking a knife into you that you don't seem to mind too much," remarked a congressional opponent. His candor sometimes offended people with whom he differed, but his eagerness to keep disagreements professional rather than personal usually salved bruised feelings. Most people seemed to find his straightforwardness refreshing, if somewhat unusual for a politician. Even those who fiercely disagreed with the Illinois senator still respected his intellect and passionate devotion to the causes in which he believed.[2]

Douglas felt very strongly about the need for politicians to conduct their affairs in an ethical manner and tried to apply Quaker teachings to public life. Very early each morning, he reposed in silence for thirty minutes or so to consider what good things—and bad things—he had done the day before. He had, noted his administrative assistant Howard E. Shuman, an obsession about honesty. When a telephone call came from someone he wished to avoid, he would step into the hallway before allowing his secretary to tell the caller that he had gone out of the office. On one occasion, the senator received a hostile visit from William McChesney Martin, chairman of the Federal Reserve Board, about a statement Douglas had supposedly made that attributed Martin's restrictive monetary policies to a desire to aid big banks. Martin said that he wished to give Douglas the opportunity to deny the statement. "Well, I don't remember saying those things," retorted Douglas, "but since I've thought them many times, I probably said them." The flustered Martin turned abruptly and left the office.[3]

As chairman of the Joint Economic Committee, according to another Shuman anecdote, Douglas clashed bitterly with Secretary of the Treasury George Humphrey while conducting hearings into the economic policies of the Eisenhower administration. The two men argued heatedly for hours about taxation policy, and with Douglas getting the better of the exchange Humphrey became increasingly imperious. Douglas returned to his office and announced bitterly: "I hate George Humphrey. I hate the Republicans." The next morning, he called Shuman into his office and apologized for his angry outburst. He said very earnestly: "You know, yesterday I said I hate the Republicans and I hate George Humphrey. I must apologize for that. I withdraw that. I take it back. . . . I must not have hate in my heart."[4]

Douglas's piety and ingenuousness, though generally regarded as enviable, left him open to charges of superciliousness. As he did battle for civil rights, depressed area legislation, and other social welfare measures, Douglas spoke of moral imperatives and by implication impugned the motives of those who opposed him. Rival politicians sometimes interpreted his unquestioning zeal as self-righteousness, a charge that his wife Emily told him contained some merit. (After a particularly contentious exchange on the Senate floor, an exasperated Robert Kerr asked Douglas if he considered himself to be Jesus Christ.) At a time when public figures rarely released the particulars of their personal finances, Douglas's annual disclosure statements must have irritated other politicians; after all, if Douglas insisted upon being so forthcoming, why not his peers? He admitted that, while devoted to fighting the good fight, he might have evinced an air of superiority. In some measure, he felt, this regrettable aspect of his public image owed to his single minded pursuit of a set of goals without consideration of how others in Congress might be affected. Douglas understood how others could interpret his zealotry for a holier-than-thou smugness. Given the righteousness of his causes and the strength of the opposition, though, he believed his unwavering advocacy to be fully justified.[5]

Even though the Democratic party won a majority in Congress in 1954 and maintained control of the legislative branch for the remainder of the decade, conservative forces continued to exercise control on Capitol Hill. Paul Douglas and other northern liberals in the Senate chafed under the dictatorial control of Majority Leader Lyndon B. Johnson and other southern barons who ruled the institution's key committees. Douglas's positions on civil rights, labor, housing, and a host of other issues not only set him at odds with President Eisenhower but frequently with the leadership of his own party. Indeed, his low standing with the members of the Senate leadership could be measured in their determination to keep him out of influential positions. Although he willingly accepted his status as an outsider in the Senate's clubby atmosphere and continued to work hard as a lonely crusader for largely unpopular causes, Douglas deeply regretted that his unpopularity kept him from being appointed to the Senate Finance Committee, a position he had coveted ever since his original appointment to the Labor Committee. Because of his experience with the formulation of social security legislation in the 1930s, his standing as a nationally renowned economist, and his familiarity with unemployment compensation and welfare, he was arguably the most qualified senator to serve on that committee. Yet his outspoken advocacy of closing tax loopholes, as well as his prominence as an opponent of oil depletion allowances, made him unacceptable to the members of the Senate Steering Committee who made the appointments under the close supervision of the majority leader.[6]

During Douglas's first seven years in the Senate, the leadership frequently ignored seniority and found one pretext after another to deny his appointment to the Finance Committee. When he arrived in 1949, the lone opening on the committee went to another freshman, Robert Kerr of Oklahoma. Several years later, the Select Committee chose George Smathers of Florida, who had been elected to the Senate two years after Douglas. When Lyndon Johnson could not find anyone to fill the next opening, he exercised his prerogative as majority leader to become a member of any committee by appointing himself. Then Douglas was passed over so that Alben Barkley, who had left Congress to become vice president under Harry S Truman and had then been reelected to the Senate in 1954, could regain his old seat on the Finance Committee. The next opening went to Clinton Anderson of New Mexico, who had equal seniority with Douglas but who had requested the appointment less often in the past. Ignoring the practice of choosing the applicant with the longest-standing interest in a vacancy, the Select Committee explained that it had chosen Anderson because of their last names (Anderson coming before Douglas alphabetically). Douglas finally secured a seat on the committee after Barkley died in 1956 and liberal columnist Doris Fleeson wrote a series of articles detailing Johnson's machinations against the Illinois senator. By the time that Johnson finally relented, Kerr had risen to second in seniority on the committee. His appointment having been delayed for seven years, Douglas took his seat as the lowest-ranking Democrat on the fifteen-member committee.[7]

Douglas gamely endured the hostility of the Senate leadership and continued to fight uphill battles, determined to advance liberal causes on a number of fronts. Critical of the Republican administration's elitist economic policies, he introduced legislation that allowed small businesses uprooted by urban renewal to purchase or lease commercial or industrial facilities when they were relocated into new areas of the city, and (with Senator John F. Kennedy of Massachusetts) he sponsored a bill expanding unemployment compensation. He championed a four-year extension of the Reciprocal Trade Act with the elimination of some restrictions on trade, believing that such a program benefited American consumers. Yet he opposed the Trade Agreements Act of 1958 because of what he considered its excessive favoritism toward the oil and natural gas industries, clashing verbally on the Senate floor with longtime nemeses Robert Kerr and Russell Long.[8]

Douglas also took exception to the Trade Agreements Act because of its dubious protection of a wide range of domestic industries. Always eager to lampoon unjustifiable expenditures for the benefit of special interests, he took the Senate floor to discuss the unusual commodities deemed worthy of tariff protection because of their purported importance for national security. With mock sincerity, he inquired about the essentiality of spring clothespins, wood screws, blue mold cheese, groundfish filets, glace cherries, and coconuts. With special relish, he ruminated about the nation's need for an adequate supply of pregnant mare's urine. "It is difficult for me to understand how this product can be protected," he lamented. "This is tariff protection with a vengeance." Thanks to his devastating critique, the Senate eliminated many of the more questionable items from the law's list of protected items. The bill passed 69–20, and despite its remaining imperfections Douglas ended up voting for it.[9]

Douglas's vigilant attention to safeguarding workers' interests led to his concern with the questionable administration of pension funds. In 1954 the Senate Labor and Public Welfare Committee's welfare and pension funds subcommittee, chaired by Irving M. Ives (Republican, New York), had commenced hearings on the operation of union welfare funds, and the investigation had continued the following year when Douglas assumed the subcommittee chairmanship. In its 1956 report, in which it noted that employee welfare and pension plans had "grown up like Topsy," the subcommittee reported having found evidence of some illegal and unethical practices. "While we found the great majority of the plans to be honestly and responsibly operated," Douglas said, "the gross abuses discovered in some cases and the clear opportunity for abuse in others in our opinion called for remedial action." In the course of its far-ranging probe, the subcommittee had posed questions about the pension funds operated by some of the giants of American industry, including the Teamsters Union and General Motors. Douglas became convinced that, because of private enterprise's inability or unwillingness to police its own affairs, the problem called for action by the federal government.[10]

In 1958 the Senate Labor and Public Welfare Committee reported the Welfare and Pension Plans Disclosure Act, which had been sponsored by Douglas, Ives, and John F. Kennedy. The measure required business firms and trade unions to report to the federal government all financial data concerning their employee welfare and pension plans. Douglas emphasized that the bill was neither a "cure-all" nor a regulatory bill but simply a law that required government to act as a watchdog. "Just as sunlight often acts as a disinfectant," he told the Senate, "we believe disclosure will tend to deter many of the kinds of abuses our investigation revealed." The Senate passed the bill by a vote of 88–0, and President Eisenhower signed it on April 28. In 1962 Congress passed and President Kennedy signed into law a series of amendments that gave the bill teeth, providing enforcement along with the requirement of disclosure, empowering the secretary of labor to investigate possible abuses and supplying criminal penalties for kickbacks, embezzlement, false statements, and conflict-of-interest payments.[11]

On May 2, 1958, Douglas introduced for the first time a bill to create a public recreation preserve in the Indiana Dunes southeast of Chicago. A quarter of a century earlier, when much of the twenty-five miles of uninterrupted Indiana shoreline at the southern tip of Lake Michigan from Gary to Michigan City remained untouched by industrial development, he and Emily had built a cottage in the dunes for summer retreats. Over the years, Douglas had become passionate about the unspoiled beauty of the majestic dunes—even as steel mills, slag heaps, and railroad yards had gradually metastasized along the lakefront. A tiny state park of 2,300 acres, which had been bequeathed by Julius Rosenwald and other philanthropic Chicagoans early in the century, offered the only public access to the lake in Indiana. By the late 1950s, only 3.75 miles remained undeveloped, and naturalists feared that this remaining sanctuary would be disfigured as the shoreline had been from Chicago to Gary farther west. The last small section of lakefront land, which had been purchased by the Bethlehem and National Steel Companies, seemed to be headed for development. At the request of the Save the Dunes Council, a nonpartisan citizens group located in northern Indiana, Douglas introduced legislation authorizing the government to purchase the land from the steel companies and create an Indiana Dunes National Lakeshore under the jurisdiction of the National Parks Service.[12]

Douglas became the champion of the Indiana Dunes because neither of the state's Republican senators, Homer Capehart and William Jenner, cared to challenge the powerful economic interests intent on developing the Lake Michigan shoreline. Indiana politicians accused Douglas of improperly prying into the affairs of a neighboring state to advance Chicago's economic interests by inhibiting its competitor's development as a steel center and shipping port. Douglas found allies among nature lovers, environmentalist groups, and scientists concerned with the pernicious effects of pollution, but arrayed against him was a powerful combination of industrialists. Because the preservation of the dunes meant slowed economic activity and the loss of jobs, many residents of Indiana expressed ambivalent feelings about the issue. In 1958 the Douglas bill garnered little support and remained in committee, but he vowed to continue fighting for the dunes in future congressional sessions. The struggle to establish an Indiana Dunes national park would be one of his longest and ultimately most fulfilling crusades.[13]

In 1959 he became involved in another environmental issue that he defined in terms of the people versus the interests. The Senate Interior Committee reported a bill authorizing construction of the San Luis irrigation unit as part of the Central Valley water project in California. Despite the support for the bill by the state's two senators, Republican Thomas Kuchel and Democrat Clair Engle, progressive legislators for whom he had great respect, Douglas raised a strenuous objection on the Senate floor. As Douglas explained, Section 6A of the bill would exempt landowners from the historic 160-acre limitation imposed by the Newlands Act of 1902. In other words, he asserted, the exemption for the San Luis project would perpetrate a "system of big landed estates" and especially benefit a 120,000-acre tract of land held by the Southern Pacific Railway, a financial leviathan that had dominated politics in California for decades. Kuchel and Engle denied Douglas's charges and questioned the federal government's authority to impose its reclamation law upon a state's economic development. On May 12 the Senate passed the bill with Douglas's amendment, thereby temporarily defending the water rights of small landowners.[14]

Douglas also became a persistent critic of President Eisenhower's inability to craft a coherent program to combat the recession plaguing the nation in the late 1950s. Faced with an increase in the inflation rate in 1957, the Eisenhower administration responded with budget cuts and a more restrictive monetary policy. The severe budgetary retrenchment plunged the nation into its deepest recession since World War II. In 1958 the number of unemployed exceeded five million for the first time since 1940 (more than 7 percent of the workforce), and Douglas contended that the Employment Act of 1946 compelled the federal government to initiate ameliorative economic measures. He acknowledged the usefulness of a public works program to stimulate the economy during recessions but feared that Republican lassitude would undermine any pump-priming efforts and that any hasty creation of spending programs would be "too little and too late." The best course of action, he believed, would be a tax cut, which would not have as positive a long-term effect but would bring more immediate relief than a large-scale public works endeavor. Douglas proposed a $6 billion tax cut largely targeted for lower and middle income groups that, he speculated, would increase economic activity by putting more disposable income in the hands of the economic classes likeliest to spend it. The proposal foundered, but Douglas had established himself as the leading proponent of a tax cut as the liberal answer to stalled economic growth, a position that he continued to champion with more success under Democratic administrations in the 1960s. In the meantime, his energetic involvement with the economic situation led to his selection in 1959 as the chairman of the Joint Economic Committee of Congress—an appointment acquiesced to by Lyndon Johnson only after his choice for the chairmanship, John Sparkman of Alabama, declined the post.[15]

In his quest to raise the nation out of its economic doldrums, Douglas became convinced that certain geographical areas suffered the most (during periods of recession but also at other times) and therefore required special attention. His interest in such depressed areas stemmed largely from firsthand knowledge of conditions in the poorer counties of southern Illinois where a legion of unemployed miners had vacated played-out coal mines and the consolidation of farmland had uprooted thousands of tenant farmers. He also learned about the plight of unemployed loggers and lumbermen in the cutover timberlands of the Upper Great Lakes states; idle miners in the iron ranges north of Duluth, Minnesota, and the anthracite and bituminous mines of Pennsylvania; jobless textile workers in New England mills; displaced sharecroppers in the agrarian South; and impoverished Native Americans living in dire poverty on southwestern and great plains reservations. Fiercely attached to their homes and communities, these victims of modernization commonly refused to leave even though their standards of living plummeted. While many conservatives discouraged involvement by the state and spoke approvingly of a Malthusian economic adjustment of the market, Douglas believed that the unemployed deserved the aid of the federal government no less than did citizens of distant lands who received foreign aid from the United States.[16]

In 1955 Douglas had introduced a depressed areas bill that went first to the Senate's Labor Committee and then to a subcommittee that he chaired. After a series of hearings, the committee reported the bill favorably in June 1956. The Senate passed the bill by a vote of 60–30, but the House Rules Committee prevented action on the measure during the session. The following year, he introduced a similar measure that provided $275 million in loans and grants for seventy-two labor market areas characterized by chronic unemployment and poverty. The measure earmarked funds for renewal of industrial facilities, new construction projects, technical assistance, and training for the unemployed. The bill went to the Banking and Currency Committee where it met the determined opposition of the chairman, J. William Fulbright (Democrat, Arkansas). Reputedly opposed to area redevelopment legislation because of the threat to low-wage, antiunion states like Arkansas posed by the resuscitation of worn-out industrial regions, Fulbright stacked the Production and Stabilization Subcommittee with opponents of the bill. For more than a year, the bill remained stalled as Douglas futilely negotiated with Fulbright.[17]

The legislative impasse dissolved in early 1958 when Senator Frederick Payne (Republican, Maine) joined forces with Douglas and introduced essentially the same bill in the full committee. After a heated exchange— Douglas called Fulbright a "deep-freeze artist," and Fulbright accused the bill's sponsor of having been "derelict in his duty"—the committee passed the Douglas-Payne bill. Both houses of Congress passed the bill, but President Eisenhower responded with a veto. In his veto message, Eisenhower charged that the legislation departed from the principle of home rule, diminished local responsibility, invested the federal government with too much authority, and suffered from inadequate funding. He minimized the severity of the recession and denied the need for a tax cut to stimulate consumption. The president likewise suggested that economic problems in depressed areas could be addressed adequately through loans under the Small Business Investment Act of 1958. Douglas rued Eisenhower's unimaginative response to economic problems and vowed to continue the fight on behalf of depressed areas.[18]

While seeking legislative solutions to a variety of economic problems, Douglas continued to devote the lion's share of his time to the cause of civil rights. Only partially satisfied with the Civil Rights Act of 1957 and unwilling to grant the defenders of the status quo any respite, he urged immediate continuation of the assault on segregation. On February 10, 1958, on behalf of himself and a bipartisan group of fifteen other senators, Douglas introduced a civil rights bill that principally sought to restore Section III to the previous year's legislation; that is, the new bill authorized the U.S. attorney general to initiate civil actions for preventive relief against those who deprive persons of their rights to equal protection of the laws on the basis of race, religion, or national origin. First and foremost, Douglas's bill proclaimed the federal government's legal and moral responsibility to aid in public school desegregation. Employing a carrot-and-stick approach, the bill provided federal funds to assist school districts willing to pursue desegregation and also conferred upon the Justice Department the power to file compliance actions against school systems where all efforts to secure compliance had failed.[19]

Opposition to the civil rights bill surfaced immediately. Many liberals and moderates argued that Douglas had committed a grievous error in hurriedly pressing the civil rights initiative so soon after the passage of the landmark 1957 law. Progress on the racial front would come through gradual, incremental change, went the argument, not through ill-timed legislation that would only irritate the southern senators who were still smarting from the previous year's setback. Extremism from the left, they argued, played into the hands of southern hard-liners by alienating the well-intentioned but cautious masses whose support was essential for lasting change. A more moderate approach was needed, claimed the South's progressive voices, for the customs of the centuries could not be swept away suddenly with governmental edicts. Virginia Durr, one of the most prominent progressive voices in the South, wrote Douglas to offer her views on the necessity of carefully modulated action. Although she agreed fully with Douglas's goals, Durr said, she hoped that northern liberals would take into account the sensitive situation in the southern states and proceed accordingly. "The pressure on people who take a stand against segregation [in the South] is terrific," she noted, "and we sometimes feel we are completely abandoned by the rest of the country." She hoped that he "will try to understand the problem here . . . and not make the South feel it is again the persecuted and injured part of the country."[20]

Similarly, journalists and editorial writers expressed their concern with Douglas's introduction of new civil rights legislation. Writing in the *Washington Evening Star,* William S. White called Douglas one of the "political villains" whose actions in the Senate exacerbated race relations in the nation. The *Chicago Sun-Times* editorialized that "the new civil rights bill . . . is so certain to stir controversy that it seems unwise to rock the Congressional boat with it at this time." Congressional and other boats needed to be rocked "at this time," Douglas responded, because interposition, nullification, and massive resistance had continued unabated after the passage of the Civil Rights Act of 1957. In an editorial, "A Stitch in Time," the *Christian Century* likewise recommended forgoing any new legislation. Frank W. McCulloch, Douglas's administrative assistant, responded with a lengthy letter informing the journal's editor, Harold E. Fey, that the editorial was based on "an incomplete understanding of Senator Douglas's new civil rights bill and the gravity of the active forces working against law and order." As in other communications emanating from Douglas's office, McCulloch's stern missive emphasized the widespread use of massive resistance in the South and the moral imperative to continue fighting for a just cause.[21]

The civil rights bill met staunch resistance in Congress as well and eventually perished in the Judiciary Committee. (The substance of the bill later became Part IV of the Civil Rights Act of 1964.) At the same time, senatorial opponents of civil rights launched their own legislative counterattack in a somewhat circuitous fashion. Congressional conservatives had been unhappy with a number of U.S. Supreme Court decisions in the mid-1950s, particularly rulings that expanded civil liberties and extended federal jurisdiction at the expense of state governments. In the minds of many traditionalists, the Supreme Court under the leadership of Chief Justice Earl Warren had been making rather than interpreting laws. As Republican senator William H. Jenner of Indiana charged, the "extreme liberal wing of the Court" had "become a majority; and we witness today the spectacle of a court constantly changing the law, and even changing the meaning of the Constitution, in an apparent determination to make the law of the land what the Court thinks it should be." In 1958 the House of Representatives passed a series of bills limiting the power of the Court, and Jenner and John Marshall Butler (Republican, Maryland) followed suit in the Senate. The Butler-Jenner bill, which had been drafted primarily with an eye toward curbing the Supreme Court's support of civil liberties, quickly became a favorite of southern senators who opposed the Warren court's *Brown* decision. After the Judiciary Committee favorably reported the bill, Majority Leader Johnson lent his support.[22]

Senate liberals found the Butler-Jenner bill reprehensible on a number of levels, but Douglas especially feared the chilling effect it would have on the school desegregation effort. Along with Hubert Humphrey of Minnesota, Thomas Hennings of Missouri, and John Carroll of Colorado, he vigorously defended the Supreme Court in debate on the Senate floor. After two days of spirited discussion, the Senate defeated the measure, which Jenner had submitted as an amendment to an innocuous House bill, by a vote of 49–41. Emboldened by the outcome and determined to press the advantage, Douglas immediately introduced an amendment to the same House bill that expressed Congress's "full support and approval" of Supreme Court decisions opposing racial segregation. Before a vote could be taken on Douglas's amendment, however, the Senate voted to lay aside the House measure and never resumed its consideration. Acknowledging that the Butler-Jenner bill failed largely because of its introduction at the very end of the legislative session, when senators were eager to return home for the fall campaign, Douglas still felt considerable satisfaction in having defended the Supreme Court's school desegregation decision. He also saw the episode as another clear-cut example of why the battle for civil rights should continue without delay.[23]

That summer, Douglas and eleven other senators (most notably Democrat Hubert Humphrey and Republicans Jacob Javits and Clifford Case) expressed their intention to amend Rule XXII at the beginning of the next legislative session. This early announcement, Douglas said, would allow the Senate membership several months to consider the appropriateness of his determination to eradicate the "sands in the gears of democracy." By the same token, the early announcement of the liberals' intention would undercut the inevitable claims by southerners that the abrupt introduction of a resolution at the start of the legislative session did not give the membership sufficient time to reflect upon the proposed action. On January 7, 1959, the bipartisan coalition of civil rights advocates would seek to attain two goals: to establish the right of the Senate to determine its own rules at the outset of each session and to allow a simple majority of the Senate to bring cloture to debate so that the filibuster could not obstruct democratic governance. Long an unconscionable barrier to fair and effective deliberation, Douglas concluded, Rule XXII must be eliminated. He summarized his point with a paraphrase from Lewis Carroll:

> A rule XXII change every other day
> A rule XXII change yesterday
> A rule XXII change tomorrow
> But never a rule XXII change today.[24]

In place of Rule XXII, the liberals advanced a compromise between the existing arrangement that required a two-thirds majority for cloture (sixty-four votes) and a simple majority. They proposed that, during a filibuster, a minimum of sixteen senators could file a petition imposing a one-hour time limit on each speaker; passage of such a measure would require a two-thirds majority by the senators present and voting. Absent a two-thirds vote, debate could be limited fifteen days later by a majority of the Senate's entire membership. In that case, debate would be halted only after each senator had the opportunity to speak for an additional hour, and then the matter before the membership would come to a final vote. This procedure, Douglas posited, allowed for full discussion by all interested senators but imposed finite and reasonable limits on debate.[25]

Opposition to the liberals' proposal mounted in the days before the opening of the Eighty-sixth Congress. Majority Leader Lyndon Johnson spoke of a counterproposal that would have reinstated the two-thirds rule for cloture that had pertained in the Senate from 1917 to 1949. As Douglas pointed out, all eight attempts at cloture during those years had ended in failure, even though heavy majorities (but not two-thirds majorities) favored cloture in two instances in 1950. He particularly regretted influential columnist Walter Lippmann's rejection of the liberals' initiative in a December 25, 1958, *Washington Post* column. Lippmann candidly conceded that Johnson's alternative offered scant change from the existing system and admitted that Douglas's new proposal allowed for full debate. Instead, his opposition stemmed from the argument that, in order to avoid tyranny by a majority, a two-thirds cloture rule was necessary to protect the rights of a minority. Such thinking, which Douglas characterized as being "in the tradition of John C. Calhoun," seemed especially regrettable coming from an influential establishment spokesman noted for "the thoughtful character of his general comments on national and world events." Lippmann's opposition underscored the difficulties facing the liberal bloc of civil rights crusaders.[26]

On January 7, 1959, anticipating the attempt of the liberals to alter the cloture rules, Johnson introduced a resolution at the outset of the Eighty-sixth Congress's first session that would alter Rule XXII in a much less substantive way. His resolution changed the number of senators needed to invoke cloture from "two-thirds of the Senators duly chosen and sworn" to "two-thirds of the Senators present and voting." Douglas responded with an amendment that would alter Rule XXII along the lines he had sketched the previous summer, allowing for a majority vote on cloture after fifteen days of debate. For the next four days, senators debated the relative merits of the Johnson and Douglas plans, and on January 12 the membership rejected the amendment by a vote of 67–28. A crestfallen Douglas commented:

> This has been a black day for the people of the United States. The majority has virtually said that in the foreseeable future there will be no meaningful civil rights legislation. It has said that a small minority of the Senators can prevent action desired by a majority of the Senators, and a still larger majority of the people of the country.

Later that day, Johnson's resolution passed by a vote of 72–22. Some liberals, the ones Oregon Senator Wayne Morse called the "half-a-loafers," voted for the resolution believing that the change proposed by Johnson represented a modest advance over the prevailing situation. Still committed to the principle that a simple majority should be empowered to invoke cloture, a disappointed Douglas voted no.[27]

On January 29, Douglas and thirteen other liberals introduced a civil rights bill patterned almost exactly after the measure that had been rejected the previous year. The heart of the bill remained a provision for adding the proposed Section III of the Civil Rights Act of 1957, thereby investing the federal government with the authority to accelerate public school desegregation. Not surprisingly, southern foes of civil rights took the offensive. North Carolina Senator Sam Ervin charged:

> If the Douglas bill should be enacted into law, it would destroy the system of government which has prevailed in the United States since the adoption of our Constitution. It proposes to place all state governments, all municipal governments and all county governments in the United States under the supervision of the Attorney General of the United States, who is to be given authority superior to that of duly elected state and local officials in all areas which can possibly be construed by usurpation or otherwise to fall within the domain covered by the 14th Amendment.[28]

Lyndon Johnson introduced a civil rights bill that extended the life of the Civil Rights Commission, created a Federal Community Relations Service to moderate between rival factions in desegregation disputes, established criminal penalties for transportation of explosives across state lines used in interracial violence, and granted subpoena powers to the Justice Department in the investigation of voting rights cases, but most notably made no mention of support for school desegregation decisions. Characterizing the Johnson bill as "definitely a step backward," civil rights attorney Joseph L. Rauh, Jr., called it a "patent attempt to sweep the real issue of desegregation under the rug until after the 1960 election." Another alternative to the Douglas bill surfaced when the Eisenhower administration submitted a measure that provided for the extension of the Civil Rights Commission but conspicuously omitted any mention of Section III of the 1957 law. Administration officials cited promising developments in public desegregation in Virginia and prescribed inaction and watchful waiting, a position that led Rauh to accuse the Eisenhower administration of having "thrown in the towel on civil rights." The Douglas bill, the only acceptable alternative to liberals, remained submerged in the Judiciary Committee as the first session of the Eighty-sixth Congress concluded. When Douglas and several other senators threatened to attach civil rights amendments to unrelated bills and thereby prolong the lengthy legislative session, Johnson and Minority Leader Everett M. Dirksen jointly announced that they would allow debate on civil rights legislation during the next session, no later than February 15, 1960. For the second straight year, Congress produced no legislation to modify or extend the Civil Rights Act of 1957.[29]

The second session of the Eighty-sixth Congress convened on January 6, 1960, amid great expectations about renewed discussion of civil rights, with interest in the topic increasing after the first of the sit-ins occurred in Greensboro, North Carolina, on February 1. Discussion throughout the legislative session focused on the means to help African Americans register and vote. In its 1959 report, the Civil Rights Commission had addressed the issue by recommending that the president be empowered to appoint temporary federal registrars to assist African Americans in states where racial discrimination existed. Hubert Humphrey of Minnesota introduced such a bill in the Senate, outlining the procedures: When the president received nine sworn complaints of discrimination from one district, he would refer them to the Civil Rights Commission for investigation. If the commission found validity in any complaints, the president would appoint a federal employee living in or near the district to register all persons eligible to vote in federal elections regardless of race.[30]

President Eisenhower balked at the registrar plan, however, saying, "I don't even know whether it is constitutional." Instead, the administration favored the use of "referees" instead of "registrars" in a markedly different process. Whereas the Civil Rights Commission had fashioned an administrative procedure to be handled within the executive branch, the president's plan required action by the federal courts. If the U.S. attorney general found evidence of discrimination, Eisenhower proposed, he could bring suit under the Civil Rights Act of 1957. If a federal judge hearing the case found a pattern or practice of illegal electoral activity, he could appoint a referee who would gather evidence from potential voters who had been disfranchised. The judge would then issue a decree authorizing the aggrieved parties to vote, and the referee would observe the elections to ensure the legal outcome. Local election officials refusing to comply would be subject to contempt of court proceedings.[31]

Senate liberals quickly found fault with the administration's plan to employ referees rather than registrars. They suspected that the court process would be cumbersome and time consuming and that federal judges in the South might well not be enthusiastic participants in civil rights actions. Placing an administrative procedure in a judicial setting might be unconstitutional, they also suggested. Chary liberals raised several practical questions about the intricate procedure outlined by the administration: Might not the tortuous court proceedings be overwhelming for poor, uneducated African Americans in rural southern backwaters? Was it fair that qualified voters should have to hack their way through such a legal thicket in order to exercise their rights? To civil rights advocates on and off Capitol Hill, it seemed that the legalistic referee plan defeated the original objective of creating a quick and simple procedure for identifying and registering disfranchised African Americans.[32]

Dissatisfaction with elements of both the referee and registrar plans led Douglas and Jacob Javits to introduce yet another proposal. Under the Douglas-Javits bill, the president would possess broader authority to eradicate racial discrimination at the polling place. Free to act without any judicial or administrative proceedings, the president would possess the authority to appoint federal registration officials in any locality where he believed racial discrimination was being practiced. Because the intent of civil rights legislation at that juncture was to register voters and not to prosecute election officials, the framers of the bill contended, the president should be armed simply with clear administrative authority to expand the voting rolls. This aggressive approach, which garnered little support in 1960, became the crux of the voting rights bill passed by Congress five years later.[33]

As promised, Majority Leader Johnson initiated the discussion of civil rights on February 15. Because the Senate Judiciary Committee still failed to report the bill it held from the previous year's deliberations, Johnson invited senators to offer civil rights amendments to an obscure House bill being considered by the Senate that would allow the U.S. Army to lease unused officer's quarters at Fort Crowder, Missouri, to local public schools. With the support of Minority Leader Everett Dirksen, the vote to consider the bill's civil rights amendments passed by a vote of 61–28.[34]

Beginning on February 29, eighteen southern senators mounted a fili-buster that lasted until March 8. During those nine days, the Senate met around the clock except for a fifteen-minute recess on March 2 and a full-day recess on Sunday, March 6. According to the schedule formulated by Richard Russell, each southern senator would have to speak for four hours and then be accorded a two-day rest before being called upon to orate again. The participating southerners kept cots in their offices where they took naps until obligated to return to the floor. To break the spirit of their liberal antagonists, the southerners frequently initiated the calling of the roll by suggesting the absence of a quorum. Such action not only provided a rest for southern orators but also forced the liberals to respond in sufficient numbers to avoid adjournment. (An adjournment was useful for filibusterers because, when the Senate reconvened, several time-consuming formalities had to be conducted.) The eighteen southerners, who often stayed away while the liberals answered quorum calls at all hours of the night, averaged only sixteen appearances at the thirteen roll call votes and fifty quorum calls they initiated. As intended, the filibuster took a heavier toll on the northerners than on the southerners.[35]

On March 8, acting for a bipartisan group of thirty senators, Douglas and Jacob Javits offered a petition to invoke cloture to end the filibuster. Majority Leader Johnson and Minority Leader Dirksen spoke against clo-ture during the lengthy discussion that followed, and on March 10 the Senate voted 53–42 against the petition. With 64 votes necessary for clo-ture (two-thirds of the senators present and voting), the liberals fell 22 votes short—a sobering result for Douglas and an indication that resis-tance to effective civil rights legislation remained strong.[36]

Majority Leader Johnson announced that the Senate leadership fa-vored a moderate civil rights bill devoted primarily to voting rights that also found acceptance in the White House. Believing that just such a bill would emerge from the House, he urged senators to wait until House Bill 8601 arrived in the Senate. The modest House bill, which passed on March 24, featured a voting referee plan patterned closely after the ad-ministration's proposal. Johnson assigned the bill to the Judiciary Com-mittee but mandated that a recommendation be rendered within five days. The Judiciary Committee appended a number of amendments to the House bill, the most important of which dealt with the nature of the hearings to be conducted by a federal election referee. In the original version, ex parte hearings (without cross-examination) would be con-ducted so that African Americans seeking to vote would not be subjected to intimidating public tribunals. The amendment provided for hearings to be held in a public place with state and county registrars being given the opportunity to attend with legal counsel. In effect, the action of the Judiciary Committee further weakened the referee procedure.[37]

The Senate approved virtually all of the Judiciary Committee's amendments with but one notable exception—the hearings conducted by the federal official would be held ex parte but in public proceedings. Majority Leader Johnson successfully moved that the several attempts by liberals to amend the referee plan be tabled. Douglas and Jacob Javits twice sought to revive Section III by proposing that the U.S. attorney general be authorized to bring injunction suits to prevent equal protection of the laws, but they failed by votes of 55–38 and 56–34. The Senate passed the bill on April 8, and the House agreed to the Senate's amendments on April 21. In a subdued ceremony attended by only two officials from the Justice Department and no one from Congress, President Eisenhower signed the Civil Rights Act of 1960 on May 6.[38]

As with the law passed three years earlier by Congress, the Civil Rights Act of 1960 proved disappointing to reformers. Douglas said that the outcome of the eight weeks of debate in the Senate reminded him of the ancient fable of a mountain that labored and labored, only to bring forth a mouse. Senator Joseph S. Clark of Pennsylvania called the product of Congress's arduous labors "a weak Republican bill, watered down by southern and southwestern Democratic votes." The NAACP's Thurgood Marshall said disgustedly, "[The Civil Rights Act of 1960] isn't worth the paper it's written on." His colleague at the NAACP, Roy Wilkins, concluded that the bill "makes it harder and not easier for Negroes to vote." Describing the referees' plan, which supposedly enhanced the prospects of voting for African Americans, he went on to say: "The Negro has to pass more check points and more officials than he would if he were trying to get the United States gold reserves in Fort Knox. It's a fraud."[39]

Senator Strom Thurmond of South Carolina happily concurred with Wilkins's assessment, contending that the Senate actions created "a pattern of defeat for the NAACP and its spokesmen." Senator Harry F. Byrd of Virginia concluded as well that "the result has been a victory for the South." Inside and outside the halls of Congress, the prevailing wisdom not only saw the bill as a victory for southern opponents of civil rights and another disappointing defeat for reformers but also suggested that the outcome owed to the political sagacity of the southerners and the ineptitude of the liberals. Newspaper columnist Joseph Alsop flatly blamed the congressional liberals for the law's shortcomings, saying that they were "less interested in the dusty legislative process than in striking noble, popular postures." Similarly, in a magazine article entitled, "The Professionals Win Out Over Civil Rights," Anthony Lewis argued that the liberals ended up with a bill of little substance by unrealistically demanding too much and not evidencing a willingness to compromise. Liberals possessed the moral high ground, but they lacked the political skills to produce effective legislation.[40]

Douglas vigorously rejected the picture painted by these political commentators of a cadre of wily southerners outmaneuvering an earnest but inept coalition of northern liberals. He felt that the putative inflexibility by the liberals had nothing to do with the outcome of the legislative struggle for civil rights. Instead, he argued, four factors had doomed the bill. First, the administration and the Republican congressional leadership wanted the passage of some legislation in an election year but would not threaten their alliance with southern conservative Democrats by insisting on a meaningful law. Second, the Democratic congressional leadership also wanted some sort of bill but similarly would not antagonize the powerful southerners in the party who controlled so many important committees by virtue of their seniority. Third, after once again using the threat of the filibuster and employing other delay tactics, the powerful southerners retreated a bit to ensure passage of a bill that actually resulted in very little change. Fourth, some Democratic senators from rural northern states with virtually no African American populations forged practical alliances with the conservatives in the party rather than with the liberals, whose concerns with race seemed remote and ideological. In short, Douglas believed, the liberals lost because other groups cooperated in order to construct a modest bill. The liberals just did not have the votes.[41]

The liberals' disappointment notwithstanding, the Senate had passed its second civil rights bill in four years. According to Douglas, passage of the Civil Rights Act of 1960 constituted a significant achievement "because of its symbolic importance as another step toward equal justice for all our citizens, more than its probable, actual effectiveness." Better to win small victories than no victories at all. Meanwhile, he noted, the battle against the filibuster must continue in coming congressional sessions, for the chances of passing truly meaningful civil legislation remained slender as long as the southerners could rely on Rule XXII. More vigorous executive leadership on this issue would be extremely helpful, he believed, and the 1960 election held the promise of a more progressive presence in the White House. "Despite our temporary defeat," he concluded, "we cannot yield to cynicism or despair. There are no second-class children of God. There should be no second-class American citizens."[42]

Throughout the legislative struggles over civil rights during the Eisenhower years, conservative columnists and other political pundits frequently contrasted the performance of two of the Senate's preeminent Democrats, Lyndon Johnson and Paul Douglas—and usually to the former's benefit. As majority leader, Johnson used power effectively to squeeze out of a divided Senate two civil rights measures that, for all of their limitations, provided measurable steps forward. By contrast, Douglas and his liberal cohorts advanced unrealistic goals and legislated less effectively because of their zealotry. Douglas took exception to such a simplistic characterization of the civil rights struggle in Congress. On moral grounds, he felt obliged to attack segregation and discrimination ardently, but this was not the starry-eyed crusade of a political naïf. He believed in the efficacy of persistent pressure against the forces of reaction, convinced that unwavering advocacy would prove effective in time. "I believed," he said, "that even if every battle was unsuccessful, constant but peaceful struggle would hasten the ultimate coming of needed reforms." Just as Americans could not ignore the sit-ins and freedom rides, the rancorous struggles between the southern segregationists and the liberals in the U.S. Congress captured the headlines and thereby educated the public about civil rights issues. The partial legislative advances of 1957 and 1960 constituted necessary preliminaries to the more significant breakthroughs that would come later—and, indeed, made those subsequent victories possible.[43]

As committed as ever to the promulgation of civil rights, Douglas also pursued other legislative initiatives in the second session of the Eighty-sixth Congress. On January 6, 1960, for example, he introduced a "truth in interest" bill designed to provide consumers with accurate information about the interest charged by various lending institutions. Douglas's concern with the issue had originated several decades earlier when William T. Foster, president of Reed College, first spoke to him about the need for legislation to protect debtors from rapacious creditors. His interest resurfaced during his brief service on the National Recovery Administration's code authority for the consumer-finance industry. At that earlier time, he had criticized finance companies for publishing their interest rates in monthly rather than annual rates. With prevailing monthly interest rates in the early 1930s advertised as being 3 1/2 percent, consumers often failed to understand that the annual rates actually stood at 42 percent. Douglas had recommended that finance companies publicize their annual rates and charge interest only on the unpaid balance of the loan, a pair of unwelcome suggestions that quickly led to his exit from the committee.[44]

At the end of 1959, Douglas reported to his constituents, Americans owed $183 billion in personal debt, $52 billion of which emanated from consumer credit (autos, personal loans, charge accounts, and the like). In almost every instance, the borrower simply did not know the total cost of receiving the loan, and in many cases this ignorance resulted from the widespread use of deceptive methods of reporting interest rates and the price of credit. Often the practice of quoting monthly interest rates rather than annual percentages misled debtors; at other times, lenders quoted loans as "so much down and so much per month" but never revealed the actual interest rate. Less scrupulous lenders employed a host of other tactics to mislead potential customers. Douglas's bill stipulated that lenders provide all borrowers with two basic facts: the total charges for the cost of the money being lent and an expression of these charges as an annual interest rate on the unpaid balance.[45]

Douglas's bill received the avid support of labor unions, credit unions, and other consumer groups, but it generated intense opposition from banking and other lending institutions. He emphasized that his disclosure bill would not regulate credit or attempt to set any ceilings on interest rates but only sought to provide consumers with full and accurate data so that they could make informed choices. Nevertheless, critics charged that such disclosure would confuse the public and impose needless costs on the purveyors of credit. President Eisenhower's Commerce Department opposed the bill, arguing that the provision of annual interest rates would be misleading to the public and that state laws dealing with credit regulation and usury already existed in abundance. In 1960 the bill remained bottled up in the Committee on Banking and Currency, whose chairman, A. Willis Robertson of Virginia, spoke openly against its passage.[46]

Just as he sought to protect consumer interests, Douglas defended taxpayers by continuing to uncover waste in the federal government. Because of his unwavering opposition to communism, he never questioned the nation's need for a strong military, but he saw the armed forces as guilty of gross inefficiency and needless extravagance. His periodic investigations and calls for reform invariably met with stony silence from the Eisenhower Defense Department. "I was forced to conclude that the much-touted Republican desire for economy was mostly verbal," Douglas said, "and, in practice, the party did not want to tangle with the vested interests of the military or of other government services." His queries in 1958 and 1959 revealed that the armed forces paid extraordinary sums of money for the routine purchase of goods because of the cozy relationships between military procurement officers and supply companies. Hundreds of high-ranking officers in the army and navy had retired and then gone to work for the private companies that sold their products to the military. As these new civilians dealt with their former colleagues in the armed forces, competitive pricing gave way to interest peddling and higher prices. On June 17, 1959, Douglas reported in Congress that one hundred corporations with 74 percent of the defense contracts awarded by the Pentagon employed 721 retired military officers above the rank of colonel in the army or captain in the navy. Such specificity lent credence to Douglas's accusations, but Congress resisted his call for legislative restrictions and instead directed the military leadership to adopt appropriate administrative solutions.[47]

Convinced that nothing had changed to reduce the abuses, Douglas resumed his campaign against waste in the military the next year. He obtained a number of invoices for military purchases and had his staff price the commodities in local stores. On June 13, 1960, he cited ten examples from the invoices in a Senate speech to demonstrate how the government's contract purchases at wholesale prices cost far more than everyday retail transactions by civilians. The military had paid $21 for lamp sockets that could be bought at a hardware store for a quarter, for example, and $250 for an electric relay line that cost the public a mere $40. These discrepancies, at once shocking and laughable, thoroughly exposed the foibles in the system of military procurement, yet not everyone appreciated Douglas's investigative work. Military apologists and other cold warriors lambasted his muckraking as inimical to the national defense because, they charged, he forced the Defense Department to ignore matters of national importance in order to defend minor purchases. Douglas believed that his efforts may have had one positive result, in that the negative publicity may have led President Eisenhower in his farewell address to warn the American public against the pernicious influence of the "military-industrial complex."[48]

Meanwhile, Douglas continued his work for depressed area legislation. In 1959, along with thirty-eight cosponsors, he submitted an area redevelopment bill that provided for the administration of the program by an autonomous federal agency and allocated $390 million for various area redevelopment enterprises in seventy urban areas and three hundred poor rural counties. With some modifications, the Senate passed the bill in March 1960, as did the House in May. (In order to make the bill more palatable to the notoriously parsimonious Republican administration, the House trimmed the appropriations to $251 million.) On May 13, 1960, however, the president vetoed the measure. In his veto message, Eisenhower opposed the creation of an Area Redevelopment Agency and instead recommended that the program be administered in the Department of Commerce. He further warned that the Douglas bill wasted money and inhibited local initiative. In short order, the administration sent Congress an alternative bill with the much lower price tag of $80 million that limited area redevelopment initiatives to urban areas, contained no programs for rural areas, and eliminated several other provisions of the Douglas bill. Douglas scoffed at the scaled-down administrative measure, saying, "It appears to me that the Administration has proposed this hollow shell of a bill primarily in an effort to wash the blame from their hands for the defeat of effective area redevelopment legislation."[49]

In the closing days of the legislative session, the Subcommittee on Production and Stabilization of the Senate Committee on Banking and Currency held hearings to attempt a reconciliation with the administration so that area redevelopment legislation could yet be passed by the Eighty-sixth Congress. Testifying for the administration, Secretary of Commerce Frederick H. Mueller evidenced little desire for compromise, exhibiting what Douglas called a "take-it-or-leave-it attitude" throughout the unproductive negotiations. In addition, a frustrated Douglas noted, the administration had stalled the bill's revisions by responding so slowly to congressional requests for cooperation. Asked by the chairman of the Banking and Currency Committee for reports on the administration's proposals, officials at the Departments of Commerce and Labor delayed for more than a month before producing the information. Then Secretary Mueller castigated Congress for failing to produce revised area redevelopment legislation in a timely fashion, implying that the Democratic majority bore the responsibility for the failure to pass a law. Douglas concluded that Eisenhower and the Republicans were playing politics on the eve of the 1960 election by offering false hopes of cooperation to produce a bill. Determined in his last days in the White House to hold tightly to the purse strings, Eisenhower had no intention of signing the kind of extensive bill that Congress wanted; the bartering with Congress was merely a charade. "If I am re-elected," Douglas promised, "I will reintroduce the bill with a $390 million authorization, and, if we elect John Kennedy, we can be sure he will sign it and will do everything he can to help."[50]

The unsuccessful effort to secure area redevelopment legislation punctuated for Douglas a frustrating eight years of dealing with the Eisenhower administration. The Illinois Democrat, who saw the White House during those years as a bastion of Republican conservatism, had emerged as one of the president's most persistent critics. He believed that Eisenhower had erred in refusing to endorse the Supreme Court's landmark *Brown* decision, in using his authority to steer Congress away from meaningful civil rights legislation, in opposing a series of area redevelopment bills, in turning resource-rich offshore lands over to the adjacent states for development, in declining to initiate bold economic measures to offset a troublesome and lingering recession, and in neglecting the health and welfare of the nation's indigent population. Douglas seldom questioned Eisenhower's judgment on foreign affairs but disagreed fundamentally with the president's conservative domestic policies. He liked Eisenhower well enough on a personal level but questioned his detached leadership style and wondered whether he had the courage to exercise leadership on tough political issues. He saw Eisenhower as "a gentle person, not a bad man. His main fault was lack of vigorous leadership. His Presidency was bland like my diet, cup custard and soup."[51]

The end of the Eisenhower presidency excited Douglas, as did the prospect of returning a liberal Democrat to the White House. By 1960 he had become an enthusiastic supporter of the party's nominee, John F. Kennedy. Douglas had met Kennedy a few times when he served in the House of Representatives but became much better acquainted with him when he moved to the Senate in 1953. The two served together for many years on the Labor Committee before Douglas switched to the Finance Committee. In his first few years in the Senate, Douglas felt, Kennedy exhibited unusual caution, kept a low profile, and associated himself with few causes. Douglas thought that Kennedy had a fine mind but seemed somewhat disengaged from Senate affairs. He also felt that Kennedy later benefited from the tutelage of Theodore Sorenson, a gifted writer and policy expert who had served as a staff employee for a subcommittee Douglas had chaired. When the subcommittee finished its work, Douglas arranged for Sorenson to join Kennedy's permanent staff. By the late 1950s, Douglas and Kennedy had developed a closer relationship because of their shared interest in area redevelopment. In 1956, after Douglas had steered the area redevelopment bill through the Labor Committee and then moved to the Finance Committee, Kennedy took over and acted as floor manager for the measure. The two senators collaborated throughout the Eisenhower years in the unsuccessful attempt to bring federal aid to depressed areas.[52]

By 1959 Douglas had decided that Kennedy had established himself as the Democratic party's best presidential candidate and, at the urging of one of Kennedy's staff members, wrote a magazine article urging the Democratic party not to hesitate in nominating a Roman Catholic for president. Also that year, Douglas introduced Kennedy to the most influential Illinois Democrats at a luncheon in Springfield and then to a larger gathering of the party faithful at the state fairgrounds. In 1960 Douglas hosted the presidential aspirant during two other trips to Illinois, one in Chicago and the other downstate. He strongly suspected that Adlai Stevenson would emerge as a presidential candidate at the Democratic National Convention in Los Angeles and that Illinois delegates would be subjected to considerable pressure to support him. Douglas thought that Kennedy would be a much better candidate. Not wishing to have to take a stance in opposition to Stevenson, he declined to attend the convention. He did, however, inform Richard J. Daley and Jacob M. Arvey, the leaders of the Illinois delegation, of his strong preference for Kennedy. Rejecting an eleventh-hour plea for support by Stevenson, Illinois cast an overwhelming vote for Kennedy at the convention.[53]

Kennedy campaign personnel considered Illinois a key state in the presidential election and worried about anti-Catholic sentiment there, particularly in the southern regions of the state. Douglas concurred with their assessment and reported pockets of religious prejudice in the state's Bible Belt. He spoke frequently during the campaign on the subject of religious tolerance and defended the Democratic candidate at every turn. Kennedy campaigned in Illinois for four days, and Douglas accompanied him the whole time. Although Douglas stood for reelection himself in 1960, he spent an inordinate amount of time campaigning for Kennedy. "I really devoted more time to speaking for him than I did speaking for myself," Douglas later remarked.[54]

Douglas could afford to work indefatigably in Kennedy's behalf because his own reelection campaign proceeded so smoothly. The Republican party struggled to find anyone eager to run against the popular Douglas and delayed selecting a candidate for several weeks. Two-time Republican governor William G. Stratton apparently considered making the race but finally announced that he had decided not to do so, bowing to the judgment of his advisers who doubted that he could win. The Republicans finally nominated Samuel Witwer, a nondescript attorney from Chicago with almost no political experience and less name recognition.

Witwer waged an aggressive campaign and received ample funding from wealthy conservative Republicans, but public opinion polls reported him trailing Douglas throughout the campaign. Political observers in Illinois and on the national scene considered the incumbent to be a heavy favorite for reelection.[55]

Refusing to be lulled into complacency by the glowing projections, Douglas conducted an exhausting campaign. By his estimation, he traveled roughly 40,000 miles in Illinois, delivered three hundred speeches to crowds totaling one-half million people, and shook the hands of 250,000 of them. A seasoned and enthusiastic campaigner, he worked feverishly during the six weeks before the election. As in his previous campaigns, he interacted directly with voters as much as possible, stopping by big city work sites early in the mornings and hailing individuals and small groups on busy downtown street corners in the afternoons. In small towns, he approached voters outside courthouses and at county fairs. Although he gave some prepared addresses to large assemblages, he more often spoke with much smaller groups in informal settings. At age sixty-eight, he seemed as energetic a campaigner as ever.[56]

In addition to his many campaign speeches, Douglas participated in three debates with Witwer (two broadcast from WGN television studios and one at the State Chamber of Commerce Convention). In these public addresses, he took care not to mention his opponent by name and always spoke glowingly of John F. Kennedy while talking mostly about his own record as a two-term U.S. senator. He proudly proclaimed his liberal views, never wavering in the support of progressive causes, yet reminded his constituents of his vigilant efforts to eliminate waste and graft from federal government programs. In extolling the virtues of area redevelopment legislation, he noted how much the poorer regions of Illinois stood to benefit. Although foreign affairs figured less prominently in the campaign than domestic policies, he vigorously asserted his cold war credentials and denounced communism in all of its varieties. He emphasized the seniority he had accrued in the Senate, noting that he would occupy a seat on the influential Banking and Finance Committee and chair the Joint Economic Committee if reelected. Finally, he reminded voters about the reputation for honesty and integrity he had acquired through a lifetime of public service. Author of the Senate's Code of Ethics, he had been an exemplar of honest and progressive government.[57]

The Republicans asked how such a virtuous public servant could be allied with the benighted Chicago Democratic machine. Douglas responded by praising the administrative work done by Mayor Richard J. Daley during his five years in city hall and by affirming that Daley had never asked him for any extraordinary considerations or offered improper suggestions—a claim that he repeated faithfully in subsequent years. Howard E. Shuman, Douglas's administrative assistant, confirmed that Daley seldom communicated with the senator and never sought special favors for Chicago Democrats. The two men maintained a cordial relationship, Shuman noted, and respected each other's political acumen. Such amicable relations were possible in large measure because a U.S. senator could in fact do very little for Chicago's mayor. If Douglas had occupied a post in patronage-rich Springfield, Daley might well have been more aggressive in behalf of the Cook County Democrats. With very little at stake, however, the machine could simply bask in the reflection of Douglas's glowing national reputation.[58]

One week before the election, the *Chicago Sun-Times* published the results of a public opinion poll that predicted Douglas winning by a half-million votes and Kennedy by 100,000 votes. Douglas ended up winning by 420,000 votes, his largest victory margin ever, as Kennedy triumphed by a razor-thin 8,000 votes. Douglas and Howard E. Shuman attributed Kennedy's surprisingly narrow victory to an anti-Catholic campaign conducted by Republicans in the closing days of the campaign in southern Illinois. Douglas somewhat dubiously dismissed allegations of vote fraud by the Chicago Democratic machine on behalf of Kennedy, claiming that a postelection investigation had disproved Republican charges. He would have been more accurate in saying that, owing to their own questionable practices downstate, the Republicans grudgingly accepted Kennedy's vote majorities in Chicago. Because of Douglas's landslide victory, observers noted that Kennedy rode to victory in Illinois on the senator's coattails. Douglas doubted that, but he conceded that his extensive campaigning for Kennedy surely played a significant role.[59]

Douglas felt optimistic about liberal causes after the 1960 election. The Democrats lost one seat in the Senate but still enjoyed a 64–36 plurality and maintained a 261–176 majority in the House. With the enervated Eisenhower administration departing and the youthful Kennedy eager to take the nation into New Frontiers, the possibilities for reform seemed much brighter. Civil rights remained Douglas's top priority, but he hoped to advance liberalism on several other fronts as well. After many years fighting uphill battles in a conservative wilderness, he hoped that the decade of the 1960s would bring liberals closer to the political Promised Land.[60]

Senator with Ideas

7

What a difference a President makes. Instead of battling upstream to achieve those things which I have felt were necessary, the President's support is like having the current of a mighty river flowing in the direction one wishes to go.

—Paul H. Douglas[1]

• On the December 11, 1960, edition of the NBC television news program "Meet the Press," Ned Brooks introduced Paul Douglas as the "idea man" of the Democratic party, whose unceasing proposals for liberal programs and policies had been interred in congressional committees or vetoed by an unsympathetic Republican president. Now, with the Democrats reclaiming control of the executive branch, Douglas could surely look forward to a more important role on Capitol Hill and a rewarding, collaborative relationship with the White House. Brooks might have added that the election of Lyndon B. Johnson as vice president would have been heartening to Douglas, for Johnson would no longer be dominating legislative affairs as Senate majority leader. Johnson's successor, Mike Mansfield of Montana, seemed likely to provide a more disinterested, less dictatorial style of leadership that could benefit Douglas and other liberals. In the interregnum between John F. Kennedy's election and inauguration, the Illinois senator repeatedly voiced his sense of expectant optimism.[2]

The relationship between Douglas and Kennedy had been largely a professional and not a personal one during their years together in Congress, and their reserved collegiality persisted during Kennedy's presidency. The two men came from different generations, and the twenty-five-year difference in their ages precluded a close friendship. Some of Kennedy's advisers said that he regarded Douglas as something of a father figure. Not wanting to "push himself" on the Kennedy administration, Douglas usually kept a respectful distance from the president and paid only a few calls at the White House. Denying that he and Kennedy enjoyed a particularly close friendship, Douglas said that they shared a mutual respect and admiration and that they thought alike about many issues. Their common views, he hoped, would lead to a fruitful collaboration in the coming years.[3]

Immediately after his election, Kennedy announced that his first priority as president would be to bring relief to the regions of the country especially hurt by the recent recession, and therefore on December 5 he appointed a twenty-three-member task force, with Douglas serving as chairman, to study the problem of depressed areas. Having spent considerable time during the campaign in strategically important West Virginia, Kennedy had become interested in the grinding poverty endured by the people of Appalachia and originally intended the task force to concentrate exclusively on that region. Douglas argued that area redevelopment legislation should aid the poor in a variety of locations and persuaded the president-elect to broaden the scope of the investigation. The task force conducted hearings in Washington, D.C., as well as in Charlestown, West Virginia, before formulating a program national in scope. On New Year's Day, Douglas met with Kennedy in Palm Beach, Florida, to present him with the task force's four principal recommendations: (1) an immediate increase in the quantity and variety of the surplus food distributed to the needy; (2) creation of an experimental food stamp program as a pilot project in a number of counties throughout the nation; (3) passage of depressed area legislation to combat unemployment; and (4) special attention to the needs of the Appalachian poor. Kennedy announced his support for the task force's proposals and began speaking publicly of the need for appropriate legislation. As his first official act as president, still dressed in white tie and tails on the evening of the inauguration, he signed an executive order authorizing the expansion of the surplus food initiative and instructed the Department of Agriculture to implement the food stamp program.[4]

Kennedy identified area redevelopment as his first legislative priority, and on January 5, 1961, Douglas introduced a new bill, S. 1, which had been written with the assistance of White House staffers and cosponsored by forty-three other senators. The bill sought to attract private industry into areas with high and protracted unemployment rates by providing government incentives, allocating $300 million for loans in three separate funds of $100 million each for industrial areas, rural areas, and public facilities. Unlike earlier incarnations, the bill encountered very little opposition in Congress and passed both houses by lopsided vote margins. Douglas expressed regret at two alterations made by Congress prior to passage. First, he opposed an amendment that altered the original administrative structure that, patterned after FDR's creation of an autonomous Tennessee Valley Authority, would have provided for an independent area redevelopment agency reporting directly to the president. Instead, the final version assigned the overall administration of the new agency to the Department of Commerce with the Department of Agriculture, the Rural Electrification Administration, and other federal bureaucracies responsible for various aspects of the program. Second, he felt that the elimination of one of the bill's original sections that allowed for redeveloping a particularly poor neighborhood within a generally healthy urban area limited the agency's effectiveness in cities by targeting the legislation excessively to rural areas. The final version of the bill that President Kennedy signed on May 1 authorized the Area Redevelopment Agency to spend $394 million over the next four years.[5]

In later years, Douglas defended the Area Redevelopment Act energetically against critics who denigrated its achievements. He admitted that the agency had made some mistakes; it had erred in approving the construction of some facilities that brought no economic benefits to depressed regions and had occasionally taken credit for economic revitalization in particular localities that may have been attributable to a combination of factors. On the whole, however, he believed that the agency's successes far outnumbered its failures. Certainly, the track record in the southern section of his home state had been good. New business enterprises (introduced with federal assistance) in Carbondale, Metropolis, Sparta, and other small communities in Illinois's Little Egypt brought appreciable economic benefits to the residents. Area redevelopment did not cure the nation's unemployment problem—that was never a realizable goal, Douglas averred—but it eased deplorable situations in a number of chronically depressed sites. It also served as a precursor to many of the Great Society programs that followed later in the decade.[6]

Douglas no doubt defended the Area Redevelopment Act out of a sense of paternity, a paternity that resulted from a long and painful gestation period. He had first introduced depressed area legislation in 1955 and reintroduced comparable measures every year until the passage of a bill in 1961. Douglas recognized the importance of having a Democratic president identify area redevelopment as his administration's first legislative priority—"it would not have happened without Kennedy's victory," he said—and remained grateful to his benefactor in the White House. More important, the eventual passage of the area redevelopment bill confirmed Douglas's belief in the necessity of perseverance, of ceaselessly fighting the good fight, of patiently keeping the faith and believing that political circumstances could change with time. Indeed, as Douglas and members of his staff noted, the pattern established by the Area Redevelopment Act repeated itself time and again. From proposal to enactment, a bill sponsored by Douglas commonly became a law only after his unrelenting effort for a period of six to ten years.[7]

Douglas knew that the passage of the area redevelopment bill owed in large measure to Kennedy's concern with the fate of the Appalachian poor, and he understood that the president held less interest in many of the Illinois senator's other long-standing causes. Douglas would certainly continue to fight for needed reforms but with less confidence that he would enjoy unqualified support from the White House. For example, he tempered his hopes for passing truly effective civil rights legislation with the knowledge that the president's record on that issue in the past had been somewhat uninspiring. During his years in the Senate, noted the historian Carl M. Brauer, Kennedy had been a "moderate in a moderate time" who had carefully hewed to the middle of the road on civil rights. Although he liked Kennedy very much and thought him liberal on most issues, Douglas acknowledged the president's lack of interest in racial matters. Douglas remembered that Kennedy had voted for the jury trial provision in the 1957 Civil Rights Act, probably to avoid a breach in relations with powerful southern senators. Speaking in Boston in 1958 about Kennedy and civil rights, Douglas had glossed over a mixed voting record and rendered a generally favorable assessment. In fact, however, he thought that Kennedy did not feel strongly about the need to combat racial inequality and that the issue remained for the president essentially a political problem that had to be addressed. Suspecting that the new president would want to maintain good relations with the conservative southerners in Congress, Douglas prepared to raise the civil rights banner again with determination but also with realistic expectations about the aid he would receive from the White House.[8]

On March 24, 1961, Douglas introduced the Civil Rights Bill of 1961, which essentially replicated the provisions of the bill he had advanced in 1959. The measure authorized injunctive relief in suits brought by the attorney general as originally proposed in the defunct Section III of the Civil Rights Act of 1957 and, unlike the Civil Rights Act of 1960, targeted the problem of public school desegregation. In proclaiming the urgent need to address the education conundrum, Douglas cited a December 1960 report in *Southern School News* that meticulously summarized the lack of desegregation completed in the South. According to the report, only 195,625 African American students—6.3 percent of the region's total enrollment—attended schools with white students where segregation once prevailed unchallenged. Very little desegregation had occurred in the Deep South, for more than 95 percent of the modest number of African American students attending integrated schools did so in the District of Columbia and the border states of Missouri, Maryland, West Virginia, Kentucky, Oklahoma, and Delaware. Clearly, Douglas argued, the promise of the *Brown* decision would not be fulfilled in the South without forceful intervention by the federal government.[9]

In campaigning for civil rights legislation in 1961, Douglas conceded that the two bills passed during the Eisenhower administration constituted necessary first steps toward meaningful reform, particularly in the area of voting rights, but argued that neither measure fully addressed the myriad problems of racial inequality in American life. Significant progress could be made only if the Fourteenth Amendment's protections of rights could be guaranteed to all citizens regardless of race, involving public education, of course, but also other areas of public life. Just as he had in earlier years, Douglas argued the importance of passing civil rights legislation in the context of the cold war. As he put it, taking highly visible action toward protecting human rights "would . . . help to put our moral house in order before the eyes of the world and greatly strengthen our country's leadership in the struggle for freedom in the world against communist tyranny." Enacting meaningful civil rights legislation would undermine communist propaganda charging that the delaying and dissembling in response to the Warren court's desegregation mandate betrayed the lofty principles outlined in the Declaration of Independence and the U.S. Constitution.[10]

During the 1960 presidential campaign, Kennedy had asked Senator Joseph Clark (Democrat, Pennsylvania) and Representative Emmanuel Celler (Democrat, New York) to draft civil rights bills for the next legislative session that embodied the promises made in the Democratic party's platform, and he had pledged to seek their prompt passage. The Clark and Celler bills, both introduced on May 8, 1961, outlawed poll taxes and literacy tests, authorized federal civil suits against the denial of civil rights, created a Fair Employment Practices Commission with broad powers, and invested the Civil Rights Commission with permanent status. That spring, however, White House spokesmen announced that the president would not support new civil rights legislation during his first year in office. The only portion of the Clark-Celler bills that Congress passed that year and the president signed into law extended the life of the Civil Rights Commission, which was scheduled to expire on November 9, 1961, by two years. Without the support of the administration, Douglas's bill languished in the Judiciary Committee and never made it to the Senate floor.[11]

In 1962 a group of liberal senators introduced a series of bills based upon five reports submitted the previous year by the U.S. Commission on Civil Rights. Douglas introduced the bills, which had been patterned closely on the commission's recommendations, as a package. Kenneth Keating's bill dealt with voting rights, Jacob Javits's bill involved education, Joseph Clark's bill established a Commission on Equal Employment Opportunity, Hugh Scott sponsored a housing bill, and Philip Hart submitted legislation expanding the Justice Department's role in civil rights cases. As the unofficial leader of the civil rights bloc in the Senate, Douglas acted as the principal cosponsor of all five bills. The package of laws stalled in the Senate, however, as the Kennedy administration provided token support.[12]

After nearly two years of procrastination, the president finally issued an executive order against discrimination in federally funded housing as he had promised to do during the 1960 campaign. The White House also publicly supported two civil rights bills under consideration by Congress. The first, a bill introduced on behalf of the administration that banned the arbitrary use of literacy tests in order to prohibit individuals from registering to vote in federal elections, perished as a result of a Senate filibuster. The second, a constitutional amendment abolishing the use of poll taxes in federal elections, had been considered frequently by Congress in the past. Because only five southern states continued to levy poll taxes in federal elections by 1962, Dixie's congressmen acceded to a constitutional amendment—but balked at the elimination of poll taxes by statutory enactment. (Arguing that the Constitution reserved the power to set voting qualifications to the states, southerners opposed any attempt by Congress to alter voting statutes. Thus, a constitutional amendment that eliminated the largely anachronistic poll tax would not threaten the South's ability to oppose other voting rights legislation.) In a lengthy historical analysis of disfranchisement in the South, Douglas argued in favor of eradicating the poll tax but not by constitutional amendment. When Jacob Javits's bill to eliminate poll taxes statutorily was tabled, Douglas reluctantly voted for the constitutional amendment. The amendment passed in the Senate 77–16, and the states completed ratification in 1964.[13]

Douglas continued to be frustrated with the Kennedy administration's hesitancy to provide leadership on civil rights matters. On March 12, 1963, he met with other prominent Democratic civil rights activists in the Senate (Hubert Humphrey, Joseph Clark, and Philip Hart) to consider possible courses of action. While regretting the White House's failure to provide more vigorous leadership, they unanimously consented to initiate no new policies without the imprimatur of the Kennedy administration and to refrain from making any remarks that could be interpreted as critical of the president. They agreed to support the tepid proposals on civil rights emanating from the executive branch while quietly working behind the scenes for more substantive initiatives. As well, they decided to withhold their names from any civil rights legislation sponsored by their Republican allies.[14]

Kennedy finally became engaged in the civil rights struggle when events that year in Birmingham, Alabama, compelled him to action. In April 1963, the Reverend Martin Luther King, Jr., launched a series of demonstrations, boycotts, and sit-ins in the city that civil rights activists considered the most segregated in the South. Birmingham's public safety commissioner, Eugene "Bull" Connor, ordered the arrest and incarceration of hundreds of protesters. Under Connor's orders, the city's policemen responded brutally, beating demonstrators with nightsticks and unleashing snarling attack dogs, while firemen doused African Americans with water from high-pressure hoses. Television broadcast shocking images of the mayhem, and Americans recoiled in shock at the violence perpetrated by local authorities. Bombs exploded at the home of King's brother and at a motel where civil rights leaders were thought to be staying. Kennedy worried about the negative publicity generated by the lawlessness but also expressed heartfelt outrage at the mistreatment of the civil rights advocates. The president felt that the situation had reached the point where the federal government had to "lead and not be swamped" by the events in Birmingham.[15]

The Kennedy administration introduced civil rights legislation in June 1963, and Douglas opted to support the president's initiative rather than sponsor another bill of his own. After two years of temporizing on the issue, Douglas felt, Kennedy had finally put the weight of his presidency behind a substantive civil rights measure—one that granted African Americans full access to all public facilities, invested the federal government with the authority to bring suits against local school districts to effect racial desegregation, and provided a framework for eliminating job discrimination. Throughout the summer, recognizing that the strength of the opposition owed to the potency of the bill, Douglas labored assiduously for the Kennedy civil rights initiative. On August 29, he and his wife participated in the march on Washington that culminated in King's moving "I have a dream" speech at the Lincoln Memorial. Buoyed by the spectacular turnout at the march and profoundly moved by the spirit of goodwill generated there, Douglas reiterated his commitment to help the Kennedy bill through the Senate, in a later session if not the current one. "If Kennedy had lived, " the Illinois senator later commented, "I believe he would have come out more strongly for civil rights." The president's untimely death placed the fate of civil rights legislation in the hands of Lyndon B. Johnson, a development that would leave Douglas decidedly less optimistic about future prospects for improving race relations.[16]

Just as Douglas hoped to stimulate Kennedy's interest in civil rights, so also did he seek to win the president over to the cause of income tax reform. For years, Douglas had been campaigning to close the loopholes—what he called "truckholes"—that allowed wealthy taxpayers to avoid paying their share of taxes. His efforts to reduce depletion allowances in the oil and gas industries had attracted the most attention, but he had also over the years targeted other tax inequities that favored the wealthy and deprived the federal treasury of revenue. He spoke at length about the formidable forces arrayed against taxation reform:

> It has been the extremely able who have inserted these loopholes in the tax laws. The large hearing room of the Finance Committee seats 150 persons. When we considered a tax bill, the room was full of prosperous

lawyers, graduates of great universities and of the top-ranking law schools, all working to hold what they and their clients had, and to enlarge it. In the halls outside the hearing room, the lobbyists are thick as flies, while the publicity men and the noisemakers are busily at work. Erudite professors train their students in the intricacies of the tax code so that they may help wealthy clients avoid taxes. A particular measure would mean millions to a few, but only a few cents to each of 200 million Americans.[17]

By the early 1960s, Douglas had become especially concerned with the problem of what he called "collection at the source." The American taxation system provided for collection at the source of income tax on wages and salaries through payroll withholding, a system that Douglas considered more efficient and just than the previous arrangement whereby workers paid their total taxes at the end of the year. With no comparable provisions for automatic deduction or reporting of interest income, though, the government allowed owners of stocks and bonds to declare their capital gains and pay the requisite taxes. Because of outright evasion, ignorance of the law, or simple forgetfulness, approximately 8 percent of the total dividends on stock and one-third of interest payments went unreported in 1959; the failure to collect these sums of money cost the federal treasury an estimated billion dollars that year. Douglas argued that these loopholes had to be closed.[18]

The Kennedy administration submitted a tax bill to Congress in 1962 that provided for collection at the source for the income tax on dividends and interest at the rate of 20 percent. Recipients of interest income who had too much money withheld could file for refunds quarterly rather than annually, an advantage over the system prevailing for taxpayers earning wage and salary income. This provision sparked little discussion as the House routinely passed the omnibus tax bill—a prelude, Douglas surmised, to quick and painless approval in the Senate. He could not have been more mistaken. With the bill assigned to the Senate Finance Committee, an extensive public relations campaign commenced against collection at the source for interest income. Within a month, Douglas reported, more than 65,000 letters opposing the measure poured into his office alone, most of them coming from Chicago's banks and savings and loan associations; other members of the committee reported being buried under a comparable mountain of paper.[19]

Some protesters erroneously objected to the passage of a new tax. Others inaccurately criticized the establishment of a tax on capital. To the former, Douglas responded that the Kennedy bill simply allowed for a better method of collecting an existing tax; to the latter, he noted that the tax had been and continued to be a levy on a form of income. Douglas challenged the popular notion that somehow interest did not qualify as income and asked why workers receiving wages and salaries should be taxed while those receiving income from their investments should not. Such a question with its populist shadings no doubt did little to assuage the fears of those critics who portrayed the new withholding measure as a communist plot to confiscate all private capital. To the charge that the collection of taxes at the source would be prohibitively expensive, Douglas cited a Treasury Department study that estimated the cost at $20 million (about 2 percent of the amount of unpaid revenue on interest income). "I am absolutely amazed," Douglas said, "that many of the same individuals and same groups who are constantly criticizing the size of our national debt, who are demanding that the budget be balanced, and who appeal for fiscal soundness are fighting this proposal."[20]

Despite the efforts of Douglas and Albert Gore (Democrat, Tennessee), the Senate Finance Committee voted 11–5 to expunge the withholding provision from the tax bill. When the entire Senate considered the bill, Douglas's motion to restore the provision amassed only 20 affirmative votes. Instead, the Senate approved an amendment suggested by Harry Byrd (Democrat, Virginia) obligating banks and other financial institutions to report to the Internal Revenue Service (IRS) the names of all individuals earning dividends and interest. According to Douglas's calculations, the identification of those individuals resulted in the annual collection of an additional $250 million of revenue. If withholding at the source had been adopted and the IRS had not been burdened with the collection of unpaid taxes, he estimated, $750 million more would have been generated. Chiefly concerned with obtaining a tax rebate on investment as a stimulant to economic growth, the Kennedy administration deserted the withholding provision. Although Douglas received no communication to that effect from the White House, he deduced that the president had decided not to jeopardize his tax bill for the sake of reform.[21]

In 1963 Kennedy proposed a $13.6 billion tax cut, $11 billion for individuals and $2.6 billion for corporations, precisely the kind of massive revenue reduction that Douglas had been proposing since the middle of the Eisenhower administration. In terms of reform, the original bill limited itemized personal deductions, cut capital gains taxes, and proposed tax advantages for the aged and people with physical handicaps. Douglas became its foremost champion in the Senate Finance Committee, but as in past years he felt that the tax cut should be accompanied by reforms that would bring greater equity to the income tax system. In 1963, reported Douglas's assistants, the IRS failed to collect taxes amounting to $40 billion on $115 billion of income. According to the U.S. Treasury, 197 persons earning more than $100,000 paid no taxes that year. Of those wealthy people, 32 earned more than $500,000, and 20 earned more than a million dollars. Douglas contended that a fair tax bill should eliminate the loopholes and other irregularities that allowed the wealthy to avoid paying their fair share in what was supposed to be a progressive tax system based upon ability to pay.[22]

As in 1962, in Douglas's view, the Kennedy administration exhibited insufficient enthusiasm for tax reform and appeared too willing to compromise in order to obtain approval for a tax cut. In hearings before the Senate Finance Committee, Douglas lectured Secretary of the Treasury Douglas Dillon on the administration's lack of resolve in protecting the bill's "timid" reforms. Douglas told Dillon that, "by not having a virile stance in favor of tax reform, you have permitted the reform provisions to be gutted. When you throw the tax reform overboard, you just permit the pirates to take over the ship." Kennedy seemed to be unwilling to curtail the traditional favors afforded the extractive industries and the deductions granted wealthy individuals. To Douglas's chagrin, reductions in depletion allowances, unlimited charitable deductions, and the capital gains tax had been bargained away in the House in order to pass the tax bill. "Very frankly," Douglas warned, "if this bill gets any worse, it is going to be very difficult for some of us to vote for it. It is going to be very difficult for some of us to vote for it as it is."[23]

When the 1963 congressional session closed, the tax bill remained in the Senate Finance Committee. Partisan sniping from the Republicans and disquietude on the part of liberals who sought to restore reforms that had been bleached from the bill in the House slowed progress in Kennedy's last days in the White House; the tax reduction came in 1964 under President Johnson's leadership. Douglas approved of the economic theory behind the tax cut and supported it as public policy but rued the paucity of reforms attending its passage. Looking back years later, he lamented his inability to reform the tax system, saying:

> Can and will the people under the best system of government in the world, and with an able and high-minded Congress, ever be able to protect the public interest in tax matters and enforce equal justice for all? I must admit that the eighteen years have, on the surface, been disillusioning. We have made a few improvements during that time and may have saved a billion dollars or more a year, but the big loopholes and truckholes remained.[24]

Because of the abstruse financial issues involved, Douglas believed, reformers found it very difficult to galvanize the public in favor of income tax reform. On the other hand, most consumers had had frustrating experiences with credit and tended to be more receptive to his advocacy of truth in lending legislation. Convinced that he enjoyed broad public support, he reintroduced a bill in 1961 that required full disclosure (in dollars and percentages) of the cost of buying on credit. Specifically, the bill mandated that total finance charges be spelled out clearly and that the interest charges be calculated as a simple annual percentage of the declining unpaid balance. Spokesmen for the U.S. Chamber of Commerce, the American Bankers Association, and the American Bar Association spoke in opposition, characterizing installment credit regulation as a state and not a federal matter. One of the bill's severest critics, a representative of the National Foundation for Consumer Credit, an organization underwritten by a consortium of finance companies, complained that, "for every fraudulent transaction the bill might prevent, it would kill a hundred perfectly sound sales." Douglas dismissed these dire predictions as unsubstantiated and countered that the Federal Reserve Board, the Federal Trade Commission, the Federal Home Loan Bank Board, the Department of the Treasury, and the Department of Health, Education, and Welfare had all endorsed the bill.[25]

Throughout 1961, the truth-in-lending bill remained under consideration by the Senate Banking and Currency Committee where Chairman A. Willis Robertson (Democrat, Virginia) openly expressed his opposition to what he derisively called one of Douglas's "pet schemes." Robertson claimed that the Kennedy administration had only given "lip service" to the bill and that the testimony given by financial institutions "gave very definite reasons for claiming that [Douglas's] proposals were impractical." In his March 14, 1962, message to Congress, President Kennedy endorsed the substance of the bill but recommended that enforcement be assigned to the Federal Trade Commission rather than the Federal Reserve Board (as provided in Douglas's bill). On September 6 of that year, however, the Production and Stabilization Subcommittee of the Banking and Currency Committee voted by a 5–4 margin not to recommend the bill. Speaking for himself and the four Republicans who outvoted the other four Democrats on the subcommittee, Robertson explained that no national demand for the legislation existed. In 1963 Douglas dutifully submitted another bill but, even with White House support, could not get the legislation out of committee.[26]

For Douglas, protection of the consumer naturally entailed action against monopolies. Wary of the economic and political power wielded by gigantic corporations, in the early 1960s he advanced a proposal to divide General Motors and U.S. Steel into several smaller corporations. He conceded that these industrial behemoths should be allowed to enjoy the advantages of vertical integration, but the combination of horizontal units should be banned. In fact, he argued, the implementation of such limitations by government could well benefit the largest economic entities. Split into three or four moderate-sized concerns, for example, U.S. Steel would benefit from better communication than it had as one giant enterprise. Not surprisingly, Douglas failed to convince the corporate management at General Motors and U.S. Steel of the efficacy of his plan, nor did he enlist many converts in the U.S. Senate. He concluded that the antitrust battle could be fought most effectively by the judiciary and applauded the Supreme Court's 1961 order that the Du Pont family divest itself of controlling interest in General Motors.[27]

The problem of monopoly disturbed Douglas when the Senate considered legislation regulating the emerging telecommunications industry in outer space. The successful launching of space satellites promised not only significant breakthroughs in communications capabilities but also vast profits for those who controlled the networks. Under the guidance of Robert Kerr and John O. Pastore (Democrat, Rhode Island), the Senate Commerce Committee approved the administration's bill in 1962 awarding monopoly control to a private corporation that allowed for a modicum of government regulation. In fact, a group of ten Democratic senators (Wayne Morris and Maureen Neuberger of Oregon, Estes Kefauver and Albert Gore of Tennessee, E. L. Bartlett and Ernest Gruening of Alaska, Russell Long of Louisiana, Ralph Yarborough of Texas, Quentin Burdick of North Dakota, and Joseph Clark of Pennsylvania) saw the Communications Satellite (COMSAT) bill as nothing more than a front for the American Telephone and Telegraph Company (AT&T). Instead, they recommended the creation of a public corporation (like the Atomic Energy Commission) that would own satellites and lease them to private corporations. Determined to avoid an immediate vote on the COMSAT bill, the small group of dissidents obtained the floor and conducted an impromptu filibuster for several days.[28]

Senate Majority Leader Mike Mansfield censured the antimonopolists and ordered a continuous session in an effort to break the filibuster. Douglas caustically noted the asperity with which Mansfield had condemned the filibusterers after exercising far more forbearance when southerners had behaved similarly in their opposition to civil rights legislation. Initially uncertain how he would vote on the complex COMSAT bill, Douglas refrained from joining the filibusterers but heatedly objected to the treatment they received from the Senate leadership. At one juncture, he stayed away from the Senate floor so that a quorum could not be achieved for a vote on cloture. He and Emily left Washington, D.C., so that he could not be found and then returned to the capital only after the Senate had recessed for lack of a quorum. The majority leader finally filed a cloture petition, and on August 14 the Senate voted 73–27 to invoke cloture. Douglas voted not to curtail debate.[29]

The filibuster defeated, the Senate passed the COMSAT bill on August 17 by a vote of 66–11. Skeptical of the conditions under which the newly created private corporation would operate and concerned that the lack of government control would give the new monopoly free rein, Douglas joined the other liberals in voting against the measure. For Douglas and the other dissidents, however, the outcome proved not altogether disappointing. For only the fifth time in history and the first time in thirty-five years, the Senate had voted under Rule XXII to limit debate. (Following the lead of Richard Russell, southerners voted not to invoke cloture but then voted for the bill itself.) The willingness of so many senators to invoke cloture on the COMSAT bill gave hope that such a result could be produced in the continuing civil rights struggle.[30]

Along with his efforts on behalf of consumers, Douglas hoped to enlist Kennedy in his attempt to save the Indiana Dunes. As a senator, Kennedy had played a leading role in creating a national park on the Cape Cod peninsula in his home state of Massachusetts, and Douglas expected that that would make the president sympathetic to a plan for the creation of a similar protected area on the shores of Lake Michigan. Kennedy refrained from embracing the Indiana Dunes cause, however. "Try as we might," lamented Douglas, "we could never get the warm support of the Kennedy administration, and without it, we could do nothing." Douglas met with Kenneth O'Donnell, one of the president's top aides, to argue his case but felt that he made little headway. He suspected that O'Donnell, like Kennedy himself, held the provincial easterner's view that nothing in the Midwest could compare with the great natural beauty of the Atlantic shoreline. Moreover, Douglas suspected that Kennedy had tentatively agreed that the new Democratic governor of Indiana could acquire land on the lakefront for the construction of a harbor. At the same time, the National and Bethlehem Steel companies announced their plans for erecting new blast furnaces and finishing mills near the projected harbor site at Burns Ditch.[31]

Fearing that the White House was preparing to approve the new port, Douglas hastily arranged a meeting with the president. Showing Kennedy photographs of the affected area, he advanced his most persuasive arguments for preservation of the dunes. The nation's rapidly expanding metropolitan areas desperately needed recreational areas close by, Douglas argued, and the vast national parks of the American West stood thousands of miles away from the population centers of the East and Midwest. (The Outdoor Recreation Resources Review Commission had made the same argument in its report to the president in 1961.) The Indiana Dunes could be for Chicago what Kennedy had helped create for Boston at Cape Cod, an accessible escape for the crowded urban masses. Because the steel companies intended to build automated mills along Lake Michigan, Douglas informed Kennedy, the threatened loss of jobs in the industry led the United Steelworkers of America to oppose the northern Indiana development. Douglas believed the meeting went well and left the White House "feeling that at least he would not oppose us." In a major address to Congress on conservation on March 1, 1962, the president recommended that Congress create an Indiana Dunes National Lakeshore.[32]

The struggle over the dunes continued throughout 1962 despite Kennedy's endorsement of a national lakeshore. The U.S. Corps of Engineers surveyed the land at Burns Ditch and prepared plans for the construction of a deepwater harbor built with $25.6 million of federal funds. The *Washington Post* observed that the fate of the dunes remained unsettled because Indiana political leaders succumbed to the industrialists' slogan, "payrolls, not picnics." House Minority Leader Charles Halleck of Indiana, an avid proponent of industrial development in the dunes, accused the Bureau of the Budget of suppressing a favorable report on the Burns Ditch harbor for political reasons, and his Republican colleague from Indiana, Representative J. Edward Roush, charged that "jealous" Illinois officials, fearing "competition from another port on Lake Michigan," were responsible for the logjam.[33]

Allying himself with Douglas and the environmentalists, Ray J. Madden, Democratic representative from Indiana, urged that the harbor be built instead in his Lake County district farther west along the Lake Michigan shore. "I do not think that the taxpayers . . . should help build a port for (former Secretary of the Treasury) George Humphrey's National Steel Corporation," he commented. The mayors of several northwestern Indiana communities—Gary, East Chicago, Whiting, and Hammond—supported Madden, realizing that new steelworks in the nearby dunes would compete with their own struggling steel factories. The scientific community assailed the despoilers and endorsed Douglas's plans for a park by signing a petition circulated by W. J. Beecher, director of the Chicago Academy of Sciences, and Dr. Charles Olmstead, chairman of the Department of Botany at the University of Chicago. Another 250,000 citizens submitted petitions to Congress urging that the dunes be preserved.[34]

On February 4, 1963, Douglas reintroduced the bill to create the Indiana Dunes National Lakeshore that he had introduced two years earlier. The 1961 version, which had been endorsed by the National Park Service and the Department of the Interior and been reported favorably by the Bureau of the Budget in 1962, authorized the secretary of the interior to create a national lakeshore park of 9,000 acres (5.39 miles of shoreline) that would include bathing beaches, a nature preserve, and areas for camping, picnicking, fishing, canoeing, hiking, and horseback riding. As before, Douglas saw his legislation blocked by the Indiana congressional delegation (with the exception of Representative Madden) and publicly condemned by the Bethlehem and National Steel Companies as well as by other potential investors in industrial expansion.[35]

Later that year, at the direction of President Kennedy, Elmer Staats, the deputy director of the Budget Bureau, and Lee White, a member of the White House staff, worked out a compromise proposal for the Indiana Dunes. The Kennedy plan attempted to satisfy both sides in the controversy by creating an approximately 10,000-acre national park in the dunes and funding a harbor at another location in northwestern Indiana. This arrangement satisfied Douglas and the Democratic members of the Indiana congressional delegation as well as the legions of civic groups that had fought to save the dunes. Acting for the administration, Senator Henry Jackson (Democrat, Washington) introduced the measure along with Douglas and the Democratic Indiana senators, Birch Bayh and Vance Hartke. House Minority Leader Charles Halleck opposed the bill, however, as did the steel companies seeking to situate the harbor at Burns Ditch. The Inland Steel Company, which stood to lose land at the site of the new harbor, also repudiated the Kennedy compromise. The bill passed in the Senate by a voice vote, but the House failed to take action, and the measure eventually died at the end of the Eighty-eighth Congress. Kennedy's attempt to resolve the dispute failed, and the fate of the dunes remained as indeterminate as before.[36]

While Douglas continued to devote most of his time in the Senate to economic and social welfare issues, he maintained his reputation as a devout cold warrior by supporting all of President Kennedy's cold war initiatives. He agreed with the new president that the threat of communist aggression remained grave throughout the world and endorsed the bellicose language in Kennedy's inaugural address that warned other nations of America's readiness to defend freedom globally. Douglas termed the Bay of Pigs episode a "crushing defeat"—a "miserably planned and executed" enterprise—but noted that Kennedy had felt constrained to follow the plan concocted by the Eisenhower administration. Moreover, Douglas asserted, Kennedy manfully accepted blame for the setback rather than singling out the principal party responsible for the fiasco, the Central Intelligence Agency. Douglas lauded Kennedy's bold action in the Cuban Missile Crisis, praising his calm resolve in forcing the Soviets to remove their missiles while still providing Nikita Khrushchev with the opportunity to save face, and credited the president's "warm and determined" speech in Berlin with giving the West Germans the courage to preserve freedom in the western sector of that city.[37]

Having favored more aggressive support for France in Indochina than President Eisenhower had been willing to countenance in the early 1950s, Douglas fully backed Kennedy's containment strategy in South Vietnam. (In fact, he thought that Eisenhower had erred in declining to send U.S. troops to the aid of embattled French forces at Dien Bien Phu in 1954.) Douglas saw much wisdom in the domino theory and felt that the fall of South Vietnam would surely lead to successful communist incursions in the Malay peninsula and India. The Indian ambassador to the United States had matter-of-factly informed him that her country would inevitably fall to the communists, Douglas recalled, if the forces of democracy allowed the first domino to fall in Southeast Asia. Thus, he thought his support for a strong U.S. presence in an obscure nation thousands of miles removed from North America justified on the basis of a real, if yet unappreciated, threat to free governments far beyond the immediate borders of South Vietnam.[38]

Douglas's fierce anticommunism surfaced prominently in his continued opposition to U.S. recognition of the People's Republic of China. Although he had favored diplomatic recognition of the USSR following his 1927 visit to that communist nation, he argued that the hostile foreign policy established by the brutally repressive regime in China argued for a different policy by the United States in the 1950s and 1960s. In Douglas's view, the People's Republic of China had become a second communist police state bent on world domination. To oppose granting recognition to the Mao Tse-tung government, he joined the Committee of One Million, a bipartisan organization composed primarily of Republican conservatives. As a member of that organization's executive committee, he insisted that funding be acquired only from individuals and specifically that no direct or indirect financial contributions be accepted from the Nationalist Chinese government in Taiwan. He likewise fervently opposed membership in the United Nations for the People's Republic of China, dismissing the argument that the nation's huge population dictated recognition as a practical matter. "I have never believed," he said, "that the magnitude of wrong-doing justifies the crime." His membership in the Committee of One Million occasionally proved embarrassing, especially when the organization impugned the motives of those groups like the National Council of Churches that favored recognition, but he remained implacably opposed to any alteration of U.S. policy toward the communist government in China—a position maintained by Kennedy as well.[39]

While supporting a firm policy of containment, however, Douglas continued to monitor defense spending to ensure the efficient use of American defense dollars. Shortly after President Kennedy announced the appointment of Robert S. McNamara as secretary of defense, Douglas sent the new cabinet member a letter suggesting a number of reforms in military spending. The senator recommended more competitive bidding instead of the negotiated contracts with single suppliers that had been commonplace in the past, the closing of antiquated military installations around the country, and a reorganization of military stores, among other changes. Expecting the same kind of hostility he had experienced from the Pentagon in the past, Douglas was pleasantly surprised when McNamara responded promptly and enthusiastically. At the defense secretary's invitation, Douglas agreed to serve on an informal committee that would meet four times annually to consider problems of military spending. Along with the other members of the committee, Douglas entered into a fruitful collaboration with McNamara that lasted for several years.[40]

Already determined to streamline military operations and willing to endure the inevitable protests emanating from the military establishment, McNamara eagerly accepted many of the recommendations made by the Douglas committee. Central to the reform effort, McNamara assented to the formation of a centralized supply agency for the military, thereby reducing the frequency of unnecessary purchases as well as the number of personnel employed in supply services. He also increased the number of contracts awarded on the basis of competitive bidding and disposed of a number of unnecessary installations, bases, and munitions plants. As a consequence of such rigorous cost cutting, the defense secretary boasted of saving several billion dollars annually in military expenditures. Announcing the saving of $4.8 billion in the fiscal 1965 budget, he said: "The Department of Defense cost-reduction program . . . owes much of its inspiration to . . . Senator Douglas."[41]

Douglas enjoyed good relations with the Democratic administration and supported its initiatives in almost every instance but dissented vigorously when, in 1962, President Kennedy openly supported Senate Minority Leader Everett M. Dirksen's reelection over Democrat Sidney Yates. Douglas thought very highly of the liberal Yates, who had achieved a solid record in the House of Representatives, and considered Dirksen an unimaginative conservative prone to tailor his views to shifting public opinion. Kennedy had achieved a comfortable working relationship with Dirksen and purportedly did not want to see archconservative Bourke Hickenlooper of Iowa become minority leader if Dirksen lost. The president told Douglas that "Dirksen was about the best Republican Senate leader that we could expect." During the campaign, Kennedy, Vice President Johnson, and Senate Majority Leader Mike Mansfield all implied that the White House supported Dirksen, a betrayal of a loyal Democrat that Douglas considered unconscionable. Illinois newspapers carried pictures of Dirksen chatting amiably with Kennedy at a Capitol Hill cocktail party, accompanying the president to a Washington Senators' baseball game, and attending a formal White House reception for congressional luminaries. Dirksen enjoyed a wellspring of publicity generated by a Democratic president while Yates had to plead for a photo opportunity with Kennedy. "I was dispirited," Douglas complained, "that the administration should treat so shabbily a good candidate who supported the forward-looking practices of our Democratic Party."[42]

Immediately following Dirksen's reelection, Douglas sent Kennedy a scathing memorandum that criticized the White House and the Senate Democratic leadership for its machinations against Yates. He upbraided Mansfield and Hubert Humphrey for their "glowing praise" of Dirksen on the eve of the election but reserved his most abrasive comments for the president himself. Douglas lambasted the several highly publicized favors Kennedy granted the minority leader and the comments from "high White House sources" that Yates had no chance of winning the election. He especially resented the president's acceptance of Dirksen's key amendments to the 1962 tax bill, concessions that he charged had more to do with politics than public policy. He received no denials from the White House and grudgingly accepted the Kennedy-Dirksen entente as an unpleasant political reality. Overall, he felt, it was a relatively minor blemish on the generally enviable Kennedy record.[43]

Douglas was conducting public hearings on truth-in-lending legislation in Boston when he received the news of Kennedy's assassination. Like countless other Americans, he felt shock and sadness upon hearing the report. "Then, and ever since," he commented, "I felt that something of grace and charm had gone out of political life." Looking back on Kennedy's years in the White House, Douglas recognized the president's shortcomings and predicted that future generations of revisionist historians would have no trouble demystifying much of the Camelot legend. "He was not superhuman," Douglas conceded, "and he had many faults, as he would have been the first to acknowledge." Generally, however, Kennedy had shown evidence of growth in office, Douglas believed, and his performance had improved gradually during those brief years. A brilliant but remote politician's expedience seemed to be giving way to increased insight and empathy, promising greater reforms in the future. Douglas concluded:

> I would say that as John Kennedy became progressively more aware of the problems which the American people faced, he became much more sympathetic towards helping people. We should remember that he grew up in a wealthy family, went to a selective private school and to Harvard, and that until he went into the service, he was in a sense insulated from the ordinary problems and difficulties which people face and unacquainted with the economic and social handicaps under which large numbers of Americans labor. As he realized these human difficulties of poverty, unemployment, unequal power, deprivation of opportunities to rise in the world, this developed him and he moved, I think, progressively onward and became more and more of an advocate of human rights and less a somewhat cold patrician.[44]

Because of his abiding affection for the president, Douglas tempered his public criticisms of the Kennedy administration and spoke wistfully of what might have been achieved had the tragedy in Dallas not occurred. Privately, Douglas conceded that the promise of the Kennedy presidency remained largely unrealized in 1963. The legislative record of the previous two years could best be described as disappointing, the passage of an area redevelopment bill outweighed by the continued inability to achieve success with such perennials as civil rights, truth in lending, saving the Indiana Dunes, and income tax reform. Most worrisome to Douglas, Kennedy's death elevated to the presidency the perennial scourge of the liberals and his own personal nemesis, Lyndon Johnson. In the wake of Kennedy's assassination, the promise of the New Frontier seemed to be fading.

On Behalf of the Great Society

8

As President [Lyndon Johnson] followed a much different course from what he had followed as Majority Leader. I had lamented his becoming President because I could not see how he would change rapidly enough, so I hadn't counted on Johnson. As President, he was a progressive. No one could have been more vigorous than he, both on civil rights and on the position of the poor and the much abused.

—Paul H. Douglas[1]

• During the Eisenhower years, Paul Douglas and Lyndon Johnson had been at loggerheads repeatedly in the U.S. Senate. The two men clashed most dramatically over civil rights matters, but they had also been on opposite sides regarding such issues as the oil depletion allowance and tax reform. They hailed from different wings of the Democratic party and often found common ground a remote destination. Douglas charged that Johnson and his cohorts in the congressional leadership perverted the principles enunciated by their party. As Senate majority leader, Johnson wielded power ruthlessly and found Douglas's independence irritating. Douglas bridled at Johnson's heavy-handedness and, applying the Quaker practice of speaking truth to power, railed against what he perceived to be abuses of power by the Senate leadership. "We used to have a saying about Johnson," remembered Douglas's administrative assistant, Howard E. Shuman. "We gave him an orchard, and he gave us an apple." In part, their difficult relations stemmed from their vastly different personalities. Shuman believed that Johnson simply could not fathom Douglas's unbending loyalty to ideas and unwillingness to barter behind the scenes. Shuman noted:

> The Senator got little of the minor goodies other people got. Of course, Mr. Douglas didn't want them. Johnson never could understand what Douglas wanted. Johnson had everybody's number—women, wine,

rooms, bills, patronage, whatever—he never understood Mr. Douglas because the only thing Mr. Douglas wanted Johnson to do was to carry out the party's program. Johnson could not understand why somebody would stand for principle.[2]

The uneasy relationship between the two men continued after Johnson became vice president in 1961. Immediately following his selection as majority leader at the outset of the Eighty-seventh Congress, Mike Mansfield stunned the other Senate Democrats by moving that Johnson be named permanent presiding officer of the party caucus. Such an action would have given a member of the executive branch an unprecedented amount of influence in the legislature, as outraged liberals quickly asserted. Mansfield's motion, which senators and onlookers alike presumed had been conceived by Johnson, seemed to be additional evidence of the designing vice president's unquenchable thirst for power. The previously quiescent Democratic meeting erupted into a donnybrook with Douglas, Albert Gore of Tennessee, and Joseph Clark of Pennsylvania leading the opposition to Mansfield's proposal. Aghast that Johnson would attempt such a bold power play and that the new majority leader would go along, Douglas denounced the proposal in uncompromising fashion. Although Mansfield's motion passed by the comfortable margin of 46–17, Johnson bristled at the liberals' flinty opposition. "I now know the difference between a caucus and a cactus," an enraged Johnson said. "In a cactus all the pricks are on the outside."[3]

To Douglas's surprise, Johnson moved quickly after becoming president to mend fences with his former antagonist. Announcing his intention of enacting a sweeping program of liberal reform, Johnson indicated his desire to work closely with Douglas and the other Senate liberals with whom he had clashed so bitterly in the past. On January 24, 1964, he wrote a warm "Dear Paul" letter to Douglas that offered the hope of a new relationship between the two men. The letter read:

> Since Harold Ickes, I don't know of a liberal I admire more than you. I say this because of your generous and sincere approach to the problems that confront our country and the depth of your convictions.
>
> You are one of those rare men in public life who can be both liberal and progressive without being a wastrel.
>
> The many speeches that you have made on saving pennies have inspired me to save dollars.
>
> I know that you have never felt particularly close to me but now the new responsibility I have draws me closer to you. Whenever you think I am making a mistake just pick up the phone, call me and tell me what you are thinking.[4]

Admittedly baffled by what he perceived to be a dramatic shift in Johnson's political views, Douglas nevertheless prepared to take advantage of the fortuitous development. He never fully understood the reasons for the president's nascent progressivism, unable to decide whether Johnson's move to the left emanated from political considerations or genuine personal growth. In other words, he wondered whether Johnson recognized the need to appear more liberal in order to receive votes from outside the South in 1964 or whether the view from the White House had inevitably broadened the narrow parochial interests of a regional politician. Either way, Douglas concluded, it seemed best not to worry excessively about politicians' motives but rather to judge them on the consequences of their actions. In fact, the rapprochement between the two Democrats lasted for just a few years, and Douglas believed that the problems of the Johnson administration's last days resulted from the president's reversion to the secretive behavior he had practiced as Senate majority leader. In early 1964, however, Douglas enthusiastically accepted the olive branch extended by Johnson.[5]

Douglas and Johnson first collaborated successfully on civil rights, an issue that had separated them bitterly in past years. "I knew that if I didn't get out in front on this issue," Johnson later told an interviewer, "[the liberals] would get me." In the winter of 1963–1964, the president charged Attorney General Nicholas Katzenbach with revising the civil rights bill John F. Kennedy had unsuccessfully introduced the previous year. The new version invested the Justice Department with the power to enforce antidiscrimination measures in voting and employment as well as to terminate segregation in public education. The Democratic Study Group, a collection of liberals from both the House and the Senate, demanded and received two additional provisions in the civil rights bill—the right of people of all races to be served in places of "public accommodation" and the allocation of federal funds for enforcement of the law. Heavily influenced by the urging of church groups and civil rights organizations, the Democratic Study Group demanded that the bill guarantee nondiscriminatory service in restaurants, hotels, department stores, rest rooms, and other public places, and the administration accepted the additions. Douglas observed that liberals had long been calling for just such empowerment of the federal government, and he eagerly endorsed the new civil rights bill.[6]

Although the dramatic events of the civil rights movement had clearly altered the political climate in the nation and public opinion polls reported that a substantial majority of the population favored passage of more substantial civil rights legislation, liberals realized that southern obstructionists in the Senate could still utilize a formidable array of procedural tricks—especially the filibuster—to deflect the will of the majority. As in the past, the wily Richard Russell needed thirty-four votes to forestall the two-thirds majority necessary for cloture, and that meant the attraction of a dozen votes from senators outside of the South. In 1957 and again in 1960, the redoubtable Russell had worked with the majority leader to dilute civil rights legislation, but in 1964 such cooperation would be impossible. From his post in the White House, Lyndon Johnson led the fight against the southern position with the aid of the new majority leader, Mike Mansfield. Russell knew that the political calculus in the Senate had changed to the detriment of the segregationists' cause.[7]

Fully committed to the passage of the civil rights law, Johnson and his White House staff worked closely day after day with sympathetic Democrats and Republicans in the House of Representatives. As expected, the bill passed there with relative ease, and Johnson and the Democratic leadership prepared for the bitter struggle that they expected to follow in the Senate. The president proclaimed his absolute determination to win the battle regardless of his senatorial opponents' resolve. "They can filibuster until hell freezes over," he said defiantly. "I'm not going to put anything on that floor until this is done." Mansfield plotted strategy in close tandem with Minority Leader Everett M. Dirksen, Douglas's Illinois colleague who had not compiled an impressive record on civil rights but who had decided that public opinion now demanded effective legislation. Civil rights, he said, had become "an issue whose time has come." Mansfield chose Hubert Humphrey, majority whip and one of the Senate's longtime proponents of civil rights, to act as floor manager of the bill. Working with Minority Whip Thomas Kuchel of California, Humphrey tirelessly guided the liberal forces against the filibuster that Russell ordered. Douglas assumed responsibility for the portion of the bill (Title IV) that dealt with the desegregation of public schools; he presented the case for Title IV on the Senate floor and assisted Humphrey in responding to questions about the measure. He also participated fully in strategy sessions and engaged eagerly in floor debates but appeared somewhat less visible than he had in earlier civil rights struggles in the Senate. Pleased that Johnson had been able to forge such bipartisan unity, Douglas readily accepted a secondary role in the 1964 crusade. Humphrey and Russell became the major protagonists in the civil rights drama, with Dirksen, Kuchel, and Mansfield playing the key supporting roles.[8]

The southerners' filibuster dragged on for more than five hundred hours spread across seventy-five days, the longest debate in Senate history, before the administration felt confident enough to invoke Rule XXII. On June 8, 1964, Mansfield and Dirksen filed a cloture petition, and two days later the Senate voted 71–29 to end debate on the civil rights bill. A few days later, the bill passed by a margin of 73–27. The measure outlawed discrimination in public places ranging from theaters and restaurants to hospitals, libraries, and playgrounds. The act threatened the withdrawal of federal funds from schools and other institutions that practiced racial discrimination and authorized the U.S. attorney general to file lawsuits on behalf of parents alleging discrimination in public schools. It also extended the life of the Civil Rights Commission and created a Community Relations Service. On July 2, one year and thirteen days after Kennedy had first requested the legislation from Congress, Johnson signed the historic Civil Rights Act of 1964 in the East Room of the White House. After the signing, the president handed out seventy-two pens as souvenirs to the legislators and other public figures who had been most instrumental in the bill's passage. A smiling Douglas gratefully accepted one.[9]

Despite Douglas's sense of satisfaction, the passage of the Civil Rights Act of 1964 must have been for him somewhat of a bittersweet victory because of the acclaim afforded Everett Dirksen. The national media fulsomely praised the Senate minority leader for his critically important role in stitching together the bipartisan alliance that smashed the southern filibuster. The thirty-three Republicans in the Senate held the key to obtaining cloture, and Dirksen could deliver a number of the votes needed to end the filibuster. As a powerful broker whose opposition could have been lethal, the junior Illinois senator emerged as a surprising hero of the civil rights cause. Previously lampooned as an oleaginous politician who enjoyed bloviating for the galleries and often portrayed as something of a political chameleon, Dirksen suddenly found himself widely praised as a prescient statesman willing to put the national interest before partisan and personal concerns. *Time* magazine put Dirksen's picture on its cover and, hyperbolically claiming that "he practically wrote the [bill]," credited him with engineering the civil rights breakthrough. On the other hand, longtime civil rights advocates appreciated the irony of celebrating the role played by Dirksen. A staunch and lethal opponent of many of the 1964 law's particulars just a few years earlier, the minority leader scrambled aboard the civil rights bandwagon very late in the parade to passage. Although he never publicly complained about the situation, said Illinois Democratic state senator Paul Simon, Douglas privately expressed bemusement at the accolades showered upon such a late convert to the civil rights cause. According to Simon, "Douglas recognized the importance of Dirksen's help, but privately and understandably resented the great attention given to Dirksen for his belated assistance, while Douglas, who had labored so long and so hard for the cause, received almost no mention."[10]

The eleventh-hour assistance provided by Everett Dirksen notwithstanding, Simon argued, "no one other than Martin Luther King is more responsible than Paul Douglas for the passage of the 1964 Civil Rights Act." Simon's claim was based on the judgment that passage of such a legislative landmark would have been impossible without the decade-long preparatory work performed by Douglas, without passage first of the 1957 and 1960 laws that acted as beachheads in the civil rights advance. Throughout much of the 1950s, Douglas stood with a mere handful of liberals in the Senate in his advocacy of civil rights, and their lonely, frustrating crusade proved indispensable. By the mid-1960s, Douglas remained every bit as devoted to racial equality, but he no longer stood out. He was surrounded by the many politicians who had by then embraced the liberal cause. He believed, though, that keeping the issue on the legislative docket year after year, despite continued setbacks, had raised the awareness of a generally indifferent citizenry. While Douglas and his liberal allies had remained steadfast, the congressional leadership of the Democratic party finally turned from outright hostility to wholehearted advocacy. Although he felt that he and other congressional liberals had been shortchanged by the national media, Douglas reveled in the passage of the Civil Rights Act of 1964. He considered the significant role he played in dismantling Jim Crow institutions to be his greatest contribution to national life.[11]

Although the passage of the 1964 law constituted a signal achievement, civil rights activists continued their assault on racial inequality. The leaders of several civil rights organizations noted that, for all its virtues, the 1964 bill failed to guarantee voting rights for African Americans in the South where local registrars continued to employ a variety of methods to disfranchise eligible voters by the thousands. In Mississippi several civil rights groups cooperated to form the Council of Federated Organizations (COFO) with the goal of registering black voters and establishing "Freedom Schools" for African American children. COFO's "Freedom Summer" campaign of 1964 gained national attention as nearly a thousand volunteers, many of them idealistic college students from northern campuses, streamed into the Magnolia State to challenge another incarnation of southern racial inequality. Concerned about preserving Democratic unity in that year's election, President Johnson opposed the Freedom Summer activities and withheld federal protection from the vulnerable activists. As state and local law enforcement officials regularly looked the other way or responded sluggishly to calls for intervention, civil rights foes conducted a campaign of terror in Mississippi, beating eighty volunteers, killing six, shooting three others, and burning or bombing thirty-five homes, churches, and other buildings.[12]

As part of its campaign to secure full political rights for black people, COFO founded the Mississippi Freedom Democratic Party (MFDP) and selected a full slate of delegates to represent the state at that year's Democratic National Convention in Atlantic City, New Jersey. (In contrast to the regular Democratic party's all-white delegation, the MFDP's thirty-four-member delegation included thirty African Americans.) The members of the MFDP group pledged their loyalty to the president and the Democratic platform, whereas the all-white delegation lambasted the Civil Rights Act of 1964 specifically and the party platform generally. Yet, fearful that a walkout of the regular Mississippi delegation would drive out other southern delegations and split the convention over the race issue, Johnson opposed the seating of the MFDP delegation. Instead, he offered a compromise of sorts by which two MFDP members would be seated as at-large representatives of the state along with the regular Mississippi delegation. In addition, the others would be allowed to remain as nonvoting observers, and the party would amend convention rules to prevent racial discrimination in 1968. Although leading liberals like Hubert Humphrey and Walter Reuther and civil rights leaders like Martin Luther King, Jr., and Bayard Rustin urged the MFDP to accept Johnson's offer, the indignant black Mississippians demurred. "We didn't come all this way for no two seats," replied Fannie Lou Hamer, who had emerged as the group's spokeswoman at the convention. The party effected the Johnson compromise even as some white Mississippi and Alabama delegates walked out of the convention hall in protest that the president had even negotiated with the MFDP.[13]

Douglas saw the wrangle over the seating of the MFDP group as a nightmare that seemed to be tearing civil rights forces apart into resentful and bitter factions. He proposed to the convention that, as a better alternative than the deal proffered by the president, both delegations should be seated with each delegate awarded one-half of a vote. He regretted that the party favored the Johnson proposal over his own and that the MFDP refused to accept any compromise. While he acknowledged that the African Americans had made a strong moral case for representing their state, he also felt that the promise of free and nondiscriminatory selection procedures for future conventions constituted a real breakthrough. The whole affair sickened him and provided more evidence that the disfranchisement of African Americans remained an important issue that had to be confronted.[14]

In January 1965, Martin Luther King, Jr., mobilized the Southern Christian Leadership Conference (SCLC) to protest such practices in Selma, Alabama, a city of 29,000 where only 355 of 15,000 blacks of voting age had been allowed to register. After sadistic Alabama law enforcement authorities repeatedly and brutally beat and arrested nonviolent protesters, King organized a protest march from Selma to the state capital of Montgomery fifty-six miles away. On March 7, sheriff's deputies and Alabama state troopers abruptly terminated the procession, wading into the demonstrators and violently driving those who could still walk back to the church where the march originated. The shocking spectacle of "Bloody Sunday" triggered a national outpouring of revulsion and indignation and again brought to the floor of Congress the issue of voting rights.[15]

Even as congressmen and administration aides began discussing the contours of new voting rights legislation, King prepared to lead another demonstration on March 9 in defiance of local authorities. Thousands of people sympathetic to the civil rights cause from around the country rushed to Selma to participate in the second march. Emily Taft Douglas decided to join the demonstration along with Jane Ickes (the widow of Harold Ickes) and another friend. Douglas urged his wife not to go, arguing that no one could guarantee her safety against the irrational southern mob and cruel policemen who would surely confront the marchers, but he could not dissuade her. With grave misgivings, he accompanied Emily and her friends to the airport for their flight to Alabama. "The next thirty-six hours," he recalled, "were frightening." The march began with the senator's wife walking next to King at the head of the procession and continued for only a short distance before, according to a prearranged, secret agreement between King and federal mediators, the marchers turned around and retraced their steps into the city. No violence ensued, and Douglas proudly proclaimed that "the civil-rights groups had won, and my wife had helped." A subsequent march begun on March 21 culminated in thousands of civil rights supporters arriving at Montgomery, the first capital of the Confederacy.[16]

On March 15, in a fiery speech to a joint session of Congress broadcast live on prime-time television, President Johnson called for passage of a new voting rights law. Concluding emotionally, he proclaimed the desperate need for an end to bigotry and injustice and promised that "we shall overcome." Although impressed by Johnson's speech and heartened by the president's inspiring rhetoric, Douglas introduced his own voting rights bill that differed somewhat from the administration's measure. (Douglas's bill banned poll taxes and stipulated that federal action could be triggered in areas where less than one-fourth of voting-age African Americans had been registered to vote by 1964.) When the administration's bill quickly became the focus of congressional attention, however, Douglas pledged his support. The bill passed in the House by a lopsided margin of 333–85. In the Senate, southerners staged a filibuster that lasted for twenty-five days before a cloture vote of 70–30 ended debate; the Senate then passed the bill 77–19. On August 6, Johnson signed the Voting Rights Act of 1965 in the same room of the Capitol where Abraham Lincoln had signed the Emancipation Proclamation just over a century earlier.[17]

During the signing ceremony, Johnson singled Douglas out by calling him to the forefront of the assembled dignitaries and presenting him with a pen—a salute to the senator whose pathbreaking work for voting rights had finally come to fruition. Indeed, those who appreciated irony recognized that one of the key provisions of the 1965 law—the employment of federal voting registrars—had originated with Douglas's 1960 bill and been opposed by Johnson. The Voting Rights Act of 1965, which covered federal, state, and local elections, empowered the Justice Department to eliminate discriminatory registration tests in southern counties where a majority of the voting-age population had been disfranchised and to dispatch federal registrars to ensure compliance. In short, the law did exactly what Douglas had been prescribing for years—insinuating the federal government into southern elections to eradicate the last vestiges of Jim Crow from the polling place.[18]

From 1964 through 1966, Douglas and other liberals vied with conservatives over a related issue, reapportionment. In 1962 the U.S. Supreme Court had issued a ruling in *Baker v. Carr* that mandated the redrawing of state and congressional voting districts to reflect more accurately the population changes that had occurred in the twentieth century. Such a reconfiguration of voting districts by the states inevitably allocated more representation to cities and suburbs at the expense of rural areas—and, conservative defenders of the old political elites feared, more representation for African Americans and other minorities at the expense of white voters. Opponents of the *Baker v. Carr* ruling had proposed amendments to state constitutions that would require apportionment on a population basis in only one of that state's two legislative houses (thereby preserving disproportionate representation for entrenched minorities in state governments). In a 1964 decision, *Reynolds v. Sims,* the Supreme Court had upheld the principle of "one man–one vote" by requiring that the membership of both houses of a bicameral legislature be based on population. At its 1964 national convention, the Republican party had included in its platform a plank calling for a constitutional amendment nullifying the Supreme Court's apportionment decisions. That year the party's presidential candidate, Barry Goldwater, made reapportionment a major issue in his campaign, excoriating the Supreme Court for tyranny in the *Baker* and *Reynolds* cases.[19]

Douglas's interest in reapportionment had originated decades earlier. While teaching at Amherst College in the 1920s, he had started writing a book on the subject but never completed the project. Immediately after the Second World War, he had helped to underwrite the cost of a lawsuit *(Colegrove v. Green)* to compel the Illinois legislature to reapportion congressional seats. The U.S. Supreme Court refused to grant a writ of certiorari, but *Colegrove v. Green* led to similar litigation in a host of states with malapportioned legislatures. Fifteen years later, the Court agreed to consider a suit brought by Nashville residents against the State of Tennessee *(Baker v. Carr)*. Thus, as Douglas saw it, the direct line of descent between the *Colegrove* and *Baker* cases gave him a special interest in upholding the Court's reapportionment rulings.[20]

On July 23, 1964, Everett Dirksen introduced into the Senate a constitutional amendment that reserved for the states the exclusive power to determine the apportionment of their legislatures and expressly provided that only one house of a bicameral legislature be apportioned by population. One day after Dirksen introduced the bill, without even the formality of hearings, the Senate Judiciary Committee approved it by a vote of 10–2. To the dismay of Douglas and other liberals, Senate Majority Leader Mike Mansfield became a cosponsor of the Dirksen amendment (after some modest changes had been incorporated). Afraid that Mansfield could help to muster the kind of bipartisan support that would result in the hasty passage of the amendment, Douglas and a few other Democratic liberals—Joseph Clark of Pennsylvania, Philip Hart of Michigan, Wayne Morse of Oregon, Abraham Ribicoff of Connecticut, and Gaylord Nelson and William Proxmire of Wisconsin—launched a "mild" filibuster against the amendment (they allowed interruptions in the extended debate to consider other legislation). In the course of the debate, Douglas characterized the proposals to overturn the Supreme Court's decisions as the product of "emotion and, in a sense, prejudice." In particular, he attributed the antiapportionment sentiment to "resentment against the Supreme Court for all its civil rights decisions; . . . fear on the part of entrenched, petty peanut politicians that they would not be re-elected to the state legislatures if the districts were properly apportioned."[21]

On September 10, after twelve days of debate, the Senate voted 63–30 to reject a cloture motion introduced by Dirksen. As a means of breaking the impasse, Senators Hubert Humphrey, Jacob Javits of New York, and Eugene McCarthy of Minnesota introduced a "sense of Congress amendment" suggesting that the states be given time by the courts to comply with the recent Supreme Court reapportionment rulings and to consider possible constitutional amendments recommended by Congress regarding apportionment in state legislatures. Calling the Humphrey-Javits-McCarthy substitute measure "an abject thing" without "a binding word" in it, Dirksen urged its rejection, and on September 15 a coalition of Republicans and southern Democrats did so by a vote of 42–40. Senator Strom Thurmond (Democrat, South Carolina) then substituted for the Dirksen-Mansfield amendment an even more extreme measure that had earlier passed the House, introduced by Representative William M. Tuck (Democrat, Virginia). The Tuck bill denied the authority of federal or state courts to deal in any way with apportionment issues in the states. Douglas argued that acceptance of the Tuck bill would deny the Supreme Court the power to invoke the Fourteenth Amendment's equal protection clause, as it had done in the reapportionment cases. "The choice between the Tuck bill and the Dirksen amendment is similar to the choice between being killed by hanging and being killed by shooting," concluded Douglas. "And I reject both methods." The Senate defeated the Tuck bill, 56–21.[22]

On September 23, to end the "gross impotence and demeaning futility" that had pervaded the Senate since August 13, Mansfield offered his own "sense of Congress amendment" as a substitute for the Dirksen-Mansfield rider. The compromise, an attachment to a foreign aid authorization bill, urged (but did not order) federal district courts to allow the states up to six months to comply with reapportionment directives. Predicting that the courts would ignore such a nonbinding directive from Congress, Dirksen opposed the measure; for the very same reason, Douglas voted for it. The innocuous proposal carried by voice vote in the Senate, but the House-Senate conference rejected the Mansfield rider, and the foreign aid authorization bill became law without mention of reapportionment. Dirksen promised to resurrect the issue when Congress reconvened the next year.[23]

In 1965 Dirksen again took the offensive, introducing in the Judiciary Committee a constitutional amendment that permitted the states to apportion seats in one house of their legislatures according to factors other than population. When he failed to garner a favorable vote, the majority leader sought to bypass the committee by attaching his constitutional amendment on the Senate floor to a joint resolution of Congress creating a National American Legion Baseball Week. Again Douglas led the opposition, this time joined most prominently by Joseph Clark, William Proxmire, Birch Bayh of Indiana, and Joseph Tydings of Maryland. As well, the Senate liberals received support from urban-based industrial unions and consumer groups. Calling the Dirksen amendment "the 'stalking horse' of those who wish to preserve the rotten borough system in the state legislatures of the United States," Douglas argued that the people possessed an inalienable right to approximate equality of representation, a right that could not be surrendered in a popular referendum. He warned that if the Senate approved Dirksen's profoundly undemocratic scheme the malapportioned state legislatures would ratify the amendment and then draft the reapportionment plans for submission to the voters. Under such a design, conservative defenders of the status quo could easily protect their own entrenched interests. In a tense roll call vote conducted on August 4, the fifty-nine affirmative votes cast in the Senate fell seven shy of the two-thirds majority necessary for passage of a constitutional amendment. Within days, however, Dirksen successfully forced a new reapportionment bill out of committee and onto the Senate calendar for consideration in the next year's session.[24]

True to his word, in 1966 Dirksen championed reapportionment for the third year in a row, forming the Committee for Government of the People and introducing another constitutional amendment into the Senate; again, Douglas led the opposing forces. With forty-six of the fifty states having already reapportioned their legislatures to meet the Supreme Court's strictures, both supporters and opponents of the Dirksen measure thought it likely in 1966 that the Senate was considering the constitutional amendment for the last time. In his closing arguments against the amendment, Douglas criticized his opponents as defenders of privilege who feared state legislatures that truly represented the populace. Private utility companies, corporations opposed to organized labor, and financial interests seeking to avoid the payment of their share of taxes—these forces, he charged, had underwritten the campaign for legislative reapportionment. On April 20, after a week of debate, the Senate voted and again fell seven votes short of the two-thirds majority necessary for passage.[25]

Three times defeated in Congress, the advocates of reapportionment took another tack by conducting a public relations campaign in the hope of calling a special national convention. By 1969, thirty-three state legislatures (one short of the necessary two-thirds) had called for a national convention to consider reapportionment, but the movement ebbed after Dirksen's death that year and never achieved success. Douglas remained convinced that reapportionment would have been profoundly harmful to American democracy and took great pride in having played a major role in its legislative defeat. At the same time, he predicted that rapid suburban growth would benefit conservative Republicans in the future. He foresaw the formation in state legislatures of anticity blocs composed of rural and suburban interests largely indifferent to the pressing urban problems of poverty, crime, race, housing, and unemployment. "The domestic future of the country," he warned a few years later, "now depends largely on whether the suburbs will recognize and carry out a common program for dealing with metropolitan problems, both urban and suburban."[26]

The struggle over reapportionment underscored the tension that existed between Douglas and Dirksen. The two Illinois senators maintained a distant, proper relationship that reflected the vast differences in their political philosophies; they conferred infrequently and rarely cooperated on legislation of interest to the people of their home state. Beneath their surface cordiality, Douglas and members of his staff held Dirksen in low esteem. (Howard Shuman said of the Republican's abilities: "He was born to be a funeral orator.") Because they hailed from the same state, a natural rivalry developed between the two men—one a devout liberal and the other a passionate conservative. Dismissive of the notion that Dirksen's chummy, clubhouse style of politics produced better results than his own independent style, Douglas took great pleasure in winning the head-to-head battles over reapportionment in 1964–1966.[27]

While marshaling liberal forces in the Senate to combat the threat posed by reapportionment, Douglas continued to work for the causes he had advanced in previous years. Most gratifying to him, the long struggle to preserve a portion of the Indiana Dunes finally ended in success. On September 29, 1964, the Senate passed Douglas's bill to establish the

11,292-acre Indiana Dunes National Lakeshore and authorized $23 million for the necessary land acquisition at a site somewhat distant from the proposed harbor at Burns Ditch. By this compromise, Douglas had obtained the agreement of the Birmingham and National steel companies that would lose prime land but not the section they most coveted. The site approved by the Senate included a tract of land owned by the Inland Steel Company, which fought against the compromise. In the House of Representatives, Minority Leader Charles Halleck remained opposed to the creation of any national park on the Lake Michigan shoreline, and the legislative session ended before the bill could be brought to a vote.[28]

In 1965 Douglas stipulated that funds appropriated for the construction of the Burns Waterway Harbor be contingent upon the establishment of a dunes national lakeshore. He received the support of Indiana's two senators, Democrats Birch Bayh and Vance Hartke, both of whom supported the national lakeshore as well as the harbor, and again the dunes bill passed with relative ease. In the House Public Works Committee, however, Charles Halleck succeeded in divorcing the national lakeshore and the harbor project—a condition absolutely unacceptable to Douglas, who feared that his opponents would pass legislation creating a harbor but no parkland. Douglas and Bayh devised compromise language that blocked appropriation of federal funds for harbor construction until both the Senate and the House had a chance to vote on the Indiana Dunes and harbor bills during the same congressional session. Such language stopped short of requiring the passage of a dunes bill before a harbor could be built but ensured that no House committees could forestall consideration of Douglas's legislation.[29]

In a February 23, 1966, message to Congress on conservation and recreation, President Johnson requested that legislation be passed creating fourteen new national parks and lakeshores—including the Indiana Dunes National Lakeshore. Even with administration support, however, passage of a bill in the House remained problematic because of Halleck's determined opposition. With the intervention of Vice President Hubert Humphrey and Speaker of the House John McCormack, the bill moved successfully from the Rules Committee to the House floor. Still, the bill may have failed had not Halleck committed a strategic error: On October 11, seeing that supporters of the bill lacked sufficient votes for passage, McCormack asked for a postponement on the vote until the 14th and an inattentive Halleck inexplicably agreed. On the latter date, a number of liberal Democrats who had been in their home districts campaigning for reelection returned to the Capitol to vote on the administration's controversial demonstration cities bill and provided the winning margin for the dunes bill. Halleck's foul-up resulted in the measure's passage. The legislation authorized the establishment of the Indiana Dunes National Lakeshore on 8,721 acres (including 478 acres owned by the Inland Steel Company) in Porter and La Porte Counties thirty-five miles from Chicago and appropriated $27.9 million for land acquisition. President Johnson signed the bill on November 5, 1966, more than eight years after Douglas introduced the first measure to save the dunes, and commented: "It took the foresight and determination of the 89th Congress—and the tireless of work of Senator Paul Douglas—to save the last remaining portion of this lakeshore area. . . . Our entire nation is made richer by this Act I have signed today."[30]

The eight-year struggle to save the dunes ended not in absolute victory but in the kind of qualified success that Douglas had learned characterized the give-and-take of national politics. Reluctantly, he and the other conservationists had had to reconcile themselves to the fact that the national lakeshore would not be located precisely at the site that they had originally selected, and they had to accept as the price of obtaining the natural refuge the creation of a new harbor nearby that would serve an expanding industrial region. Congressional delay had resulted in the incremental loss, year after year, of sections of unspoiled wilderness to industrial expansion and residential development, so that the national lakeshore finally created by law presented a sharp contrast with a surrounding environment that had grown more cluttered over the years. Still, despite the limitations imposed on his legislative triumph, Douglas celebrated the preservation of a significant portion of the Indiana Dunes. It had been a great achievement, he felt. In later years, Douglas often laughingly told of how, when he first went to Congress, he had hoped to save the world. After he had been there several years, he just hoped to save the country. By the end of his career in the Senate, he concluded, he just wanted to save the Indiana Dunes. In limited fashion, he did.[31]

Douglas continued to work for another of his perennials, truth-in-lending legislation, but with less satisfactory results. President Johnson endorsed the bill shortly after taking office with the stipulation that truth in lending be administered by the Federal Trade Commission; Douglas, who had designated the Federal Reserve Board as the appropriate supervisory agency, readily concurred with the change as a necessary cost of obtaining the administration's support. As in previous years, the bill ran headlong into the opposition of the powerful chairman of the Senate's Banking and Currency Committee, A. Willis Robertson (Democrat, Virginia). The Production and Stabilization Subcommittee, chaired by Douglas, passed the bill by a vote of 5–4 on March 16, 1964. The next day, Robertson wrote Douglas enumerating the bill's many defects and concluded by saying: "I intend to cooperate with you to bring the bill before the full Committee in plenty of time for action this session, with the expectation that, when the members of the Committee have had an opportunity to review the extensive hearings, the bill will be rejected by the Committee." Yet, despite Robertson's promise to allow the full committee to consider truth in lending, Douglas bristled as two months went by without action. On May 21, he sent Robertson a tart letter of protest, saying:

> I do not believe that the Committee can continue to be run in such a way as to favor those bills that the chairman personally favors and to hinder action on those bills which I and others on the Committee may favor, but which the chairman opposes. The issue . . . is not the truth-in-lending bill or any other bill before the Committee, but simply the question of fair committee procedure and adequate guidelines to insure that all members are treated equitably.

Douglas added that he would seek consideration of the bill at the next regularly scheduled committee meeting on May 25. On the Senate floor, Robertson called Douglas's letter "very bitter if not insulting" and expressed his indignation at its contents. He also canceled the May 25 committee meeting. When the committee finally met on June 23, its membership recommitted the bill to the Production and Stabilization Subcommittee, effectively sidetracking it for the balance of the congressional session.[32]

In 1965 Chairman Robertson utilized a new tactic to derail truth-in-lending legislation. When the new Congress convened following the previous year's elections, the Banking and Currency Committee membership changed to ten Democrats and four Republicans to reflect the new Democratic majority of 68–32 in the Senate. Instead of conforming to the five–two ratio of Democrats to Republicans in forming subcommittees, however, Robertson selected seven Democrats and three Republicans. Because the new committees contained ten members rather than seven, the possibility of tie votes existed—and ties defeated bills in subcommittees. To the Production and Stabilization Subcommittee, which would consider truth-in-lending legislation, Robertson assigned Republicans Wallace F. Bennett of Utah, John G. Tower of Texas, and Strom Thurmond of South Carolina, all proven opponents of Douglas's bill. Along with five liberal Democrats, he assigned himself and Edward V. Long of Missouri, a conservative banker and owner of a savings and loan establishment who opposed any economic regulation of credit by government. The new configuration of the subcommittee inevitably resulted in a tie vote on the Douglas bill and therefore a negative recommendation to the entire committee.[33]

Reporting that financial institutions had extended approximately $75 billion in installment credit to consumers in 1965 alone, President Johnson recommended at the outset of the 1966 legislative session that Congress pass effective truth-in-lending legislation. Although Johnson declined to introduce a consumer credit bill, administration spokesmen indicated that the 1965 Douglas bill would be satisfactory. Even with the strongest presidential endorsement to date, though, the Senate Banking and Currency Committee again failed to take action. Having been defeated in the Democratic primary election that year, A. Willis Robertson spent his lame duck session in the Senate working as hard as ever against truth in lending. By the end of 1966, Douglas seemed no closer to breaking the impasse.[34]

Douglas's continuing battle for tax reform produced mixed results. In 1964 the Senate Finance Committee approved a bill passed in the House that lowered the corporation income tax rate over a two-year period from the standard rate of 52 percent to 48 percent. Douglas had introduced an amendment to lower the rate only to 50 percent and to use the revenue saved to reduce certain federal excise taxes, but the committee had opted by a vote of 11–2 for the House formula. The committee also rejected a provision in the House bill that would have lowered the rate on capital gains; in alliance with President Johnson, who sought to hold the capital gains tax rate steady, Douglas carried the battle onto the Senate floor. At his insistence, the full Senate voted on the capital gains cut, the only one of the 153 amendments recommended by the Finance Committee to be considered separately. Douglas asked for a formal roll call vote so that the strength of the opposition to a reduction would limit the chances of the House conferees restoring the capital gains tax cut at a later stage. The Senate passed the bill 77–21, and the successful fight to forestall any reduction in capital gains taxes made the law more palatable to Douglas.[35]

As in previous years, Douglas devoted most of his time to domestic legislation while advocating generous expenditures for a strong national defense. At a time when many liberals openly questioned President Johnson's decision to wage war in Vietnam, Douglas firmly supported the administration's policies in Southeast Asia. He attributed the rising level of protest against the war on college campuses to the impetuousness of youth. He also expressed dismay at the influence of the New Left antiwar movement upon the Americans for Democratic Action (ADA), an organization with which he had been closely affiliated for years. In his view, the strength of the organization had always been its dedication to the principle that communism posed a serious danger to democratic societies, and he feared that that steadfastness appeared to be eroding. His continued involvement in the affairs of the ADA, he wrote John Kenneth Galbraith, would be conditional upon a firm "non-Communist, anti-Communist, anti-totalitarian pledge as a requirement for membership."[36]

As an unreconstructed nationalist, Douglas also took a highly publicized stand in 1965 against what he considered to be the anti-American pronouncements and actions of French president Charles De Gaulle. In

Douglas's view, De Gaulle had committed a number of offenses against the United States, including the refusal to dispatch an adequate number of French troops to North Atlantic Treaty Organization (NATO) armies, the recognition of the People's Republic of China and North Vietnam, and the obstruction of cooperative trade relationships between the United States and the European Common Market. The most egregious transgression, Douglas believed, came when De Gaulle ordered state-controlled French banks to demand payment of $400 million of gold in 1964 and an additional $544 million in 1965 from the U.S. treasury. While France was entitled to demand payment of these debts in gold, Douglas argued, such action by a purported ally was shocking—especially because much of the adverse balance of payments in the United States owed to the extensive post–World War II expenditures on military aid and economic assistance from which France had benefited. In response to De Gaulle's actions, Douglas recommended a discontinuation of aid to former French colonies, limitations on the travel of U.S. citizens in France, the reduction of U.S. forces in NATO armies, and an insistence that France repay its World War I debts, which had been long since forgotten but technically not forgiven. Relations between the De Gaulle regime and the United States remained strained during the Johnson presidency, and Douglas continued to urge a tough policy against the French.[37]

In addition to the work he did for his own causes, Douglas avidly backed many of Johnson's Great Society measures. Long a supporter of federal health care for the aged, Douglas became one of the foremost advocates in the Senate for the administration's Medicare bill, which had narrowly failed to pass in 1964 and was reintroduced in 1965. The bill's basic health plan increased taxes for social security—and required some deductions—to subsidize hospitalization and nursing care for people over the age of sixty-five, providing up to ninety days of hospital care, one hundred days of nursing-home care, one hundred home-health-care visits, and outpatient diagnostic service. The bill's supplementary health plan paid 80 percent of the cost of a variety of health services after a $50 annual deduction. Douglas lamented that the bill did not provide fully for the payment of physicians' or surgeons' fees and wished that Medicare could provide for longer hospital stays, medical treatment outside of hospitals, and more generous stipends so that patients could avoid deductible payments, but he supported the administration's bill as the best that could be obtained at the time. He scoffed at the American Medical Association's characterization of Medicare as socialized medicine, noting that physicians would still be individually hired and individually compensated. Indeed, he predicted, medical doctors would profit handsomely under the new law because of the increased volume of cases available for treatment. Patients formerly treated as indigents would be charged regular prices, for the government and not the individual would be responsible for payment. The same would be true for Medicaid, the companion legislation that offered the states federal funds for medical treatment of indigent patients of all ages.[38]

After passage in the House, the Medicare bill went to the Senate Finance Committee where Douglas quickly became embroiled in a heated battle over the issue of specialist payments. With the encouragement of the White House, he offered an amendment supporting the American Hospital Association against the American Medical Association (AMA) in a dispute that bitterly divided the health care industry. Citing the need to reduce the financial burden on aged persons for medical care, Douglas's amendment specified that charges by RAPP (Radiologists, Anesthesiologists, Pathologists, and Physiatrists) specialists would be covered by the basic health insurance plan only when billed through hospitals. The AMA condemned the amendment for proposing to make these specialists "coerced employees." As an AMA lobbyist informed the Finance Committee, "Medical care is the responsibility of physicians, not hospitals." Testifying in favor of the measure, which would limit Medicare's price tag, the general counsel for the Department of Health, Education, and Welfare pointed out that the specialists normally enjoyed a monopoly of hospital business yet sought the status of independent practitioners while avoiding the competition to which other practitioners were subjected. The Finance Committee members agreed and approved the Douglas amendment. Later, the House-Senate Conference Committee agreed to payment of RAPP specialists under the supplementary Medicare plan rather than the basic plan.[39]

The thorny question of specialist payments having been decided, Douglas admitted to making "the second big mistake of my senatorial career." Russell Long of Louisiana, the ranking Democrat on the committee, submitted an amendment that removed the sixty-day limit on Medicare coverage for elderly patients with catastrophic illnesses. Believing Long to be ingenuous in his presentation to the committee, Douglas joined the majority in approving the amendment by an 8–6 margin. Disconcerted by the fact that the committee's staunch opponents of the bill had all voted with him, Douglas immediately returned to his office and began to reconsider his vote. Calculating the number of elderly people in the population and the daily costs of hospital care, he quickly realized that the Long amendment would be financially untenable. Worse, he felt, the amendment would "turn the nation's hospitals into warehouses for the senile." Attaching such costly requirements to the bill had been a way of making Medicare so expensive that taxpayers would find it unacceptable. "I saw that I had made a mistake," Douglas lamented. "I simply hadn't understood the proposal."[40]

Douglas returned to the committee, announced that he had made a mistake in voting for the Long amendment, and called for a reconsideration. Because of an irregularity in counting proxy ballots, the committee readily agreed to another vote. (Just as he had done with the McCarran internal security bill fifteen years earlier, Douglas believed, he had been afforded the opportunity to rectify a serious mistake.) When the second vote resulted in defeat for the disputed amendment, Long successfully introduced an alternative measure imposing a ten-dollar-a-day deductible that Douglas and other liberals voted against. Even with that unfortunate addition, Douglas voted to recommend the bill to the entire Senate where it passed by a vote of 68–21. President Johnson took Douglas and several other influential legislators to Independence, Missouri, for the signing of the bill in the presence of Harry S Truman, who had fought unsuccessfully for an early form of Medicare fifteen years earlier. The National Council of Senior Citizens recognized Douglas and Clinton Anderson of New Mexico as the two senators most responsible for securing the law's passage.[41]

Douglas recognized the law's imperfections and hoped that they could be corrected in the future. He regretted that the cost of prescription medicine had not been included in Medicare benefits and feared that the failure to affix upper limits on the services performed by medical personnel would lead to spiraling costs in health care. He found most immediately disturbing the expressions of anger and disappointment by physicians and the attendant rumors that these doctors would refuse to accept Medicare patients or otherwise seek to sabotage the new program. In a speech delivered shortly after the law's signing, he said:

> We've had a lot of reports about doctors planning to raise their fees so that the "reasonable" charges prevailing in their area would be higher. Of course, as soon as the bill was passed, they said it would never work and that the administration would be to blame for its failure. We'll know where the blame lies—and so will the people. The doctors of this country say they have a sacred trust. I hope they keep it.[42]

In 1966 Douglas also agreed to serve as Senate spokesman for another important administration bill, the controversial "open occupancy" bill. Douglas had introduced a civil rights bill on February 10 that dealt with jury selection in civil rights cases, civil indemnification for plaintiffs in civil rights cases, and extension of FEPC provisions, but failed to deal with racial discrimination in housing. Increasingly, he devoted his time to the administration bill, a less comprehensive measure that focused on the question of de facto segregation resulting from discriminatory real estate practices. As long as potential buyers and tenants were turned away because of their race, Douglas noted, racial segregation would be perpetuated not only in housing but also in education. If northerners condemned the South for failure to comply expediently with recent

Supreme Court decisions and legislative advances, they must be prepared to address the festering problems associated with de facto segregation in big cities such as Chicago, Detroit, and Cleveland.[43]

While Douglas argued the merits of open housing in the Senate Judiciary Committee, the House passed a version of the administration's bill that applied only to dwellings containing more than four units. Recognizing that such legislation exempted single-family dwellings and would therefore have little impact on the residential suburbs where racial segregation was most firmly entrenched, Douglas and other liberals expressed their disappointment but reluctantly endorsed the House measure. On the Senate floor, open occupancy encountered the full force of a bipartisan anti–civil rights coalition that had lost to the liberals in 1964 and 1965 but remained a formidable opponent. Leading the forces arrayed against additional civil rights legislation, Everett Dirksen characterized the bill as an unwarranted attack on property rights. So recently an indispensable leader in the coalition that made passage of landmark civil rights laws possible, Dirksen seemed to be guided by what Douglas termed his "weathervane sensitivity" in determining that open housing was not an idea whose time had come. Without the influence of the Senate minority leader, the bill's supporters could not muster the votes to break the filibuster mounted by southerners. Although Douglas estimated that the liberals had the votes to pass the open housing bill, the filibuster prevented a vote from being taken in 1966.[44]

That year the Johnson administration also sent to Congress the Demonstration Cities (Model Cities) Act, which Wright Patman (Democrat, Texas) and Douglas introduced in the House and the Senate, respectively. The bill, an ambitious attempt to address the problems plaguing the nation's blighted cities, authorized grants to participating communities for 80 percent of the cost of programs involving housing and neighborhood renovation, health care, education, crime prevention, and recreation; the president estimated the total cost of the six-year program to be $2.3 billion. Throughout the spring and early summer months of 1966, the administration experienced great difficulty in finding a senator willing to steer the bill through committee and serve as its floor manager. Although Douglas had introduced the bill, he faced a difficult reelection campaign that year and expressed concern about being closely associated with such a volatile measure at that time. John Sparkman of Alabama, the Senate's other leading spokesman for liberal housing legislation, likewise stood for reelection that year; eventually, the task fell to Edmund Muskie (Democrat, Maine). Douglas voted for the bill and spoke in its behalf on the Senate floor but understood the wisdom of having Muskie assume the high profile role of floor manager.[45]

Although Douglas had won his three previous senatorial elections by generous margins, he expected a very different situation in 1966. In talking with voters and other politicians, he feared that the political pendulum in the United States was beginning to swing rightward. Already he discerned a reaction against the Great Society measures passed by Congress in the previous two years, as evidenced by the fierce resistance to the open housing law in Washington and indeed throughout the land. White flight to the suburbs, in part a reaction to the liberal legislation of recent years, guaranteed the continued separation of the races. Crises had erupted along Chicago's affluent North Shore when two suburbs, Deerfield and Kenilworth, attempted to exclude blacks and Jews from purchasing homes. Martin Luther King, Jr.'s attempt to take his civil rights campaign into the urban North met fierce resistance in Chicago where white ethnic homeowners in the bungalow belts staged ugly, violent counterdemonstrations, and Mayor Richard J. Daley defended the turf of his white constituents. Douglas needed to look no further than his own backyard to view the first manifestations of white backlash to the Great Society.[46]

As Douglas clearly saw, political reaction, resurgent Republicanism, and suburban sprawl mixed together to form a combustible compound that portended ill for liberal Democrats, and, again, the evidence was very visible in Illinois. By 1965, while the population of Chicago had remained fairly steady at approximately 3.5 million, the number of people residing in suburban Cook County had risen to an estimated 2 million. The population of neighboring DuPage County, whose leaders proudly identified it as the nation's strongest Republican county, neared 500,000, and the other collar counties, McHenry and Lake, experienced comparable growth rates. The explosive population increase of suburban Chicago in the postwar era meant that by the mid-1960s, two-thirds of the state's people resided within fifty miles of that city's central business district; fully half of those people lived in the suburbs, and the number was growing. Would these suburbanites exercise their growing influence at the polls in 1966 by returning one of the Senate's premier liberals to Washington for another six years? Douglas secretly admitted to having doubts.[47]

As a candidate for a fourth term, Douglas also suspected that his age would be a liability. At age seventy-four, he enjoyed good health generally and continued to work twelve-hour days in the Senate. In fact, he noted, his health in 1966 probably was much better than it had been during his 1954 campaign when he suffered from undulant fever. Still, he acknowledged, "I could not quarrel with my birth certificate." And, as he also freely admitted, his white hair, craggy features, and poor posture gave the impression of a man descending rapidly into old age. Political columnist Stewart Alsop noted that "sometimes, when he is tired after a long day, [Douglas's] face seems to fall, like a bloodhound's, and he looks older than his age." If he won reelection in 1966, he would be eighty years old when his fourth term ended—a fact that would no doubt concern some voters. Finally, he suspected that, in their senatorial primary, the Republicans had bypassed State Treasurer William J. Scott in favor of forty-seven-year-old Charles H. Percy at least in part to draw a sharp contrast between their youthful candidate and the septuagenarian incumbent.[48]

Douglas had run against Republicans of modest distinction in his three earlier senatorial campaigns, but, as he clearly recognized, Charles Percy would be a formidable opponent. Matinee idol handsome, articulate, wealthy, and ambitious, Percy seemed like the perfect candidate to topple a liberal Democratic icon like Douglas. Percy came from a well-to-do family, but his father had lost a fortune in the stock market crash of 1929. After working his way through the University of Chicago—and, he claimed, enrolling in an economics class taught by Professor Douglas— Percy went to work at the Bell and Howell Camera Company and shot up the corporate ladder to become its president at the age of twenty-nine. During his meteoric rise to the top, he had elevated Bell and Howell from an obscure firm with modest assets to a multinational corporation and had become a legend in American business circles. He had also become good friends with Dwight D. Eisenhower and helped the national Republican party with such tasks as fund-raising and platform writing. In short order, leading Republicans were touting the "boy wonder" of Illinois as presidential material subject to his winning one of the major elective offices in the state. In 1964 Percy ran for governor and lost narrowly to incumbent Otto Kerner while outpolling Republican presidential candidate Barry Goldwater in Illinois by more than a half-million votes. Almost immediately after that loss, Percy began campaigning for the Senate seat held by Douglas, and Republicans nationwide lent their moral and financial support.[49]

Feeling uncharacteristically vulnerable and facing the prospect of having to wage a draining campaign against a tough opponent, Douglas seriously considered retirement from the Senate. When Congress adjourned in 1965, he toured Illinois to discuss issues and sound out the voters about his possible reelection. He reported having received a gracious reception everywhere in the state, including promises of financial contributions for the upcoming campaign. Mayor Richard J. Daley pledged the full resources of the Chicago Democratic machine, a vital necessity for winning a statewide election. Most important in convincing Douglas to run again, he said, was his desire to conclude a number of crusades left unfinished. In January 1966, when he announced his intention to seek reelection, legislation saving the Indiana Dunes had still not been secured, and the fate of truth in lending remained in jeopardy. He saw Medicare as incomplete and intended to introduce complementary legislation that would add the cost of prescription drugs to a list of benefits provided the elderly. He also believed in the necessity of additional civil rights legislation and feared the erosion of progress in that area if the Republicans secured majorities in the House and Senate. Unfinished business overrode his reluctance to enter a bruising campaign, and Douglas agreed to seek reelection.[50]

In the early stages of the campaign, Douglas explicated fully the achievements of his eighteen years in Washington and spoke repeatedly about the Democratic successes of the Kennedy and Johnson presidencies. Economic growth in the 1960s had far outpaced the recession-riddled Eisenhower years, he contended, and as an economist who had been urging the aggressive use of fiscal as well as monetary policy since the 1950s he could claim some of the credit for the increased production of goods and services. Illinois citizens had benefited from this economic growth, he reminded the voters, for factory workers in Chicago, Rockford, Peoria, and other industrial communities took home fatter paychecks just as the state's farmers earned higher prices as a consequence of what he termed Democratic prosperity. At the same time that able-bodied wage earners improved their economic conditions, Douglas proudly proclaimed, he had personally advanced the cause of society's unfortunates for whom government often served as the provider of last resort. More public housing for the indigent, Medicare and Medicaid for the sick, area redevelopment for chronically depressed regions, and civil rights for African Americans constituted a partial list of the liberal laws he had successfully championed. His record certainly impressed those who approved of Great Society liberalism. He was, Martin Luther King, Jr., said, "the greatest of all senators."[51]

To offset Douglas's estimable reputation, Percy presented himself as a youthful innovator who would bring energy and new ideas to the Senate. Dressing informally on the campaign trail with his collar unbuttoned, swimming in Lake Michigan, and dancing for hours at ethnic festivals, he seemed to be taking every opportunity to underscore his youth and vigor. Concerned about the age issue, Douglas brought Robert Kennedy into Illinois to campaign in his behalf. Unfortunately, felt Paul Simon, the picture of the boyish-looking Kennedy and Douglas standing side by side may have dramatically reinforced the significant difference in their ages. An Illinois Democrat suggested the hiring of a young woman to file a paternity suit against Douglas. "It will eliminate the age issue overnight," the party loyalist assured Simon. Douglas demurred. Nevertheless, the age issue continued to nettle the Douglas campaign, which countered by seeking to portray Percy's youth and inexperience as liabilities. "There's a young man in a hurry," said Emily Taft Douglas of her husband's opponent, "lacking political convictions and political experience but trying to start his political career at the top. That might be nice for the young man, but why should Illinois swap a record of achievement for shifting promises?"[52]

Percy's campaign initially focused on two related issues, flaws in the economy and Douglas's support of U.S. intervention in Vietnam. To Democratic claims of spectacular economic growth, low unemployment, and higher wages, Percy responded with statistics outlining an 8 percent increase in the cost of living during the Johnson years. While Douglas dismissed concerns about the rising inflation rate with repeated references to the general level of prosperity, Percy campaign workers distributed to housewives shopping bags emblazoned with the slogan, "Fight High Prices." Expect an end to good economic times, Percy warned Illinois voters, for the Democrats had purchased gaudy economic growth rates at consumers' expense. The situation would surely worsen, because President Johnson's steady escalation of the war in Vietnam indicated his stubborn insistence on having generous quantities of guns and butter at the same time. As an alternative to a deepening American presence in Southeast Asia, Percy vaguely called for a meeting of Asian powers, including the People's Republic of China, to settle the questions of sovereignty in Vietnam. His proposal for an All-Asian Peace Conference on Vietnam generated considerable discussion during the campaign, but Percy never responded to requests for more specificity.[53]

Although polling results indicated that Percy's condemnation of the Johnson administration's Vietnam policy resonated with a significant and growing number of voters, Douglas never wavered in his support of the president. He wholly endorsed the policy of halting communist aggression everywhere and believed that a failure to do so in Vietnam would result in the consequent loss of India, Indonesia, the Philippines, and Japan. He recognized the need to exercise caution in order to curtail direct involvement by the Soviet Union and the People's Republic of China but nevertheless insisted that the threat to Southeast Asia necessitated a firm U.S. response. His blueprint for U.S. involvement in South Vietnam specifically favored the restriction of bombing to military targets and opposed an invasion of North Vietnam. In short, he endorsed the steps taken by President Johnson in 1965–1966. "I am as much opposed to the bombing of the people of Hanoi and the use of nuclear bombs," he summarized, "as I am to putting our tail between our legs and scuttling out of South Viet Nam." Douglas knew that his unequivocal stand on Vietnam troubled many voters on the left, especially young people on college campuses, but he insisted on facing the issue squarely and often in his campaign. Believing that candidates should not just tell their audiences what they wanted to hear, he ignored his aides' advice and went out of his way to address the Vietnam situation in all of his campaign addresses—and at greatest length in front of the most hostile groups.[54]

By the fourth of July, the polls showed Douglas and Percy running even, but thereafter two developments shifted public opinion toward the Republican. In the first, a series of events in Chicago elevated the cause of civil rights to the forefront of the campaign—ironically with negative consequences for Douglas. In July a race riot in Chicago led Mayor Daley to summon the National Guard, and even after the restoration of order a residue of bitterness remained in the city. The situation worsened in August when Martin Luther King, Jr., and his followers staged a series of protest marches in white neighborhoods of the Northwest and Southwest Sides that staunchly opposed integration. Embattled white homeowners, who had invariably supported Mayor Daley's Democratic machine in the past and could normally have been expected to vote for Douglas, expressed their displeasure at the senator's racial liberalism. The tense civil rights confrontations in the summer of 1966 left many whites uneasy about the direction the civil rights movement seemed to be heading, an uneasiness that Republicans skillfully exploited. Speaking for Percy at the Illinois State Fair on September 20, Michigan congressman Gerald Ford's remarks invoked the spirit of the rising white backlash in the country. He asked, "How long are we going to abdicate law and order—the backbone of any civilization—in favor of a soft social theory that the man who heaves a brick through your window or tosses a firebomb into your car is simply the misunderstood and underprivileged product of a broken home?"[55]

At the same time, militant blacks criticized Douglas for not having marched alongside King in Chicago and suggested that his shopworn liberalism had outlived its usefulness in the expanding civil rights struggle. The Reverend James Bevel, King's chief of staff in the Chicago campaign, underscored the militants' dissatisfaction with the Democrats, saying: "We are going to march until every white man in the suburbs votes Republican." Specifically asked whom he favored in the Illinois senate race, Bevel answered, "the younger man." Noting that the Percy forces had quickly taken advantage of the racial unrest in Chicago, Douglas lamented: "They are trying to get the young Negroes to oppose me on the ground that I haven't done enough, and to get the Whites to oppose me on the ground that I had done too much."[56]

By the end of August, open occupancy—or, as Douglas called it, "freedom of residence"—had become the most volatile issue of the campaign. Having been a cosponsor of the administration's civil rights bill earlier that year and having testified in favor of the bill's open housing provision, he could hardly equivocate as the controversy in Congress played out in his home city. Douglas continued to argue passionately that persons of good standing should not be denied the opportunity to acquire decent housing solely on the basis of their race; such discrimination simply contradicted the tenets of the Constitution's Bill of Rights, he affirmed. To the consternation of his advisers, Douglas seemed to take a perverse pleasure in proclaiming that position in front of the most antagonistic audiences. When speaking before notoriously conservative business groups and white homeowners associations, he insisted on confronting the issue straightforwardly and even in many cases making it the centerpiece of his remarks.[57]

Percy approached the open housing issue much differently. During the 1964 campaign, he had opposed a statewide open occupancy law and promised to veto any such measure if elected governor. At the outset of the 1966 senatorial campaign, however, Percy announced that he had changed his view and accepted the necessity of open housing legislation. Yet later that summer, as the issue became a lightning rod for white backlash sentiments, he modified his position by advocating open housing restrictions only on buildings with more than six units and thereby exempting the predominantly Republican suburbs. Percy told Republican loyalists that his opponent simply wanted to go "too far and too fast." Douglas and his aides charged that Percy continued to advocate open occupancy while addressing black audiences but pledged his opposition to residential desegregation while speaking to white suburban groups. They also suspected that Percy knew about and never took any action to curb a covert Republican campaign (based upon word of mouth and the secret distribution of leaflets) to tarnish the Democrats on the open housing issue. A frustrated Douglas stopped short of calling Percy a bigot but said that the Republican was "blowing kisses to the racists."[58]

In early October, Robert Sabonjian, the Democratic mayor of Waukegan, a gritty industrial city north of Chicago in Lake County, announced his write-in candidacy for senator. Following a two-day racial disturbance in that city in August, Sabonjian had blamed the unrest on civil rights demonstrators, calling them "scum, winos, and junkheads." He further excoriated Douglas's position on open housing specifically and his civil rights record generally. Sabonjian's belated emergence in the Illinois senate race mirrored in microcosm George Wallace's presidential candidacy, for both disaffected Democrats provided conservative whites disinclined to vote Republican with an alternative to voting for liberal Democrats. Indeed, the results of a *Chicago Sun-Times* survey in Waukegan indicated that voters who intended to cast their ballots for Sabonjian would be likelier to desert Douglas than Percy. Once predominantly a southern concern, civil rights was beginning to take root in northern cities by the mid-1960s, and Douglas became one of the first liberal politicians to encounter the electoral problems associated with the struggle against de facto segregation.[59]

For Douglas, the second unfortunate development of the campaign came in an unexpected and tragic fashion on September 18. Campaigning in East Saint Louis, the Democrat learned that Percy's twenty-one-year-old daughter Valerie had been beaten and stabbed to death in her Kenilworth home. Douglas immediately sent a telegram to the Percy family expressing his condolences and announced that he would suspend his campaign indefinitely. Percy responded that he could not expect his opponent to stop campaigning for long and urged Douglas to resume at his convenience. Douglas answered that he felt it only proper to wait for an extended period of time. The senator returned to Washington, and, for the next several weeks, accounts of the Percys' bereavement and the police investigation of the murder dominated the news. From the moment they received the news of the murder, Douglas and his aides believed that Percy would benefit politically from the tragedy. Inevitably, the press directed its attention at the Republican candidate's brave struggle to resume a campaign under the most heartbreaking of circumstances. The death of Valerie Percy seemed to humanize her grieving father. Previously viewed as a cold, aloof millionaire, Percy became to many voters a more sympathetic man who acted with grace and courage during the grueling campaign. No one knew how to measure the impact of Valerie Percy's death on election day, but some sort of sympathy vote seemed very likely.[60]

After a hiatus of several weeks, Percy returned to the hustings and resumed making the charges of unethical behavior he had begun leveling at Douglas before his daughter's death. In August, Percy had objected to a photograph of himself crossing a union picket line during the 1964 gubernatorial campaign that, he charged, had been distributed by Douglas. Percy vehemently argued that he had not crossed a picket line and that the photo had been a fake. Douglas just as adamantly denied circulating the snapshot and, being unable to locate a copy, questioned whether it actually existed. Nevertheless, Douglas noted, Percy had crossed a picket line two years earlier, and the sworn testimony of union officials provided the proof. In a similar instance, Percy had accused Douglas of distributing a leaflet, which had originally been printed in 1964, charging him with opening a Bell and Howell factory in Japan that resulted in the loss of jobs for Illinois workers. Again Douglas had denied involvement in the leaflet's distribution but added that Percy had in fact been responsible for situating a new factory in a foreign country.[61]

After the campaign's resumption in October, Douglas campaign workers obtained copies of leaflets distributed by Percy in Chicago's black wards that pledged his support for open occupancy and then dispersed the materials in white wards and suburbs. Douglas asserted that such evidence proved that his opponent had been saying different things to different audiences instead of maintaining consistent positions on the issues. The Percy campaign somewhat comically threatened legal action on the basis that the pamphlet had been illegally used outside of a designated geographical area; Douglas responded by noting sardonically, "So far as I know, this is the first time in political history that a candidate has objected to the distribution of his own literature." On the Saturday before the election, Percy announced that he would file charges with the Committee on Fair Campaign Practices, a nonpartisan group in

Washington dedicated to ethical election practices. Percy also accused Douglas of smearing him by calling him anti-Catholic. The Republican had recently criticized the provisions of an education bill passed by Congress that permitted the teaching of public and private school students together in nonsectarian buildings, and Douglas charged that the substance of his opponent's objections favored public schools over parochial schools. Percy claimed that Douglas's comments bespoke charges of religious bigotry, an imputation that the Democrat vigorously denied. The deluge of charges on the very eve of the election—"when the truth can't catch up with a lie"—seemed highly suspicious to the Democrats. "Percy smeared Mr. Douglas by charging us with smearing him," said Howard E. Shuman, "probably the oldest trick in political campaigning."[62]

In the last weeks before the election, the *Chicago Sun-Times* published the results of a series of public opinion polls conducted exclusively in the suburbs west of Chicago. Because the newspapers polled registered voters only in rock-ribbed Republican communities, the results showed Percy with a substantial lead over Douglas. The repeated publication of the dispiriting poll numbers undermined the enthusiasm of Douglas's supporters, the Democrats felt, and contributed to a bandwagon effect for Percy. The Democrats bitterly complained to the newspaper and urged the publication of polling data from Douglas's strongholds in Chicago and southern Illinois, but no changes ensued. Douglas and his aides resented how Marshall Field, the partisan owner of the *Sun-Times*, had used his newspaper to aid the Republican cause. This seemed to be a clear case, Douglas and his aides believed, where public opinion polls shaped public opinion rather than simply assessing it.[63]

As the electoral contest drew to a close, Douglas charged that his opponent had conducted a vacuous campaign devoid of substance. "It's very hard to detect what Mr. Percy stands for," Douglas said. "He's carried out a campaign of almost studied ambiguity." The Republican offered a vague plan for addressing the Vietnam conundrum and no concrete programs for economic growth. He seemed only interested in glad-handing and photo opportunities. "I would say he's conducting intellectual guerilla warfare," concluded Douglas. By contrast, the incumbent stood on the ideas he had articulated for the previous eighteen years. He closed his political advertisements with the statement, "You know where he stands."[64]

On election day, Paul and Emily Douglas voted early and then toured ward headquarters and polling places on Chicago's South and Southwest Sides. Sensing a strong backlash vote in the city's white residential enclaves and hearing of unusually heavy voting in the suburbs, Douglas concluded that he would lose. Even precincts in his own Fifth Ward seemed to be closely contested, with Percy forging small electoral majorities in some of them. After a three-hour nap that afternoon, Douglas awoke to find his pessimistic projections accurate. He lost by more than four hundred thousand votes, winning in Chicago by a modest 185,000 (compared to his 525,000 victory margin of 1960) and losing in the suburbs by 280,000; he even lost his home precinct, 148–128. At one o'clock in the morning, he addressed a gathering of loyal friends and supporters in the basement of the Conrad Hilton Hotel. After extending the obligatory congratulations to his victorious opponent and thanking the Democrats who had worked hard for him in the campaign, he closed with some general remarks about his senatorial career. He said:

> I want to thank the voters of Illinois for the privilege of representing them for eighteen years and of fighting for the causes in which I believe. Some of these causes have triumphed; others, I believe, will ultimately prevail. . . . I leave public life with no regrets. I would not change a vote or a position. I shall continue to work on behalf of those causes in which I believe, and I shall always remain your friend, just as you have remained mine.[65]

The nation's political pundits and editorial writers judged the outcome of the Illinois senatorial race highly significant, although no consensus developed to explain fully how such a highly respected national leader like Douglas could have lost so overwhelmingly to a largely untested politician like Percy. The Republican surely benefited from an outpouring of sympathy over his daughter's murder. His campaign artfully drew attention to the incumbent's advanced age, and perhaps some voters responded positively to the notion that Douglas had served the state well for many years but the time had come for a fresh face and new ideas. The senator's relentless support of the increasingly unpopular war in Vietnam puzzled some liberals—although his consistent opposition to the spread of communism should have made his position on Vietnam predictable—and undoubtedly cost him votes on the political left. The Democrats detected wholesale defections from the liberal Jewish community on Chicago's North Side solely on that issue. Douglas's apostasy on Vietnam, which had come to be a litmus test for many liberals, overshadowed all of the progressive stands he had taken in the previous eighteen years in Congress.[66]

Douglas himself believed that the issue of race, a cause in which he had invested so much of his energy as a senator, had at last done him in. His unwavering support of open occupancy served as a lightning rod for the growing number of white voters caught up in the backlash against civil rights, and the emerging Black Power movement left him alienated from many African American voters. Although more than 75 percent of the voters in Chicago's predominantly black wards voted for Douglas, many blacks expressed their discontent with the Daley machine's oppressive policies by staying home on election day. More damaging to the Democrat was the discontent among white voters. In the eight white ethnic wards of the Northwest and Southwest Sides where King had led open-housing marches, the voting support that Douglas had enjoyed in 1960 plummeted six years later. Between 1960 and 1966, Douglas lost 108,310 votes in those eight wards. In 1960 he had carried all of the wards, whereas in 1966 he lost all but two. The explosive issue of race proved to be a valuable asset to Percy, an attractive candidate who ran a savvy—and cynical—campaign.[67]

If, as some observers theorized, the political winds in the country were beginning to shift away from New Frontier–Great Society liberalism, then Douglas may well have been one of the first casualties of the change. The 1966 elections produced some notable advances for a revitalized Republican party that picked up three seats in the Senate, forty-seven seats in the House, and eight governorships. In California, disgruntled voters selected Ronald Reagan for governor over two-time incumbent Edmund "Pat" Brown, and Georgia voters chose the virulently racist Lester Maddox for governor. In Alabama, where state law prohibited the reelection of George Wallace as governor, the electorate conveniently found a surrogate, Wallace's wife, Lurleen. Another period of reform in American history was drawing to a close, and the electorate had grown tired of change. No one in Washington had been more unabashedly liberal in the preceding generation than Douglas, and he made an inviting target at the outset of a conservative renaissance. Assaying the outcome of the Illinois senatorial contest, political columnist Stewart Alsop suggested, "Paul Douglas is a dragon slayer who has run out of dragons to slay." Perhaps it would be more accurate to say that the electorate no longer saw the need to rid themselves of dragons.[68]

After the Senate

9

Old age brings losses of dear ones as well as physical afflictions, and also perhaps a darkening of the horizon. Certainly there is much wrong with the world today. Nevertheless, I see bright spots. . . . On the personal level I have the happiness of congenial work, congenial friends, and my home with Emily.

—Paul H. Douglas[1]

• When Paul and Emily Douglas returned to Washington, D.C., after the 1966 election, a crowd of two hundred met them at the airport. The gathering included a large contingent from the Greater Washington Labor Council along with other representatives from various union locals, the National Council of Senior Citizens, and a handful of local reporters. Vice President Hubert Humphrey and Senator Ernest Gruening also joined the welcoming assemblage. When the Douglases entered the airport terminal, members of the crowd cheered, applauded, and waved banners and signs. While a reporter from a Chicago television station conducted a short interview with Douglas, the onlookers waited patiently in the background. Finally, Douglas stepped to a microphone and briefly thanked the crowd for the gesture of affection. "Nothing in my whole life," he said quietly, "has touched me so much." Then Humphrey briskly escorted Paul and Emily Douglas to a car that would drive them to their Washington home. The touching tableau, which had taken only a few minutes, signaled the end of Douglas's eighteen-year career in the Senate.[2]

Douglas needed, first of all, to decide on a way to support himself and his wife. He might have considered returning to a teaching career at the University of Chicago, but no offer came from the institution. Other colleges and universities, including the University of Illinois, the University of Hawaii, the University of California at Los Angeles, Williams College, and his alma mater, Bowdoin College, attempted to recruit him to their faculties, but he chose another academic appointment instead. Douglas accepted an offer from Harry Gideonse, an old friend from Chicago who had become chancellor at the New School for Social Research in New York City, to teach part-time at that university. (The first term, he taught a graduate seminar, "Current Economic and Political Problems," with an enrollment of twenty specially selected students.) Gideonse also prevailed upon Douglas to become the unpaid chairman of the board of Freedom House, a liberal organization devoted to the promulgation of democratic institutions. At the same time, Douglas accepted an offer to host a television series, "In Our Time," produced in New York City. He quickly settled into a schedule that allowed him to fulfill his obligations in New York City from Monday through Wednesday and spend the remainder of the week at his Washington, D.C., home.[3]

Even as he sought to create a new life, Douglas remained intensely interested in public affairs and sought to do whatever he could outside the Senate to advance the causes to which he had been dedicated for many years. He still spoke often, for example, about the need for the adoption of a code of ethics in Congress. Public concern with the quality of public life in Washington could be allayed, he suggested, with the implementation of two reforms: (1) annual disclosure of income and capital assets by members of Congress; and (2) tax-funded national election campaigns. Appalled at the outrageous amounts of money spent in the 1966 elections, he feared the consummation of an unholy marriage between influence-peddling representatives of big business and morally lax politicians. "These costs are no longer under control," he said. "It was estimated that Mr. [Nelson] Rockefeller's last campaign cost $5,000,000. That's an extraordinary amount of money for an ordinary man to raise. A candidate must be wealthy or look for wealthy benefactors. Few large benefactors give without expectation of a later harvest."[4]

Douglas also kept informed about the fate of legislation that he had previously championed in the Senate. Even though Congress had passed a bill in 1966 to save the Indiana Dunes, he remained concerned that the proponents of industrial development along the southern shoreline of Lake Michigan would try to subvert his achievement. In December 1966, he wrote a lengthy and detailed letter to Secretary of the Interior Stewart Udall outlining the measures he thought should be employed to safeguard the development of the national lakeshore. He warned Udall that opponents of the park had pledged to introduce legislation that would remove land approved by Congress from the planned area of development. At the same time, he urged President Johnson to oppose Bethlehem Steel's proposal to fill in several hundred acres of Lake Michigan between the Burns Waterway Harbor and the national lakeshore. He likewise opposed bills submitted to the Indiana legislature to grant railways the right of way to lay track through the lakeshore area and to construct an airport there. When he received the $5,000 Murray-Green

Award for public service in 1969, he donated $2,000 of the grant to the Save the Dunes Council for the acquisition of additional lakefront land. Not only did the reformers need to be vigilant to protect the national lakeshore, he believed, but they could best protect the parkland by adding acreage whenever possible.[5]

Douglas maintained a keen interest in truth-in-lending legislation as well. He initially despaired that his defeat in 1966 would end the legislative struggle he had launched years before, but, to his great relief, other liberals in Congress took up the cause in his absence. Early in the 1967 legislative session, Senator William Proxmire of Wisconsin introduced a truth-in-lending bill patterned almost exactly after the bill that Douglas had submitted the previous year. Proxmire altered the language in a few places and exempted short-term revolving loans from the requirements for disclosure of annual rates but essentially tampered very little with the legislation that Douglas had crafted. Kenneth Gray, who had previously served as Douglas's aide and who then held the position of administrative assistant to Vice President Hubert Humphrey, assured Douglas that "this is your bill in every respect." Opponents of the bill concurred. The Proxmire bill "isn't materially different from the Douglas bill," noted a representative of the National Consumer Finance Association. Because A. Willis Robertson no longer chaired the Senate's Banking and Currency Committee, Proxmire and Douglas hoped the legislation might finally make it to the Senate floor, where passage seemed likely.[6]

Robertson had assigned truth-in-lending legislation to the Production and Stabilization Subcommittee in previous years, but in 1967 the bill went to the Financial Institutions Subcommittee chaired by Proxmire. The subcommittee issued a favorable report on June 8, and Douglas served as the Banking and Currency Committee's first witness during the hearings that followed. He staunchly rejected the claims of the bill's opponents that truth in lending would undermine the commercial credit industry, saying, "There is simply no evidence that consumers will rise up in mass revolt if they are told the truth." Dismissing the notion that truth in lending constituted some kind of radical threat to capitalist institutions, he said:

> The basic philosophy behind truth in lending is a belief in free enterprise and in the price system. But if markets are to function properly, there must be a free flow of information. Perfect competition requires perfect information. Of course, perfect competition does not exist anywhere in our economy. Nevertheless, it is an ideal towards which public policy should work.[7]

The former senator expressed his delight and surprise at the cordial reception he received from former colleagues on the committee, who asked few questions of their witness and on June 29 voted unanimously to approve the measure. The entire Senate reacted in much the same fashion, and on July 11 the truth in lending bill passed, 92–0. Senators who had bitterly opposed earlier versions of the bill could now say that they had voted for the 1967 law on the first try.[8]

In the House of Representatives, Leonor K. Sullivan (Democrat, Missouri) introduced a more stringent bill than the one passed by the Senate. Her version restored the deleted sections on revolving credit and made advertisers legally culpable for disseminating misleading information about credit rates. Douglas testified before the Subcommittee on Consumer Affairs of the House Banking and Currency Committee, which Sullivan chaired, and lavishly praised her bill as "intrinsically superior" to the Senate bill. The House Banking and Currency Committee reported the measure on December 13, two days before the adjournment of Congress, thereby delaying floor action until the following year. On February 1, 1968, the House passed the bill by a vote of 383–4. During the consideration of the Senate and House bills at conference, Proxmire and Sullivan worked in tandem to defend the stronger version. On May 22 the two chambers of Congress adopted the conference report that granted the liberals what they wanted—a provision requiring disclosure of interest rates on all revolving charge accounts on both an annual and monthly basis.[9]

At the invitation of President Johnson, Douglas went to the White House for the signing of the truth-in-lending law on May 29, 1968. As he entered the East Room for the signing ceremony, many longtime opponents of the bill, most notably representatives of the American Bankers Association, rushed forward to offer enthusiastic congratulations. Already, he mused, the critics of financial disclosure had begun to deny their prolonged opposition. Such historical revisionism notwithstanding, the press reported what Senator Proxmire and Representative Sullivan underscored in their remarks that day—that the enactment of truth-in-lending legislation owed to the indefatigable efforts of Paul Douglas during six discouraging years. Again, success had come "in the fullness of time."[10]

Douglas also persisted in his support of U.S. involvement in Vietnam even though the war grew more unpopular each year. In 1967 he served as the organizing chairman of the Committee for Peace with Freedom in Vietnam, a bipartisan group devoted to the preservation of a noncommunist government in South Vietnam. Beginning with 140 charter members, including former president Dwight D. Eisenhower and General Omar Bradley, the organization quickly increased its membership to 1,500. While opposing a unilateral withdrawal of U.S. troops, the Committee for Peace with Freedom in Vietnam under Douglas's direction recommended meaningful land reform in South Vietnam and sought to reform the unsatisfactory government there. Still, despite the many shortcomings of the ruling class in South Vietnam and the rising level of dissatisfaction with the war at home, Douglas remained resolute in his defense of President Johnson's policies in Southeast Asia. He continued to affirm the efficacy of the domino theory and warned that the fall of Vietnam would spark a series of communist insurgencies in nations throughout the Pacific. To charges that the increasing cost of the war was beginning to harm the U.S. economy, he responded adamantly: "How can anyone say that a nation with an income of more than $800 billion can't afford a $30 billion war?"[11]

Douglas disagreed with those who argued that Johnson needed to raise taxes in order to fund the Vietnam War. He acknowledged that a growing federal deficit was causing inflation but felt that cutting federal spending in other areas such as highway construction and the space program should reduce the shortfall. More important, the threat of inflation allowed him to return to one of his favorite crusades—the need for income tax reform. Tax increases would be unnecessary and the federal deficit would melt away, he argued, if the government closed the plethora of existing loopholes and the corporate rich simply paid their taxes. As he had so often throughout his senatorial career, Douglas laid the blame principally on the inequities surrounding capital gains taxes and depletion allowances. If those two abuses could be remedied, he argued, the government could reduce the deficit to a modest $6-8 billion, roughly 1 percent of the gross national product. In alliance with United Auto Workers president Walter Reuther, Douglas continued to speak out publicly for corrections to the flawed tax system.[12]

In the two years after he left the Senate, Douglas spent most of his time serving as chairman of the Commission on Urban Problems. Authorized by Congress under Section 301 of the Housing and Urban Development Act of 1965 and granted an appropriation of $1.5 million, the commission sought to investigate the worsening conditions of the nation's cities with particular emphasis on housing. Douglas assumed the task at the request of President Johnson, who had insisted that he did not want a whitewash and promised the commission members total freedom in conducting their inquiries. Johnson formalized the appointment on January 12, 1967, and requested that he be given the commission's final report by December 31, 1968. For nearly two years, Douglas and the other fifteen members of the commission conducted an intensive investigation of urban life, assembling data at its temporary quarters in Washington, D.C., and receiving testimony from approximately 350 witnesses in twenty-two cities around the country, including New Haven, Boston, Pittsburgh, Detroit, East Saint Louis, and Los Angeles.[13]

Despite President Johnson's promises of full cooperation from other federal agencies, the Commission encountered sustained opposition from the Department of Housing and Urban Development (HUD) and its secretary, Robert Weaver. Even before Douglas had agreed to participate and the other members of the commission had been chosen, the HUD bureaucracy had resisted its creation. When Johnson could not be dissuaded, Weaver relented but argued that the commission should report to him rather than to the president and attempted to reduce its operating budget. Further, Weaver sought to specify what the commission could study (building and housing codes, zoning, taxation, and development standards) and what stood outside its bailiwick (housing programs and broader urban issues). Douglas reaffirmed the commission's independence with White House staffers before proceeding with the investigation. Even so, Weaver and his associates persisted in criticizing the commission throughout its two-year existence. "Weaver had made a poor record," Douglas later commented, "and he didn't want to be criticized."[14]

Weaver opposed allowing the commission to conduct hearings in various urban locations, Douglas believed, because such intense scrutiny would reveal HUD's shortcomings in administering housing programs in the nation's ghettos. Douglas had eagerly supported President Kennedy's selection of Weaver to head the Housing and Home Finance Agency (HHFA) as well as President Johnson's later decision to nominate him as the first secretary of HUD (and the first African American to serve in a presidential cabinet). Douglas had, in fact, spearheaded the confirmation effort in the Senate when a group of southerners opposed Weaver. In the years following the appointment, Douglas believed, Weaver proved to be a timid and ineffective administrator. Every year, the HUD secretary presented a new program to the Senate Finance Committee, Douglas asserted, but little progress ensued in the quest to improve the nation's housing stock. Douglas saw him as a cautious bureaucrat unwilling to challenge entrenched interests on behalf of poorly housed citizens. Perhaps, the senator speculated, Weaver wanted desperately, as the highest-ranked African American in the federal government, to avoid seeming too militant. Weaver's reluctance to allow a comprehensive investigation of HUD's effectiveness suggested to Douglas that his misgivings about the public housing program would prove well founded.[15]

Indeed, the commissioners received testimony from a steady stream of disgruntled public housing residents, community organizers, civil rights activists, and others who excoriated HUD as a remote, ineffective bureaucracy that had constructed low-income housing at a snail's pace and then responded indifferently to tenants' complaints. Witnesses further lambasted the urban renewal program administered by HUD for its wholesale destruction of housing in modest neighborhoods and wholly inadequate construction of affordable replacement units. Municipal officials and other bureaucrats predictably defended the federal government's efforts in the field of housing, but the majority of witnesses—especially unscheduled speakers who took the opportunity afforded by the commission to speak extemporaneously—painted a disappointing picture of government indifference and lassitude.[16]

The commission collected information during the combustible summer months of 1967 when cities blazed with civil rights protest. The violence and destruction in urban America that year made a profound impression on the commission members, who, as Robert Weaver and others at HUD no doubt feared, wrote a report that freely took the federal government to task for its failures. The massive final report, consisting of more than two hundred policy recommendations packed into five hundred pages of text, stopped somewhat short of blaming the "red hot summers" of the 1960s on the inadequacies of federal bureaucracies but left little doubt that the promise of national housing programs had gone unfulfilled. The Taft-Ellender-Wagner Act of 1949, of which Douglas had been one of the primary advocates, prescribed the construction of 135,000 new public housing units a year for six years, a total of 810,000 units by 1955; under HHFA's and HUD's torpid direction, local housing authorities had completed just 500,000 units in nearly twenty years. The report was equally condemnatory of urban renewal. It read:

> Instead of a grand assault on slums and blight as an integral part of a campaign for "a decent home and a suitable living environment for every American family," [urban] renewal was and is too often looked upon as a federally financed gimmick to provide relatively cheap land for a miscellany of profitable or prestigious enterprises.[17]

The commission provided a plethora of recommendations, many of which could be described as excessively ambitious. First, in conjunction with the charge that HUD had built far too few houses in the preceding generation, the commission called for the construction of 2.0–2.5 million housing units each year. Of these, 500,000 units should be devoted to low- and moderate-income families unable to secure satisfactory lodging in the private housing market. These units should be built on scattered sites throughout metropolitan areas to foster integration. In addition, the commission report recommended the construction of low-rise public housing and outlined a series of steps to be taken to improve the quality of life for residents of extant high-rise projects. Most provocatively, the commission urged that, if state and local housing authorities failed to make satisfactory progress in meeting the housing needs of low- and moderate-income families, the federal government should assume control and become the builder of last resort. In all, the recommendations constituted a ringing endorsement of the liberal vision for improving urban America by calling for a larger role by the federal government and the investment of increasing amounts of the nation's resources in the fight to save the cities.[18]

The members of the commission found the imposing task of completing the report on schedule exceedingly difficult, in large measure because of the disappointing quality of support provided by the staff. (Douglas commented that the commission had a superb staff; half of it was superbly good, and half of it was superbly bad.) Because some members of the group hesitated to write critically about HUD's performance, Douglas undertook the composition of the housing and urban renewal sections himself. He worked at a grueling pace seven days a week for five months and finally finished those chapters just a half hour before leaving for the Democratic National Convention in Chicago. He found little opportunity for rest or recuperation as a delegate-at-large at the tempestuous convention and complained about feeling ill throughout his stay in Chicago. During a nominating speech for one of the presidential candidates, he fainted and had to be carried to a room under the platform for emergency medical care. When a physician hastily conducted a cursory examination and concluded that the episode was not life threatening, Douglas insisted upon returning to the floor so that he could cast his vote for Hubert Humphrey in the balloting for the presidential nomination. After the convention, he complained of exhaustion and intestinal discomfort but maintained a busy schedule campaigning throughout the nation for Humphrey. At the same time, he continued to work daily on the commission report and, after the campaign concluded, increased the tempo of his writing and editing.[19]

By the fall of 1968, the commission had published reports of its hearings and individual studies of particular topics, so the tenor of its conclusions had become widely known. In early November, Douglas forwarded copies of the final report to Secretary Weaver and President Johnson. He also wrote Joseph Califano, Johnson's special assistant in charge of domestic programs, to request a meeting with the president so that the commission could formally present its report. Douglas quickly concluded that the report had found no warmer reception in the White House than it had in HUD offices. For nearly a month, Califano returned none of Douglas's telephone calls and studiously avoided any contact with him. The two finally met at the White House on December 3. After Douglas waited for more than an hour before being admitted to the adviser's office, Califano described President Johnson's displeasure with the report's conclusions. He asked how many members of the commission had signed the report, and, contradicting Weaver's reports of acrimony and contentiousness on a bitterly divided commission, Douglas replied that there had been no dissenters. Califano instructed Douglas to submit the report formally to President-elect Richard Nixon. Douglas refused, noting that the law prescribed that the report be submitted to the president by December 31 and arguing that Johnson owed a formal meeting to the commission members who had devoted so much time and effort to the study. Affronted at the president's refusal to meet with the commission, Douglas announced that he would unilaterally release the report to the press on December 15:

"I can't tell the President that," Califano replied.

"I don't care what you tell the President," Douglas rejoined. "But I am telling you. We are releasing the report."[20]

HUD staffers attempted to suppress the report, but Douglas and members of the commission staff sent photocopies of the materials to the *Washington Post,* the *New York Times,* and the major wire services; they also handed out foot-thick mimeographed copies to reporters and other interested parties. On December 15 excerpts from the report appeared on the front page of the *New York Times* and hundreds of other daily newspapers throughout the country. On December 31, in response to the mandate outlined in the Housing and Urban Development Act of 1965, the secretary of HUD submitted the commission report to Congress—but, to Douglas's chagrin, the version sent to Capitol Hill contained less than half of the full report. Robert Wood, who had replaced Weaver as HUD secretary several months earlier, refused to provide Congress with the portions of the study that criticized public housing, urban renewal, and other HUD initiatives. Wood explained that he had simply excised the sections that had gone beyond the commission's charter. Douglas regretted that such censorship not only eliminated much of the commission's analysis of urban travails but also expunged more than fifty detailed recommendations that could have proved useful to congressional policymakers.[21]

The contretemps surrounding the report of the National Commission on Urban Problems seems in retrospect perfectly predictable. Always fiercely independent and accustomed in Congress to taking the role of outsider, Douglas promised to compose an objective report that would be comprehensive if not politic. No less surprising was Lyndon Johnson's sensitivity to criticism. The White House had, after all, given an equally frosty reception several months earlier to the Report of the National Advisory Commission on Civil Disorders, the so-called Kerner Commission Report. A lame duck president in his last days in office with disastrously low ratings in public opinion polls—a proud man frustrated over his inability to extract the nation from a highly unpopular war—could not have welcomed criticism of yet another aspect of his administration. Johnson would not abide the accusation that so little progress had been made in the quest to house the poor during his five years in the White House. Nevertheless, to the members of the commission who had invested two years of their lives in the report's preparation, his actions seemed petty and self-serving. "He reverted to the Johnson of his Senate period, 1949-60," Douglas concluded sadly.[22]

While working for the Commission on Urban Problems, Douglas also gathered information for and began the writing of two books. The first,

In Our Time, hailed from the television program of the same name that he hosted in New York City. A collection of eight essays dealing with problems confronting contemporary America, the book divided into two sections. The first part contained four essays on topics of particular interest to Douglas during his senatorial career—tax loopholes, oil shale ownership rights, truth in lending, and political ethics and the cost of elections. The second half of the volume dealt with poverty and discussed how the world's richest nation must summon the will to provide for its poorest citizens. Part rigorous analysis and part clarion call to action, *In Our Time* very much reflected the author's commitment to liberal principles. Suffused with optimism, the book acknowledged the severity of the problems confronting the nation but also affirmed Douglas's belief in the basic decency of the American people. After all, he posited, he had seen often in his long senatorial career how the political process could indeed work to reform a flawed system.[23]

The writing of the second book, his autobiography, proved to be exacting and time-consuming. The septuagenarian found that his imperfect recall of events decades past often made historical accuracy difficult to attain. He regretted that he had to write substantial portions of the manuscript after having donated his papers to the Chicago Historical Society, forcing him to operate "from a very imperfect memory." Recognizing the likelihood that his manuscript contained factual errors, he sent chapters to friends and former colleagues for proofreading; their lengthy, detailed responses confirmed the wisdom of his cautious approach. For example, he sent chapters dealing with civil rights to Joseph Rauh, whose thorough editing saved the book from a host of errors (particularly concerning Douglas's indispensable contributions to the 1957, 1960, and 1964 civil rights laws). Rauh apologized to Douglas for making such copious suggestions for revision and hoped his "comments do not appear carping because they were not so intended. You were the leader of the fight for Civil Rights legislation in Congress, and we as your messenger boys want to make sure this comes through clearly and accurately."[24]

Douglas's progress on his autobiography slowed because of a series of health problems that began shortly after he left Congress and plagued him for the remaining years of his life. Physicians never fully identified the reasons for his fainting spell at the 1968 Democratic National Convention, and he reported feeling ill for months thereafter. In December 1968 a bout with Asiatic flu resulted in heart and lung complications that lingered interminably. He recovered enough to deliver several commencement addresses at universities in the spring of 1969 but found himself tiring easily and losing his memory. On August 11, 1969, he suffered a stroke and had to be hospitalized for several weeks; when he returned home, several months of intensive physical therapy produced grudging progress that allowed for a partial return to normal activity for a time. He finished the autobiography many months behind schedule, and its publication finally came in 1971.[25]

Increasingly slowed by failing health in the early 1970s and self-conscious about his crippled appearance caused by the stroke, Douglas spent great amounts of time at his Washington home and infrequently engaged in public affairs. In the spring of 1970, he made a rare public appearance to accept an honorary doctorate at the Chicago campus of the University of Illinois. When Mayor Daley had proposed the creation of the campus in the 1960s, Douglas had opposed the site just southwest of the Loop because the original plans had called for the bulldozing of Jane Addams's historic Hull House. A compromise had preserved the settlement house on the university campus, but a residue of bitterness remained between Douglas and the university administration. He interpreted the offer of an honorary degree as a peacemaking gesture on the part of the university and, therefore, despite his health problems, decided to accept the honor at the spring 1970 commencement exercises.[26]

The event became clouded in controversy because of Douglas's well-known support of the war in Vietnam. A group of University of Illinois students and faculty members wrote Douglas demanding to know his current position on the war and threatening some form of action if his answer displeased them. Hoping to avoid an embarrassing public demonstration at the university's commencement, Douglas volunteered to cancel his appearance. The university chancellor refused to appease the protesters, however, and insisted that the honorary degree be conferred as planned. Douglas offered to participate in an open forum to discuss the war, but the protesters refused. When the chancellor presented Douglas the honorary degree, approximately fifty protesters (out of an estimated fifteen thousand in attendance) rose silently and left the auditorium. Douglas praised the university for its restraint in handling the situation and noted approvingly that the dissenters had been allowed to exercise their freedom of speech in a wholly appropriate way; he also expressed an appreciation for their opposition to the war. The episode, he said, had been trying but constructive.[27]

Later that year, Douglas's name surfaced in the newspapers because of his agreement to serve as chairman of the National Citizens' Committee to Aid the Families of General Motors Strikers. As chairman of the seventy-eight member committee, which included other leading Democratic politicians such as Hubert Humphrey, George McGovern, Edward Kennedy, Edmund Muskie, Birch Bayh, and Philip Hart, Douglas led the fund-raising drive to aid the families of United Automobile Workers (UAW) who were engaged in a prolonged strike against the General Motors Corporation. He emphasized that the members of the committee were not taking sides in the strike but simply seeking to provide humanitarian aid to the strikers' families. "I strongly feel that strikes should be settled on their merits," he wrote in a fund-raising letter, "and not be resolved on the basis of hunger and deprivation imposed on the children and wives of the strikers." The committee required a minimum of traveling, and most of his efforts in behalf of the cause involved letter writing.[28]

With time to devote again to scholarly investigations, Douglas turned his attention to the relationship between labor and capital in determining prices that he had considered nearly fifty years earlier. The Cobb-Douglas function, which had been greeted with considerable skepticism by many economists in the 1920s, had been widely accepted in Europe, Japan, and Australia, as well as the United States, in the ensuing years. Working with other economists during his retirement years, Douglas extended the study of labor and prices in Australia to 1970 in the hope of refining earlier conclusions and extending the analysis to new fields of inquiry. He found gratifying the widespread appreciation within economic circles for the pioneering work he had done decades before, but he had little time and could not muster the energy to attempt much scholarly work in the years after leaving Congress.[29]

During the early 1970s, Douglas receded steadily from public view. In 1971 he endured another lengthy stay in a hospital after suffering a stroke while swimming. A series of disabling strokes followed, and advancing years and declining health greatly limited his physical exertions. Unable to walk any appreciable distance alone, he became confined to a wheelchair and eventually to a bed. "It has been a humbling experience," he told an interviewer in 1974. "I think loneliness is the chief lament of old people, particularly old people who have been slowed up by disability." His devoted wife Emily faithfully monitored his care as his vigor slowly ebbed. After months of steady deterioration, he died of respiratory failure in his Washington, D.C., home on September 25, 1976, at the age of eighty-four.[30]

Liberal Crusades

10

I wanted to represent the general public interest. It is frequently not represented. The power Establishment in the Senate is on the whole biased against the public interest. The small taxpayers—people of low income, of minority groups—are individually weak. The special interests, producing interests, are . . . organized. In the struggle between concentrated private interest and diffused general interest, the private interests have all the resources and drive they need to win.

—**Paul H. Douglas**[1]

• Paul Douglas's commitment in the U.S. Senate to battle the interests on behalf of society's powerless reflected a lifelong attraction to the cause of the underdog. Convinced that modern industrial societies did not provide adequately for the working masses and the indigent, he gravitated in his early years toward a political radicalism that proposed sweeping changes in the American socioeconomic system. Complaining that "the main mass of the general public and even of the academic profession stand by as mere spectators and allow without protest the power juggernauts to conquer," he flirted with different varieties of socialism without ever joining the Socialist party. By the mid-1930s, he moved along with other radicals into the left wing of the Democratic party. Heartened by the New Deal's achievements, especially in the "Second New Deal" of 1935, and wary of the rising threat of totalitarianism in Europe, he cast his lot with a liberalism situated firmly within the American political mainstream. Right-wing Republicans who red-baited him in later decades were correct in noting the earnestness of his youthful radicalism, but they failed to see how thoroughly he had rejected that extremism for a more conventional liberalism.[2]

Douglas's liberalism embraced not only a passion for domestic reform but also a fervent dedication to the containment of communism internationally. As an avid champion of the limited welfare state and a fierce cold warrior, he allied himself with the Union for Democratic Action (UDA) and its successor, the Americans for Democratic Action (ADA). In full agreement with other leading members of the ADA such as Reinhold Niebuhr, Joseph Rauh, and Arthur Schlesinger, Jr., he renounced the Quaker policy of nonviolent resistance to aggression and unapologetically expressed a willingness to use force against communism. The lessons of World War II and the opening years of the cold war convinced him of the inefficacy of pacifism and bred a conviction that appeasement could only lead to widespread human suffering and defeat for democracy. "Thermopylae was necessary," he concluded, "that Socrates might practice his dialectic."[3]

Douglas's implacable anticommunism commingled with an equally strong nationalism that left some liberals uneasy. Followers of Henry Wallace and others who called for less belligerence in the government's relations with communist nations accused Douglas of bellicosity, no more so than during his defense of U.S. military involvement in Vietnam. Critics asserted that his willingness to commit U.S. troops to battle communism in remote corners of the globe betrayed a dearth of sympathy for anticolonialism and Third World revolutions, a lack of understanding for the complex world of international relations. Even those who lauded his assumption of forthright positions on sensitive issues and appreciated the tenacity with which he clung to unpopular causes thought his anticommunism excessive and his patriotism overwrought. In 1963, for example, a member of the U.S. mission to the United Nations complained to Adlai Stevenson about an impolitic speech Douglas had delivered to the Women's American Organization for Rehabilitation through Training (ORT) at the Grand Ballroom of the New York Hilton Hotel. Speaking at length about all the good works effected in an entirely disinterested fashion by the United States and the inexcusable ingratitude shown by nations throughout the world, Douglas singled out Britain, France, Italy, and Tunisia for especially execrable behavior—even as the United Nations delegates from those countries listened in rising outrage. Noting that "nobody can be more self-righteous than Paul when he puts his mind to it," U.N. functionary Clayton Fritchey reported to Stevenson that Douglas delivered such speeches extolling America's selfless humanitarianism at least once a year and could not be deterred from doing so. His unabashed flag-waving, usually done in front of appreciative groups in Illinois, could be a diplomatic blunder when repeated before more cosmopolitan audiences.[4]

Though Douglas unashamedly praised the United States in international forums, he never hesitated to enumerate the nation's shortcomings in providing for the health and welfare of all its citizens. He used America's disappointing record on race relations, which, he argued, "adversely affect the struggle of freedom against tyranny in the world," as the primary example of how much remained to be achieved. Douglas told the Senate:

> With the Communists reaching out to the uncommitted people of the Middle East and Africa and Southeast Asia, each housing riot in Illinois, each school riot in Kentucky, and each bombing of a pastor's home or intimidation of a would-be Negro voter in Alabama or Mississippi becomes not only an affront to human dignity here in this country, but a defeat for freedom in its tough world struggle for survival.[5]

He persistently called for the American people to live up to the promise offered by the Declaration of Independence and the Constitution, urging reform of a system of government that remained flawed in many critical respects. "Where are the champions of the people?" he asked rhetorically, for he fully intended to fulfill that role in Congress. Reconciled to being excluded from the inner sanctum of the Senate, he gloried in his lonely—and sometimes solitary—crusades on behalf of the people. Unafraid to assume an unpopular position or champion a cause that had as yet attracted few supporters, he eagerly adopted the Quaker practice of speaking truth to power.[6]

Because Douglas frequently fought for unpopular causes and suffered an untold number of setbacks, a popular image arose of him as an ineffective senator who spent more time tilting at windmills than marshaling electoral coalitions. According to some of his congressional opponents and conservative members of the Washington press corps, he was one of a number of effete liberals on Capitol Hill who displayed more skill delivering speeches and striking righteous poses than legislating. Douglas bridled at such a characterization, both because he thought it unfair to the causes for which he fought and because he considered it an inaccurate description of what transpired in the Senate. "Long periods of public education are needed before these issues are accepted," he explained. "I see my own role . . . primarily as one of introducing and trying to develop these much-needed but controversial issues so that they eventually gain success."[7]

The record substantiates Douglas's contention that his approach often proved fruitful. Richard L. Strout, the author of the *New Republic*'s T. R. B. column, observed: "He won many of his struggles; others, he lost. Yet what is astonishing is how so many of the so-called 'lost causes' of yesterday have become in a few years the commonplaces of today." His list of successes included truth in lending, area redevelopment, the Indiana Dunes National Lakeshore, Medicare, and many other measures for which he labored for many years before achieving breakthroughs. He even managed to win some battles that seemed truly hopeless. For twenty-five years, he attacked the most sacred of all tax loopholes, the 27 1/2 percent oil depletion allowance. Time after time, his amendments to tax bills prescribing reductions in the considerations given the oil companies suffered overwhelming defeats. In 1969, two years after he left the Senate, a tax measure cut the oil depletion allowance to 22 percent; in 1975, the largest oil companies lost the depletion allowance altogether while smaller firms retained a less generous write-off. Hubert Humphrey, widely believed to have been the most effective liberal legislator of the post–World War II era, said: "No man had his name on more major issues, major bills, and major legislation, than Paul Douglas." Herbert Lehman praised Douglas even more effusively, saying: "By long odds the most useful and inspiring Senator of my time was Paul H. Douglas of Illinois. . . . The ablest Senators all agreed, the best-informed newspaper correspondents all agreed, that the strongest man in the Chamber has been Mr. Douglas."[8]

Nothing better illustrated the value of Douglas's persistence than the passage of civil rights legislation. To be sure, the legislative breakthroughs cannot be understood apart from the grassroots civil rights movement that stirred the nation's conscience, but Douglas was surely correct in underscoring the important work done on Capitol Hill during the decade before the passage of landmark bills in 1964 and 1965. According to the testimony of prominent civil rights leaders, Douglas was the key congressional figure. Clarence Mitchell, the Washington bureau chief of the NAACP, put it simply: "Without Paul Douglas, we would have no civil-rights legislation as we know it today. He was the leader of the Senate team from 1949 into the early '60's." Joseph L. Rauh concurred, saying, "Though he unselfishly conferred the accolade of Mr. Civil Rights on others, his was the head and the heart of the victorious march for decency of the Fifties and Sixties. For us, Paul Douglas will always be Mr. Civil Rights." Mitchell, Rauh, and other civil rights leaders remembered Douglas humiliated and reduced to tears when he lost a Senate vote 76–6 in 1956 on the issue of the filibuster, recalled how he introduced civil rights measures and demanded discussion of racial equality when others counseled inaction, and appreciated how he accepted compromise in the short run but continued to work for more sweeping reform in the long run. They dismissed caricatures of Douglas as an impractical idealist whose rigidity worked against modulated change and knew that his unwillingness to settle for less made more possible. Civil rights became his greatest legacy.[9]

Ever the realist, Douglas understood that reform came in fits and starts, and he acknowledged failures as well as successes. His crusade to improve the efficiency of military spending produced modest results, for example. His flamboyant battles against pork-barrel legislation, he readily admitted, resulted in appreciative newspaper headlines but also in lopsided roll call defeats. Unable to persuade his senatorial colleagues to set aside the parochial interests of their home states, he finally surrendered. "I just had to give up," he said. "I couldn't take it any longer. For about ten years, I hit my head against a . . . wall. The people want it; they expect it; heaven help the legislator who does not deliver."[10]

Douglas's fight against congressional logrolling, the practice of regularly disclosing the details of his own finances, pioneering work on composing standards for ethics in government, political independence, and reputation for blunt honesty marked him as a man of singular probity in the nation's capital. Known as "the conscience of the Senate," he took forceful positions and never equivocated in front of hostile audiences. His persona undoubtedly contributed significantly to the political success he enjoyed in Illinois, a large and diverse state that sent a number of conservative Republicans to Washington at the same time that Douglas won three senatorial elections. Secure in his core of support among intellectuals, middle-class reformers, and the Chicago Democratic machine, Douglas also appealed successfully to many voters as a paragon of integrity who could be trusted to represent the state's interests in the national government. Without a doubt, Illinois voters saw him as an unabashed liberal; they also saw him as an honest and diligent public servant. Douglas's status as a straight-talking, issues-oriented politician served him well in an era before personal celebrity, pithy sound bites, and lavish campaign chests became the prerequisites for political office seeking.

During his senatorial career, Douglas found it possible to champion the causes that mattered deeply to him. His proposals for using the tools of economics to enhance American prosperity—and extend its reach to include a broader cross section of the population—emanated directly from his own academic work. His very personal fight to save the Indiana Dunes was more than a broad-based commitment to environmentalism. His advocacy of consumer interests, as evidenced especially in the truth-in-lending legislation, harkened back to his New Deal work in the 1930s. His crusade for civil rights reflected a commitment to improve American society by doing what he believed to be the right thing. Communism needed to be opposed globally because of its wickedness, its terrible potential to damage people's lives. The firm belief that these crusades mattered kept him striving even when the political climate seemed foreboding.

Most of all, Paul Douglas's senatorial career reflected his fervent belief in liberalism as an instrument for improving the commonweal. Imbued with the optimistic Quaker view of mankind's essential goodness, he felt that democracy offered the best hope for the regulation of human interaction. Life necessitated constant struggle but held out the promise of great reward. He spoke with optimism of the nation's future:

> The basic decency of the vast majority of the American people has enabled us in the past to overcome temporary epidemics of racism and class prejudice. . . . I am sufficiently optimistic to believe that we can surmount our present problems and come safely into harbor.[11]

Notes

1: PROFESSOR AND SOCIAL ACTIVIST

1. Jerry M. Anderson, "Paul H. Douglas: Insurgent Senate Spokesman for Humane Causes, 1949–1963" (Ph.D. diss., Michigan State University, 1964), pp. 21–22.

2. Paul H. Douglas, *In the Fullness of Time: The Memoirs of Paul H. Douglas* (New York: Harcourt Brace Jovanovich, 1971), pp. 3–4.

3. Ibid., p. 5.

4. Anderson, "Paul H. Douglas," p. 3 (quotation).

5. Douglas, *In the Fullness of Time,* pp. 6–8.

6. Anderson, "Paul H. Douglas," p. 6; "The Making of a Maverick," *Time* 55 (Jan. 16, 1950), p. 16.

7. Douglas, *In the Fullness of Time,* p. 9.

8. Ibid., pp. 18–20; Anderson, "Paul H. Douglas," pp. 6–7.

9. Douglas, *In the Fullness of Time,* pp. 23–24.

10. Ibid., pp. 24–25; Anderson, "Paul H. Douglas," p. 9.

11. Anderson, "Paul H. Douglas," p. 8 (first quotation); Douglas, *In the Fullness of Time,* p. 25 (second quotation).

12. Douglas, *In the Fullness of Time,* pp. 28–29.

13. Ibid., p. 32.

14. Ibid., p. 36 (quotation); Joe Alex Morris, "Senator Douglas: Hard-Boiled Idealist," *Saturday Evening Post* 222 (Aug. 6, 1949), p. 108.

15. Douglas, *In the Fullness of Time,* p. 34; Anderson, "Paul H. Douglas," p. 11.

16. Douglas, *In the Fullness of Time,* pp. 35–36.

17. Ibid., p. 37; Devere Allen, ed., *Adventurous Americans* (New York: Farrar and Rinehart, 1932), p. 182.

18. Douglas, *In the Fullness of Time,* p. 37. Several observers of Douglas's career have commented on the significance of his Quaker beliefs. Cabell Phillips commented in 1951 that "Douglas's concept of morality of public duty and human relationships has remained patterned on those of John Woolman" ("Paul Douglas—Instinctive Liberal," *New York Times Magazine,* June 24, 1951, p. 10). See also Mortimer Smith, "Senator Paul H. Douglas," *American Mercury* 71 (July 1950), pp. 28–29; and Morris, "Senator Douglas," p. 27.

19. Allen, ed., *Adventurous Americans,* pp. 181–82; Douglas, *In the Fullness of Time* p. 45. See the following articles written by Douglas at the close of World

War I: Paul H. Douglas, "Absenteeism in Labor," *Political Science Quarterly* 34 (December 1919), pp. 591–608; Paul H. Douglas, "Computation of Labor Turnover," *American Economic Review* 10 (March 1920), pp. 106–8; Paul H. Douglas, "Definition of Conditions of Labor," *Quarterly Journal of Economics* 33 (August 1919), pp. 725–29; Paul H. Douglas, "Development of System of Federal Grants in Aid," *Political Science Quarterly* 35 (June 10, 1920), pp. 255–71; and Paul H. Douglas, "Labor Administration in the Shipbuilding Industry during War Time," *Journal of Politics and Economics* 27 (1919), pp. 45–47, 362–96; and Paul H. Douglas, "Shop Committees: Substitute for, or Supplement to, Trade-Unions?" *Journal of Political Economy* 29 (February 1921), pp. 89–107.

20. Douglas, *In the Fullness of Time,* pp. 45–46.

21. Douglas's dissertation was published in Faculty of Political Science of Columbia University, ed., *Studies in History, Economics, and Public Law* 95 (New York: Columbia University Press, 1921).

22. Douglas, *In the Fullness of Time,* 77. Some materials on Douglas's teaching are found in the Paul H. Douglas Papers, box 305, Chicago Historical Society, Chicago, Illinois.

23. Edmund Whittaker, *Schools and Streams of Economic Thought* (Chicago: Rand McNally, 1960), p. 323; Anna Rothe, ed., *Current Biography, 1949* (New York: H. W. Wilson, 1950), p. 167; Paul H. Douglas and Dorothy Douglas, "What Can a Man Afford?" *American Economic Review* 11 (December 1921), pp. 1–118; Paul H. Douglas, Curtice N. Hitchcock, and Willard E. Atkins, *The Worker in Modern Economic Society* (Chicago: University of Chicago Press, 1923).

24. Paul H. Douglas, *Wages and the Family* (Chicago: University of Chicago Press, 1925).

25. Paul H. Douglas, *Real Wages in the United States, 1890–1926* (New York: Houghton Mifflin, 1930); Paul H. Douglas, *The Movement of Money and Real Earnings in the United States, 1926–1928* (Chicago: University of Chicago Press, 1931).

26. Douglas, *In the Fullness of Time,* pp. 47–48.

27. Ibid., p. 70 (quotations); Daniel Horowitz, *Betty Friedan and the Making of the Feminine Mystique: The American Left, the Cold War, and Modern Feminism* (Amherst: University of Massachusetts Press, 1998), p. 146. Dorothy Wolff Douglas's devotion to the Communist party was rumored to have been a major cause of the friction in the marriage. A Federal Bureau of Investigation informant identified her as a Communist in the 1930s, and in 1953 she invoked the Fifth Amendment in refusing to respond to questioning by the House Committee on Un-American Activities about her membership in the Communist party. A copy of her 731-page FBI file, Freedom of Information Privacy Act No. 914121, is in my possession.

28. Douglas, *In the Fullness of Time,* p. 76; Daniel Horowitz, *Betty Friedan and the Making of the Feminine Mystique,* p. 51; *New York Times,* Dec. 11, 1968; FBI file on Dorothy Wolff Douglas.

29. Morris, "Senator Douglas," p. 107. Douglas claimed that, despite his demand that no Communists be allowed on the trip, a "confirmed fellow traveler" was included at Coyle's invitation (*In the Fullness of Time,* p. 50).

30. Smith, "Senator Paul H. Douglas," p. 29 (quotation); Douglas, *In the Fullness of Time,* pp. 50–54; Allen, ed., *Adventurous Americans,* pp. 188–90. Two years after the trip to the Soviet Union, Douglas analyzed the economic successes

of the Russian economy at a major luncheon of the Foreign Policy Association and recommended recognition of the USSR (*New York Times,* Jan. 20, 1929).

31. Anderson, "Paul H. Douglas," pp. 29–30.

32. *New York Times,* Aug. 25, 1928 (first and second quotations); Paul H. Douglas, "Why I Am for Thomas and Why a Vote for Anyone Else Is Thrown Away," *New Republic* 56 (Oct. 24, 1928), p. 270 (third quotation). After the 1928 election, Douglas continued to lobby for the creation of a labor party. See, for example, *New York Times,* Feb. 10, 1930.

33. Paul H. Douglas, "Lessons from the Last Decade," in Harry W. Laidler and Norman Thomas, eds., *The Socialism of Our Time* (New York: Vanguard Press and the League for Industrial Democracy, 1929), pp. 29–57.

34. The standard biography of Insull remains Forrest McDonald, *Insull* (Chicago: University of Chicago Press, 1962). In 1929 Douglas was offered the secretaryship of the National Child Labor Committee, a post that he likely turned down because of the increasing amount of time he spent on the Insull affair. Paul H. Douglas to Florence Kelley, Nov. 26, 1929, Records of the National Consumers League, box B12, folder II-D, Paul H. Douglas Correspondence, Manuscript Division, Library of Congress, Washington, D.C.

35. McDonald, *Insull,* pp. 252–59.

36. Paul H. Douglas, "Chicago's Persistent Traction Problem," *National Municipal Review* 18 (November 1929), pp. 669–75; Linda J. Lear, *Harold L. Ickes: The Aggressive Progressive, 1874–1933* (New York: Garland Publishing, 1981), p. 338; Paul H. Douglas, "Statement by Paul H. Douglas on the Traction Situation, December 29, 1933," Douglas Papers, box 295, folder 6; Paul H. Douglas, untitled statement, n.d., Harold L. Ickes Papers, box 37, folder "People's Traction League, 1929–30–2," Manuscript Division, Library of Congress, Washington, D.C. (quotation). Douglas presented an exceptionally detailed analysis of Insull's traction scheme to the Chicago Forum on Nov. 20, 1932. See Paul H. Douglas, "The Challenge of the Insull Smash," Nov. 20, 1932, Douglas Papers, box 293, folder "Reports, Press Releases, Etc."

37. Harold L. Ickes to Oscar Hewitt, July 27, 1929, Ickes Papers, box 37, folder "People's Traction League, 1925–1930–1"; *Chicago Tribune,* July 29, 1929; Lear, *Harold L. Ickes,* pp. 334–35; Douglas, "Chicago's Persistent Traction Problem," pp. 672–73; McDonald, *Insull,* p. 260.

38. McDonald, *Insull,* p. 261; Douglas, *In the Fullness of Time,* p. 71 (quotation). The Douglas-Ickes correspondence is found in the Ickes Papers, box 37, folder "People's Traction League, 1925–1930–2." See, for example, the letters of May 29, June 6–7, 1930.

39. Lear, *Harold L. Ickes,* pp. 360–61; Douglas, *In the Fullness of Time,* p. 60.

40. Lear, *Harold L. Ickes,* p. 361; Douglas, *In the Fullness of Time,* pp. 59–61.

41. Morris, "Senator Douglas," p. 109.

42. Douglas, "Statement by Paul H. Douglas on the Traction Situation," pp. 2–3; Douglas, *In the Fullness of Time,* p. 61 (quotation).

43. Douglas, *In the Fullness of Time,* pp. 62–63.

44. Ibid., p. 63 (quotation).

45. *New York Times,* Aug. 1, 1932; Anderson, "Paul H. Douglas," p. 34 (quotation).

46. Frances Perkins, *The Roosevelt I Knew* (New York: Harper and Row,

1946), pp. 104–5; Paul H. Douglas, *The Coming of a New Party* (New York: Whittlesey House, McGraw-Hill, 1932), pp. 83–84, 171 (quotation); Douglas, *In the Fullness of Time,* pp. 71–72.

47. Douglas, *Coming of a New Party,* pp. 26–37, 204, 216 (quotation on p. 195); "United Conference for Progressive Political Action," 1933, Thomas R. Amlie Papers, box 10, folder 5, State Historical Society of Wisconsin, Madison, Wisconsin.

48. *New York Times,* June 27, 1934; Edward L. Schapsmeier, "Dirksen and Douglas of Illinois: The Pragmatist and the Professor as Contemporaries in the United States Senate," *Illinois Historical Journal* 83 (summer 1990), p. 78, n. 10; Douglas, *In the Fullness of Time,* p. 64 (quotation). For his assessment of the NRA and other early New Deal programs, see Paul H. Douglas, "The New Deal after Ten Weeks," *World Tomorrow* 16 (June 1933), pp. 418–19. Even while working for the NRA, Douglas was publicly critical of the agency. See, for example, his comments in the *New York Times,* Jan. 7, 1934.

49. *New York Times,* Nov. 17, 1933; Douglas, *In the Fullness of Time,* pp. 64–65.

50. Richard L. Strout, "Paul Douglas: Senator with Ideas," *New Republic* 121 (Sept. 5, 1949), p. 13; Paul H. Douglas, *The Problem of Unemployment* (New York: Macmillan, 1931); *New York Times,* May 24, 1931; Paul H. Douglas, *Standards of Unemployment Insurance* (Chicago: University of Chicago Press, 1933).

51. Paul H. Douglas, *The Theory of Wages* (New York: Macmillan, 1934).

52. Paul H. Douglas, *Controlling Depressions* (New York: W. W. Norton, 1935); Paul H. Douglas, "The Economics of Unemployment Relief," *American Economic Review* 23 Supplement (March 1933), p. 54. Douglas's family wages plan was also explained in Allen, ed., *Adventurous Americans,* pp. 185–88.

53. Paul H. Douglas, "Social Security for Today," *Christian Century* 51 (Nov. 28, 1934), p. 1515; Paul H. Douglas, "The Political Stabilization of Workers' Incomes through Unemployment Insurance," *Annals of the American Academy of Political and Social Science* 153 (March 1931), p. 102; Douglas, *Standards of Unemployment Insurance;* Schapsmeier and Schapsmeier, "Paul H. Douglas," p. 313; Paul H. Douglas tapes 1–9, Douglas Papers; Douglas, *In the Fullness of Time,* p. 74. As early as 1930, Douglas was writing to Senator Robert F. Wagner about the drafting of national social security legislation. See, for example, Paul H. Douglas to Robert F. Wagner, June 14, 1930, Legislative Files, Robert F. Wagner Papers, Georgetown University, Washington, D.C.

54. *New York Times,* Dec. 7, 1930; Douglas, "Political Stabilization of Workers' Incomes," pp. 99–100. Also see Roy Lubove, *The Struggle for Social Security, 1900–1935* (Pittsburgh: University of Pittsburgh Press, 1986).

55. Lubove, *Struggle for Social Security,* pp. 174–75; *New York Times,* Nov. 17, 1934, Jan. 16, 1935; Paul H. Douglas, "Security for Americans: Unemployment Insurance and Relief," *New Republic* 81 (Dec. 19, 1934), pp. 160–63; Paul H. Douglas, "Unemployment Insurance—Questions and Answers," *Christian Century* 52 (Jan. 2, 1935), pp. 12–14; Daniel Nelson, *Unemployment Insurance: The American Experience, 1915–1935* (Madison: University of Wisconsin Press, 1969), pp. 200–214; Douglas, *In the Fullness of Time,* p. 75; Paul H. Douglas, *Social Security in the United States* (New York and London: Whittlesey House, McGraw-Hill, 1936). Douglas testified before the Senate Committee on Education and Labor in 1934 at the request of Senator Wagner (Paul H. Douglas to Robert F. Wagner, Mar. 9,

1934, Wagner Papers, Legislative Files). Subsequent to his experiences with the national legislation, Douglas was the principal author of the Illinois Unemployment Insurance Act of 1937 (Anderson, "Paul H. Douglas," pp. 49–50).

56. The best biography of Thompson is Douglas Bukowski, *Big Bill Thompson, Chicago, and the Politics of Image* (Urbana: University of Illinois Press, 1998). On Cermak, see Alex Gottfried, *Boss Cermak of Chicago: A Study of Political Leadership* (Seattle: University of Washington Press, 1962). On Kelly, see Roger Biles, *Big City Boss in Depression and War: Mayor Edward J. Kelly of Chicago* (DeKalb: Northern Illinois University Press, 1984).

57. *New York Times*, Feb. 16, 26, 1935; Douglas, *In the Fullness of Time*, p. 85.

58. *New York Times*, Mar. 31, 1935.

59. Ibid., July 6, 1935; Paul H. Douglas to Gerald P. Nye, July 18, 1935, Amlie Papers, box 21, folder 4. See Douglas's letters to Amlie of July 26, 1935, in box 21, folder 4, and of Aug. 3, 1935, in box 21, folder 5, of the Amlie Papers.

60. Douglas, *In the Fullness of Time*, pp. 102–3. On the Memorial Day Massacre, see Biles, *Big City Boss in Depression and War*, pp. 61–64.

61. Douglas, *In the Fullness of Time*, pp. 78–84; Schapsmeier, "Dirksen and Douglas of Illinois," p. 80, n. 12 (quotation).

62. Schapsmeier and Schapsmeier, "Paul H. Douglas," pp. 314–16.

2: INTO THE POLITICAL ARENA

1. Paul H. Douglas to John J. Gunther, Feb. 5, 1957, Americans for Democratic Action Papers, Legislative File, box 21, Paul Douglas folder, State Historical Society of Wisconsin, Madison, Wisconsin.

2. Biles, *Big City Boss in Depression and War*, pp. 103–5; Harold L. Ickes, *The Secret Diary of Harold L. Ickes: The Inside Struggle, 1936–1939* (New York: Simon and Schuster, 1954), pp. 431–32 (quotation). Douglas discussed the extent of corruption in Chicago in an interview he gave to the Columbia University Oral History Research Office. See interview 3 (Sept. 13, 1974) of the Douglas interview in the Columbia University Oral History Project.

3. Biles, *Big City Boss in Depression and War*, pp. 67–69; Ickes, *Secret Diary of Harold L. Ickes*, pp. 512–15, 523; Douglas, *In the Fullness of Time*, pp. 85–86.

4. Douglas, *In the Fullness of Time*, p. 86; Rothe, ed., *Current Biography, 1949*, p.167 (quotation).

5. Douglas, *In the Fullness of Time*, p. 87; Schapsmeier, "Dirksen and Douglas of Illinois," p. 79, n. 11. Douglas had been working against the Kelly-Nash machine for years, even writing influential figures in Washington to see what could be done to cleanse Chicago politics and government. See, for example, Paul H. Douglas to Robert F. Wagner, Sept. 28, 1933, Wagner Papers, Legislative Files.

6. On Hyde Park, see Dominic A. Pacyga and Ellen Skerrett, *Chicago: City of Neighborhoods* (Chicago: Loyola University Press, 1986). On changing black voting patterns, see Roger Biles, "'Big Red in Bronzeville': Mayor Ed Kelly Reels in the Black Vote," *Chicago History* 10 (summer 1981), pp. 99–111; and William J. Grimshaw, *Bitter Fruit: Black Politics and the Chicago Machine, 1931–1991* (Chicago: University of Chicago Press, 1992).

7. Douglas, *In the Fullness of Time*, pp. 87–89.

8. Ibid., pp. 87–88.

9. *Chicago Tribune,* Mar. 1, Apr. 5, 1939; Douglas, *In the Fullness of Time,* pp. 89–90; "Making of a Maverick," p. 18.

10. Len O'Connor, *Clout: Mayor Daley and His City* (New York: Avon Books, 1975), p. 127 (quotation); Douglas, *In the Fullness of Time,* pp. 91–92.

11. "Making of a Maverick," p. 18 (quotations); Douglas, *In the Fullness of Time,* pp. 96–99; Morris, "Senator Douglas," p. 109.

12. Douglas, *In the Fullness of Time,* pp. 92–94; "Making of a Maverick," p. 18; Douglas, "Running for Office Means What It Says," *New York Times Magazine,* Sept. 5, 1948, p. 6.

13. Douglas, *In the Fullness of Time,* p. 95.

14. "Speech by Alderman Paul H. Douglas at Final Vote of City Council opposing Passage of Traction Ordinance," June 19, 1941, Douglas Papers, box 296, folder 13; *Chicago Tribune,* June 20, 1941; Douglas, *In the Fullness of Time,* p. 97. The ordinance was ratified in a public referendum on June 1, 1942, but, echoing some of the same concerns about the measure raised by Douglas in the city council, the Illinois Commerce Commission quashed the plan the following year. David M. Young, *Chicago Transit: An Illustrated History* (DeKalb: Northern Illinois University Press, 1998), p. 106.

15. Douglas, *In the Fullness of Time,* pp. 97–99.

16. Schapsmeier, "Dirksen and Douglas of Illinois," pp. 80–81; Douglas, *In the Fullness of Time,* pp. 104–5; Paul H. Douglas to Franz Boas, Sept. 20, 1940, Douglas Papers, box 113, folder "Ab. Linc. Rep. Club Attack"; *New York Times,* May 31, 1941.

17. In response to my Freedom of Information Act request, the FBI released its 256-page file on Douglas. The contents of the file, Freedom of Information Privacy Act No. 911987, are in my possession.

18. Paul H. Douglas to Adlai E. Stevenson, Jan. 8, 1942, Adlai E. Stevenson to Paul H. Douglas, Jan. 21, 1942, and Paul H. Douglas to Adlai E. Stevenson, Jan. 27, 1942, all in Adlai E. Stevenson Papers, box 25, folder 11, Princeton University, Princeton, New Jersey; John Bartlow Martin, *Adlai Stevenson of Illinois* (Garden City, N.Y.: Doubleday, 1976), pp. 199–200.

19. *Chicago Tribune,* Jan. 15, 1942; Biles, *Big City Boss in Depression and War,* pp. 119–21. Douglas charged that the Kelly-Nash machine tried to "buy" him by offering the nomination for the Second District seat in the House of Representatives held by McKeough if he would not run for the U.S. Senate. *Chicago Sun* clipping, May 7, 1942, in Douglas Papers, box 286, scrapbook "Candidate for U.S. Senate (1942)."

20. Harold L. Ickes to Paul H. Douglas, Jan. 4, 1943, Ickes Papers, box 160, Paul H. Douglas folder; Douglas, *In the Fullness of Time,* p. 108 (quotation).

21. Morris, "Senator Douglas," p. 109.

22. Ibid., p. 110.

23. Paul H. Douglas to Harold L. Ickes, Apr. 23, 1942, Ickes Papers, box 160, Paul H. Douglas folder; Schapsmeier, "Dirksen and Douglas of Illinois," p. 81; Douglas, *In the Fullness of Time,* pp. 108–9; *Chicago News* clipping, Apr. 15, 1942, in Douglas Papers, box 286, scrapbook "Candidate for U.S. Senate (1942)."

24. Paul H. Douglas to Adlai E. Stevenson, Apr. 17, 1942, Adlai E. Stevenson to Paul H. Douglas, Apr. 24, 1942, and Paul H. Douglas to Adlai E. Stevenson, Apr. 28, 1942, all in Stevenson Papers, box 25, folder 11; Frank Knox to Harold L. Ickes,

Dec. 31, 1942, and Harold L. Ickes to Paul H. Douglas, Jan. 4, 1943, both in Ickes Papers, box 160, Paul H. Douglas folder; Douglas, *In the Fullness of Time,* pp. 109–11.

25. Anderson, "Paul H. Douglas" (first quotation); Paul H. Douglas to Adlai E. Stevenson, Jan. 27, 1942, Stevenson Papers, box 25, folder 11 (second quotation).

26. Douglas, *In the Fullness of Time,* pp. 111–18; Paul H. Douglas to Harold L. Ickes, Aug. 14, 1943, Ickes Papers, box 160, Paul H. Douglas folder; Paul H. Douglas to Adlai E. Stevenson, Sept. 30, 1943 (quotation), and Adlai E. Stevenson to Paul H. Douglas, Oct. 29, 1943, both in Stevenson Papers, box 25, folder 11.

27. Douglas, *In the Fullness of Time,* pp. 121–22; "Making of a Maverick," p. 18; Douglas Committee Campaign Release, Oct. 30, 1948, Douglas Papers, box 515, folder "October 30, 1948"; Morris, "Senator Douglas," p. 27 (quotation).

28. Douglas, *In the Fullness of Time,* pp. 122–23; Douglas Committee Campaign Release, Oct. 30, 1948, Douglas Papers, box 515, folder "October 30, 1948."

29. Anderson, "Paul H. Douglas," p. 67; Douglas, *In the Fullness of Time,* pp. 126, 181–82.

30. *New York Times,* Sept. 7, 1945; Paul H. Douglas, "Are There Laws of Production?" *American Economic Review* 38 (March 1949), pp. 1–41; Douglas, *In the Fullness of Time,* pp. 127–28.

31. Morris, "Senator Douglas," p. 110; Cabell Phillips, "Presenting Mrs. Douglas and Mrs. Douglas," *New York Times Magazine,* Feb. 18, 1945, pp. 20, 41; *Chicago Tribune,* Oct. 23 (quotation), Nov. 7, 1946; *New York Times,* Nov. 7, 1946.

32. On the 1947 mayoral election, see Biles, *Big City Boss in Depression and War,* pp. 145–50. Also see Arnold R. Hirsch, "Martin H. Kennelly: The Mugwump and the Machine" in Paul M. Green and Melvin G. Holli, eds., *The Mayors: The Chicago Political Tradition* (Carbondale: Southern Illinois University Press, 1987), pp. 126–43.

33. Paul H. Douglas to Adlai E. Stevenson, Sept. 30, 1943, and Adlai E. Stevenson to Paul H. Douglas, Oct. 29, 1943, both in Stevenson Papers, box 25, folder 11; Frank W. McCulloch to James Loeb, Jr., Dec. 10, 1947, Americans for Democratic Action Papers, Chapter Files, box 13, folder "Chicago Chapter Corr. 1947, Oct.–Dec."; Board of Directors Meeting Minutes, Dec. 9, 23, 1947, Independent Voters of Illinois Papers, box 2, folder "1947 May–Dec.," Chicago Historical Society, Chicago, Illinois.

34. Martin, *Adlai Stevenson of Illinois,* p. 274.

35. "Gentleman and Scholar," *Time* 51 (Jan. 12, 1948), p. 61; Martin, *Adlai Stevenson of Illinois,* p. 277 (first quotation); Douglas, *In the Fullness of Time,* p. 129 (second quotation).

36. Samuel Shaffer, *On and off the Floor: Thirty Years as a Correspondent on Capitol Hill* (New York: Newsweek Books, 1980), p. 15 (first quotation); Rothe, ed., *Current Biography, 1949,* p. 167 (second quotation); "Making of a Maverick," pp. 18–19 (third quotation).

37. *Chicago Tribune,* Nov. 4, 1948; Douglas, *In the Fullness of Time,* p. 130.

38. Richard Norton Smith, *The Colonel: The Life and Legend of Robert R. McCormick, Indomitable Editor of the Chicago Tribune* (Boston: Houghton Mifflin, 1997), pp. 442 (quotation), 479.

39. "Where Does Paul H. Douglas Stand?" *New Republic* 118 (Feb. 16, 1948), p. 10; Schapsmeier, "Dirksen and Douglas of Illinois," p. 81 (quotation); "Douglas: His Policy," *New Republic* 118 (June 28, 1948), pp. 20–21.

40. Douglas, "Running for Office Means What It Says," pp. 5–7; Rothe, ed., *Current Biography, 1949,* pp. 167–68; "Douglas: His Policy," p. 20.

41. "Douglas: His Policy," p. 21 (first quotation); Anderson, "Paul H. Douglas," p. 85 (second quotation).

42. Interview with Howard E. Shuman, pp. 217–19, Senate Historical Office, Washington, D.C.

43. Biles, *Big City Boss in Depression and War,* p. 151 (quotation); Douglas, *In the Fullness of Time,* pp. 133–35. On the 1948 Democratic National Convention, see Irwin Ross, *The Loneliest Campaign: The Truman Victory of 1948* (New York: New American Library, 1968).

44. Douglas, *In the Fullness of Time,* p. 134.

45. Ibid., p. 136.

46. Martin, *Adlai Stevenson of Illinois,* p. 295; Douglas, *In the Fullness of Time,* p. 136; interview with Shuman, pp. 75–76. Neither the Douglas nor the Stevenson Papers contain any correspondence between the two men during the 1948 campaign.

47. *Chicago Tribune,* Sept. 14 (quotations), 19, 21, 23, 1948; "Champaign, Ill. Speech by Paul H. Douglas," Douglas Papers, box 114, folder "Reply to Cong. Busbey." In its coverage of the 1948 election results, the *Tribune* again referred to Douglas as a former leader of the Socialist party and also erroneously reported that he switched to the Democratic party after the leftward turn of the Roosevelt administration in 1933 (*Chicago Tribune,* Nov. 4, 1948).

48. Rothe, ed., *Current Biography, 1949,* p. 167; "Making of a Maverick," p. 19 (first and second quotations); Morris, "Senator Douglas," p. 119 (third quotation).

49. "Democrats at Twilight," *Newsweek* 32 (Oct. 18, 1948), p. 37; Douglas, *In the Fullness of Time,* pp. 138–39.

50. Douglas, *In the Fullness of Time,* pp. 139–40.

51. *Chicago Tribune,* Nov. 4, 1948; Anderson, "Paul H. Douglas," pp. 88–89; "Corn for the Colonel," *New Republic* 119 (Nov. 15, 1948), p. 7; "Democrats at Twilight," p. 38. Also see the analysis of the 1948 campaign in Steven M. Gillon, *Politics and Vision: The ADA and American Liberalism, 1947–1985* (New York: Oxford University Press, 1987), pp. 55–56.

52. James Loeb, Jr., to Paul H. Douglas, Dec. 2, 1948, Americans for Democratic Action Papers, Administrative File, box 33, Paul Douglas folder.

3: PRECOCIOUS FRESHMAN SENATOR

1. Paul H. Douglas, "Report from a Freshman Senator," *New York Times Magazine,* Mar. 20, 1949, p. 74.

2. Lawrence A. Yates, "Fair Deal" in Richard S. Kirkendall, ed., *The Harry S. Truman Encyclopedia* (Boston: G. K. Hall, 1989), p. 124 (quotation).

3. Alonzo L. Hamby, *Beyond the New Deal: Harry S. Truman and American Liberalism* (New York: Columbia University Press, 1973), chap. 11; Robert C. Byrd, *The Senate, 1789–1989: Addresses on the History of the United States Senate* (Washington, D.C.: Government Printing Office, 1988), p. 593; Douglas, *In the Fullness of Time,* pp. 197–214. Also see Edward L. Schapsmeier and Frederick H. Schapsmeier, "Scott W. Lucas of Havana: His Rise and Fall as Majority Leader in the United States Senate," *Journal of the Illinois State Historical Society* 70 (November 1977), pp. 302–20.

4. Douglas, "Report from a Freshman Senator," p. 10; *Chicago Tribune,* Sept. 25, 1976; Strout, "Paul Douglas: Senator with Ideas," p. 14 (first and second quotations); Phillips, "Paul Douglas—'Instinctive Liberal,'" p. 10 (third quotation).

5. Paul H. Douglas, "Report from a Freshman Senator," pp. 10, 14.

6. Morris, "Senator Douglas," p. 110.

7. T. R. B., "Washington Wire," *New Republic* 120 (Mar. 14, 1949), p. 4; Douglas, *In the Fullness of Time,* pp. 214–15; "The Fair Deal Falters," *New Republic* 120 (Feb. 21, 1949), p. 5.

8. T. R. B., "Washington Wire," p. 3; Anderson, "Paul H. Douglas," pp. 230–31; Schapsmeier and Schapsmeier, "Scott W. Lucas of Havana," pp. 308–9; Hamby, *Beyond the New Deal,* p. 313.

9. *Congressional Record,* 81st Cong., 1st sess., Mar. 17, 1949, 95, pt. 2:2665–67. Also see Paul H. Douglas, "Address by Senator Paul H. Douglas, National Convention of Americans for Democratic Action," Hotel Sherman, Chicago, Illinois, Apr. 9, 1949, Douglas Papers, box 515, folder 4/9/49.

10. Hamby, *Beyond the New Deal,* p. 313 (first quotation); Douglas, *In the Fullness of Time,* p. 269 (second quotation).

11. Press release, June 9, 1949, Douglas Papers, box 515, folder 6/9/49; "Making of a Maverick," p. 19; "The Fair Deal Falters," pp. 5–6; Douglas, *In the Fullness of Time,* p. 269.

12. *U.S. Statutes at Large,* 63, pt. 1:413 (first quotation); *Congressional Record,* 81st Cong., 1st sess., Apr. 19, 1949, 95, pt. 4:4730 (second quotation); *New York Times,* Apr. 20, 1949; Thomas Sancton, "Housing and Segregation," *Nation* 168 (Apr. 30, 1949), p. 490. The most thorough description of the legislative battle over housing legislation in 1949 appears in Richard O. Davies, *Housing Reform during the Truman Administration* (Columbia: University of Missouri Press, 1966).

13. Davies, *Housing Reform,* p. 107; *Congressional Record,* 81st Cong., 1st sess., Apr. 20, 1949, 95, pt. 4:4802.

14. Paul H. Douglas, "A Senator's Vote: A Searching of the Soul," *New York Times Magazine,* Apr. 30, 1950, p. 42; *Congressional Record,* 81st Cong., 1st sess., Apr. 21, 1949, 95, pt. 4:4850–57 (quotation); Richard O. Davies, *Defender of the Old Guard: John Bricker and American Politics* (Columbus: Ohio State University Press, 1993), p. 138; Paul H. Douglas, "Address by Senator Paul H. Douglas of Illinois In Opposition to the Bricker Amendment to the Housing Bill," Douglas Papers, box 515, folder 4/21/49.

15. Douglas, *In the Fullness of Time,* p. 272.

16. Strout, "Paul Douglas," p. 15; Sancton, "Housing and Segregation," p. 491.

17. Strout, "Paul Douglas," p. 15.

18. Anderson, "Paul H. Douglas," pp. 234–35; Douglas, *In the Fullness of Time,* pp. 269–70. An angry Senator McKellar complained that Douglas had earlier urged in committee hearings the deepening and widening of the Cal-Sag canal in Illinois; Douglas responded that he reserved the right to represent his state in a committee but still serve the national interest on the Senate floor (*In the Fullness of Time,* p. 252).

19. Anderson, "Paul H. Douglas," p. 235; "Senator Douglas Meets the Press," *American Mercury* 69 (September 1949), pp. 322–23. In January 1949, Douglas said that some new taxes would be necessary to balance the budget, but by May he concluded that budget cuts would be sufficient and dismissed the

need for a tax increase. Transcript of "The American Forum of the Air," Jan. 31, 1949, Douglas Papers, box 515, folder "1/31/49 The American Forum of the Air."

20. Douglas, *In the Fullness of Time*, p. 313.

21. *New York Times*, Dec. 8, 1949; Monte M. Poen, *Harry S. Truman versus the Medical Lobby: The Genesis of Medicare* (Columbia: University of Missouri Press, 1979), pp. 161–62.

22. *New York Times*, Dec. 8, 1949; Poen, *Truman versus the Medical Lobby*, pp. 168–69 (quotations).

23. Douglas, *In the Fullness of Time*, pp. 351–53.

24. Ibid., pp. 354–55; Press release, Aug. 10, 1949, Douglas Papers, box 515, folder 8/10/49 (quotation); *Congressional Record*, 81st Cong., 1st sess., June 1, 1949, 95, pt. 6:7064–71, Aug. 10, 1949, 95, pt. 8:11176–86.

25. Douglas, *In the Fullness of Time*, pp. 414–17; James T. Patterson, *Mr. Republican: A Biography of Robert A. Taft* (Boston: Houghton Mifflin, 1972), pp. 432–33.

26. "Making of a Maverick," p. 16; Patterson, *Mr. Republican*, p. 440; Press release, n.d., Douglas Papers, box 515, folder "9/49 Pageant Magazine Poll."

27. Robert Wallace, "New Gouge for Consumers," *New Republic* 122 (Mar. 13, 1950), p. 11; Anne Hodges Morgan, *Robert S. Kerr: The Senate Years* (Norman: University of Oklahoma Press, 1977), pp. 61–62.

28. Douglas, *In the Fullness of Time*, p. 235.

29. Joseph P. Harris, "The Senatorial Rejection of Leland Olds: A Case Study," *American Political Science Review* 45 (September 1951), pp. 676–90; *Congressional Record*, 81st Cong., 1st sess., Oct. 12, 1949, 95, pt. 11:14368 (quotations); Morgan, *Robert S. Kerr*, pp. 73–74. Douglas prefaced his support of Leland Olds by explaining that he knew and revered the nominee's father, George D. Olds, who had for fifty years been a professor of mathematics, dean, and president of Amherst College (*Congressional Record*, 81st Cong., 1st sess., Oct. 12, 1949, 95, pt. 11:14386).

30. "High Ride for Gas," *Time* 55 (Apr. 10, 1950), p. 20; Douglas, *In the Fullness of Time*, p. 465 (first quotation); "On the Natural Gas Bill, S. 1498," Mar. 29, 1950, Douglas Papers, box 176, folder "Cong. Speeches & Statements, 1950"; Morgan, *Robert S. Kerr*, p. 86 (second and third quotations). Also see Paul H. Douglas to H. Clay Tate, Aug. 2, 1950, Douglas Papers, box 176, folder "Douglas Correspondence 1950–52."

31. "High Ride for Gas," p. 20; *New York Times*, Apr. 6, 1950; Morgan, *Robert S. Kerr*, p. 99 (quotation).

32. Hamby, *Beyond the New Deal*, pp. 346–48; Morgan, *Robert S. Kerr*, p. 102 (quotation).

33. "Steamboat Comin' Roun' de Bend," *Time* 55 (May 1, 1950), pp. 18–19; Charles Mangel, "Paul Douglas: Man Ahead of His Time," *Look* 31 (June 13, 1967), p. 108 (quotation); interview with Shuman, p. 254.

34. Randolph E. Paul, *Taxation in the United States* (Boston: Little, Brown, 1954), p. 559.

35. Ibid., p. 566 (quotation); Douglas, *In the Fullness of Time*, pp. 424–25.

36. Paul, *Taxation in the United States*, pp. 609–18; Douglas, *In the Fullness of Time*, pp. 425–26; "The Senator and the Expense Account," *Business Week*, Oct. 13, 1951, p. 172.

37. See Richard M. Fried, *Nightmare in Red: The McCarthy Era in Perspective* (New York: Oxford University Press, 1990).

38. "For Internal Security," *New Republic* 123 (Aug. 21, 1950), pp. 7–8; "Excess of Zeal," *Nation* 171 (Aug. 19, 1950), pp. 158–59; William S. Tanner and Robert Griffith, "Legislative Politics and 'McCarthyism': The Internal Security Act of 1950," in Robert Griffith and Athan Theoharis, eds., *The Specter: Original Essays on the Cold War and the Origins of McCarthyism* (New York: New Viewpoints, 1974), p. 181; *Congressional Record*, 81st Cong., 2d sess., Sept. 8, 1950, 96, pt. 11:14411 (quotation).

39. Tanner and Griffith, "Legislative Politics and 'McCarthyism,'" pp. 183–84; *Congressional Record*, 81st Cong., 2d sess., Sept. 8, 1950, 96, pt. 11:14424; Thomas C. Reeves, *The Life and Times of Joe McCarthy: A Biography* (New York: Stein and Day, 1982), p. 331.

40. Douglas, *In the Fullness of Time*, p. 307 (first, second, and fourth quotations); Reeves, *Life and Times of Joe McCarthy*, p. 331 (third quotation).

41. "Statement by Senator Paul H. Douglas of Illinois," Douglas Papers, box 113, folder "Internal Security"; Reeves, *Life and Times of Joe McCarthy*, p. 331. In January 1951, Douglas proposed that citizens questioned by congressional committees be allowed to file statements as part of the official record, to summon corroborative witnesses, and to cross-examine their accusers. Richard M. Fried, *Men against McCarthy* (New York: Columbia University Press, 1976), p. 194.

42. "The Senate's Most Valuable Ten," *Time* 55 (Apr. 3, 1950), p. 20; Anderson, "Paul H. Douglas," pp. 247–48.

43. Schapsmeier, "Dirksen and Douglas of Illinois," pp. 74–84; Schapsmeier and Schapsmeier, "Scott W. Lucas of Havana," p. 313 (quotations); Douglas, *In the Fullness of Time*, pp. 561–62; Martin, *Adlai Stevenson of Illinois*, pp. 456–60.

44. "The Fin of the Shark," *Time* 57 (Jan. 22, 1951), p. 16; *Congressional Record*, 82d Cong., 1st sess., Jan. 15, 1951, 97, pt. 1:231–33; Paul H. Douglas, "Our Foreign Policy in the Present International Crisis," Douglas Papers, box 516, folder 1/15/51.

45. Paul H. Douglas, "Our Foreign Policy in the Present International Crisis," Douglas Papers, box 516, folder 1/15/51; Anderson, "Paul H. Douglas," p. 255 (quotation); *Congressional Record*, 82d Cong., 1st sess., Jan. 15, 1951, 97, pt. 1:233–51; "The Fin of the Shark," pp. 17–18.

46. Douglas, *In the Fullness of Time*, pp. 497–98; Paul H. Douglas to "Dear Friend," Apr. 13, 1951, Douglas Papers, box 516, folder 4/13/51 (first quotation); *New York Times*, May 27, 1951 (second quotation); Paul H. Douglas to George C. Marshall, July 10, 1951, Douglas Papers, box 517, folder "7-10-51 Marshall Letter."

47. Interview with Paul H. Douglas, interview 2, Sept. 10, 1974, Columbia University Oral History Project, p. 12.

48. *New York Times*, July 7, 22, Aug. 10, 1950; Donald R. McCoy, *The Presidency of Harry S. Truman* (Lawrence: University Press of Kansas, 1984), p. 279; Randall Bennett Woods, *Fulbright: A Biography* (Cambridge: Cambridge University Press, 1995), pp. 160–61.

49. Paul H. Douglas, *Ethics in Government* (Cambridge, Mass.: Harvard University Press, 1952), p. 5; David McCullough, *Truman* (New York: Simon and Schuster, 1992), p. 864 (first and second quotations); William McGaffin,

"'Ferocious Independent' at 70," *New York Times Magazine,* Mar. 25, 1962, p. 44 (third quotation); interview with Paul H. Douglas, interview 2, pp. 12A–13; Douglas, *In the Fullness of Time,* p. 223 (fourth and fifth quotations).

50. Douglas, *In the Fullness of Time,* pp. 223–24 (quotations); McCullough, *Truman,* p. 864.

51. *New York Times,* May 13, 1951; Douglas, *In the Fullness of Time,* pp. 223–24; interview with Paul Douglas, interview 2, p. 14 (quotation).

52. "Statement of Sen. Paul H. Douglas (D., Ill.) on Nominations for Federal Judgeships in U.S. District Court for Northern Illinois," July 27, 1951, Douglas Papers, box 517, folder 7/27/51.

53. "Statement of Senator Paul H. Douglas (D., Ill.), August 10, 1951," Douglas Papers, box 298, folder "Stevenson Memorandum/U.S. Dist. Judgeships"; McCoy, *Presidency of Harry S. Truman,* p. 277.

54. Harry S Truman to Paul H. Douglas, Aug. 2, 1951, and Paul H. Douglas to Harry S Truman, Aug. 4, 1951, both in Douglas Papers, box 298, folder "Douglas-Truman Correspondence, 1948–52."

55. Douglas, *Ethics in Government,* p. 47.

56. Douglas considered Truman "one of our near-great Presidents" and noted happily that historians have concurred. "I have had the pleasure of personally telling him this several times," he noted, "but I am sure that he continued to cherish his dislike [of Douglas]" (*In the Fullness of Time,* p. 226). Shortly before Truman left office, Douglas wrote him a letter lauding his achievements and expressing regret that the two men had not enjoyed better relations; Truman wrote a gracious response in which he noted his admiration for Douglas's courage and ability. Paul H. Douglas to Harry S Truman, n.d., and Harry S Truman to Paul H. Douglas, Jan. 9, 1953, both in Douglas Papers, box 298, folder "Douglas-Truman Correspondence, 1948–52."

57. Estes Kefauver to Paul H. Douglas, Mar. 29, 1951, and Paul Simon to Paul H. Douglas, Mar. 8, 1951, both in Douglas Papers, box 233, folder "Douglas for President"; Phillips, "Paul Douglas—'Instinctive Liberal,'" p. 10; Lucille Sharkey to Paul H. Douglas, Feb. 5, 1951, Douglas Papers, box 426, file "Douglas for Secretary of State"; Sollace Mitchell to Paul H. Douglas, Feb. 10, 1951, and Paul H. Douglas to Sollace Mitchell, Feb. 15, 1951, both in Douglas Papers, box 426, folder "Douglas for Commissioner of Baseball." The Douglas Papers, especially box 233, contain dozens of letters in which Douglas denied any interest in running for president and ordered supporters to cease their activities in his behalf.

58. Shuman reported that members of the eastern establishment including the chief executive officer of City Bank, *Time* publisher Henry Luce, and one of the Rockefellers offered Douglas one million dollars for his campaign chest if he agreed to run for president. Douglas met with them in New York City and declined their offer (interview with Shuman, pp. 79–81).

59. Paul H. Douglas to Walter J. Dennis, Aug. 23, 1951, Douglas Papers, box 233, folder "Douglas for President Oregon State Primary"; Paul H. Douglas to Henry P. Slane, editor, *Peoria Journal,* Mar. 19, 1951, Douglas Papers, box 233, folder "Douglas for President."

60. *New York Times,* Sept. 11, 1951; "A Senator Screams," *Time* 58 (Sept. 24, 1951), p. 26 (quotation); "Frustration in the Senate," *Commonweal* 54 (Sept. 21,

1951), p. 564; Douglas, *In the Fullness of Time*, p. 320; "How Douglas Cracked," *Newsweek* 38 (Sept. 24, 1951), p. 24.

    61. Douglas, *In the Fullness of Time*, p. 320.

4: POLITICS IN THE AGE OF MCCARTHY

    1. Press release by Paul H. Douglas, July 30, 1954, Douglas Papers, box 519, folder "July 30, 1954."

    2. *New York Times*, Dec. 27, 1951; Paul H. Douglas to Floyd Maxwell, May 29, 1952, Adolf A. Berle, Jr., to Paul H. Douglas, May 21, 1952, and Paul H. Douglas to Adolf A. Berle, Jr., May 26, 1952, all in Douglas Papers, box 233, folder "Douglas for President May 1952"; Douglas, *In the Fullness of Time*, p. 563.

    3. On Kefauver's career, see Joseph Bruce Gorman, *Kefauver: A Political Biography* (New York: Oxford University Press, 1971).

    4. Douglas acknowledged that differences existed between himself and Kefauver—he noted, for example, that he "went further" on civil rights and that Kefauver supported the Atlantic Union more enthusiastically—but overall felt the Tennessean was the best choice for liberals. Paul Douglas, "Why I'm for Kefauver," *Collier's* 130 (July 19, 1952), p. 57.

    5. Press release, Feb. 10, 1952, Douglas Papers, box 517, folder 2/10/52; Anderson, "Paul H. Douglas," pp. 256–57; Gorman, *Kefauver*, p. 118 (quotation).

    6. Martin, *Adlai Stevenson of Illinois*, pp. 482–83; Paul H. Douglas to Adlai E. Stevenson, Oct. 26, 1951, and Adlai E. Stevenson to Paul H. Douglas, Apr. 19, 1952, both in Stevenson Papers, box 25, folder 11; Douglas, *In the Fullness of Time*, pp. 562–63.

    7. Douglas, *In the Fullness of Time*, pp. 563–64; interview with Paul H. Douglas, interview 2, Sept. 10, 1974, Columbia University Oral History Project, pp. 16–17. Douglas aide Howard Shuman believed that Douglas not only spoke with Stevenson confidants but also actually received the governor's personal assurances that he would not run for president that year; Douglas does not mention in his autobiography any direct conversation with Stevenson (interview with Shuman, p. 78).

    8. Douglas, *In the Fullness of Time*, pp. 564–65. On Stevenson's reluctant candidacy, see Martin, *Adlai Stevenson of Illinois*, chap. 7; and Roger Biles, "Jacob M. Arvey, Kingmaker: The Nomination of Adlai E. Stevenson in 1952," *Chicago History* 7 (fall 1979), pp. 130–43.

    9. Speech by Senator Paul H. Douglas, July 21, 1952, Douglas Papers, box 517, folder "July 21, 1952."

    10. "The Liberal Democrats Take Their Stand," *New Republic* 127 (July 28, 1952), p. 5; Douglas, *In the Fullness of Time*, p. 565.

    11. Martin, *Adlai Stevenson of Illinois*, pp. 592–95; Douglas, *In the Fullness of Time*, p. 565.

    12. Douglas, *In the Fullness of Time*, pp. 565–66.

    13. Ibid., pp. 566–67; *New York Times*, July 26, 1952; "The Big Battle," *Time* 60 (Aug. 4, 1952), p. 11; Paul H. Douglas to Adlai E. Stevenson, telegram, July 26, 1952, Stevenson Papers, box 25, folder 11.

    14. Douglas, *In the Fullness of Time*, p. 567; Paul H. Douglas to Adlai E. Stevenson, Sept. 13, 1952, and Paul H. Douglas to Adlai E. Stevenson, telegram,

Nov. 5, 1952 (quotation), both in Stevenson Papers, box 25, folder 11.

15. "Talking It Over: America's Immigration Policy and the McCarran-Walter Bill," June 1, 1952, Douglas Papers, box 517, folder "June 1, 1952"; *Congressional Record,* 82d Cong., 2d sess., May 19, 1952, 98, pt. 4:5410–25.

16. *Congressional Record,* 82d Cong., 2d sess., July 1, 1952, 98, pt. 7:8716–36; Douglas, *In the Fullness of Time,* pp. 355–57.

17. *Congressional Record,* 82d Cong., 2d sess., July 2, 1952, 98, pt. 7:8888–92; Douglas, *In the Fullness of Time,* pp. 357–58.

18. Press release, Feb. 27, 1952, Douglas Papers, box 517, folder 2/27/52; Anderson, "Paul H. Douglas," p. 261 (first quotation); release of speech, Feb. 24, 1952, Douglas Papers, box 517, folder "February 24, 1952" (second quotation).

19. Text of speech, Jan. 7, 1953, Douglas Papers, box 518, folder "Cloture Jan. 7, 1953" (quotation). Douglas discussed these issues fully in an article that he wrote before Congress convened and appeared in the *New Republic* shortly after the session opened (Paul H. Douglas, "The Fight against the Filibuster," *New Republic* 122 [Jan. 12, 1953], pp. 6–8).

20. Douglas, *In the Fullness of Time,* pp. 277–78; *Congressional Record,* 83d Cong., 1st sess., Jan. 7, 1953, 99, pt. 1:202–6, 232.

21. Gary W. Reichard, *The Reaffirmation of Republicanism: Eisenhower and the Eighty-third Congress* (Knoxville: University of Tennessee Press, 1975), chaps. 1–2.

22. Reichard, *Reaffirmation of Republicanism,* pp. 148–49. Also see Ernest R. Bartley, *The Tidelands Oil Controversy: A Legal and Historical Analysis* (Austin: University of Texas Press, 1953).

23. Reichard, *Reaffirmation of Republicanism,* pp. 149–50; press release, Mar. 1, 1952, Douglas Papers, box 517, folder "March 1, 1952."

24. *Congressional Record,* 83d Cong., 1st sess., Apr. 10, 1953, 99, pt. 3:3049–50. Douglas objected to the claim that the bill's opponents had staged a filibuster. Although a true filibuster was designed to prevent a vote, he maintained, the liberals in this instance were simply trying to delay a vote so that the Senate and the public could be educated about the legislation's impact (*In the Fullness of Time,* p. 469).

25. Douglas, *In the Fullness of Time,* pp. 428–33; *Congressional Quarterly Almanac, 1958* (Washington, D.C.: Congressional Quarterly, 1958), p. 265; *Congressional Quarterly Almanac, 1959* (Washington, D.C.: Congressional Quarterly, 1959), pp. 201–2; *Congressional Quarterly Almanac, 1960* (Washington, D.C.: Congressional Quarterly, 1960), p. 364.

26. *Congressional Record,* 83d Cong., 1st sess., July 16, 1953, 99, pt. 7:8953–54; press release, July 16, 1953, Douglas Papers, box 518, folder 7/16/53. A vast historical literature has grown up around McCarthyism. See, for example, Richard H. Rovere, *Senator Joe McCarthy* (New York: Harper and Row, 1959); Fried, *Men against McCarthy;* Fried, *Nightmare in Red;* and Ellen Schrecker, *Many Are the Crimes: McCarthyism in America* (Boston: Little, Brown, 1998). On Eisenhower and McCarthyism, see Jeff Broadwater, *Eisenhower and the Anti-Communist Crusade* (Chapel Hill: University of North Carolina Press, 1992).

27. Rovere, *Senator Joe McCarthy,* p. 13 (first quotation); Allida M. Black, *Casting Her Own Shadow: Eleanor Roosevelt and the Shaping of Postwar Liberalism* (New York: Columbia University Press, 1996), p. 169 (second quotation); Fried, *Men against McCarthy,* p. 186 (third and fourth quotations).

28. Fried, *Men against McCarthy,* p. 297. Douglas discussed his feelings about McCarthy in his autobiography, *In the Fullness of Time,* pp. 249–52. In an effort to save the U.S. Marine Corps from being terminated by legislative fiat, Douglas drafted a bill that guaranteed the perpetual existence of at least four divisions of Marines. He calculated that to ensure the measure's passage he needed Joseph McCarthy's support. The Wisconsin senator sent word that Douglas must approach him on the Senate floor, in full view of the press gallery and all of their colleagues, and publicly ask for his support. Douglas found the prospect extremely distasteful, but his love for the Marines prevailed and he satisfied McCarthy's conditions for the needed support (interview with Shuman, pp. 99–100; Douglas, *In the Fullness of Time,* pp. 347–48).

29. Fried, *Nightmare in Red,* pp. 129–30; Douglas, *In the Fullness of Time,* p. 251; "Ten Try For Chance to Replace Douglas," *Life* 36 (Feb. 22, 1954), p. 34. The ten Republican aspirants were John Crane, Lar Daley, Edgar Elbert, Herbert Geisler, Edward Hayes, Julius Klein, Park Livingston, Joseph Meek, Deneen Watson, and Austin Wyman.

30. Hubert Cordier, "Campaigning with Television: The Speaking of Senator Paul H. Douglas in the 1954 Campaign" (Ph.D. diss., University of Illinois, 1955), pp. 10–11; Elmer Gertz, "Shall the Meek Inherit? Douglas Faces a Fight," *Nation* 179 (Oct. 23, 1954), p. 362. On McCormick and the *Tribune,* see Smith, *The Colonel: The Life and Legend of Robert R. McCormick.*

31. Theodore H. White, "Pivotal Campaign in Illinois: Joe Meek vs. Paul Douglas," *Reporter* 11 (Oct. 7, 1954), p. 35; Cordier, "Campaigning with Television," p. 10; "Mr. Retail v. the Professor," *Time* 63 (Apr. 26, 1954), p. 28 (first and second quotations); "Opposites in Illinois," *Time* 64 (Oct. 25, 1954), p. 15 (third, fourth, fifth, and sixth quotations).

32. Joseph T. Meek to Everett M. Dirksen, Dec. 24, 1953, Joseph T. Meek Papers, box 1, folder "Senatorial Race May 1953–February 1954," Chicago Historical Society, Chicago, Illinois. On Dirksen, see Byron C. Hulsey, *Everett Dirksen and His Presidents: How a Senate Giant Shaped American Politics* (Lawrence: University Press of Kansas, 2000); and Schapsmeier, "Dirksen and Douglas of Illinois," pp. 74–84.

33. Cabell Phillips, "Communique on the Illinois Campaign," *New York Times Magazine,* Sept. 26, 1954, p. 14.

34. "Formal Announcement of Candidacy of Joe Meek," Nov. 15, 1953, Meek Papers, box 1, folder "Senatorial Race May 1953–February 1954"; Phillips, "Communique on the Illinois Campaign," p. 79 (first quotation); White, "Pivotal Campaign in Illinois," p. 36 (second quotation); Gertz, "Shall the Meek Inherit?" p. 361 (third quotation).

35. *Chicago Sun-Times* clipping, Oct. 14, 1954, Douglas Papers, box 114, folder "McCarthy Era Smears on Douglas"; "Bushwhackers Work on Douglas," *New Republic* 131 (Nov. 1, 1954), p. 5; news release, n.d., Douglas Papers, box 114, folder "Articles pertaining to P.D.'s Marine Service, Etc."; Norman Thomas to Paul H. Douglas, July 1, 1954, Douglas Papers, box 428, folder "Norman Thomas, 1954" (quotation); Cordier, "Campaigning with Television," p. 80.

36. *Chicago Tribune,* Oct. 27, 1954; "Bushwhackers Work on Douglas," p. 5.

37. Statement by Paul H. Douglas, July 30, 1954, Douglas Papers, box 519,

folder "July 30, 1954"; *New York Times,* May 15, 1953; Cordier, "Campaigning with Television," p. 120 (quotation); "Douglas Answers Doctor's Health Insurance Query," Douglas Papers, box 519, folder "July 20, 1954"; *St. Louis Post-Dispatch* clipping, Sept. 26, 1954, Stevenson Papers, box 25, folder 11. The Bricker Amendment, which Eisenhower strongly opposed, limited the president's power to make treaties and other international agreements and increased the role of Congress in the conduct of foreign affairs; the amendment narrowly failed (Reichard, *Reaffirmation of Republicanism,* pp. 51–52). On Eisenhower and public housing, see Roger Biles, "Public Housing in the Eisenhower Administration," *Mid-America* 81 (winter 1999), pp. 5–25.

38. Douglas, *In the Fullness of Time,* p. 569; *Chicago Tribune,* Oct. 26, 31, 1954. See Paul H. Douglas, *Economy in the National Government* (Chicago: University of Chicago Press, 1952).

39. *Chicago Tribune,* Oct. 25, 1954; Hulsey, *Everett Dirksen and His Presidents,* p. 72 (first quotation); Phillips, "Communique on the Illinois Campaign," p. 74 (second quotation); William S. White, *Citadel: The Story of the U.S. Senate* (New York: Harper and Brothers, 1956), p. 150.

40. *Chicago Tribune,* Sept. 24, Oct. 31, 1954; *New York Times,* Sept. 19, 1954; Hulsey, *Everett Dirksen and His Presidents,* p. 79.

41. Joseph McCarthy to Joe Meek, Nov. 1, 1954, and Joseph McCarthy to Paul H. Douglas, Nov. 1, 1954, both in Meek Papers, box 3, folder "Senatorial Race Nov.-Dec. 1954"; *Chicago Tribune,* Nov. 2, 1954; Douglas, *In the Fullness of Time,* p. 251.

42. *Chicago Tribune* clipping, n.d., Stevenson Papers, box 25, folder 11; Douglas, *In the Fullness of Time,* p. 568. Also see the *Chicago Tribune*'s articles and editorials during the two weeks preceding the November 2 election.

43. Douglas, *In the Fullness of Time,* p. 569 (quotation); Joseph T. Meek to Robert Humphreys, Dec. 3, 1954, Meek Papers, box 3, folder "Senatorial Race Nov.–Dec. 1954."

44. Richard Lewis, "Illinois," *Nation* 179 (Nov. 13, 1954), p. 419; White, "Pivotal Campaign in Illinois," p. 38.

45. *Chicago Tribune,* Nov. 7, 1954; White, "Pivotal Campaign in Illinois," p. 38. Despite their earlier differences, Adlai Stevenson endorsed Douglas, donated $500 to his campaign, and gave a number of speeches for him throughout the state. Adlai E. Stevenson to Paul H. Douglas, May 3, 1954, Paul H. Douglas to Adlai E. Stevenson, Aug. 25, 1954, and Paul H. Douglas to Adlai E. Stevenson, Nov. 11, 1954, all in Stevenson Papers, box 25, folder 11.

46. This view of Douglas's reelection is confirmed by the endorsements he received from several Illinois newspapers. See, for example, the undated clippings from the *Decatur Sunday Herald and Review,* the *Fulton Journal,* and the *Freeport Journal-Standard* in the Stevenson Papers, box 25, folder 11.

5: THE CIVIL RIGHTS MOVEMENT IN THE SENATE

1. "Why the Anderson-Aiken Amendment Should Be Defeated," Douglas Papers, box 94, folder "Civil Rights 1957."

2. Paul H. Douglas, "The Right to Vote," *Atlantic Monthly* 200 (December 1957), p. 42 (quotation).

3. Douglas, *In the Fullness of Time,* p. 280; Allan Nevins, *Herbert H. Lehman and His Era* (New York: Charles Scribner's Sons, 1963), p. 400; interview with Paul H. Douglas, July 25, 1957, p. 3, Columbia University Oral History Research Office.

4. Paul H. Douglas to "Dear Friend," n.d., Douglas Papers, box 101, folder "1956 Civil Rights Letter."

5. Douglas, *In the Fullness of Time,* p. 568. Lyndon Johnson made light of Douglas's illness, sarcastically referring to him "writhing on his couch." Douglas's aide Howard E. Shuman dismissed that unflattering description as Johnson's typical attempt to belittle Douglas (interview with Shuman, pp. 89–90).

6. Douglas, *In the Fullness of Time,* p. 148 (quotation); interview with Shuman, pp. 328–31.

7. Paul H. Douglas to "Dear Friend," n.d., Douglas Papers, box 101, folder "1956 Civil Rights Letter."

8. "Freed from Federal Control?" *Congressional Digest* 34 (June–July 1955), pp. 175, 177; "Statement of Senator Paul H. Douglas Accompanying Analysis of Contradictions of Proponents of the Fulbright Bill," Douglas Papers, box 521, folder "January 24, 1956" (quotation); Douglas, *In the Fullness of Time,* p. 466; Woods, *Fulbright,* pp. 202–4.

9. Douglass Cater, "How the Senate Passed the Civil-Rights Bill," *Reporter* 17 (Sept. 5, 1957), p. 9; Douglas, "Right to Vote," p. 42; Douglas, *In the Fullness of Time,* pp. 281–82; Robert F. Burk, *The Eisenhower Administration and Black Civil Rights* (Knoxville: University of Tennessee Press, 1984), p. 163.

10. Howard E. Shuman, "Senate Rules and the Civil Rights Bill: A Case Study," *American Political Science Review* 51 (December 1957), p. 956; Gilbert C. Fite, *Richard B. Russell, Jr., Senator from Georgia* (Chapel Hill: University of North Carolina Press, 1991), p. 336; *Congressional Record,* 84th Cong., 2d sess., July 24, 1956, 102, pt. 10:14228 (quotation).

11. Hubert H. Humphrey to Adaline G. Franks, July 31, 1956, Hubert H. Humphrey Papers, Senatorial Files, box 127, folder "Civil Rights," Minnesota Historical Society, St. Paul, Minnesota (Humphrey quotation); Douglas, *In the Fullness of Time,* p. 283 (Douglas quotation).

12. Clarence Mitchell to Paul H. Douglas, telegram, July 25, 1956, Humphrey Papers, Senatorial Files, box 127, folder "Civil Rights."

13. Paul H. Douglas to William McCormick Blair, May 3, 1956, Stevenson Papers, box 25, folder 11; Douglas, *In the Fullness of Time,* pp. 283–84; John Bartlow Martin, *Adlai Stevenson and the World: The Life of Adlai E. Stevenson* (Garden City, N.Y.: Doubleday, 1977), pp. 348–49; interview with Douglas, July 25, 1957, p. 4; Joseph L. Rauh to Paul H. Douglas, Aug. 13, 1970, Joseph L. Rauh Papers, box 8, folder "Gen. Corr. D 1968–72," Library of Congress, Manuscript Division, Washington, D.C.

14. Douglas, *In the Fullness of Time,* pp. 284, 570; Paul H. Douglas to Adlai E. Stevenson, Nov. 7, 1956, Stevenson Papers, box 25, folder 11. Stevenson carried only seven states, including six from the Old Confederacy—North Carolina, South Carolina, Georgia, Alabama, Mississippi, and Arkansas (Martin, *Adlai Stevenson and the World,* p. 391).

15. Memorandum, n.d., Douglas Papers, box 522, folder "11/56 Background Memorandum concerning Majority Rule in the Senate"; "Question of Limiting U.S. Senate Debate," *Congressional Digest* 36 (February 1957), pp. 39–40;

Gilbert Ware, "The National Association for the Advancement of Colored People and the Civil Rights Act of 1957" (Ph.D. diss., Princeton University, 1962), pp. 85–88; Shuman, "Senate Rules and the Civil Rights Bill," p. 960.

16. "Question of Limiting U.S. Senate Debate," pp. 51–53; Paul H. Douglas, "Stop the Filibuster," *America* 96 (Jan. 5, 1957), p. 383.

17. Interview with Howard E. Shuman, p. 143.

18. *Congressional Record,* 85th Cong., 1st sess., Jan. 4, 1957, 103, pt. 1:215; Hubert H. Humphrey to Walter P. Reuther, Jan. 22, 1957, Humphrey Papers, Senatorial Files, box 136, folder "Civil Rights" (first quotation); Paul H. Douglas to "Dear Friend," n.d., Douglas Papers, box 89, folder "Civil Rights S. 810 Data—Wright Speeches" (second quotation).

19. "Special Report: Civil Rights Legislation," *Congressional Quarterly,* May 6, 1960, p. 752; Shuman, "Senate Rules and the Civil Rights Bill," pp. 961–62.

20. Paul H. Douglas to "Dear Friend," n.d., Douglas Papers, box 89, folder "Civil Rights S. 810 Data—Wright Speeches"; "Special Report," p. 752; Douglas, *In the Fullness of Time,* p. 285 (quotation).

21. "Special Report," pp. 752–53; Shuman, "Senate Rules and the Civil Rights Bill," pp. 963–65; Hubert H. Humphrey to Paul H. Douglas, June 27, 1957, Humphrey Papers, Senatorial Files, box 136, folder "Civil Rights." In his memoirs, Douglas does not refer to Hennings by name, identifying him only as an alcoholic member of the Judiciary Committee; Howard E. Shuman makes the reference explicit in his oral history interview for the Senate Historical Office (Douglas, *In the Fullness of Time,* p. 290; interview with Shuman, p. 122).

22. "Special Report," pp. 752–53; *Congressional Record,* 85th Cong., 1st sess., June 20, 1957, 103, pt. 7:9827; Gayle B. Montgomery and James W. Johnson, *One Step from the White House: The Rise and Fall of Senator William F. Knowland* (Berkeley: University of California Press, 1998), p. 216 (quotation).

23. Douglas, *In the Fullness of Time,* p. 287; Robert Dallek, *Lone Star Rising: Lyndon Johnson and His Times, 1908–1960* (New York: Oxford University Press, 1991), pp. 521–22.

24. Paul H. Douglas to "Dear Friend," n.d., Douglas Papers, box 89, folder "Civil Rights S. 810 Data—Wright Speeches"; "Special Report," pp. 753–54.

25. Douglas, "Right to Vote," p. 43; Paul H. Douglas to Jean Taft Douglas, June 27, 1957, Douglas Papers, box 428, folder "June 1957."

26. *Congressional Record,* 85th Cong., 1st sess., July 2, 1957, 103, pt. 8:10771; Joseph L. Rauh to Paul H. Douglas, Aug. 13, 1970, Rauh Papers, box 8, folder "Gen. Corr. D 1968–72" (first quotation); "Some Excerpts from the Discussion of the Civil Rights Bill in the United States Senate," Douglas Papers, box 103, folder "Suggested Releases—Speech Outlines, Etc." (second, third, and fifth quotations); Douglas, *In the Fullness of Time,* p. 288 (fourth and sixth quotations); Paul H. Douglas to "Dear Friend," n.d., Douglas Papers, box 89, folder "Civil Rights S. 810 Data—Wright Speeches"; Douglass Cater, "The Senate Debate on Civil Rights," *Reporter* 17 (Aug. 8, 1957), pp. 37–40.

27. Dallek, *Lone Star Rising,* pp. 522–23 (Eisenhower quotation); Stephen E. Ambrose, *Eisenhower: The President* (New York: Simon and Schuster, 1984), pp. 407–8 (Ambrose quotation).

28. Fite, *Richard B. Russell, Jr.,* p. 339; Burk, *Eisenhower Administration and Black Civil Rights,* p. 171 (first quotation); Ware, "The National Association for

the Advancement of Colored People and the Civil Rights Act of 1957," p. 116 (second quotation).

29. Douglass Cater, "Senate Debate on Civil Rights," p. 39; Shuman, "Senate Rules and the Civil Rights Bill," pp. 970–72; "Why the Anderson-Aiken Amendment Should Be Defeated," Douglas Papers, box 94, folder "Civil Rights 1957"; "Why Title III of the Civil Rights Bill Should Be Retained and Why the Anderson-Aiken Amendment Should Be Defeated," Douglas Papers, box 523, folder "July 24, 1957."

30. "Why the Anderson-Aiken Amendment Should Be Defeated;" *Congressional Record,* 85th Cong., 1st sess., July 24, 1957, 103, pt. 9:12565.

31. Douglas, *In the Fullness of Time,* p. 289; Fite, *Richard B. Russell, Jr.,* p. 337 (quotation).

32. "Speech and Brief of Hon. Paul H. Douglas," Apr. 18, 1957, Rauh Papers, box 25, folder "Civil Rights Act of 1957"; Paul H. Douglas to "Dear Friend," n.d., Douglas Papers, box 89, folder "Civil Rights S. 810 Data—Wright Speeches."

33. Shuman, "Senate Rules and the Civil Rights Bill," p. 972 (first quotation); Cater, "How the Senate Passed the Civil Rights Bill," pp. 11–12; Dallek, *Lone Star Rising,* p. 525 (second quotation).

34. Paul H. Douglas to "Dear Friend," n.d., Douglas Papers, box 89, folder "Civil Rights S. 810 Data—Wright Speeches."

35. *Congressional Record,* 85th Cong., 1st sess., Aug. 1, 1957, 103, pt. 10:13356; Shuman, "Senate Rules and the Civil Rights Bill," p. 974.

36. "Remarks by Senator Paul H. Douglas prior to Vote on Final Passage of Civil Rights Bill," Aug. 7, 1957, Douglas Papers, box 91, folder "*FWM*—Work File—Personnel Proposals—Key Clips, Etc." (first quotation); Paul H. Douglas to Walter Reuther, Aug. 8, 1957, Douglas Papers, box 710, folder "1957 100 R 01 Civil Rights August Only" (second quotation).

37. Joseph L. Rauh to Paul H. Douglas, Aug. 13, 1970, Rauh Papers, box 8, folder "Gen. Corr. D 1968–72"; "Special Report," p. 754. Voting against the bill were Senators Byrd, Eastland, Ellender, Ervin, Fulbright, Hill, Holland, Johnston, Long, McClellan, Morse, Robertson, Russell, Scott, Sparkman, Stennis, Talmadge, and Thurmond; all except Wayne Morse of Oregon hailed from southern states (*Congressional Record,* 85th Cong., 1st sess., Aug. 7, 1957, 103, pt. 10:13900).

38. "Special Report," p. 754; Douglas, *In the Fullness of Time,* p. 290; Douglas, "Right to Vote," p. 43.

39. Burk, *Eisenhower Administration and Black Civil Rights,* p. 173 (first quotation); Dallek, *Lone Star Rising* (second and third quotations).

40. Cater, "Senate Debate on Civil Rights," p. 39 (first quotation); Shuman, "Senate Rules and the Civil Rights Bill," p. 975 (second quotation). In August 1957, Russell said that he had "enjoyed a full and satisfying life but that he would give up the remainder of it if such a sacrifice would 'guarantee the preservation of a civilization of two races of unmixed blood in the land I love'" (Fite, *Richard B. Russell, Jr.,* p. 343).

41. Douglas, *In the Fullness of Time,* pp. 290–91; Violet M. Gunther to Joseph L. Rauh, Jr., Aug. 25, 1958, Americans for Democratic Action Papers, Legislative File, box 48, Joseph L. Rauh folder. The consensus among his biographers is that Johnson worked to pass a civil rights bill in 1957 in order to transform himself from a regional leader into a politician of national stature and that

Richard Russell and others went along to make Johnson a viable presidential candidate who could attract support outside of the South. See, for example, Dallek, *Lone Star Rising,* pp. 517–19; Paul K. Conkin, *Big Daddy from the Pedernales: Lyndon Baines Johnson* (Boston: Twayne, 1986), pp. 139–42; and Bruce J. Schulman, *Lyndon B. Johnson and American Liberalism: A Brief Biography with Documents* (Boston: Bedford Books, 1995), pp. 51–53.

42. Steven F. Lawson, *Black Ballots: Voting Rights in the South, 1944–1969* (New York: Columbia University Press, 1976), p. 196 (first quotation); Paul H. Douglas to Norman Thomas, Aug. 22, 1957, Douglas Papers, box 710, folder "1957 100 R 01 Civil Rights August Only" (second quotation); "Address of Senator Paul H. Douglas in Accepting the Sidney Hillman Award," Nov. 12, 1957, Douglas Papers, box 523, folder "Nov. 12, 1957" (third quotation).

43. Paul H. Douglas to "Dear Friend," n.d., Douglas Papers, box 89, folder "Civil Rights S. 810 Data—Wright Speeches"; Douglas, "Right to Vote," p. 44 (quotation).

6: UNDAUNTED CRUSADER FOR CIVIL RIGHTS

1. "Senator Douglas Reports," n.d., Douglas Papers, box 91, folder "August 1960."

2. Phillips, "Paul Douglas—'Instinctive Liberal,'" p. 10; interview with Shuman, pp. 424–25; "Idea Man for the Democrats," *Business Week,* May 26, 1955, pp. 128–34; McGaffin, "'Ferocious Independent' at 70," pp. 38–48; Mangel, "Paul Douglas: Man Ahead of His Time," pp. 103–110; *Chicago Tribune,* Sept. 25, 1976 (quotation). For examples of Douglas's income disclosures, see *New York Times,* June 12, 1966; and "Senator Douglas Reports," April 1964, Douglas Papers, box 530, folder "April 1964."

3. Douglas, *In the Fullness of Time,* p. 154; interview with Shuman, p. 86 (quotation).

4. Interview with Shuman, pp. 85–86.

5. Mangel, "Paul Douglas: Man Ahead of His Time," p. 106; Douglas, *In the Fullness of Time,* pp. 194–95.

6. Interview with Shuman, p. 203; Michael Foley, *The New Senate: Liberal Influence on a Conservative Institution, 1959–1972* (New Haven: Yale University Press, 1980), pp. 12–13.

7. Interview with Shuman, pp. 204–6; Douglas, *In the Fullness of Time,* p. 427.

8. Anderson, "Paul H. Douglas," pp. 296–301; Douglas, *In the Fullness of Time,* pp. 475–79.

9. Shaffer, *On and off the Floor,* p. 247; *Congressional Quarterly Almanac, 1958,* p. 454.

10. Press release, Apr. 16, 1956, Douglas Papers, box 522, folder 4/15/56; *Congressional Quarterly Almanac, 1962* (Washington, D.C.: Congressional Quarterly, 1962), p. 522 (first quotation); *Congressional Record,* 85th Cong., 2d sess., Apr. 23, 1958, 104, pt. 6:7060 (second quotation).

11. *Congressional Record,* 85th Cong., 2d sess., Apr. 23, 1958, 104, pt. 6:7062 (quotation); *Congressional Quarterly Almanac, 1962,* p. 521.

12. "Speech By Senator Paul H. Douglas on His Bill to Preserve the Indiana Dunes by Making Them a National Monument—Instead of Allowing Them to Be

Taken Over for Steel Mills," May 26, 1958, Douglas Papers, box 524, folder "May 26, 1958"; Douglas, *In the Fullness of Time,* pp. 76–77.

13. Douglas, *In the Fullness of Time,* pp. 536–38.

14. *Congressional Quarterly Almanac, 1959,* p. 266 (quotation); Douglas, *In the Fullness of Time,* pp. 366–71.

15. Iwan W. Morgan, *Deficit Government: Taxing and Spending in Modern America* (Chicago: Ivan R. Dee, 1995), pp. 81–82; "The Case for a General Tax Cut," June 18, 1958, Douglas Papers, box 524, folder "June 18, 1958"; *New York Times,* Mar. 13, 1958; "Plumping for Faster Growth," *Business Week* 1535 (Jan. 31, 1959), pp. 23, 24; "Senator Douglas Tackles Inflation Problems," *U.S. News and World Report* 46 (Feb. 6, 1959), p. 22.

16. Douglas, *In the Fullness of Time,* pp. 512–15.

17. John Bibby and Roger Davidson, *On Capitol Hill: Studies in the Legislative Process* (New York: Holt, Rinehart, and Winston, 1967), pp. 197–204.

18. Douglas, *In the Fullness of Time,* pp. 205 (quotation), 516–18; "History of Legislative and Federal Action respecting Distressed Areas," n.d., Douglas Papers, box 62, folder 62–3; Morgan, *Deficit Government,* p. 83; "Copy of President Eisenhower's Message Accompanying Veto of S. 3683, the Area Redevelopment Bill," Sept. 6, 1958, Douglas Papers, box 525, folder 9/6/58; "Refutation by Senator Douglas of President Eisenhower's Veto Memorandum on the Area Redevelopment Bill," n.d., Douglas Papers, box 68, folder "Area Redevelopment Bills 1958–1959—Statements."

19. "Statement of Senator Paul H. Douglas on the Introduction in the Senate of the Civil Rights Act of 1958," n.d., Douglas Papers, box 523, folder "February 10, 1958"; *Congressional Record,* 85th Cong., 2d sess., Feb. 10, 1958, 104, pt. 2:1912; Paul H. Douglas to "Mr. Chairman," June 20, 1958, Rauh Papers, box 25, folder "Civil Rights Act of 1958."

20. Virginia Durr to Paul Douglas, Feb. 11, 1958, Douglas Papers, box 94, folder "Civil Rights—1957–58—Misc."

21. Paul H. Douglas to William S. White, Aug. 29, 1958, Douglas Papers, box 711, folder "100 R 01 1958, Civil Rights General (July–Aug)" (first quotation); *Chicago Sun-Times,* Feb. 15, 1958 (second quotation); Paul H. Douglas to editor, *Chicago Sun-Times,* Feb. 25, 1958, Douglas Papers, box 93, folder "Civil Rights—1958, etc." (third quotation); "A Stitch in Time," *Christian Century* 75 (Feb. 26, 1958), pp. 245–47; Frank W. McCulloch to Harold E. Fey, Mar. 3, 1958, Douglas Papers, box 93, folder "Civil Rights—PHD Test'y—House—1958" (fourth quotation).

22. *Congressional Quarterly Almanac, 1958,* pp. 293–94; Douglas, *In the Fullness of Time,* p. 309. Douglas failed to mention the Civil Rights Act of 1958 at all in the first draft of his autobiography but did so briefly in the final version at the urging of Joseph L. Rauh (Joseph L. Rauh to Paul H. Douglas, Aug. 13, 1970, Rauh Papers, box 8, folder "Gen. Corr. D 1968–72").

23. *Congressional Quarterly Almanac, 1958,* pp. 294–95; Douglas, *In the Fullness of Time,* pp. 309–10.

24. Violet M. Gunther to Joseph L. Rauh, Jr., Aug. 25, 1958, Americans for Democratic Action Papers, Legislative File, box 48, Joseph L. Rauh folder; "Statement by Senators Case, Douglas, Humphrey, Javits," Sept. 23, 1958, Douglas Papers, box 213, folder "Work File—Rule 22 Cloture 1958–59"; *Congressional Record,* 85th Cong., 2d sess., July 28, 1958, 104, pt. 12:15274, 15277 (quotation).

25. "The 86th Congress and Civil Rights," Dec. 16, 1958, Douglas Papers, box 89, folder "Civil Rights S. 810 data—Wright speeches."

26. Paul H. Douglas to Walter Lippmann, Dec. 5, 1958, Douglas Papers, box 213, folder "Work File—Rule 22 Cloture 1958–59"; Paul H. Douglas to editor, Letters to the Editor Column, *Washington Post* and *Times-Herald*, Dec. 26, 1958 (quotations).

27. *Congressional Record,* 86th Cong., 1st sess., Jan. 7, 9, 12, 1959, 105, pt. 1:8, 287, 489–90, 494.

28. "Speech of Senator Paul H. Douglas in the United States Senate on Introduction of Civil Rights Act of 1959," Jan. 29, 1959, Rauh Papers, box 25, folder "Civil Rights Jan–March 1959." Also see "Statement of Senator Paul H. Douglas before the Subcommittee on Constitutional Rights of the Senate Judiciary Committee in Support of S. 810, the Civil Rights Act of 1959," Mar. 19, 1959, ibid.; "Senator Sam Ervin Says," Feb. 8, 1959, Douglas Papers, box 103, folder "Recent Significant Speeches Civil Rights, 1958–9."

29. *Congressional Quarterly Special Report: Civil Rights Legislation* (Washington, D.C.: Congressional Quarterly, 1960), pp. 759–61; "Civil Rights Groups Say Douglas Bill Is Cure to Cancer of Segregation," Apr. 8, 1959, Douglas Papers, box 103, folder "Recent Significant Speeches Civil Rights, 1958–59" (quotations); "Senator Douglas Reports," n.d., Douglas Papers, box 89, folder "Civil Rights S. 810 data—Wright speeches." For an item-by-item comparison of the three bills, see Leadership Conference on Civil Rights, "Summary Comparison of the Three Most Widely Discussed 'Civil Rights' Bills," Douglas Papers, box 93, folder "Civil Rights Bills 1959." Also see Burk, *Eisenhower Administration and Black Civil Rights,* pp. 241–43.

30. Daniel M. Berman, *A Bill Becomes a Law: The Civil Rights Act of 1960* (New York: Macmillan, 1962), pp. 35–36.

31. Ibid., pp. 44–46.

32. Ibid., pp. 46–47; *Congressional Quarterly Special Report,* p. 767.

33. Berman, *Bill Becomes a Law,* pp. 51–52. In his autobiography, Douglas says that he decided on this course of action because of a conversation he had with a southern segregationist who frankly said that African Americans would vote in the South only with the exercise of such power by the federal government. This southerner, whom Douglas does not name, said that he would deny ever offering such advice if Douglas recounted their conversation (*In the Fullness of Time,* pp. 293–94). Douglas's aide, Howard E. Shuman, identified the southerner as Louisiana senator Russell Long (interview with Shuman, pp. 146–47).

34. Berman, *Bill Becomes a Law,* pp. 39, 56.

35. *Congressional Quarterly Special Report,* pp. 765–70.

36. "Senator Douglas Reports," n.d., Douglas Papers, box 91, folder "August 1960."

37. Berman, *Bill Becomes a Law,* p. 100.

38. "Senator Douglas Reports," n.d., Douglas Papers, box 91, folder "August 1960"; Burk, *Eisenhower Administration and Black Civil Rights,* p. 246.

39. "Senator Douglas Reports," n.d., Douglas Papers, box 91, folder "August 1960"; Berman, *Bill Becomes a Law,* pp. 108 (Clark quotation), 117 (Marshall quotation); *Congressional Quarterly Special Report,* p. 763 (Wilkins quotations).

40. *Congressional Quarterly Special Report,* p. 763 (Thurmond quotation); Berman, *Bill Becomes a Law,* pp. 107 (Byrd quotation), 122 (Alsop quotation); Anthony Lewis, "The Professionals Win Out over Civil Rights," *Reporter* 22 (May 26, 1960), p. 27.

41. Paul H. Douglas, "Liberals and Civil Rights," *Reporter* 22 (June 23, 1960), p. 10.

42. Anderson, "Paul H. Douglas," p. 313 (first quotation); Paul H. Douglas, "The 1960 Voting Rights Bill: The Struggle, the Final Results, and the Reasons," *Journal of Intergroup Relations* 1 (summer 1960), p. 86 (second quotation).

43. Douglas, *In the Fullness of Time,* p. 283 (quotation).

44. Interview with Paul H. Douglas, Nov. 1, 1974, pp. 13–14, Lyndon B. Johnson Presidential Library, Austin, Texas; Paul H. Douglas, *In Our Time* (New York: Harcourt, Brace, and World, 1967), pp. 95–96.

45. "Senator Douglas Reports," n.d., Douglas Papers, box 213f, folder "Douglas Statements 1960."

46. Ibid.; Under Secretary of Commerce to A. Willis Robertson, Apr. 7, 1960, Douglas Papers, box 213d, folder "Misc. Correspondence 1960"; Douglas, *In the Fullness of Time,* p. 523.

47. Douglas, *In the Fullness of Time,* p. 321 (quotation); *Congressional Record,* 86th Cong., 1st sess., June 17, 1959, 105, pt. 8:11040–41.

48. *Congressional Record,* 86th Cong., 2d sess., June 13, 1960, 106, pt. 9:12414–16; Douglas, *In the Fullness of Time,* pp. 321–23.

49. "Senator Douglas Reports," n.d., Douglas Papers, box 526, folder "November 1959 PHD Reports: Area Redevelopment"; Paul H. Douglas, untitled speech, *Congressional Digest* 38 (February 1959), pp. 48–52; "Senator Douglas Reports," n.d., Douglas Papers, box 526, folder "July 15, 1960 Area Redevelopment" (quotation).

50. "Statement by Senator Paul H. Douglas on Area Redevelopment Hearings," n.d., Douglas Papers, box 68, folder "Area Redevelopment Bill 1960—His Statements" (first and second quotations); "Opening Statement by Senator Paul H. Douglas," Aug. 18, 1960, ibid.; *Congressional Record,* 86th Cong., 2d sess., June 24, 1960, 106, pt. 11:14160–61.

51. "Growth without Inflation," *New Republic* 143 (Sept. 26, 1960), pp. 16–22; McGaffin, "'Ferocious Independent' at 70," pp. 44–48 (quotation).

52. Interview with Paul H. Douglas, June 6, 1964, pp. 1–6, Oral History Project, John F. Kennedy Memorial Library, Boston, Massachusetts; Douglas, *In the Fullness of Time,* p. 254.

53. Paul H. Douglas, "A Catholic Can Become President!" *Coronet* 45 (March 1959), pp. 104–11; interview with Douglas, June 6, 1964, pp. 13–17; Douglas, *In the Fullness of Time,* pp. 256–57.

54. Interview with Douglas, June 6, 1964, pp. 18–19 (quotation).

55. Douglas, *In the Fullness of Time,* p. 571; "A Survey of the Senatorial Race in Illinois," Sept. 26, 1960, Douglas Papers, box 25, folder "1960 Campaign."

56. Anderson, "Paul H. Douglas," pp. 319–20.

57. Ibid., pp. 319–20; *Congressional Record,* 86th Cong., 2d sess., July 2, 1960, 106, pt. 12:15591–93.

58. Interview with Shuman, pp. 232–33; Douglas, *In the Fullness of Time,* p. 185.

59. Douglas, *In the Fullness of Time,* p. 572; interview with Douglas, June 6, 1964, pp. 18–19; interview with Shuman, pp. 224–31.

60. Anderson, "Paul H. Douglas," p. 321.

7: SENATOR WITH IDEAS

1. Anderson, "Paul H. Douglas," p. 324.

2. Ibid., p. 314.

3. McGaffin, "'Ferocious Independent' at 70," p. 48.

4. Interview with Douglas, June 6, 1964, pp. 7–8; Douglas, *In the Fullness of Time,* pp. 518–19. The Jan. 2, 1961, issue of the *New York Times* contains the text of the task force report.

5. *Congressional Quarterly Almanac, 1961* (Washington, D.C.: Congressional Quarterly, 1961), pp. 76, 247–49; Douglas, *In the Fullness of Time,* pp. 519–20.

6. Douglas, *In the Fullness of Time,* pp. 520–22.

7. Ibid., p. 520. Douglas says that the title of his autobiography, "In the Fullness of Time," refers to the fact that fulfillment often comes quite late in a person's life. The observation could obviously refer to his entry into politics somewhat late in life and to the acclaim he received as a senator at an advanced age. The phrase "in the fullness of time" could also relate to the legislative success he enjoyed late in his career after many years of frustration.

8. Carl M. Brauer, *John F. Kennedy and the Second Reconstruction* (New York: Columbia University Press, 1977), pp. 28–29; interview with Douglas, June 6, 1964, pp. 9–12.

9. "Remarks of Senator Paul H. Douglas on the Introduction of the Civil Rights Bill of 1961," Mar. 24, 1961, pp. 1–2, Douglas Papers, box 95, folder "1961—PHD Civil Rights Bill."

10. Ibid., p. 2 (quotation).

11. *Congressional Quarterly Almanac, 1961,* p. 81.

12. *Congressional Record,* 87th Cong., 2d sess., Mar. 13, 1962, 108, pt. 3:3877–78.

13. "Speech by Senator Paul H. Douglas (D. Ill.) on a More Effective Way of Eliminating the Poll Tax than by a Constitutional Amendment," n.d., Douglas Papers, box 528, folder "April 18, 1962"; *Congressional Quarterly Almanac, 1962* (Washington, D.C.: Congressional Quarterly, 1962), pp. 404–5; Brauer, *John F. Kennedy and the Second Reconstruction,* pp. 131–32.

14. Robert D. Loevy, ed., *The Civil Rights Act of 1964: The Passage of the Law that Ended Racial Segregation* (Albany: State University of New York Press, 1997), p. 186.

15. Brauer, *John F. Kennedy and the Second Reconstruction,* p. 246 (quotation).

16. Anderson, "Paul H. Douglas," p. 338; Douglas, *In the Fullness of Time,* p. 295 (quotation). On the substance of Kennedy's 1963 bill, see Brauer, *John F. Kennedy and the Second Reconstruction,* chap. 10.

17. "T. R. B.," *New Republic* 175 (Oct. 9, 1976), p. 2.

18. Douglas, *In the Fullness of Time,* pp. 433–34.

19. Ibid., p. 434; Douglas, *In Our Time,* p. 6.

20. Douglas, *In the Fullness of Time,* pp. 434–35; *Congressional Record,* 87th Cong., 2d sess., May 21, 1962, 108, pt. 7:8809 (quotation).

21. Douglas, *In the Fullness of Time,* pp. 436–37; Douglas, *In Our Time,* p. 8; interview with Douglas, June 6, 1964, pp. 23–24.

22. James N. Giglio, *The Presidency of John F. Kennedy* (Lawrence: University Press of Kansas, 1991), pp. 137–39; Douglas, *In the Fullness of Time,* pp. 448–49.

23. Interview with Douglas, June 6, 1964, pp. 24–25; *Congressional Quarterly Almanac, 1963* (Washington, D.C.: Congressional Quarterly, 1963), pp. 497–98 (quotations).

24. Giglio, *Presidency of John F. Kennedy,* pp. 138–39; Douglas, *In Our Time,* p. 23 (quotation). Also see Douglas's detailed discussion of tax reform in Paul H. Douglas, "The Problem of Tax Loopholes," *American Scholar* 37 (winter 1967), pp. 21–43.

25. Douglas, *In the Fullness of Time,* p. 531; "The True Cost of Interest," *Time* 78 (July 28, 1961), p. 68; *Congressional Record,* 87th Cong., 1st sess., Apr. 27, 1961, 107, pt. 5:6860 (quotation).

26. A. Willis Robertson to Paul H. Douglas, Dec. 12, 1961, Douglas Papers, box 215, folder "Douglas Correspondence 1961" (quotations); *Congressional Quarterly Almanac, 1962,* pp. 70, 393.

27. Douglas, *In the Fullness of Time,* pp. 361–63, 460.

28. *Congressional Quarterly Almanac, 1962,* pp. 546–53; Francis R. Valeo, *Mike Mansfield, Majority Leader: A Different Kind of Senate, 1961–1976* (Armonk, N.Y.: M. E. Sharpe, 1999), pp. 65–66.

29. Douglas, *In the Fullness of Time,* p. 220; *Congressional Record,* 87th Cong., 2d sess., Aug. 14, 1962, 108, pt. 12:16421.

30. *Congressional Record,* 87th Cong., 2d sess., Aug. 17, 1962, 108, pt. 12:16898; Valeo, *Mike Mansfield,* pp. 67–70; Douglas, *In the Fullness of Time,* p. 220.

31. Douglas, *In the Fullness of Time,* p. 540 (quotation); "Sand versus Steel," *New Republic* 145 (Oct. 16, 1961), p. 7.

32. Interview with Douglas, June 6, 1964, pp. 21–22; Douglas, *In the Fullness of Time,* p. 540 (quotation); *Congressional Record,* 88th Cong., 1st sess., Feb. 4, 1963, 109, pt. 2:1681.

33. *Washington Post* quoted in *Congressional Record,* 88th Cong., 1st sess., Feb. 4, 1963, 109, pt. 2:1682; *Congressional Quarterly Almanac, 1962,* p. 459 (Roush quotation).

34. *Congressional Quarterly Almanac, 1962,* p. 459; *Congressional Record,* 88th Cong., 1st sess., Feb. 4, 1963, 109, pt. 2:1682–83; Paul H. Douglas, "There is Still Time to Save the Indiana Dunes," *Audubon Magazine* 64 (July 1962), pp. 192–93.

35. *Congressional Record,* 88th Cong., 1st sess., Feb. 4, 1963, 109, pt. 2:1677; *Congressional Quarterly Almanac, 1965* (Washington, D.C.: Congressional Quarterly, 1965), p. 771.

36. *Congressional Quarterly Almanac, 1965,* p. 771; interview with Douglas, June 6, 1964, pp. 22–23. In *In the Fullness of Time,* Douglas's explanation of the 1963 Kennedy compromise proposal is very confusing and somewhat misleading (540–41).

37. Interview with Douglas, June 6, 1964, p. 33; Douglas, *In the Fullness of Time,* pp. 260 (first and second quotations), 507 (third quotation).

38. Douglas, *In the Fullness of Time,* pp. 499–501.

39. Paul H. Douglas to J. W. Fulbright, July 3, 1963, Douglas Papers, box 121, folder "Committee of One Million 1966"; *Congressional Record,* 87th Cong.,

1st sess., Apr. 19, 1961, 107, pt. 5:6224 (quotation); Douglas, *In the Fullness of Time,* p. 493.

40. Douglas, *In the Fullness of Time,* pp. 323–24.

41. Ibid., p. 324; Mangel, "Paul Douglas: Man Ahead of His Time," p. 108 (quotation).

42. Edward L. Schapsmeier and Frederick H. Schapsmeier, *Dirksen of Illinois: Senatorial Statesman* (Urbana: University of Illinois Press, 1985), pp. 143–44; Hulsey, *Everett Dirksen and His Presidents,* p. 161 (first quotation); Douglas, *In the Fullness of Time,* p. 574 (second quotation).

43. Schapsmeier and Schapsmeier, *Dirksen of Illinois,* pp. 144 (first quotation), 145 (second quotation); Douglas, *In the Fullness of Time,* pp. 574–75.

44. Douglas, *In the Fullness of Time,* p. 261 (first and second quotations); interview with Douglas, June 6, 1964, pp. 31–32 (third quotation).

8: ON BEHALF OF THE GREAT SOCIETY

1. Interview with Douglas, Nov. 1, 1974, pp. 6–7.

2. Douglas, *In the Fullness of Time,* pp. 233–35; Joseph S. Clark, *The Senate Establishment* (New York: Hill and Wang, 1963), pp. 123–24; interview with Shuman, pp. 159 (first quotation), 156 (second quotation).

3. Valeo, *Mike Mansfield,* p. 13; Robert Dallek, *Flawed Giant: Lyndon Johnson and His Times, 1961–1973* (New York: Oxford University Press, 1998), p. 8 (quotation).

4. Lyndon B. Johnson to Paul H. Douglas, Jan. 24, 1964, Douglas Papers, box 424, folder "Kennedy Letters."

5. Douglas, *In the Fullness of Time,* pp. 234–35; interview with Douglas, Nov. 1, 1974, p. 7.

6. Doris Kearns, *Lyndon Johnson and the American Dream* (New York: Signet, 1976), p. 191 (quotation); Douglas, *In the Fullness of Time,* pp. 295–96.

7. Charles Whalen and Barbara Whalen, *The Longest Debate: A Legislative History of the 1964 Civil Rights Act* (Cabin John, Md.: Seven Locks Press, 1985, p. 236.

8. Dallek, *Flawed Giant,* p. 117 (first quotation); Valeo, *Mike Mansfield,* p. 122; *Congressional Quarterly Almanac, 1964* (Washington, D.C.: Congressional Quarterly, 1965), p. 367 (second quotation); Hugh Davis Graham, *The Civil Rights Era: Origins and Development of National Policy, 1960–1972* (New York: Oxford University Press, 1990), pp. 142–43; interview with Shuman, p. 326. The "captains" assigned to manage the various titles of the bill were Philip Hart for Title I (voting rights); Warren Magnuson for Title II (public accommodations); Wayne Morse for Title III (attorney general's powers); Douglas for Title IV (public school desegregation); Edward Long for Title V (Civil Rights Commission); John Pastore for Title VI (cutoff of federal funds); Joseph Clark for Title VII (equal employment opportunity); and Thomas Dodd for Titles VIII, IX, and X (Community Relations Service and miscellaneous provisions). Loevy, ed., *Civil Rights Act of 1964,* p. 183.

9. *Congressional Record,* 88th Cong., 2d sess., June 10, 1964, 110, pt. 10:13327; Valeo, *Mike Mansfield,* pp. 158–64.

10. Interview with Shuman, p. 327; "The Covenant," *Time* 83 (June 19, 1964), p. 18 (first quotation); Paul Simon, *P.S.: The Autobiography of Paul Simon* (Chicago: Bonus Books, 1999), p. 292 (second quotation).

11. Simon, *P.S.*, p. 292 (quotation); Douglas, *In the Fullness of Time*, pp. 298–99.

12. James T. Patterson, *Grand Expectations: The United States, 1945–1974* (New York: Oxford University Press, 1996), pp. 552–54. On the Freedom Summer in Mississippi, see Doug McAdam, *Freedom Summer* (New York: Oxford University Press, 1988); and John Dittmer, *Local People: The Struggle for Civil Rights in Mississippi* (Urbana: University of Illinois Press, 1994).

13. Patterson, *Grand Expectations*, pp. 554–56.

14. Paul H. Douglas to Russell W. Nash, Sept. 22, 1964, Douglas Papers, box 721, folder "100 R 04 Negro Rights August."

15. Patterson, *Grand Expectations*, pp. 579–82.

16. Ibid., pp. 581–82; Douglas, *In the Fullness of Time*, pp. 296–97 (quotations).

17. Patterson, *Grand Expectations*, pp. 582–84; Douglas, *In the Fullness of Time*, p. 297 (quotation); *Congressional Quarterly Almanac, 1965*, p. 541.

18. Interview with Shuman, p. 325.

19. *Congressional Quarterly Almanac, 1964*, p. 390; Douglas, *In the Fullness of Time*, pp. 550–53.

20. Douglas, *In the Fullness of Time*, pp. 546–49.

21. *Congressional Record*, 88th Cong., 2d sess., July 23, 1964, 110, pt. 13:16689; *Congressional Quarterly Almanac, 1964*, p. 393.

22. *Congressional Quarterly Almanac, 1964*, pp. 393–96; "Excerpt from Debate, August 21, 1964," *Congressional Digest* 44 (January 1965), p. 19 (quotation).

23. *Congressional Quarterly Almanac, 1964*, pp. 396–97; Peter Irons, "The Race to Control the States," *Progressive* 29 (May 1965), pp. 11–13.

24. *Congressional Record*, 89th Cong., 1st sess., July 29, 1965, 111, pt. 14:18849; "When One Person, One Vote Came Up," *U.S. News and World Report* 59 (Aug. 16, 1965), p. 20; *Congressional Quarterly Almanac, 1965*, pp. 52–30; Douglas, *In the Fullness of Time*, pp. 555–57; Irons, "Race to Control the States," p. 14 (quotation).

25. *Congressional Quarterly Almanac, 1966* (Washington, D.C.: Congressional Quarterly, 1966), pp. 505–8; Schapsmeier and Schapsmeier, *Dirksen of Illinois*, p. 180.

26. Douglas, *In the Fullness of Time*, p. 558.

27. Interview with Shuman, p. 306.

28. Paul H. Douglas, "Our Best Chance to Save the Indiana Dunes," *Audubon Magazine* 66 (March 1964), pp. 112–14; *Congressional Quarterly Almanac, 1964*, p. 476.

29. *Congressional Quarterly Almanac, 1965*, pp. 771–72.

30. Public Law 89-761, 89th Congress, S. 360, Nov. 5, 1966, Douglas Papers, box 534, folder "Nov. 5, 1966"; *Congressional Quarterly Almanac, 1966*, p. 657 (quotation); Douglas, *In the Fullness of Time*, pp. 542–43.

31. "Statement of Senator Paul H. Douglas on the Indiana Dunes National Lakeshore," Apr. 14, 1966, Douglas Papers, box 144, folder "Reports, Pamphlets, Statements, Etc.—1966."

32. Paul H. Douglas to Philip A. Hart, Feb. 5, 1964, Douglas Papers, box 223, folder "Reports, Pamphlets, Statements, Etc.—1964"; A. Willis Robertson to Paul H. Douglas, Mar. 17, 1964, Douglas Papers, box 223, folder "Douglas Correspondence, 1964" (first quotation); *Congressional Quarterly Almanac, 1964*, p. 584

(second quotation); *Congressional Record,* 88th Cong., 2d sess., May 22, 1964, 110, pt. 9:11728 (third quotation); "Fact Sheet on Truth-in-Lending Bill," May 25, 1964, Douglas Papers, box 223, folder "Douglas Correspondence 1964."

33. James Deakin, "How to Out-Fox the Majority," *New Republic* 152 (Feb. 27, 1965), pp. 13–14.

34. *Congressional Quarterly Almanac, 1966,* p. 351; Douglas, *In the Fullness of Time,* pp. 532–33.

35. *Congressional Quarterly Almanac, 1964,* pp. 527–32. Also see Douglas, "Problem of Tax Loopholes," pp. 21–43.

36. Paul H. Douglas to John Kenneth Galbraith, June 13, 1967, Rauh Papers, box 11, folder "June–Dec. 1967."

37. Paul H. Douglas, "What Shall We Do About de Gaulle?" *New Republic* 152 (June 12, 1965), pp. 7–10; "Senator's Indictment of de Gaulle: Excerpts from Address, June 3, 1965," *U.S. News and World Report* 58 (June 14, 1965), p. 8; Douglas, *In the Fullness of Time,* pp. 485–90.

38. "For Medicare under Social Security," Feb. 10, 1964, Douglas Papers, box 530, folder 2/10/64; *Congressional Quarterly Almanac, 1965,* pp. 236–37; Douglas, *In the Fullness of Time,* pp. 394–97.

39. Theodore R. Marmor, *The Politics of Medicare* (Chicago: Aldine, 1970), p. 71.

40. Paul H. Douglas, "American Hospital Association Strongly Urges Reinstatement of Services of Medical Specialists as Reimbursable Costs under Medicare," Douglas Papers, box 530, folder 4/6/65; Richard Harris, *A Sacred Trust* (New York: New American Library, 1966), p. 199 (quotations); Douglas, *In the Fullness of Time,* pp. 394–95.

41. Harris, *Sacred Trust,* p. 204; Douglas, *In the Fullness of Time,* pp. 395–96; Mangel, "Paul Douglas: Man Ahead of His Time," p. 103.

42. Douglas, *In the Fullness of Time,* pp. 396–97; Harris, *Sacred Trust,* p. 218.

43. "Statement by Senator Paul H. Douglas in Support of S. 2923 before Senate Committee on Judiciary—June 9, 1966," Douglas Papers, box 95, folder "1966—Civil Rights."

44. Douglas, *In the Fullness of Time,* pp. 302–3.

45. *Congressional Quarterly Almanac, 1966,* pp. 216–18; Patterson, *Grand Expectations,* pp. 648–49.

46. Douglas, *In the Fullness of Time,* p. 579. On the confrontation between Daley and King in Chicago, see Roger Biles, *Richard J. Daley: Politics, Race, and the Governing of Chicago* (DeKalb: Northern Illinois University Press, 1995), especially chap. 6; and James Ralph, Jr., *Northern Protest: Martin Luther King, Jr., Chicago, and the Civil Rights Movement* (Cambridge, Mass.: Harvard University Press, 1993).

47. Douglas, *In the Fullness of Time,* p. 578.

48. Ibid., p. 579 (first quotation); Stewart Alsop, "Percy vs. Douglas: The Blighted Campaign," *Saturday Evening Post* 239 (Nov. 5, 1966), p. 28 (second quotation).

49. Peter M. Deuel, "A Boy Wonder Grows Up," *Nation* 203 (Oct. 17, 1966), p. 374; Richard T. Cooper, "The Hardest Campaign of Paul Douglas' Career," *New Republic* 155 (Oct. 22, 1966), p. 9.

50. "Speech by Senator Paul H. Douglas before League of Women Voters, Chicago, Illinois—October 19, 1966," Douglas Papers, box 43, folder "League of Women Voters"; Douglas, *In the Fullness of Time,* pp. 581–82.

51. "Speech by Senator Paul H. Douglas before League of Women Voters"; Douglas, *In the Fullness of Time*, p. 585 (quotation).

52. Cooper, "Hardest Campaign of Paul Douglas' Career," p. 9; Simon, *P.S.*, 82 (quotation); Paul Douglas tapes 10–14, Chicago Historical Society, Chicago, Illinois.

53. Cooper, "Hardest Campaign of Paul Douglas' Career," p. 9; Deuel, "Boy Wonder Grows Up," p. 375.

54. News release, Mar. 20, 1966, Douglas Papers, box 531, folder "March 20, 1966"; "Douglas and the Devil Theory," *Nation* 202 (Oct. 17, 1966), p. 315; speech, n.d., Douglas Papers, box 43, folder "Vietnam Speech"; Douglas, *In the Fullness of Time*, pp. 583–84; interview with Shuman, p. 296.

55. Interview with Douglas, Nov. 1, 1974, p. 16; Thomas Byrne Edsall and Mary D. Edsall, *Chain Reaction: The Impact of Race, Rights, and Taxes on American Politics* (New York: W. W. Norton, 1991), p. 51.

56. Interview with Shuman, p. 158 (first quotation); Douglas, *In the Fullness of Time*, p. 585 (second quotation); "WGN Interview with Senator Paul H. Douglas concerning Charles Percy's 'Liar' Charges," Aug. 25, 1966, p. 4, Douglas Papers, box 532, folder "August 25, 1966" (third quotation).

57. Douglas, *In the Fullness of Time*, p. 587.

58. Paul H. Douglas, "Statement on Open Occupancy," Douglas Papers, box 534, folder 10/25/66; interview with Shuman, pp. 157–58; Douglas, *In the Fullness of Time*, pp. 588 (first quotation), 591 (second quotation).

59. Deuel, "Boy Wonder Grows Up," p. 374; Cooper, "Hardest Campaign of Paul Douglas' Career," p. 10 (quotation); Douglas, *In the Fullness of Time*, pp. 588–89.

60. Interview with Shuman, pp. 233–36; Cooper, "Hardest Campaign of Paul Douglas' Career," p. 9; Paul H. Douglas to Charles and Lorraine Percy, telegram, Sept. 17, 1966, Charles Percy to Paul H. Douglas, telegram, Sept. 21, 1966, and Douglas news release, Sept. 21, 1966, all in Douglas Papers, box 36, folder "Percy-Douglas Correspondence on Murder—1966."

61. "WGN Interview with Senator Paul H. Douglas concerning Charles Percy's 'Liar' Charges," pp. 1–2; Douglas, *In the Fullness of Time*, pp. 591–92.

62. Paul H. Douglas, telegram to Fair Campaign Practices Committee, Nov. 5, 1966, Douglas Papers, box 534, Folder 11/5/66 (first quotation); *Chicago Tribune*, Nov. 6, 8 (second quotation), 1966; interview with Shuman, p. 236 (third quotation); Douglas, *In the Fullness of Time*, pp. 591–92.

63. Interview with Shuman, pp. 237–39; Douglas, *In the Fullness of Time*, p. 590. Douglas received the endorsement of the *Chicago American*. "We Are for Douglas," Oct. 11, 1966, Douglas Papers, box 533, folder 10/11/66.

64. Paul Douglas tapes 10–14.

65. *Chicago Tribune*, Nov. 9, 1966; Douglas, *In the Fullness of Time*, pp. 592–93.

66. Douglas, *In the Fullness of Time*, pp. 592–94; interview with Shuman, p. 293.

67. Edsall and Edsall, *Chain Reaction*, p. 61; "T. R. B. from Washington," *New Republic* 155 (Nov. 26, 1966), p. 4.

68. Philip A. Klinkner, with Rogers M. Smith, *The Unsteady March: The Rise and Decline of Racial Equality in America* (Chicago: University of Chicago Press,

1999), pp. 280–81; Patterson, *Grand Expectations,* p. 650; Alsop, "Percy vs. Douglas," p. 28 (quotation).

9: AFTER THE SENATE

1. Douglas, *In the Fullness of Time,* p. 617.

2. "T. R. B. from Washington," *New Republic* 155 (Nov. 26, 1966), p. 4.

3. Douglas Papers, box 424, folder "Job Offers—Pending"; *New York Times,* Feb. 7, 1967; Douglas, *In the Fullness of Time,* pp. 597–98. He remained on the faculty at the New School for Social Research from 1967 to 1970.

4. Mangel, "Man Ahead of His Time," p. 104.

5. Paul H. Douglas to Stewart Udall, Dec. 22, 1966, and Paul H. Douglas to Lyndon B. Johnson, Dec. 22, 1966, both in Douglas Papers, box 145, folder "Douglas Correspondence 1966"; Paul H. Douglas to Thomas B. Dustin, Mar. 31, 1969, and Paul H. Douglas to Robert C. Byrd, Aug. 5, 1969, both in Douglas Papers, box 145, folder "Indiana Dunes 1969 Save the Dunes Council."

6. Kenneth E. Gray to Paul H. Douglas, Feb. 24, 1967 (first quotation), and "New Push Set for Truth-in-Lending Bill," Apr. 7, 1967 (second quotation), both in Douglas Papers, box 225, folder "Reports, Pamphlets, Statements 1967"; Douglas, *In the Fullness of Time,* p. 533.

7. "New Push Set for Truth-in-Lending Bill"; *Congressional Quarterly Almanac, 1967* (Washington, D.C.: Congressional Quarterly, 1968), p. 720 (quotations).

8. "New Push Set for Truth-in-Lending Bill"; Douglas, *In the Fullness of Time,* p. 533.

9. "Testimony of Paul H. Douglas before the House Subcommittee of Consumer Affairs (Banking and Currency)," Aug. 7, 1967, Douglas Papers, box 225, folder "Douglas Statements 1967"; Douglas, *In the Fullness of Time,* p. 534; *Congressional Quarterly Almanac, 1968* (Washington, D.C.: Congressional Quarterly, 1968), pp. 207–11.

10. Douglas, *In the Fullness of Time,* pp. 534–35.

11. Ibid., pp. 608–11; "An Interview with Former Senator Paul Douglas," *Forbes* 101 (Mar. 1, 1968), p. 50 (quotation).

12. "Interview with Former Senator Paul Douglas," pp. 50–51; Douglas, *In the Fullness of Time,* p. 607.

13. Paul H. Douglas et al., *Building the American City: Report of the National Commission on Urban Problems* (New York: Frederick A. Praeger, 1969), p. vii; Douglas, *In the Fullness of Time,* p. 598.

14. Howard E. Shuman, "Behind the Scenes . . . and Under the Rug," *Washington Monthly* (July 1969), pp. 16–18; Douglas, *In the Fullness of Time,* p. 599; interview with Douglas, Nov. 1, 1974, p. 15 (quotation).

15. Douglas, *In the Fullness of Time,* pp. 405–8.

16. Shuman, "Behind the Scenes . . . and Under the Rug," p. 18–20.

17. Douglas et al., *Building the American City,* pp. 13–14, 153.

18. Ibid., pp. 180–92. Douglas advocated increased government support for housing in other venues as well. He explored this theme, for example, when delivering the Moskowitz lectures at New York University in 1968; the lectures were published the following year as part of an anthology on urban affairs. See

William E. Zisch, Paul H. Douglas, and Robert C. Weaver, *The Urban Environment: How It Can Be Improved* (New York: New York University Press, 1969).

19. Interview with Shuman, p. 400; *New York Times,* Aug. 29, 1968; Simon, *P.S.,* p. 252; Douglas, *In the Fullness of Time,* pp. 600–601. It is unclear exactly what caused Douglas to faint, but Paul Simon believed that Douglas might have suffered a small stroke (Simon, *P.S.,* p. 252).

20. Paul H. Douglas to Joseph Califano, Nov. 11, 1968, Douglas Papers, box 349, folder "Commission—1969"; Shuman, "Behind the Scenes . . . and Under the Rug," pp. 20–21; interview with Shuman, p. 406.

21. Shuman, "Behind the Scenes . . . and Under the Rug," pp. 21–22; *New York Times,* Dec. 15, 1968; Douglas, *In the Fullness of Time,* pp. 604–5.

22. Douglas, *In the Fullness of Time,* p. 605 (quotation).

23. Douglas, *In Our Time.* The book was insightfully reviewed in the *New York Times,* Nov. 24, 1968.

24. Joseph L. Rauh to Paul H. Douglas, July 29, 1970, Joseph L. Rauh to Paul H. Douglas, Aug. 13, 1970 (Rauh quotation), and Paul H. Douglas to Joseph L. Rauh, Aug. 26, 1970, all in Rauh Papers, box 8, folder "Gen. Corr. D 1968–72." In his autobiography's acknowledgments, Douglas thanks a number of people for checking sections of the manuscript for accuracy—Kenneth Gray on the Indiana Dunes, Ezra Levin on health issues, Jonathan Lindley on depressed areas legislation, Walter Rybeck on housing, Paul Taylor on land monopoly, and Howard Shuman on a number of topics, in addition to Joseph Rauh on civil rights and civil liberties (*In the Fullness of Time,* p. xiii).

25. *New York Times,* Aug. 22, 1969; Douglas, *In the Fullness of Time,* pp. 612–13.

26. Douglas, *In the Fullness of Time,* p. 613.

27. Ibid., pp. 613–14.

28. *New York Times,* Oct. 25, 1970; Paul H. Douglas to "Dear Friend," n.d., Wilbur J. Cohen Papers, box 208, folder 16, State Historical Society of Wisconsin, Madison, Wisconsin.

29. Interview with Paul H. Douglas, Columbia University Oral History Research Office, 1977, pp. 5–8; Douglas, *In the Fullness of Time,* pp. 614–15.

30. Interview with Douglas, 1977, pp. 1–2 (quotation); *Chicago Tribune,* Sept. 25, 1976; *New York Times,* Sept. 25, 1976.

10: LIBERAL CRUSADES

1. Mangel, "Paul Douglas: Man Ahead of His Time," p. 106.

2. "TRB," *New Republic* 175 (Oct. 9, 1976), p. 2 (quotation).

3. "What Senator Paul Douglas Learned," *Life* 60 (June 17, 1966), p. 6 (quotation). On the ADA, see Gillon, *Politics and Vision.*

4. Jane Dick to Adlai Stevenson, Oct. 15, 1963, and Clayton Fritchey to Adlai Stevenson, n.d., both in Stevenson Papers, box 25, folder 11.

5. *Congressional Digest* 36 (April 1957), pp. 116–18. The connection between civil rights and America's cold war policies has been made in several recent studies. See, for example, Mary L. Dudziak, *Cold War Civil Rights: Race and the Image of American Democracy* (Princeton: Princeton University Press, 2000); Brenda Gayle Plummer, *Rising Wind: Black Americans and U.S. Foreign Affairs,*

1935–1960 (Chapel Hill: University of North Carolina Press, 1996); and John David Skrentny, "The Effect of the Cold War on African-American Civil Rights: America and the World Audience, 1945–1968," *Theory and Society* 27 (April 1968), pp. 237–85.

6. "TRB," p. 2 (quotation).

7. Mangel, "Paul Douglas: Man Ahead of His Time," p. 106 (quotation).

8. "A Memorial Service for Paul Howard Douglas, the Friends Meeting House, Washington, D.C., September 27, 1976," Rauh Papers, box 33, subject file, Paul H. Douglas folder (first quotation); "TRB," p. 2; *New York Times,* Sept. 25, 1976 (second quotation); *Congressional Record,* 86th Cong., 2d sess., July 2, 1960, 106, pt. 12:15592 (third quotation).

9. Mangel, "Paul Douglas: Man Ahead of His Time," p. 103 (first quotation); "A Memorial Service for Paul Howard Douglas" (second quotation).

10. Mangel, "Paul Douglas: Man Ahead of His Time," p. 106.

11. *New York Times,* Nov. 24, 1968.

Bibliographical Essay

Any study of Paul Douglas's life should begin with his papers at the Chicago Historical Society. The massive collection is essential to an understanding of his public career, and the bulk of the materials deal with the senatorial years. Unfortunately, the papers are confusingly arranged and therefore very difficult to use at first. Boxes contain two sets of identifying numbers, and researchers must recognize the more recent—and more accurate—set of numbers when using the finding guides. Fortunately, the helpful staff at the Chicago Historical Society can provide the necessary guidance. In addition to examining correspondence, draft speeches, newsletters, and assorted government documents, students of Douglas's life can listen to a series of audio tapes (recordings of speeches and radio broadcasts) in the manuscript collection; they can also view clips from the Chicago Historical Society's WGN Film Archive.

Other manuscript collections should be consulted as well. Paul Douglas and Adlai E. Stevenson corresponded sporadically for nearly a quarter of a century; their letters are contained in Stevenson's Papers at Princeton University's Seeley G. Mudd Library. The Harold L. Ickes Papers at the Manuscript Division of the Library of Congress are useful in describing Douglas's participation in the battle against Samuel Insull. The Joseph L. Rauh Papers, also in the Library of Congress's Manuscript Division, provide material on civil rights. On the same topic, see the Hubert H. Humphrey Papers at the Minnesota Historical Society. The Joseph Meek Papers at the Chicago Historical Society provide material on the 1954 senatorial election. Several manuscript collections shed light on Douglas's many and varied reform activities. See, for example, the Records of the National Consumers League and the Hugo L. Black Papers at the Library of Congress; the Americans for Democratic Action Papers, the Wilbur J. Cohen Papers, and the Thomas R. Amlie Papers at the State Historical Society of Wisconsin; the Robert F. Wagner Papers at Georgetown University; and the Independent Voters of Illinois Papers at the Chicago Historical Society.

Douglas talked about his experiences in a number of oral history interviews. See interview transcripts in the John F. Kennedy Presidential Library, Boston, Massachusetts, and the Lyndon B. Johnson Presidential Library, Austin, Texas. Also see the transcripts of two interviews conducted with Douglas, the first in 1957 and the second in 1974–75, by the Oral History Research Office at Columbia University. An oral history interview with Howard E. Shuman, Douglas's administrative assistant, is available from the Senate Historical Office, Washington, D.C. Also valuable is an interview with Lawrence O'Brien, former chairman of the Democratic National Committee, at the Johnson Presidential Library.

As a leading economist, public-spirited reformer, and elected official, Douglas published a long list of books and articles. He completed his autobiography, *In the Fullness of Time: The Memoirs of Paul H. Douglas* (New York: Harcourt Brace Jovanovich, 1971), with much difficulty. He wrote the book after donating his papers to the Chicago Historical Society and during the time that he suffered from a number of debilitating medical conditions. As a consequence, historians will find the volume somewhat disappointing for its inaccuracies and omissions. (For example, Douglas wrote virtually nothing about his important work on behalf of civil rights during the years 1958 to 1960.) Still, the book contains much valuable information, and the author reveals much about his own character through the comments he scatters throughout the narrative.

Most of Douglas's written work in the 1920s and 1930s dealt with economic matters. Among the most important are "What Can a Man Afford?" *American Economic Review* 11 (December 1921), pp. 1–118; *The Worker in Modern Economic Society* (Chicago: University of Chicago Press, 1923); *Wages and the Family* (Chicago: University of Chicago Press, 1925); *Real Wages in the United States, 1890–1926* (Boston: Houghton Mifflin, 1930); *The Movement of Money and Real Earnings in the United States, 1926–1928* (Chicago: University of Chicago Press, 1931); *The Problem of Unemployment* (New York: Macmillan, 1931); "The Partial Stabilization of Workers' Incomes through Unemployment Insurance," *Annals of the American Academy of Political and Social Science* 153 (March 1931), pp. 94–103; *Standards of Unemployment Insurance* (Chicago: University of Chicago Press, 1933); "The Economics of Unemployment Relief," *American Economic Review* 23 Supplement (March 1933), pp. 51–55; *The Theory of Wages* (New York: Macmillan, 1934); "Social Security for Today," *Christian Century* 51 (Nov. 28, 1934), pp. 1515–17; "Unemployment Insurance and Relief," *New Republic* 81 (Dec. 19, 1934), pp. 160–63; "Unemployment Insurance—Questions and Answers," *Christian Century* 52 (Jan. 2, 1935), pp. 12–14; *Controlling Depressions* (New York: W. W. Norton, 1935); and *Social Security in the United States* (New York and London: Whittlesey House, McGraw-Hill, 1936). Also, his presidential address to the American Economic Association was published as "Are There Laws of Production?" *American Economic Review* 38 (March 1948), pp. 1–41.

Douglas also wrote extensively about political affairs. For a better understanding of his early political activism, see his "Why I Am for Thomas and Why a Vote for Anyone Else is Thrown Away," *New Republic* 56 (Oct. 24, 1928), pp. 268–70; and "Chicago's Persistent Traction Problem," *National Municipal Review* 18 (November 1929), pp. 669–75. He explained his depression-era disaffection with the Democratic party in *The Making of a New Party* (New York and London: Whittlesey House, McGraw-Hill, 1932). During his years in Washington, he wrote a number of magazine articles about life in the U.S. Senate. See, for example, "Running for Office Means What It Says," *New York Times Magazine*, Sept. 5, 1948, pp. 5, 41, 42; "Report from a Freshman Senator," *New York Times Magazine*, Mar. 20, 1949, pp. 10, 72–75; "Senator Douglas Meets the Press," *American Mercury* 69 (September 1949), pp. 322–27; and "A Senator's Vote: A Searching of the Soul," *New York Times Magazine*, Apr. 20, 1950, pp. 9, 38–44. His *Ethics in Government* (Cambridge, Mass.: Harvard University Press, 1952) originated with three lectures he delivered earlier that year at Harvard University. He discussed his abiding interest in the judicious use of government resources in *Economy in the National Government* (Chicago: University of Chicago Press, 1952). He explained his choice in 1952 for a presidential candidate in "Why I'm for Kefauver," *Collier's* 130 (July 19, 1952), pp. 20, 57. His *In Our Time* (New York: Harcourt, Brace, and World, 1967) considered the reform issues that had been most important to him during his senatorial years. Also see his chapter, "Jobs: A Key to Improving the Urban Environment" in William E. Zisch, Paul H. Douglas, and Robert C. Weaver, *The Urban Environment: How It Can Be Improved* (New York: New York University Press, 1969). As chairman of the National Commission on Urban Problems, Douglas wrote large sections of its final report, *Building the American City: Report of the National Commission on Urban Problems* (New York: Frederick A. Praeger, 1969). He lauded former colleagues Philip Hart, Jerry Voorhis, and Frank Porter Graham in "Three Saints in Politics," *American Scholar* 40 (spring 1971), pp. 223–32.

Douglas sought to educate the public about civil rights in the following publications: "The Fight against the Filibuster," *New Republic* 128 (Jan. 12, 1953), pp. 6–8; "Stop the Filibuster," *America* 96 (January 5, 1957), p. 383; "The Right to Vote," *Atlantic Monthly* 200 (December 1957), pp. 37–44; and "The 1960 Voting Rights Bill: The Struggle, the Final Results, and the Reasons," *Journal of Intergroup Relations* 1 (summer 1960), pp. 82–86.

During his years in the Senate, Douglas became the subject of several journalistic profiles. See Joe Alex Morris, "Senator Douglas: Hard-Boiled Idealist," *Saturday Evening Post* 222 (Aug. 6, 1949), pp. 27, 107–10; Richard L. Strout, "Paul Douglas: Senator With Ideas," *New Republic* 121 (Sept. 5, 1949), pp. 13–15; "The Making of a Maverick," *Time* 55 (Jan. 16, 1950), pp. 16–19; Mortimer Smith, "Senator Paul H. Douglas," *American Mercury* 71 (July 1950), pp. 28–29; Cabell Phillips, "Paul Douglas— 'Instinctive Liberal,'" *New York Times Magazine,* June 24, 1951, pp. 10–12; "Idea Man for the Democrats," *Business Week* (Mar. 26, 1955), pp. 128–34; William McGaffin, "'Ferocious Independent' at Seventy," *New York Times Magazine,* Mar. 25, 1962, pp. 38–48; and Charles Mangel, "Paul Douglas: Man Ahead of His Time," *Look* 31 (June 13, 1967), pp. 103–10. Later accounts by historians include Edward L. Schapsmeier and Frederick H. Schapsmeier, "Paul H. Douglas: From Pacifist to Soldier-Statesman," *Journal of the Illinois State Historical Society* 67 (June 1974), pp. 307–23; and Edward L. Schapsmeier, "Dirksen and Douglas of Illinois: The Pragmatist and the Professor as Contemporaries in the United States Senate," *Illinois Historical Journal* 83 (summer 1990), pp. 74–84. Two unpublished doctoral dissertations contain valuable information. See Hugh Cordier, "Paul Douglas's 1954 Senatorial Campaign with Special Reference to Television" (Ph.D. diss., University of Illinois, 1955); and Jerry M. Anderson, "Paul H. Douglas: Insurgent Senate Spokesman for Humane Causes, 1949–1963" (Ph.D. diss., Michigan State University, 1964).

Douglas spoke frequently on the Senate floor, delivering lengthy prepared addresses, engaging in colloquies with other colleagues to clarify issues, and debating opponents—all of which appear in the *Congressional Record*. Abridged versions of some of his remarks can be found in assorted volumes of *Congressional Digest*. The annual editions of *Congressional Quarterly Almanac* are helpful both in delineating Douglas's activities and in providing context for understanding relevant legislative contests.

A number of books discuss the Senate during Douglas's years in Washington. Begin with William S. White, *Citadel: The Story of the U.S. Senate* (New York: Harper and Brothers, 1956), an influential volume that denigrated the performance of Douglas and other liberals. For the contrary view, consult Michael Foley, *The New Senate: Liberal Influence on a Conservative Institution, 1959–1972* (New Haven: Yale University Press, 1980); and James L. Sundquist, *Politics and Policy: The Eisenhower, Kennedy, and Johnson Years* (Washington, D.C.: Brookings Institute, 1968). Joseph S. Clark, *The Senate Establishment* (New York: Hill and Wang, 1963) also wrote disapprovingly of White's *Citadel*. Samuel Shaffer, *On and off the Floor: Thirty Years as a Correspondent on Capitol Hill* (New York: Newsweek Books, 1980) is anecdotal.

Biographies of other influential senators from the period put Douglas's career into perspective. See the following: Anne Hodges Morgan, *Robert S. Kerr: The Senate Years* (Norman: University of Oklahoma Press, 1977); Richard O. Davies, *Defender of the Old Guard: John Bricker and American Politics* (Columbus: Ohio State University Press, 1993); Gilbert C. Fite, *Richard B. Russell, Jr., Senator from Georgia* (Chapel Hill: University of North Carolina Press, 1991); Joseph Bruce Gorman, *Kefauver: A Political Biography* (New York: Oxford University Press, 1971); Gayle B. Montgomery and James W. Johnson, *One Step from the White House: The Rise and Fall of Senator William F. Knowland* (Berkeley: University of California Press, 1998); Edward L. Schapsmeier and Frederick H. Schapsmeier, "Scott W. Lucas of Havana: His Rise and Fall as Majority Leader in the United States Senate," *Journal of the Illinois State Historical Society* 70 (November 1977), pp. 302–20; Edward L. Schapsmeier and Frederick H. Schapsmeier, *Dirksen of Illinois* (Urbana: University of Illinois Press, 1985); Byron C. Hulsey, *Everett Dirksen and His Presidents: How a Senate Giant Shaped American Politics* (Lawrence: University Press of Kansas, 2000); Francis R. Valeo, *Mike Mansfield, Majority Leader: A Different Kind of Senate, 1961–1976* (Armonk, N.Y.: M. E. Sharpe, 1999); Randall Bennett Woods, *Fulbright: A Biography* (Cambridge: Cambridge University Press, 1995); Hubert H. Humphrey, *The Education of a Public Man: My Life and Politics* (Garden City, N.Y.: Doubleday, 1976); and Timothy N. Thurber, *The Politics of Equality: Hubert H. Humphrey and the African American Freedom Struggle* (New York: Columbia University Press, 1999). For Lyndon Johnson's years as Senate majority leader, see Robert Dallek, *Lone Star Rising: Lyndon Johnson and His Times, 1908–1960* (New York: Oxford University Press, 1991).

Finally, a number of recent studies by historians and political scientists shed light on post–World War II liberalism in the United States. See, for example, Iwan W. Morgan, *Beyond the Liberal Consensus: A Political History of the United States since 1945* (New York: St. Martin's Press, 1994); Alan Brinkley, *Liberalism and Its Discontents* (Cambridge, Mass.: Harvard University Press, 1998); Thomas Byrne Edsall and Mary D. Edsall, *Chain Reaction: The Impact of Race, Rights, and Taxes on American Politics* (New York: W. W. Norton, 1991); Ronald Radosh, *Divided They Fell: The Demise of the Democratic Party, 1964–1996* (New York: Free Press, 1996); David Plotke, *Building a Democratic Political Order: Reshaping American Liberalism in the 1930s and 1940s* (Cambridge: Cambridge University Press, 1996); Judith Stein, *Running Steel, Running America: Race, Economic Policy, and the Decline of Liberalism* (Chapel Hill: University of North Carolina Press, 1998); Steven M. Gillon, *Politics and Vision: The ADA and American Liberalism, 1947–1985* (New York: Oxford University Press, 1987); Patrick M. Garry, *Liberalism and American Identity* (Kent, Ohio: Kent State University Press, 1992); and Gary Gerstle, "The Protean Character of American Liberalism," *American Historical Review* 99 (1994), pp. 1043–73.

Index